Toward Entrepreneurial Community Development

Toward Entrepreneurial Community Development is about developing entrepreneurial communities, and goes beyond theories of the firm to demonstrate how local and regional society contributes in important ways to the vitality of entrepreneurs. The literature is rich with insights about leadership and culture within small and medium enterprises (SMEs), and the behaviors and attitudes of their founders, founding teams, and managers. Since most of the attention in the entrepreneurship literature is focused on firms, we wish to explore everyone else: the social environment surrounding the entrepreneur and how leadership and culture outside the firm can have pervasive effects on the business.

This book reaches across disciplinary boundaries, integrating and advancing knowledge on entrepreneurial community development. The book identifies actionable leadership strategies that can be used by literally anyone to help make a community or region a more culturally supportive, interactive home for entrepreneurial minds. We draw from original research to compare high and low-entrepreneurship communities, and present an emergent picture of how community-level actors can (or fail to) work together to support entrepreneurship in places that are culturally distant from the Silicon Valley (i.e., most places). *Toward Entrepreneurial Community Development* then offers techniques for entrepreneurial community leadership, including how to build lasting alliances, create an image, and harness the local culture for entrepreneurial advantage.

The result is a book that provides the reader with the latest advancements and techniques in entrepreneurship development in a straightforward, readable format. No matter the reader, *Toward Entrepreneurial Community Development* demonstrates how anyone, in any position, can lead a local entrepreneurship movement starting anywhere, anytime.

Michael W-P Fortunato is an Assistant Professor of Sociology and Director of the Center for Rural Studies at Sam Houston State University, USA.

Morgan R. Clevenger is an Assistant Professor of Entrepreneurship at the Jay S. Sidhu School of Business and Leadership at Wilkes University, USA.

Routledge Studies in Entrepreneurship

Edited by Susan Marlow and Janine Swail (University of Nottingham, UK)

For a full list of titles in this series, please visit www.routledge.com

This series extends the meaning and scope of entrepreneurship by capturing new research and enquiry on economic, social, cultural and personal value creation. Entrepreneurship as value creation represents the endeavours of innovative people and organisations in creative environments that open up opportunities for developing new products, new services, new firms and new forms of policy making in different environments seeking sustainable economic growth and social development. In setting this objective, the series includes books which cover a diverse range of conceptual, empirical and scholarly topics that both inform the field and push the boundaries of entrepreneurship.

5 **Enterprising Initiatives in the Experience Economy**
Transforming social worlds
Edited by Britta Timm Knudsen, Dorthe Refslund Christensen and Per Blenker

6 **Entrepreneurial Learning**
The development of new perspectives in research, education and practice
David Rae and Catherine L. Wang

7 **Entrepreneurship and Knowledge Exchange**
Edited by Jay Mitra and John Edmondson

8 **Entrepreneurship in Small Island States and Territories**
Edited by Godfrey Baldacchino

9 **Entrepreneurship and Cluster Dynamics**
Edited by Cristina Boari, Tom Elfring, and F. Xavier Molina-Morales

10 **The Habitual Entrepreneur**
Paul Westhead and Mike Wright

11 **Toward Entrepreneurial Community Development**
Leaping Cultural and Leadership Boundaries
Edited by Michael W-P Fortunato and Morgan R. Clevenger

Toward Entrepreneurial Community Development

Leaping Cultural and Leadership Boundaries

Edited by Michael W-P Fortunato
and Morgan R. Clevenger

Routledge
Taylor & Francis Group
LONDON AND NEW YORK

First published 2017
by Routledge

2 Park Square, Milton Park, Abingdon, Oxfordshire OX14 4RN
52 Vanderbilt Avenue, New York, NY 10017

Routledge is an imprint of the Taylor & Francis Group, an informa business

First issued in paperback 2019

Library of Congress Cataloging-in-Publication Data
A catalog record for this book has been requested

ISBN: 978-1-138-93554-9 (hbk)
ISBN: 978-0-367-24292-3 (pbk)

Typeset in Sabon
by Apex CoVantage, LLC

This book is dedicated to my mentors, Diane McLaughlin, Ted Alter, and Bunny Willits at Penn State University; to the memory of my grandfather, Bill Lawrence, an entertainer and entrepreneur *par excellence*; and most especially to Amy Schmalz, my constant inspiration and confidant who by some miracle still tolerates me each day.

– Michael

For my father, Ronald G. Clevenger, who has always been an entrepreneur, community citizen, and local leader.

– Morgan

Contents

Tables and Figures

Preface

Creating a book about entrepreneurial community ecosystems led to the opportunity of exploring key history, various models and ideas, evaluating research in multiple fields at their cross sections, and having many conversations with scholars and practitioners on the matter. What is presented in this book is a macro discussion of key topics from a 30,000-foot bird's eye view. The next product will be a case study book—including current research being conducted by the co-editors in Pennsylvania and Texas.

Toward Entrepreneurial Community Development: Leaping Cultural & Leadership Boundaries is about developing entrepreneurial community ecosystems, and goes beyond theories of the firm to demonstrate how local and regional society contributes in important ways to the vitality of entrepreneurs. The literature is rich with insights about leadership and culture within SMEs, and the behaviors and attitudes of their founders, founding teams, and managers. Since a majority of the attention in the entrepreneurship literature is focused on individuals, firms, and the strategic behaviors they exhibit, we wish to explore everyone else: the social environment surrounding the entrepreneur and how local leadership and culture can have pervasive effects on the business.

Entrepreneurial community development reaches across disciplinary boundaries, integrating and advancing knowledge on entrepreneurial community development. This book identifies actionable leadership strategies that can be used by literally anyone to help make a community or region a more culturally supportive, interactive home for entrepreneurial minds. We draw from a wide range of literature, prior research initiatives, and original research to compare high- and low-entrepreneurship communities, and present an emergent picture of how community-level actors can (or fail to) work together to support entrepreneurship in places that are culturally distant from the Silicon Valley (i.e., most places). The book then offers techniques for entrepreneurial community leadership, including how to build lasting alliances, lead ecosystems at the macro-level, and harness the local culture for entrepreneurial advantage. The result is a book that provides the reader with the latest advancements and techniques in entrepreneurship development in a straightforward, readable format. No matter the reader,

Toward Entrepreneurial Community Development demonstrates how anyone, in any position, can work with others to lead a local entrepreneurship movement starting anywhere, anytime.

This book explores what gives some communities an entrepreneurial culture, while other communities struggle to support entrepreneurship development. The book has the following aims: (1) to integrate and advance the fragmented and sometimes discordant literature on entrepreneurial communities in order to present a cohesive view of the nexus between entrepreneurship and community economic development, based in theory and research; (2) to offer an alternative approach to a "prescription" for entrepreneurial communities, demonstrating multiple viable paths toward entrepreneurialism rooted in a citizen-driven culture of place; (3) to provide an overview of entrepreneurial community development and leadership through the current day, as an educational guide or classroom text for students and researchers; (4) to offer strategies for both formal and informal community leaders for building alliances from scratch, empowering entrepreneurs and creating forums and platforms for their voices to be heard, and keeping busy people coming back for more; (5) to develop real, actionable implications and suggestions for individuals as diverse as researchers, economic development practitioners, entrepreneurs, and policy makers; and (6) to tackle the sometimes complex theoretical world of entrepreneurship in plain language that is accessible to anyone.

M. W-P Fortunato & M. R. Clevenger

Contributors

Nicole D. Breazeale is an assistant professor of sociology at Western Kentucky University. Her research explores topics related to rural development and agricultural change, with a focus on entrepreneurship. She was a co-PI on a USDA National Institute of Food and Agriculture grant [2011–68006–30807] on rural entrepreneurship in Kentucky and is lead author on the first article to come out of that research, which was recently published in *Community Development*. She received her Ph.D. in community and environmental sociology from the University of Wisconsin-Madison

Morgan R. Clevenger is an assistant professor of entrepreneurship at the Jay S. Sidhu School of Business and Leadership at Wilkes University. He received his Ed.D. in educational leadership and policy analysis at the University of Missouri-Columbia. Additionally, he attained an MBA from the College of Business & Economics and a bachelor of science degree in journalism from the Reed College of Media, both at West Virginia University. Clevenger's research interests include entrepreneurship, entrepreneurial communities, family business, corporate entrepreneurship, nonprofit management, corporate citizenship, philanthropy, and higher education.

Michael W-P Fortunato is an assistant professor of sociology and director of the Center for Rural Studies at Sam Houston State University. He received his Ph.D. degree in rural sociology and master of science in community economic development from Penn State University. Fortunato grew up in his grandfather's Pittsburgh-based entertainment business, Alanna Records, and went on to launch Fortunet Entertainment, Inc. in New York City. While based in New York, his travels took him into many historically important rural communities in the northeast United States. Fortunato's professional interests include finding ways to infuse community development practice with high levels of creativity, enthusiasm, and compassion. His research focuses on how local culture and institutional structure shape local innovation, entrepreneurship, and well-being in communities both domestically and internationally, as well as how to enable transformation from legacy social systems into newer, flexible, more democratic and entrepreneurial local systems that serve the public good. By examining the differences between high- and low-entrepreneurship areas, Fortunato's research seeks to understand the attitudes of citizens as they navigate their past, imagine a better future, and catalyze fast, meaningful steps toward action and accomplishment. He uses this knowledge while conducting applied work in communities across rural Texas, and internationally, co-creating local systems and practices for overcoming obstacles, elevating citizen voices, and unleashing untapped creative potential. He has applied this work to topics ranging from business creation to interorganizational cooperation, drought management, rural broadband development, and management of invasive pests.

Kathleen Houlihan is the Founder of Degree2Career, which integrates education and workforce information and provides career opportunities to those in the networked community. She has more than 15 years of experience in education administration at three universities and she serves as a consultant for numerous businesses. She earned her Bachelor of Arts degree in psychology and her MBA from Wilkes University. Houlihan has a PhD in management information systems from Capella University.

Ronald J. Hustedde is a professor of community and leadership development at the University of Kentucky. He is also director of the Kentucky Entrepreneurial Coaches Institute, a unique leadership program that builds grassroots entrepreneurial advocates and leaders in rural Kentucky. He is also part of *E-Discovery Challenge*, an educational program for middle school and high school students in Kentucky's Appalachian communities. Those students have launched thousands of businesses that have sold products and services at community and school sales events and fairs. Hustedde has done research about rural entrepreneurship, venture capital markets, economic conflicts, leadership development, and community development. He is past president of the Community Development Society and is the recipient of many national and regional awards. He received his Ph.D. in sociology from the University of Wisconsin-Madison.

Chao Miao is an assistant professor of management at Wilkes University. He received his Ph.D. degree in management from Virginia Commonwealth University. He has taught various management classes related to entrepreneurship, leadership, foundations of management, organizational behavior, and human resource management. His research interests include entrepreneurship, leadership, emotional intelligence, personality, national culture, job attitudes and performance, and meta-analysis. His research has been published in several journals including *Entrepreneurship Theory and Practice*, *Industrial and Organizational Psychology: Perspectives on Science and Practice*, *Journal of Developmental Entrepreneurship*, *Journal of Small Business Management*, and *Personality and Individual Differences*.

Ellen E. Newell, Ph.D. is an assistant professor of psychology in the College of Arts, Humanities, and Social Sciences at Wilkes University where she teaches social psychology, statistics, and industrial organizational psychology. Her research interests center on the social psychological study of group identification, social stigmatization, and physiological and psychological well-being. Throughout her research she examines minority groups' (such as entrepreneurs) resilience in the face of social pressures and stress. In addition, she integrates socially relevant issues (e.g. LGBT+ well-being; women in STEM fields) into her study of the consequences of group identification. Her current research interests include the psychology of entrepreneurs, entrepreneurial ecosystems, psychology of women, and intergroup relations among socially devalued groups.

Acknowledgments

As scholar-practitioners, we are most grateful to the people in the communities, organizations, universities, and businesses where we have learned, worked, or volunteered. Real-world experience has been the best teacher to see and feel entrepreneurial community development.

It took considerable assistance, contributions, and coordination to produce this work. As editors we would like to acknowledge the help of all the people involved in this project and, more specifically, to the authors and reviewers that took part in the writing and review process. Without their support, this book would not have become a reality.

First, the editors would like to thank each one of the contributors. Our sincere thanks and gratitude goes to the chapter's authors who incorporated their time and expertise to these topics and key ideas relating to entrepreneurial community development. Second, the editors wish to acknowledge the valuable contributions of the peer reviewers and blind reviewers regarding the improvement of quality, coherence, and content presentation of the chapters. Many of the authors also served as referees; we highly appreciate the double task.

A world of thanks is extended to Wilkes University students who helped gather literature for this project: David Graff, Taylor Baker, Britton Heim, Kim Keller, Colleen McCabe, Emelie Meinhart, Ethan Lonstein, and Alanna Denauski, as well as to Mary Ahlstrom at Sam Houston State University for her efforts in compiling references. We would also like to thank Drs. Diane K. McLaughlin and Theodore R. Alter from Penn State for their mentorship and insights into this topic. Finally, a special thank you is extended to Ann Marie Feldmeth for copyediting and to Taylor Baker and Michelle Lehman for indexing.

Morgan R. Clevenger, Wilkes University, USA
Michael W-P Fortunato, Sam Houston State University, USA

1 An Introduction to Entrepreneurial Community Development

Michael W-P Fortunato and Morgan R. Clevenger

Entrepreneurship is a global phenomenon—a human behavioral process that can be observed across cultures, across geopolitical regions, and across vastly different kinds of people. While often lumped together into a singular grouping, entrepreneurs comprise a diverse group of human beings—as diverse as the many ventures they create (Davidsson, 2009; Gartner, 1985)—from cutting-edge, high-tech blockbuster entrepreneurs who launch paradigm-changing products and services to lifestyle entrepreneurs who enrich their communities by sharing their passions as well as from serialpreneurs strategically launching whole portfolios of companies to the accidental entrepreneur who creates something new only to find that "surprise!" someone is willing to pay for it! Entrepreneurship is a phenomenon that both delights and puzzles scholars and economic development practitioners. For anyone who cares about novelty, innovation, new offerings, product improvements, innovative services, solutions to common problems, and just plain old convenience, entrepreneurship represents the power to harness real resources and talent behind the spirit of ideation and the pursuit of opportunity—all while bearing the risk of financial, professional, and reputational loss. Schumpeter (1934) was the first economist to recognize the cyclical, chaotic, sometimes brutal world of entrepreneurship, defining entrepreneurs as the creative destroyers who shatter old markets in favor of newer, more innovative and relevant markets. A true pioneer of entrepreneurship scholarship, Schumpeter (1934) did more to clarify the role of the entrepreneur than any other single scholar of his time.

The story of entrepreneurship feels like a hero's tale (Lichtenstein & Lyons, 2010) through which a brave protagonist conquers impossible odds and great perils to solve the world's most pressing problems, or to provide value and relief to the masses. The tale revolves around the individual's struggle to seek opportunity at all cost and, using some ingenuity, the ability to find and reallocate resources strategically to exploit the opportunity (Shane, 2003). The "hero's tale" may at least partially explain why entrepreneurship is such an alluring topic for so many, and why entrepreneurial success stories frequently dominate Western media, and increasingly, global business school curricula in colleges and universities.

Entrepreneurship is fundamental to the cultural history of many nations, particularly the United States, beginning with early settlers and founding fathers (Richards & Bulkley, 2007), and later championed by immigrant classes as well (Light & Bonacich, 1991; Portes, Guarnizo, & Haller, 2002; Saxenian, 2002). Many immigrants are among the most risk-tolerant of their peers, leaving familiar surroundings with few belongings to prosper in an unknown land. Thanks to its strengthening legal protections, its burgeoning urban environments, its rich resource base, and openness to immigration, America has thus become a self-selection experiment attracting hardier risk takers from around the world, and thrusting them into an environment that embraces capitalism, self-reliance, and innovation. It is hard to imagine the course of the United States' social and economic trajectory without some of the classic innovations that have emerged since the early Industrial Revolution.

This spirit has spread to other nations as well, and self-employment has long represented the most basic, historical way that individuals would bring their talents and resources to the marketplace (Aronson, 1991). Even as of this writing, "Countries such as Hungary, Denmark, Finland, New Zealand, Sweden, Israel, and Italy all have higher startup rates than America does" (Clifton & Badal, 2014, p. 11). In developing nations across the world, entrepreneurship is increasingly seen as a path to collective prosperity and opportunities for entrepreneurship appear to be rising (Ho & Wong, 2007; Naudé, 2013). Given the importance of entrepreneurs historically and globally, it is little wonder why successful entrepreneurs receive such positive attention today.

Much deeper than the "heroism" of entrepreneuring, there is a more layered story—one where the hero does not always win, where excellent ideas can flounder if the conditions are poor, and where life-cycle phases of launch, growth, maturity, and decline continuously refresh and rejuvenate the economy—often at the cost of an entrepreneurial venture failing along the way. Few people who launch businesses rise to any level of notoriety or stardom, and for many people—especially in developing economies—necessity-driven entrepreneurship can be the only real option for making a living (Bosma & Levie, 2009). Without entrepreneurs, whole economies would surely fail, starved by the domination of large bureaucracies, unsolved societal problems, and a lack of innovative progress. Research illustrates that everything from start-up rates to failure rates, high-growth to low-growth businesses, opportunistic serial ventures to the harsh realities of necessity-oriented entrepreneurship, all vary widely from place to place (see Kelley, Singer, & Herrington, 2016 for a global perspective). The reasons for these variations are broad, ranging from differences in laws, rules, cultural norms, the nature of the marketplace, access to capital and critical infrastructure, access to key markets, beliefs about the future, the ease of starting a business, and corruption and lawfulness to name a few (Kelley et al., 2016). It can be said that *place,* and the *environmental context* in which entrepreneurship occurs, is in many ways just as important as the actions of entrepreneurs themselves. In the end, it is entrepreneurs who start businesses, but the social, environmental, economic, and institutional framework of *places* can fundamentally influence the likelihood of entrepreneurial success or failure for entire societies.

Moreover, these individualistic, heroic entrepreneurs rarely, if ever, act alone in their journey. They are often times supported by their family, their business partners, teams, and perhaps most of all, their community. In the world of business and economics, a key feature of "places" that is often overlooked in favor of an examination of market conditions is *culture*. There is a substantive literature on the impacts of national culture on phenomena like entrepreneurship, but a far lesser focus on the culture of localities and regions (Breazeale, Fortunato, Allen, Hustedde, & Pushkarskaya, 2015; Hustedde, 2007). At a far more localized level than nations, the unique culture of *communities,* based on the attributes of the *local society* and the unique *history of place*, can equally impact entrepreneurial outcomes. Wilkinson (1991) notes that, beyond the family, a person's community is his or her first introduction to society. It follows that the norms, mores, and traditions of these communities can strongly influence the entrepreneurial spirit at a local level, and the propensity of would-be entrepreneurs to launch a venture in the first place. Along with the specific culture and history of place, *local leaders* from both the public and private sector often serve as the standard-bearers of the local culture. They are frequently members of influential local organizations and are especially well positioned to create pathways to entrepreneurship, or divert attention and resources away from entrepreneurs toward other projects perceived to be more valuable. The nexus between culture, history, and leadership is a recurring theme throughout this book. The analyses presented here will help to illustrate why two neighboring towns or counties with so much in common can have very different entrepreneurship and self-employment rates as a result of dynamic forces at this nexus.

All of these concepts matter to the extent that they can influence the *actions* or *inactions* of potential and existing entrepreneurs. The deliberate cultivation of a community that fosters entrepreneurial action through a supportive culture and effective local and regional leadership is this book's definition of *entrepreneurial community development*. It is a complicated term, mostly because it consists of ideas that have a multitude of definitions, conceptualizations, and interpretations that have different meanings in different fields. Entrepreneur, community, and development are ideas that are in transformation as many disciplines seek to unpack what it means to be an entrepreneur, what it means to live and work in a community, and what constitutes development and why it matters. As one author states, "Entrepreneurship remains a complex and multidimensional research object" (Fayolle, 2014, p. 1), but this is well established in the literature. What is less well established is how anyone—from entrepreneurs to economic development professionals to researchers to local leaders—can encourage individualistic entrepreneurs to reap the benefits of working collaboratively. These interactions (among individuals and organizations) only become more complicated as "collaboration" moves to "community," which includes many actors who are not entrepreneurs, but who can play a fundamental role in supporting entrepreneurship.

The book uses the term *community* often, but this is not a term to be taken lightly. It is not only just a collection of people nor a geographic place where people live and work. According to Theodori (2005), a community has (1) a geographic dimension (i.e., a locality), (2) human life dimension (i.e., people living there), and (3) relatively complete organization (i.e., institutions and patterns of behavior that cover the broad range of human interests) (p. 663). "Each feature is a necessary but not sufficient condition for community" (Theodori, 2005, p. 663), which positions community as a variable, rather than a constant. There are varying degrees to which *community* is present at any time, and this consideration is equally true for communities of entrepreneurs. Communities are dynamic, not static. While some elements of an effective community may be present at one time, these elements may not be sufficient to provide adequate support for entrepreneurship. Similarly, any of the social actors within a community are equally capable of creating barriers to entrepreneurship as they are supports: something that Honig and Dana (2008) call communities of *dis*entrepreneurship. The culture and leadership found within communities, whose influence proliferates through human interaction in a particular geographic place, provides an important mechanism for understanding how communities of heightened entrepreneurship evolve over time.

This book, therefore, has three central themes. First, the book elevates the importance of *community* in understanding entrepreneurial action, and specifically how culture and leadership within the community contribute to experienced entrepreneurial outcomes in real places. Second, the book seeks to move beyond static models of the community toward increasingly dynamic models that evolve over time. The book uses the term *ecosystem* to describe evolutionary processes of entrepreneurship development—an idea covered extensively in Chapter 3. Finally, the book is purposive. The ideas presented here are intended to be used by practitioners and applied researchers alike. The book seeks to uncover better ways to study entrepreneurs in a community environment and to understand better the nexus between entrepreneurs and their communities. It also draws from these ideas to present relevant, actionable strategies that anyone can use to support entrepreneurship locally, focusing on ways to leap over common cultural and leadership barriers that impede entrepreneurial action.

The themes explored in this book thus revolve around two major research and practice questions. First, if entrepreneurship rates, and the rates of entrepreneurial success, vary from place to place, what does the community contribute to this variability? Second, can the cultural and leadership dynamics of a community enhance or inhibit entrepreneurship, and if so, how can a more supportive culture and leadership style be cultivated over time?

The concepts presented emphasize multidisciplinary dimensions and a historical context perspective, with an encouragement for more research—particularly qualitative sharing the essence of lived experiences. In looking at levels of analysis for entrepreneurship, much has been studied at the individual, firm, national, and global levels. The unit of analysis—and admittedly most complex—is that of the community level, thus *entrepreneurial communities*. This topic is understudied. This book expands on the knowledge of entrepreneurial community development.

Chapter Descriptions

The chapters of this book present thinking by established scholars and practitioners with expertise in their given professions on the topic of how communities can support entrepreneurship at a local and regional level. These chapters examine different dimensions of entrepreneurship development, from entrepreneurial leadership and psychology to theoretical frameworks for understanding and examining entrepreneurial communities. In the final chapter, Chapter 10, the editors explore a reflection on the content of the book, provide opportunities for additional ideas, set forth future research directions, and summarize the entrepreneurial community development discussion. In each chapter, extra attention is given to ensure that the discussion informs both research and practice simultaneously, and recognizes the promise of a development practice informed by research, and research informed by development practice (see Flyvbjerg, 2001; Schön, 1983). Provided here is brief synopsis of each chapter.

Chapter 2: Perceptions of Entrepreneurs and Community: From Historical Roots to a Contemporary Kaleidoscope

Chapter 2 creates a backdrop for the book's focus on entrepreneurs and communities and examines the entrepreneur and the community in a modern context. The chapter integrates across definitions and reviews concepts that will be used throughout the rest of the book. The chapter moves beyond the view of the entrepreneur as an "agent" working in a contextual "environment." It more soundly presents the community as a group of co-actors (i.e., both individuals and organizations) with the power to enhance—or inhibit—the ability of the entrepreneur to succeed, right down to his or her choice to launch a business in the first place. The community is thus a field of action from which leaders and champions can emerge, including those that place a very high or low value on entrepreneurial action.

Chapter 3: Models of Entrepreneurial Community and Ecosystem Development

Chapter 3 offers a review of the literature on four frameworks that describe the contextual environment in which entrepreneurs operate: facilitating conditions, national and regional policy, entrepreneurial communities, and entrepreneurial ecosystems. The chapter integrates across the current literature, comparing and contrasting these diverse models and highlighting the contributions (and gaps) of major studies within each framework category. This integration creates a starting point for understanding which ingredients, processes, and approaches are useful for studying and/or launching an entrepreneurial community, and strengthening the local environment for entrepreneurship. The chapter ends by clarifying the role of culture and leadership within each framework and why this matters for entrepreneurship development.

Chapter 4: Understanding the Impact of Culture in Entrepreneurship

Chapter 4 describes the current research at the nexus of entrepreneurship and place—otherwise referred to as "entrepreneurial geographies," with a focus on an often hidden aspect of this contextual dimension: culture. The contours of this area of scholarship are highlighted, drawing out the main insights from empirical research on this topic. In particular, differentiation between the culture and structure of society at these different levels of analysis are examined.

Chapter 5: Transformational Leadership to Build an Entrepreneurial Community

Chapter 5 demonstrates the various leadership roles played by formal and informal leaders across the community, and how transformational leadership can be more effectively harnessed to support entrepreneurship. This chapter is important for economic development readers in particular, as formal community leaders are still primarily viewed as "gatekeepers" of decision making around economic development strategy. This chapter presents a more holistic, multi-agent view, and situates transformational leadership as an important (and often overlooked) type of leadership development in the community.

Chapter 6: The Value and Process of Social Networking for Entrepreneurs

Across entrepreneurial community models, there is strong agreement that teamwork is absolutely necessary to make a community a better place for entrepreneurs. Chapter 6 demonstrates ways that anyone in a community can start building an alliance supporting entrepreneurial action. The chapter covers important elements for building meaningful strategic partnerships, giving the partnership a voice and a presence in the community, and managing competition and conflict in the process. Concepts of social network, trust, and social capital are also discussed.

Chapter 7: High- and Low-Entrepreneurial Communities: A Multiple Case Study

Chapter 7 presents an updated chapter from Fortunato's (2011) dissertation on the cultural, social, and institutional differences between high- and low-entrepreneurship communities. The chapter examines the experiences of entrepreneurs and local institutional actors across six communities in Maine, Pennsylvania, and Wisconsin—three with high rates of entrepreneurship, and three with low rates. The stories of participants reveals "many paths forward" for highly entrepreneurial communities rooted in common habits of networking and purposive interaction. Consequently, the scar of industrial development is still felt in low-entrepreneurship communities seeking to break free of an external capital-driven, wage-employment structure, thus placing a firm grip on those who would become entrepreneurs.

Chapter 8: Analysis of the Case Study Data: Considerations for Studying or Launching an Entrepreneurial Community or Ecosystem

Chapter 8 builds upon Fortunato's (2011) dissertation data from Chapter 7, examining some of the qualitative results with respect to the process of developing a more proactive entrepreneurial community. This chapter uses the case study data to identify specific techniques for leaping a variety of boundaries to entrepreneurship. Entrepreneurial actions in the Chapter 7 case studies are compared using models presented in Chapter 3 to understand the strengths and weaknesses of the four main approaches to entrepreneurial community development. This chapter is targeted toward both researchers and practitioners to discuss not only how to study entrepreneurial communities but also how to take deliberate, conscientious steps toward creating an entrepreneurial community or ecosystem in any place.

Chapter 9: Entrepreneurial Community Success: Psychological Characteristics, Experiences, and Identities

Chapter 9 provides insight about engaging entrepreneurs by cultivating a deeper understanding of entrepreneurial psychology. This chapter explores the tension between an entrepreneur's independent identity and the benefits of collective action, teams, and working groups of entrepreneurs. Through this exploration, strategies are highlighted for anyone who seeks to engage entrepreneurs and empower them with leadership in the development of an entrepreneurial community or ecosystem.

Chapter 10: Leaping Cultural and Leadership Boundaries: Catalyzing Entrepreneurial Communities

Chapter 10 summarizes the lessons learned in the book, discusses the strengths and weaknesses of the approach, and develops implications and action items for a wide variety of potential readers. We then call these individuals to action, asking them to put down the book and take the first step toward meaningful, lasting social and community change.

References

Aronson, R. L. (1991). *Self-employment: A labor market perspective*. Ithaca, NY: ILR Publishing.

Bosma, N., & Levie, J. (2009). *Global entrepreneurship monitor 2008 global report*. Boston, MA: Babson College.

Breazeale, N., Fortunato, M., Allen, J., Hustedde, R., & Pushkarskaya, H. (2015). Constructing a multi-dimensional measure of local entrepreneurial culture. *Community Development*, *46*(5), 516–540.

Clifton, J., & Badal, S. B. (2014). *Entrepreneurial strengths finder*. New York, NY: Gallup Press.

Davidsson, P. (2009). *The entrepreneurship research challenge*. Cheltenham, UK: Edward Elgar.

Fayolle, A. (2014). What we know and what we need to know in the field of entrepreneurship. In A. Fayolle (Ed.), *Handbook of research on entrepreneurship: What we know and what we need to know* (pp. 1–12). Northampton, MA: Edward Elgar.

Flyvbjerg, B. (2001). *Making social science matter: Why social inquiry fails and how it can succeed again*. Cambridge, MA: Cambridge University Press.

Fortunato, M. W-P (2011). *The individual-institutional-opportunity nexus: Examining interaction, purpose, and opportunity in rural entrepreneurship development*. (Unpublished dissertation). University Park, PA: Pennsylvania State University.

Gartner, W. B. (1985). A conceptual framework for describing the phenomenon of new venture creation. *Academy of Management Review*, *10*(4), 696–706.

Ho, Y. P., & Wong, P. K. (2007). Financing, regulatory costs, and entrepreneurial propensity. *Small Business Economics*, *28*, 187–204.

Honig, B., & Dana, L. (2008). Communities of disentrepreneurship: A comparative cross-national examination of entrepreneurial demise. *Journal of Enterprising Communities: People and Places in the Global Economy*, *2*(1), 5–20.

Hustedde, R. (2007). What's culture got to do with it? Strategies for strengthening an entrepreneurial culture. In N. Walzer (Ed.), *Entrepreneurship and local economic development* (pp. 39–58). Lanham, MD: Lexington Books.

Kelley, D. J., Singer, S., & Herrington, M. (2016). *Global entrepreneurship monitor 2016 global report*. London: Global Entrepreneurship Research Association, London Business School.

Lichtenstein, G. A., & Lyons, T. S. (2010). *Investing in entrepreneurs: A strategic approach for strengthening your regional and community economy*. Santa Barbara, CA: Praeger.

Light, I., & Bonacich, E. (1991). *Immigrant entrepreneurs: Koreans in Los Angeles, 1965–1982*. Los Angeles, CA: University of California Press.

Naudé, W. (2013). *Entrepreneurship and economic development: Theory, evidence and policy*. IZA Discussion Paper No. 7507. Retrieved from http://ftp.iza.org/dp7507.pdf

Portes, A., Guarnizo, L. E., & Haller, W. J. (2002). Transnational entrepreneurs: An alternative form of immigrant economic adaptation. *American Sociological Review*, *4*(1), 278–298.

Richards, S. T., & Bulkley, S. (2007). *Agricultural entrepreneurs: The first and the forgotten?* Research Paper #07–01. Washington, DC: The Hudson Institute.

Saxenian, A. (2002). Transnational communities and the evolution of global production networks: The cases of Taiwan, China and India. *Industry and Innovation*, 9(3), 183–202.

Schön, D. A. (1983). *The reflective practitioner: How professionals think in action*. New York, NY: Basic Books.

Schumpeter, J. A. (1934). *The theory of economic development: An inquiry into profits, capital, credit, interest and the business cycle*. Cambridge, MA: Harvard University Press.

Shane, S. A. (2003). *A general theory of entrepreneurship: The individual-opportunity nexus*. Cheltenham, UK: Edward Elgar.

Theodori, G. L. (2005). Community and community development in resource-based areas: Operational definitions rooted in an interactional perspective. *Society and Natural Resources*, *18*, 661–669.

Wilkinson, K. P. (1991). *The community in rural America*. Appleton, WI: Social Ecology Press.

2 Perceptions of Entrepreneurs and Community

From Historical Roots to a Contemporary Kaleidoscope

Morgan R. Clevenger

There has long been a focus on the importance of the role of entrepreneurship in modern societies (Acs & Audretsch, 2003; Baron & Shane, 2007; Landström, 2005; Lichtenstein & Lyons, 2001, 2010; Shane & Venkataraman, 2000; Sexton, 1997; Venkataraman, 1997). Reynolds (2007) said that entrepreneurship as a phenomenon is "a systematic, pervasive, and important feature of U.S. personal and economic life" (p. 15), and Lichtenstein and Lyons (2010) said, "Entrepreneurs are the true heroes of the U.S. economy" (p. 1). "Historically, entrepreneurship is one of the oldest activities" (Landström, 2005, p. 3). Entrepreneurship had long been considered a deviant economic function by many economists (with the exception of Marshall, Cantillon, Say, and a few others) (Mitra, 2012) and not given much attention until Schumpeter (1934) elaborated on the role of entrepreneurs in the U.S. economic landscape and their ability to innovate and cause positive disruption through new ideas and business ventures.

Today, there are more than 275 colleges and universities in the United States with degree programs in entrepreneurship. Perhaps there is more economic insecurity compared to the past generations (Florida, 2012; Scott, 2002). The 1980s saw wide corporate downsizing, and the 1990s technology growth and subsequent bubble created positive momentum for start-ups that has maintained a public perception of the importance and viability of entrepreneurs (Low, 2001). Additionally, pop culture television series focus on various facets of entrepreneurs in *Shark Tank* and *Dragon's Den, The Apprentice, How I Made My Millions,* and *The Profit*. Likewise, several other popular series highlight the stories of entrepreneurs in different industries, such as *Kitchen Nightmares, Tabitha's Salon Takeover, Flip or Flop, Flipping Out*, and *Bar Rescue*. Special attention to entrepreneurs and small businesses is spotlighted annually during National Small Business Week, occurring since 1963 (McDaniel, 2015). The U.S. Department of Commerce's Economic Development Administration also acknowledged the emphasis of entrepreneurship in 2014 by establishing the new Office of Innovation and Entrepreneurship and its National Advisory Council on Innovation and Entrepreneurship.

Entrepreneurship is both a practice of business and a field of scholarly inquiry (Baron & Shane, 2007; Bygrave, 2007; Landström, 2005; Shane & Venkataraman, 2000). As a *process*, entrepreneurship is "a field of business [that] seeks to understand how opportunities create something new . . . arise and are discovered or created by specific persons, who then use various means to exploit or develop them, thus producing a wide range of effects" (Baron & Shane, 2007, p. 7). As a *field of scholarly inquiry*, the aim is to understand this societal phenomenon better (Davidsson, 2008). Entrepreneurship is about the behaviors and processes behind the emergence of new ventures (Shane & Venkataraman, 2000).

Entrepreneurship, however, is still a young *field of study*, progressing through adolescence, and struggling with its identity (Chell & Karatas-Özkan, 2014; Churchill & Lewis, 1986; Cornelius, Landström, & Persson, 2006; Dean, Shook, & Payne, 2007; Low, 2001). As a field of study, entrepreneurship is relatively new compared to other social sciences (Chell & Karatas-Özkan, 2014; Cooper, Markman, & Niss, 2000). "The Academy of Management views entrepreneurship as a division not a discipline and likewise the British Academy of Management categorises it as an area of special interest" (Chell & Karatas-Özkan, 2014, p. 1). Interestingly enough Landström, Parhankangas, Fayolle, and Riot (2017), Stevenson and Jarillo (1990), and Shane and Venkataraman (2000) indicate entrepreneurship research has become mainstream and *is* institutionalized as a *field of study* and a *field of practice*. Landström (2005) credits both Aldrich and MacMillan for efforts in this milestone.

Entrepreneurship as a phenomenon and *field of practice* is a source of new ideas, new industries, innovation, opportunity creation, job creation, improved sector productivity, economic growth, career advancement, and a catalyst of significant social integration and mobility (Lichtenstein & Lyons, 2010; National Governors Association, 2004; Reynolds, 2007). "The field has implications not only for entrepreneurs [and scholars] but also for public policy makers, managers, and the general public" (Cooper et al., 2000, p. 115).

While the concept of entrepreneurship is complex by itself, the idea of "community" is also multifarious. Beyond the family unit, the *community* is often the place where humans get their first introduction to society (Wilkinson, 1991), and, therefore, its norms and values. This capacity specifies enormous primacy in the role of the community. "People construct community symbolically, making it a resource and repository of meaning, and a reference of their identity" (Cohen, 1985, p. 118). Wilkinson (1991) defines community as having three elements: (1) a locality, (2) a local society, and (3) a set of locally oriented collective actions. Specifically, the third concept sits at the nexus of entrepreneurship and community (Davidsson, 2015). Additionally, individuals affiliate and bond through social identity and the development of social capital (Adler & Kwon, 2002; Putnam, 2000; Stam, Arzlanian, & Elfring, 2014; Warren, 1987; Wilkinson, 1991).

Social capital is the process by which each person contributes to the overall good of society through social norms, communications and information exchange, and fulfilling obligations and expectations in some supporting social structure or relationship (Coleman, 1988; Nahapiet & Ghoshal, 1998). Smith (2001) said social capital is "the sense of attachment and quality of social networks" (p. 15). Ideally, social actors have independent goals and actions, but utilize their individual human capital to support others in an interdependent frame. Relationships are built on trust and trustworthiness in the social environment (Coleman, 1988; Tajfel, 1982; see also Clevenger, Fortunato, & Houlihan, 2017, regarding social networks, relationships, and trust). The norms of reciprocity and trust are critical in an entrepreneurial context, too, by enhancing the propensity of entrepreneurs to behave collaboratively. Social capital is important because it is a "glue" that can bind entrepreneurs to one another to explore synergies for action, and entrepreneurs to a community to build an effective, community-wide support system for entrepreneurs (as well as benefits to a community).

Social identity is the reflection of belongingness within units. Social identity creates 'in-groups' and 'out-groups.' *In-groups* are those mutually relying on one another. An *out-group* is outside the bounds of an in-group. Depending on the culture, acceptability, and embeddedness, entrepreneurs may be in an out-group initially, and later in an in-group. Ideally, entrepreneurs form a sub-community within a community. Community is about relationships. Generative relationships—focused on innovation and improvement—help to create entrepreneurial climates (Lane & Maxfield, 1996; Surie & Hazy, 2006).

Meyer and Jepperson (2000) said, "Modern culture depicts society as made up of 'actors'" (p. 100). These actors include individuals and all forms of organizations contributing to community-level concerns. Martinelli (2004) said,

> Entrepreneurship cannot be fully understood without making reference to the socio-cultural and politico-institutional context in which it arises and develops . . . The socio-cultural and politico-institutional environment influences entrepreneurial attitudes and motives, the resources that can be mobilized, the constraints and opportunities related to starting and expanding a business, and the cultural climate that can either legitimize or hinder the entrepreneurial role.
>
> (p. 55)

This "wider ecosystem" of community considers other entrepreneurs, institutions, government, and broader factors such as public policy (Corno, Lal, & Colombo, 2014; Hechavarria & Ingram, 2014; Hwang & Powell, 2005; Marti, Courpasson, & Barbosa, 2013; Renski, 2009). The broader complexity of ecological factors makes up an entrepreneurial community (Lichtenstein, Lyons, & Kutzhanova, 2004).

Chaskin, Brown, Benkatesh, and Vidal (2001) examine the resources of a community to function sustainably, as well as providing the ability to support any initiative—including entrepreneurship. The ability of a community to meet its own needs independently of excessive external support is called *community capacity* (see Wilkinson, 1991), and it involves the resources of people, business and nonprofit organizations, government, physical infrastructure, housing, education, and social capital systems that collectively improve or maintain well-being (Chaskin et al., 2001). Community systems are complex, and involve a wide range of diverse actors, often with competing ideologies and uneven patterns of human interaction (i.e., an active, well-integrated community versus a community that is segregated along race, religious, or class lines). Entrepreneurship has an important role in community (Cochran, 1949; Hustedde, 2007).

This chapter provides an overview of who entrepreneurs are and what they do, the field of entrepreneurship as both a practice of business and a field of study, the important of entrepreneurship education, the role of entrepreneurship in economic development, and the theory of community. Concerns of community and the embedded dynamics related to trust and sociological constructions are discussed. Finally, the framework of *levels of analysis* of entrepreneurship is elaborated at the micro-, meso-, and macro-levels and their interrelated significance. Such a framework provides clarity to understand individual entrepreneurs separate from their firms and then how they fit into macro considerations of industry, community, and larger levels of regional, state, national, and worldwide entities. Understanding all of these concepts is requisite in order to explore deeper the entrepreneurial community unit of analysis in the development of entrepreneurial community ecosystems to support this important function in the United States and globally.

Entrepreneurship: An Overview

Several recent texts exist that provide eloquent and lengthy historical accounts of entrepreneurship as a field of study and discuss various typologies, philosophies, and applications, including Casson, Yeung, Basu, and Wadeson's (2006) *The Oxford Handbook of Entrepreneurship*; Cooper, Markman, and Niss's (2000) *The Evolution of the Field of Entrepreneurship*; Fayolle's (2014) *Handbook of Research on Entrepreneurship: What We Know and What We Need to Know*; Sexton and Smilor's (1986) *The Art and Science of Entrepreneurship* and (1997) *Entrepreneurship 2000*; Shane's (2004) *A General Theory of Entrepreneurship: The Individual-Opportunity Nexus*; and Hébert and Link's (2009) *A History of Entrepreneurship*. Additionally, three other interesting discussions of entrepreneurship are Morris's (1998) *Entrepreneurial Intensity: Sustainable Advantages for Individuals, Organizations, and Societies;* Walzer's (2007) *Entrepreneurship and Local Economic Development;* and Swedberg's (2000) *Entrepreneurship: The*

Social Science View, which critically questions many prior ideas, frameworks, and concepts to add some devil's advocacy on the matter. Finally, some texts explain the "how to" of being an entrepreneur and creating an entrepreneurial venture from a firm-level perspective. For instance, Jain (1998) provides an excellent book discussing all facets for entrepreneurs titled *Handbook for New Entrepreneurs*. Kuratko's (2016) tenth edition of *Entrepreneurship: Theory, Process, and Practice* includes step-by-step ideas for individual entrepreneurs or corporate entrepreneurship in companies. Finally, Zacharakis, Spinelli, and Timmons's (2011) book *Business Plans That Work: A Guide for Small Business* details a straightforward approach to entrepreneurial practice.

Highlighted here are key points to serve as the basis of discussion to define entrepreneurs and entrepreneurship, explore the role of entrepreneurial education, understand the strategic investment by communities and economic development groups to emphasize entrepreneurship, explore the depth of research for entrepreneurship as a field of study, and illuminate the dynamic aspects of entrepreneurship in practice.

A Brief History

The term *entrepreneur* first appeared in 1437 in a French dictionary with three definitions: active with achievement, undertaking, or war-like activities. Some "French authors referred to the entrepreneur as someone who is tough and prepared to risk his own life and fortune" (Landström, 2005, p. 4). Risk became commonly associated with entrepreneurs in the 17th Century. In the 17th and 18th centuries, the label *entrepreneur* became associated with "technical and managerial responsibility for . . . construction" (Landström, p. 4).

The 12th-Century European economy was locked in the feudal system, so it "hampered innovation" (Landström, 2005, p. 27). Later, "entrepreneurship appeared in the economic science literature primarily through the writings of Richard Cantillon (approx. 1680–1734, an Irish-born banker who lived in Paris)" (Landström, 2005, p. 28).

The times from the American Revolution to the Gilded Age of the late 1800s and the Progressive Era of the early 1900s until World War II were particularly entrepreneurial in this regard, with American ingenuity and charisma exhibited by the great industrialists such as Andrew Carnegie, Henry Ford, J. P. Morgan, and John D. Rockefeller; inventors such as Benjamin Franklin, Thomas Edison, George Washington Carver, the Wright Brothers, George Eastman, and Alexander Graham Bell; and innovators such as Coco Chanel and Walt Disney (Norris & Bockelmann, 2000; Putnam, 2000).

Additionally during the late 1800s and early 1900s, immigrants flocked to America from all parts of Europe and other various places around the world to settle in the United States seeking a better life and opportunities that they could not find or create in their homelands—a trend that continues today (Kerr & Kerr, 2016; Portes, 1995). Individuals forge(d) a new life through entrepreneurship and maintain family firms, which continue to constitute a key role in the landscape of American business (Astrachan, 2003; Gompers, 1999; Hollander & Elman, 1988; McCann, Leon-Guerrero, & Haley, 2001; Portes, 1995; Poza & Daugherty, 2014; Sharma, Chrisman, & Gersick, 2012; Sorenson, Yu, Brigham, & Lumpkin, 2013; Zahra, 2005). Currently, 18 percent of all American businesses are owned by immigrants (McDaniels, 2015; Sandburn, 2012). These adventurous and hopeful people effectively represent cohorts of risk takers and ambition who are tolerant of the risks involved with significant relocation and starting businesses, or did so out of necessity.

Schumpeter (1934) addresses entrepreneurship from an economic standpoint, enterprise evolution, and possibilities of economic enterprise to add to Léon Walras's (1834–1910) equilibrium theory by explaining an "energy" and "enthusiasm" "that created disequilibrium in the market" (Landström, 2005, p. 32). Landström (2005) credits Baumol (1990), whose

> Basic thesis is that the supply of entrepreneurs in a society is constant but that the societal value of their self interest driven ingenuity varies according to the rewards available. This [view] indicates that, in order to encourage entrepreneurship, it is necessary to create conditions that allow the entrepreneurial pursuit of self-interest to accord with social wealth creation.
>
> (p. 37)

Kirzner (1973), on the other hand, believes in a market demand perspective to fulfill a need or gap in society. Both supply-side and demand-side functions explain the various roles of entrepreneurs and contributions to economic development (Thornton, 1999).

While entrepreneurship is found in many societies, some forms of entrepreneurship are productive and others unproductive (Baumol, 1990). Productive entrepreneurship is the positive, economic-enhancing view that serves as a catalyst in the free enterprise economy and the backbone to a democratic capitalistic society. Unproductive entrepreneurship—while creating business and generating money—is seen as black markets and illegal or immoral business activities, which cause the degradation or erosion of ethics and morals.

Entrepreneurs have been studied and yielded a wide range of different views of the entrepreneur over time—from risk taker and finder of fortune, to resource allocator, niche carver, creative destructor, opportunity-seeker, and agent of the community, perhaps.

Entrepreneurs have been seen as villains and heroes as well as pillars for the economy. Studies of entrepreneurs have emphasized the supply-side disruptor ingenuity and passion, and more recent research explores the demand side of opportunity and need fulfillment through strategic management and catalytic creation of "must have" products, services, and processes. Westhead and Wright (2013) and Zacharakis et al. (2011) group entrepreneurs "into different categories based on stage of business development" (Zacharakis et al., 2011, p. 3). For example, individuals might be nascent entrepreneurs (i.e., pre-launch mode), start-up entrepreneurs (novice), mature entrepreneurs, serialpreneurs, intrapreneurs, corporate entrepreneurs, or entrepreneurial community advocates (Kuratko, 2016; Westhead & Wright, 2013; Zacharakis et al., 2011).

Bhidé (2000) and Clifton and Badal (2014) indicate few people are born entrepreneurs willing to start businesses under any conditions. Evidence of a single personality trait leading to become an entrepreneur is not supported in empirical evidence. However, many characteristics have been identified as conduits to being a successful entrepreneur including: (1) open communication, (2) ability to leverage social networking and building relationships, and (3) creating and fulfilling mutual expectations (Aldrich & Zimmer, 1986). Entrepreneurs can be born but more than likely will be made by choice and through habits (Gartner, 1988; Gasse, 1986; Neck & Regele, 2012). Gerber (1995) leaned more toward someone having an "entrepreneurial personality" (p. 23). Florida (2012) promotes the importance of talent, which includes "skilled, ambitious, educated, and entrepreneurial people" who "are a central force in economic progress" (p. 231). Landström (2005) says an "entrepreneur must also possess competency . . . the ability to handle . . . employing empirical knowledge . . . as well as reflecting over and questioning practical experience" (p. 17).

Macke and Markley (2003) view entrepreneurs as innovative and creatively inclined human beings who strive for personal and collective social and economic successes. Landström (2005) said, "Entrepreneurship . . . demands creativity—the creation of something new that builds on the entrepreneur's readiness to learn and self-reliance, which makes the entrepreneur dare to challenge established practices" (p. 17). Kanter (1986) said creativity comes from a creative environment through "contact with other people" and "cross-fertilization" through "cross-disciplinary contact" (p. 11).

Gerber (1995) highlights three different personality faces of an entrepreneur: the dreamer, the technician, and the manager—and notes that one cannot be excellent at all three simultaneously. Gerber indicates when one decides to become an entrepreneur, that moment is an "entrepreneurial seizure" when one discovers s/he is good at something and decides to make money from it (p. 12). "The entrepreneurial personality turns the most trivial condition into an exceptional opportunity . . . the visionary . . . the dreamer . . . [with] energy . . . [and] imagination," (Gerber, 1995, p. 23). The dreamer is passionate and compelling, but may be best at people building or sales. "The technician suffering from an entrepreneurial seizure takes the work [s/]he loves to do and turns it into a job," (Gerber, 1995, p. 17). The manager is the efficient operations director and taskmaster, but loses sight of the excitement of creating through the original love of craft or use of technical skills.

Aldrich and Zimmer (1986) address two key ideas: "(1) entrepreneurship is a process and must be viewed in dynamic terms rather than in cross-sectional snapshots; and (2) entrepreneurship requires *linkages or relations* between key components of the process," (p. 3). Further, Aldrich and Zimmer describe "connections to resources and niches in an opportunity structure" (p. 3). These ideas are best illustrated by *The Timmons Model* (see Figure 2.1), which considers four key variables that must act holistically for creation and sustainability of a venture as the founder (i.e., the entrepreneur), the team executing on ideas, opportunity(ies) to fulfill a market need or create a market need, and the various resources of production (Timmons & Spinelli, 2009; Zacharakis et al., 2011). Davidsson (2015) and Timmons (1997) consider entrepreneurship as a way of thinking and approaching opportunities. These variables combine personal drive and persona, social networks, organizational dynamics, and environmental capacities to elevate all the requirements—constituting many moving dynamics—for entrepreneurship (Bygrave, 2007; Zacharakis et al., 2011).

Entrepreneurship Education

The first course in entrepreneurship on record was offered at Harvard University in 1947 with venture creation as the focus (Cooper et al., 2000). Since then, entrepreneurship education has proliferated widely and diversely (see Bae, Qian, Miao, & Fiet, 2014; Kuratko, 2005; Martin, McNally, & Kay, 2013). Fayolle and Kyro's (2008) *The Dynamics Between Entrepreneurship,*

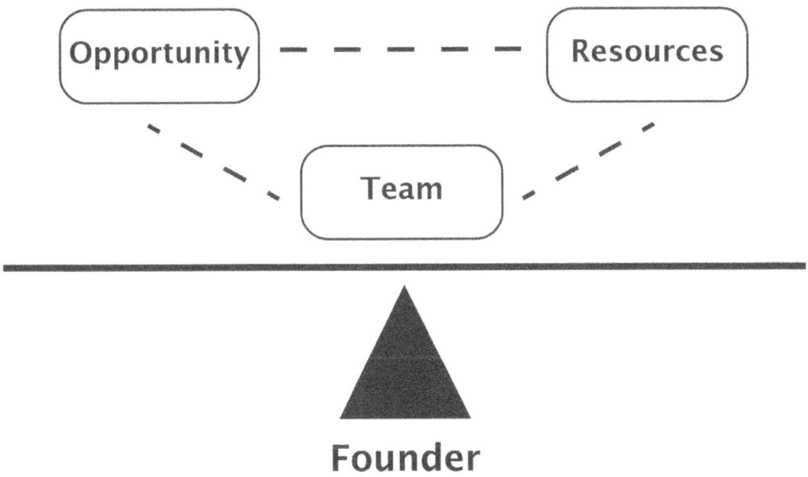

Figure 2.1 Simple Timmons Model. Concepts and their relationships include Founder (Entrepreneur), Team, Opportunity, and Resources (Adapted from *The Timmons Model: The Classically Balanced Venture*, Zacharakis et al., 2011, p. 17)

Environment, and Education provides a summary and statistics of education in the U.S. landscape. Solomon (2007) also provides an overview of entrepreneurship education and notes that entrepreneurship programs lack uniformity, and traditional business programs sometimes fail to be relevant to the needs of today's entrepreneurs or business world.

Kuckertz (2013); Kuratko, Cornwall, and Morris (2013); and Morris (2014) promote quality teaching and curriculum development focused on an innovation platform with hands-on, real-world application. Entrepreneurship should be taught differently than other business topics with more creative thinking, skill development, and teamwork through various internships and project-based learning (Kanter, 1986, 2002; Kuckertz, 2013). Guo, Chen, and Yu (2015) promote the merits of receiving a college education and how it has a positive influence on an entrepreneurial business. Their research looks at four questions. (1) What is the impact of college on becoming an entrepreneur? (2) Do self-employed people make more money than those hired by others? (3) In terms of entrepreneurs' annual income, what is the impact of college education? (4) Does college education affect women and minorities the same way it does others? The results highlight how a formal entrepreneurship education is significantly associated with being self-employed and provides a positive, significant annual income. Li and Liu's (2011) research correlates a positive relationship between undergraduates' education and employment performance. Entrepreneurship education is of an utmost importance and is a justifiable means by graduates creating or securing good jobs, which alleviates issues of being unemployable or unemployed, settling for an average job, or being forced into more formal education.

Neck and Regele (2012) explain that in the United States there is a demand for entrepreneurs in order to generate economic growth. Harrington and Maysami (2015) describe the benefits of fostering entrepreneurship in regional universities in order to boost the regional and state economic development. These colleges and universities provide a catalyst for new businesses and help to foster a flexible, creative, motivated, and well-educated workforce that may improve a local economy. Entrepreneurship is enhanced when situated near academic institutions (Florida, 2002; Pride, Hughes, & Kapoor, 2014). Narayan (2015) and Neck and Regele (2012) promote entrepreneurial education at the K–12 level as well as in higher education to support economic growth. Lichtenstein and Lyons (2001) support "building skills" in order to develop entrepreneurs (p. 7). Programs through 4-H's *EntrepreneurShip Investigation: Discover the E-Scene* series, incubatoredu.org, and Junior Achievement's *Be Entrepreneurial*® provide entrepreneurial skills in K–12 (4-H Mall, 2016; INCubatoredu®, 2016; juniorachievement.org, 2016).

While much has been emphasized in entrepreneurship education, there is opportunity for additional compilation of practices, curricula, disciplinary needs, and students' entrepreneurial abilities, such as creativity, critical thinking, critical reading, critical analysis, problem solving, social networking, and entrepreneurial leadership (Byrne, Fayolle, & Toutain, 2014; Kuratko, 2007, 2016). Much of the practice has followed the research of entrepreneurship with exploration into individual behaviors and traits, the firm or enterprise unit, and economic functionality. Missing in both teaching entrepreneurship and research in entrepreneurship is the community of practice for entrepreneurs and the sociological and contextual settings of entrepreneurs and their businesses.

Entrepreneurship and Economic Development

Economic development tries to facilitate business development to spawn the economy (Hustedde, 2007; Lane & Johnstone, 2012; National Governors Association, 2004; Parker, 2005; Renski, 2009; Schumpeter, 1934; Walzer, 2004, 2007; Walzer & Athiyaman, 2007; Young, 1971). Entrepreneurship has long been an economic development community strategy (Liñán, Fernández-Serrano, & Romero, 2013). Parker (2005) said, "The arguments for promoting entrepreneurship are so familiar that they barely need repeating. Entrepreneurship is held to stimulate competition, create innovation and jobs, generate positive externalities, and provide a route out of poverty and discrimination" (p. 37). Lichtenstein and Lyons said,

> The community's entrepreneurs and enterprises should be treated as a portfolio of related business assets and managed accordingly. This requires that economic developers approach managing their Pipelines holistically and link all segments together, not favoring certain segments over others. Economic development strategies should be targeted to specific needs, goals, and parts of the Pipeline, but this should be done in a way that sustains the entire Pipeline, its volume, and its flow.
>
> (p. 176)

Entrepreneurship is a "significant causal factor in the process of economic growth and development" (Wilken, 1979, p. 2). Some economists have historically seen entrepreneurship as nonessential and as a dependent variable, since the entrepreneur has not historically fit cleanly into economic models; by contrast, noneconomists (sociologists and psychologists) tend to believe entrepreneurship is a significant independent variable (Wilken, 1979, p. 4). Environmental conditions promoting entrepreneurship at the community level may include: (a) economic: opportunity, capital, increased income and (b) noneconomic: legitimacy of entrepreneurship, social mobility, denial of conventional routes to prestige with flexibility, marginality, social integration, security, ideology, other social factors (Baron & Shane, 2007; Wilken, 1979). Additionally, the emphasis of opportunity affects social change, the development of new markets and distribution channels, and the availability of resources and systems (Baron & Shane, 2007). Putnam (2000) said,

"Where trust and social networks flourish, individuals, firms, neighborhoods, and even nations prosper" (p. 319).

In 2004, the National Governors Association highlighted the need for more entrepreneurs. The organization—with the assistance of several experts in entrepreneurship as well as the Ewing Marion Kauffman Foundation—identified four key facets of entrepreneurship and the multifaceted emphasis for (1) a cognitive mind-set: thinking about entrepreneuring, (2) understanding behavioral processes to start new businesses, (3) the consideration of economic as well as sociological aspects of new firm formation, and (4) supporting innovation and growth with an overall approach to entrepreneurial management (National Governors Association, 2004, p. 6). The economic benefit of entrepreneurs is seen locally and regionally [through the generation of revenues], and in job creation (Haltiwanger, 2009; Low, Henderson, & Wiler, 2005; Thurik, 2009; Walzer, 2004). Shuffstall (2013) and Shuffstall and Fortunato (2013) have developed a tool to assess how entrepreneurial a community is. The tool considers reflection of entrepreneurs, institutions, and culture to support entrepreneurship.

Research and Scholarship in Entrepreneurship

From a research perspective, the field of entrepreneurship is defined as the scholarly examination of how, by whom, and with what effects opportunities create future goods, services, or processes that are discovered, created, evaluated, and exploited (Davidsson, 2008; Ireland & Webb, 2007; Shane & Venkataraman, 2000). Early research focused on entrepreneurial traits. There was a shift to policy in the 1940s. Entrepreneurship research began escalating in the late 1940s (Evans, 1949). Soltow's (1968) study on entrepreneurship illuminates various prior reviews and indicates there were no case studies done from the early years until the 1980s—the goal was simply exploratory on independent traits or concerns (e.g., psychological, sociological, economic, etc.) (Fayolle, 2014; Wortman, 1986). After personality theories, some economic theories were explored and then sociocultural perspectives and the population perspectives appeared (Aldrich & Zimmer, 1986; Fayolle, 2014). Productive and functional dependence theories and management studies later emerged (Cuevas & Carrasco, 2008; Fayolle, 2014).

Scholarship in entrepreneurship has grown since the 1950s (Chell & Karatas-Özkan, 2014). The most common approaches to early entrepreneurship research focused on survey questionnaires and interviews—but using others' tools (none unique for entrepreneurship) (Wortman, 1986). Various typologies have included: theoretical, historical, environmental, organizational, functional, and future (Wortman, 1986). Wortman's (1986) work summarizes studies over 30 years, but only 5 were on the environmental level and none for organizational levels; most were conducted on characteristics, functions in business, or corporate entrepreneurship. At that time, there was little use of "statistics in studying individual entrepreneurship" (Wortman, 1986, p. 298). Wortman encouraged use of overall frameworks instead of isolated characteristics. By the late 1980s, Low and MacMillan (1988) found that 36 percent of entrepreneurship research was focused on individuals, 4 percent on teams, 2 percent on innovation, 53 percent on the firm, and 5 percent on industry or macro-level issues. Research on entrepreneurship had been developing in various capacities and independently across different disciplines (Bygrave, 2007; Sexton, 1997; Sexton & Smilor, 1986, 1997).

To address the massive diversity across the emerging field of entrepreneurship, several major works have attempted to integrate across entrepreneurship research strands: Wortman's (1986) work, *A Unified Framework, Research Typologies, and Research Prospectuses for the Interface Between Entrepreneurship and Small Business*; Acs and Audretsch's (2003, 2011) *Handbook of Entrepreneurship Research: An Interdisciplinary Survey and Introduction,* Davidsson's (2008) *The Entrepreneurship Research Challenge*, Landström's (2005) *Pioneers in Entrepreneurship and Small Business Research*; Alvarez, Agarwal, and Sorenson's (2005) *Handbook of Entrepreneurship Research: Disciplinary Perspectives*; and Landström et al.'s (2017) *Challenging Entrepreneurship Research* are just a few examples that provide ideas, discussions, and frameworks for entrepreneurial research. In 2000, Alverez and Barney said there had been too much emphasis on entrepreneurship as a strategy for survival to develop deeper theory across the multiple facets entangled in entrepreneurship. Chandler and Lyon (2001) believe more research from the 21st Century began pushing emphasis for the creation of more sophisticated theoretical models, the opportunity for longitudinal research, and greater emphasis on multiple source data sets. Dean et al. (2007) indicate the need for more widespread dissemination of entrepreneurship research from doctoral students and faculty to better compound knowledge from so many scholars.

With all its diversity, entrepreneurship remains a bounded multidisciplinary field (Cornelius et al., 2006; Herron, Sapienza, & Smith-Cook, 1991; Ireland & Webb, 2007; Kuratko, 2007; Landström, 2014, p. 46; Low & MacMillan, 1988; Parker, 2005; Zahra, 2005) with a need for integration across economics, geography, management, finance, strategy, psychology, and sociology (Acs & Audretsch, 2003; Bygrave, 2007; Hitt & Ireland, 2000). "Entrepreneurship is a complex, heterogeneous and multilevel phenomenon, and there is a need to use knowledge from many other fields in order to understand the phenomenon," (Landström, 2014, p. 46). However, "entrepreneurship is viewed as a very applied field and unsuitable (fraught with danger) for the teaching and research activities of young scholars" (Churchill & Lewis, 1986, p. 334). Oddly, this observation is in direct contradiction to the practice of entrepreneurship itself.

The diversity of entrepreneurship research has had a chilling effect on the creation of unified theories addressing entrepreneurship as a phenomenon.

Alvarez and Barney (2000) said there is a "lack of a well-articulated, underlying theory of entrepreneurship" (p. 64). Likewise, Pittaway, Holt, and Broad (2014) provide five concerns in entrepreneurship research: (1) a lack of consistent terminology, (2) disciplinary focuses without consideration of overlaps, (3) a large range of methods leading to atheoretical explanations, (4) a need for more robust theoretical constructs, and (5) a need for greater inter-relationships between levels of analysis (p. 86). Neergaard (2007) discusses the challenging issues regarding sample sizes, methodologies, and access to entrepreneurs for research purposes. Churchill and Lewis (1986) indicate,

> Individuals actively involved in entrepreneurship have related more to the practitioner than to the university. Thus they are somewhat outside the mainstream of academic activity and are perceived as taking more from the academic community than they return to it.
>
> (p. 334)

Therefore, some researchers have been hesitant to spend the time needed to foster strong relationships with entrepreneurs—they are a moving target or like "herding cats."

More recent scholars indicate that quantitative work is not an ideal research methodology alone because entrepreneurial research ideally needs small sample sizes, and multiple viewpoints—to best illuminate the lived experience (Bygrave, 2007; Hill, 2012; Neergaard, 2007, 2014; Neergaard & Ulhøi, 2007). Bygrave (2007) said,

> No amount of regression analysis will help us understand what triggers the quantum jump [in entrepreneurial behaviors] or what happens during the quantum jump. At most, a dummy variable in regression analysis will tell us that a change has occurred. But as its name implies cannot tell us the details of why and how the change occurred.
>
> (p. 43)

Perhaps the challenge comes from understanding entrepreneurs from a qualitative standpoint as "researchers try to understand phenomena from the perspective of the participant . . . [and] researchers stress the emergence of theory from the data rather than forcing data into existing theories . . . [because] the causes of experiences are assumed to be complex and nonlinear" (Hill, 2012, p. 15). This dilemma of qualitative and quantitative methodologies gives rise to the value of mixed methods research supported by Creswell (2013, 2014) and other research scholars.

The field of study of entrepreneurship has seen a major increase in scholarship and publishing (Alvarez & Barney, 2000; Chell & Karatas-Özkan, 2014; Hayton & Cacciotti, 2014). There are now more than 50 entrepreneurship or management journals available for scholars to highlight research and serve as a venue for the development of concepts, models, theories, practice, and utilization of entrepreneurship (Carraher & Paridon, 2015). Additionally, Grégoire, Nöel, Déry, and Béchard (2006) indicate there has been growth from 1980 to 2005 for convergence in entrepreneurship theory as a basis of strong research that needs to be shared and positioned over multiple disciplines.

Despite the challenges in integrating across disciplines and finding a set of cohesive, unifying theories, the field of entrepreneurship research—as both a field of scholarly inquiry and a field of practice—needs more work (Bird, Schjoedt, & Hanke, 2014; Bygrave, 2007; Byrne et al., 2014; Chandler & Lyon, 2001; Cooper et al., 2000; Davidsson, 2008; Landström et al., 2017; Low & MacMillan, 1988; Parker, 2005; Phan, 2004; Sexton, 1997; Zahra, 2005). Kuratko, Morris, and Schindehutte (2015) summarize a framework approach to entrepreneurship research that is very helpful, but does not consider the entrepreneurial community nor ecosystem approach. Kuratko et al. do have an "integrative framework" that includes concerns such as the entrepreneur, resources, and the environment.

Levels of Analysis in Entrepreneurship

A key organizational system for entrepreneurship research can be the consideration through levels of analysis (Bird, Schjoedt, & Hanke, 2014; Bourdieu, 1977, 1984, 1987, 1990, 1998; Chandler & Lyon, 2001; Cuevas & Carrasco, 2008; Davidsson & Wiklund, 2001; Forson, Obbilgin, & Ozturk, 2014; Hechavarria & Ingram, 2014; Landström, 2005; Martinelli, 2004; Mourdoukoutas & Papadimitriou, 2002; Thornton, 1999). The three main units of consideration are micro-, meso-, and macro-levels. The *micro-level* approach is concerned with the individual: financial motive, risk-uncertainty theory, and psychological theories on optimization of the entrepreneur's behavior. The *meso-level* approach focuses on the firm's interest: wider theory including economics, social network theory, spin-off process, innovation, job creation, and all facets of management. Finally, the *macro-level* approach combines both the individual and enterprise concern within the economic system where entrepreneurial activity is located and intertwines with complexities of all other businesses, organizations, governments, policies, and systems. The macro-level 1 is that of a community, and the macro-level 2 is broader such as regional or national society, and the macro-level 3, which is worldwide.

In the context of our focus on entrepreneurs and communities, levels of analysis for entrepreneurship can be reframed in this way: *individual* (e.g., psychological and personal skills and motives); *firm* (e.g., group level interactions relating to sociological, institutional, and organizational frames); *community* (e.g., societal and culture realms, behavior similar to organizational or institutional, and environmental and ecological units); *regional, state, national, or industry* (e.g., also societal and culture with various economic and environmental exchanges); and *worldwide* (e.g., macro-culture, national society interactions, global economic intermingling, and multi-national environmental complexities) (Aldrich, 1990; Bourdieu, 1977, 1984, 1987, 1990, 1998; Chandler & Lyon, 2001; Cuevas & Carrasco, 2008; Davidsson & Wiklund, 1996, 2001; Forson, Ozbilgin, Ozturk, & Tatli, 2014; Karatas-Özkan, Yavuz, & Howells, 2014; Kutzhanova, Lyons, & Lichtenstein, 2009; Low, Henderson, & Wiler, 2005; McMullen & Shepherd, 2006; Mourdoukoutas & Papadimitriou, 2002; Ruef & Lounsbury, 2007; Sine & David, 2010; Thornton, 1999; Tolbert, David, & Sine, 2011; Trompenaars & Hampden-Turner, 2012). Additionally, other key measures of analysis may include: growth in business, innovation, opportunity recognition, and business creation (Baron & Shane, 2007; Reynolds, 2007; Ryan, 2004). These various units of analysis cluster best into Bourdieu's (1977, 1984, 1987, 1990, 1998) three units of micro, meso, and macro concerns, which were also considered by Cunningham and Lischeron (1991) and Forson et al. (2014) (see Table 2.1).

Entrepreneurship happens because of a mix of economic and noneconomic considerations: the latter is a specific set of social conditions or by

Table 2.1 Levels of Analysis in Entrepreneurship

Unit	*Level of Analysis*	*Functional Characteristics*
Macro-level 3	Worldwide level: global macro-sociological, global sociocultural, global society, global culture dynamics, global political economies	United Nations initiatives, human regulation context, global industrial relations, global business environments, global labor market dynamics, structures of resources and constraints, globalization
Macro-level 2	Environmental level: macro-sociological, regional or national sociocultural, regional or national society, regional or national culture, political economy	Social regulation context, industrial relations, legislation, macro regional and national business environments, labor market dynamics, prevailing discourses of legitimacy, structures of resources and constraints, globalization
Macro-level 1	Community level: sociological, sociocultural, sector or industry, market, community as organization, industries, ecosystem	Objective structures pertaining to the community organization and sector, industry rules and procedures, industry or sectoral patterns of legitimacy and competition, entrepreneurial networks (which may include associational, professional and organizational linkages), informal codes of conduct, community and organizational history and culture, informal rules of legitimacy

Unit	*Level of Analysis*	*Functional Characteristics*
Meso-level	Enterprise or firm level: organization	Educational, financial, cultural, and network resources; strategies used to gain capital to legitimize their presence in the field
Micro-level	Individual level: entrepreneurs and small business owners	"Great person" school; psychological entrepreneurial attributes, biographies, and motivations; management function; leadership function; intrapreneurship

Adapted and amalgamated from ideas from Bourdieu (1977, 1984, 1987, 1990, 1998); Cunningham and Lischeron (1991); Forson, Ozbilgin, Ozturk, and Tatli (2014); and Thornton (1999).

particular social and psychological factors (Wilken, 1979). Aldrich and Zimmer (1986) said, "Entrepreneurship is a social role, embedded in a social context. Investigators cannot treat entrepreneurs in isolation as autonomous decision makers or lump them together with others with similar social characteristics, without regard to context" (p. 20). Embeddedness is important to understand context and community (McKeever, Anderson, & Jack, 2014).

Each of these levels is a valuable entity to explore and understand entrepreneurship. Collectively, an integrative consideration of ideas intertwine psychology, sociology, anthropology, economics, social embeddedness, and organizational and institutional theory (Thornton, 1999). The ecology of community and a multilevel framework create a complex and beautiful kaleidoscope of concepts to illuminate and study entrepreneurship.

Micro-Level: The Entrepreneur

At the micro-level is *the individual* (i.e., psychological); contributing individuals illustrate various characteristics that then collectively contribute to local culture (Aldrich & Wiedenmayer, 1993; Brockhaus & Horowitz, 1986; Hayton, George, & Zahra, 2002; McClelland, 1961; Rauch & Frese, 2007; Weber, 1930). Entrepreneurial cognition, motivation, behavior, self-efficacy, and choice have been studied extensively (Allen & Lee, 1997; Bowser, 2016; Hansemark, 2003; Hornaday & Aboud, 1971; Mitchell et al., 2002; Nandram & Samson, 2006; Rauch & Frese, 2007; Reynolds, 2007; Tan, 2002; Westhead & Wright, 2013). Skills, technical ability, and management acumen have also been important considerations (Gerber, 1995; Kutzhanova et al., 2009; Lichtenstein & Lyons, 2010; Stevenson & Jarillo, 1990). Additionally, Thomas and Mueller (2000) explored individuals' differences across cultures including locus of control, risk-taking propensity, innovativeness, and energy. Bird, Schjoedt, and Hanke (2014) also consider performance, selling, creativity, innovation, discovery, and leadership as key factors.

"An entrepreneur is an independent being; entrepreneurship provides an opportunity for self-expression and the realization of one's passion for doing something new and different—a scope for innovation" (Jain, 1998, p. 3). Simply put, an entrepreneur is someone who takes on the risk and responsibility to own and operate a business to potentially reap a reward. "Hard work and self-improvement were believed to be the basis for 'getting ahead.' These values are somewhat differently regarded by the different social class groups" (Warren, 1987, p. 106).

Florida explains it best:

> An innovation has no value until an ambitious entrepreneur builds a business model around it and turns it into a product or service that customers will buy. If you can't turn an innovative idea into something that creates a customer, it's worthless.
>
> (p. 8)

Researchers look at entrepreneurship—and, thus, an entrepreneur—from various discipline perspectives (Bygrave, 2007; Fortunato, 2017; Gartner, Davidsson, & Zahra, 2006; Low & MacMillan, 1988). Gartner (1990) believes the central feature of entrepreneur behavior is creating a new business or venture that adds value to society. Many scholars differ in the consideration of what "adding value" constitutes. Davidsson (2008) promotes clarification as a new product, service, or process; a bundle of products or services; or attention to the price-value relation (e.g., better price, speed, or quality). Thus an entrepreneur is

> an individual or part of a group of individuals who . . . create[s] a new business venture within a place to offer a new product or service, bundle of products or services, or price/value relationship that adds value to markets.
>
> (Fortunato, 2017, p. 185)

This definition is sufficiently broad to include innovative replication, or the introduction of a prior innovation to a new geographic market, or to an old market in a new way (Davidsson, 2008; Schumpeter, 1934).

Core concepts at the micro-level emphasize innovation and the applicability to market opportunities or to create markets. *Innovation* is one of those difficult English words that encompasses many ideas. The four types of innovation for entrepreneurial purposes includes invention, extension, duplication, and synthesis (Kuratko, 2016). These concepts are illustrated in Figure 2.2. *Invention* is developing a new product, service, or process previously not in existence (e.g., Thomas Edison's invention of the light bulb). *Extension* is the improvement or addition of features to an existing product, service, or process. For example, Apple's fall 2016 introduction of the iPhone 7 compared to prior models enhanced camera functionality to match the human eye, and it eliminated a port for earphones and instead featured wireless earbuds. *Duplication*, or imitation, is introducing a similar product, service, or process as a competitor or replicating an exact idea in a new market. Imitation, for example, is when Subway develops a new sandwich, and Quiznos may quickly respond by offering a similar sandwich. Or a community that did not have Starbucks but finally has a Starbucks open is an example of duplication. Finally, *synthesis* is the process of combining two or more prior ideas into a new item or service. Creating garbage bags with drawstring technology provides the prior need for trash preparation with the technology of a drawstring (from a hoodie or gym shorts) to secure the garbage in a better fashion than gator ties.

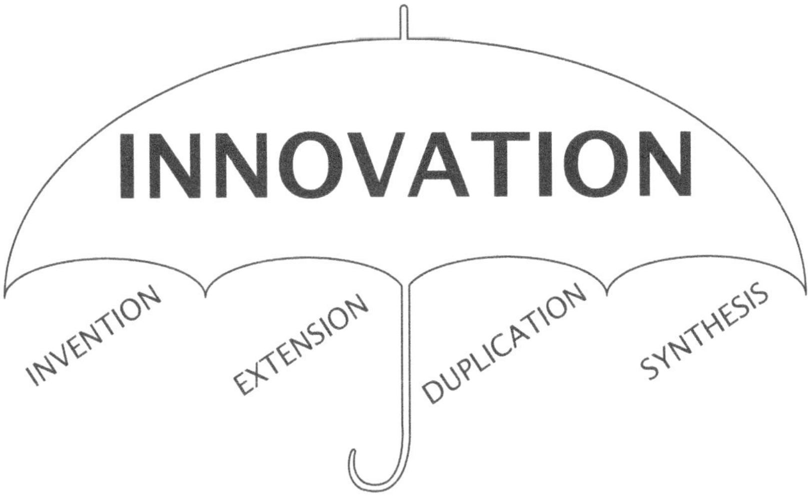

Figure 2.2 The Umbrella of Innovation is a way to view the multiple concepts of innovation, including Invention, Extension, Duplication, and Synthesis

"We need to get beyond the notion that innovation is something that only occurs among scientists working in a lab. Innovation happens anywhere and everywhere, and more often that not it comes from small things" (Florida, 2012, p. 389). Ryan (2004) said, "Innovation does not happen accidentally. Consistent, high-quality breakthroughs occur when people have access to each other (even if it's online, although live is best), can learn and collaborate together in a systematized way, and are safe to fail" (p. 38).

Feld (2012) and Isenberg (2010) believe entrepreneurs are themselves leaders. Note that leadership as a field of study and a field of practice also developed along the same time frame in social sciences as entrepreneurship with differing views. Entrepreneurial management, generative leadership, and entrepreneurial leadership are various considerations today. Relevant to entrepreneurship, first came entrepreneurial management emphasizing general function control within a firm (Stevenson & Jarillo, 1990). Generative leadership emerged next and emphasizes innovation (Lane & Maxfield, 1996; Surie & Hazy, 2006). Finally, entrepreneurial leadership has emerged and is the coordination, direction, and implementation of firm-level activities (Kuratko, 2007, 2016). Kuratko (2007) said, "Entrepreneurs are now described as aggressive catalysts for change in the world of business" (p. 1). These specific forms of leadership are important and a key to building an entrepreneurial community, and they have much in common. In a broader entrepreneurial community discussion, transformational leadership is the specific concern coordinating people to achieve a higher performance or quality level (Avolio & Bass, 1988; Burns, 1978; Clevenger & Miao, 2017). Where do these types of leadership fit in the overall leadership realm? Figure 2.3 provides a continuum to consider the extremes of leadership. On one end is autocratic leadership that is bureaucratic, closed, secretive, and high in structure. The extreme of autocratic leadership is a dictator. On the other side is a democratic leadership where openness, participative styles are found including entrepreneurial, generative, and transformational. The extreme of democratic leadership is anarchy. Laissez-faire–or non-action–lies in the middle.

Intrapreneurship is another important concept, which is the empowerment of individuals—in any type of setting—to have the ability to be innovative and approach their work with an innovative or creative mind-set (Carsrud, Olm, & Eddy, 1986; Kuratko, 2016). Intrapreneurship may be applied anywhere individuals are allowed to approach work creatively with unique perspective.

Many people disparage corporations as being anti-entrepreneurial. Lichtenstein and Lyons (2010) note, "As a nation, we seem to have collectively forgotten from where the large corporations that are our central focus of attention came from. These corporations did not spring from the earth fully

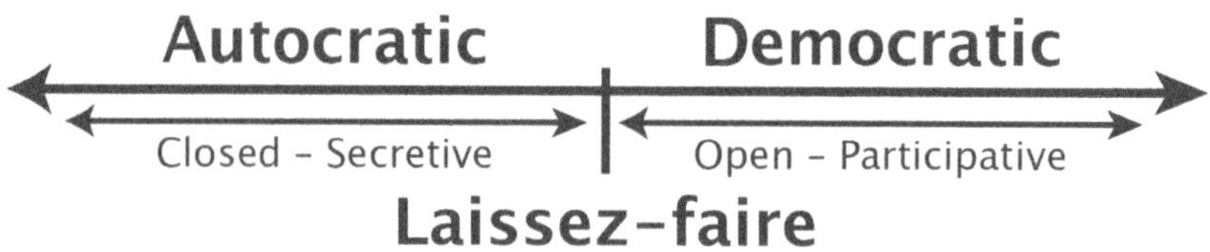

Figure 2.3 The Leadership Continuum provides a basic concept of the field of leadership to understand the situational considerations of entrepreneurial leadership, generative leadership, and transformational leadership in open, democratic leadership functions

formed" (p. 1). An economy needs a balance of firms in a pluralistic society, so entrepreneurial start-ups, small and medium enterprise, and corporations are all at various life-cycle stages and may have an entrepreneurial function (Carroll & Buchholtz, 2015). This concept demonstrates the need to give attention to all stages of the business life cycle regardless of location in rural, suburban, or urban areas (Renski, 2009).

Meso-Level: The Enterprise or Firm

As noted by Cuevas and Carrasco (2008), there is a difference between the entrepreneur and the enterprise as two discrete variables in the field of entrepreneurship. The meso-level focuses on a business *firm* or enterprise, which is a functioning organization of any size (Scott, 2002). From a firm level, key considerations of the sociological and organizational or institutional unit are portrayed in the closed system while the firm acts in the open system of the market (Casson, 2003; Kanter, 2002; Katz & Kahn, 1966; McMullen & Shepherd, 2006; Scott, 2002; Thornton & Flynn, 2003). The firm or enterprise is a unique environment with a culture created by the owners and management (Casson, 2003; Della-Giusta & King, 2006). Gerber (1995) said one's "business is nothing more than a distinct reflection" of the owner or entrepreneur (e.g., neat, hip, functional, innovative, sloppy, disorganized, greedy, etc.) (p. 5). Firms also tend to "reflect the historical conditions at the time of their founding" (Thornton, 1999, p.26).

There are two views on enterprise development and management: the resource-based theory and the firm-based theory (Alvarez & Barney, 2000; Krackhardt, 1995; Sharma & Manikutty, 2005). The *resource-based* theory considers uniqueness of the firm with nonimitable resources to create a competitive advantage. However, "mainstream economics has little to tell us about how and why some firms survive and grow and others do not" (Bhidé, 2000, p. 242). The *firm-based* view looks more at the structure of the firm and its management and operations processes regarding entrepreneurial opportunity (Krackhardt, 1995).

The shaping of a firm stems from organizational structure, culture, and management. Organizational culture is made up of the values and beliefs to which participants within the bounds of the organization contribute to and support (Bolman & Deal, 2013; Casson, 2003; Morgan, 2006). At the firm level, the entrepreneurial management or entrepreneurial leadership attention is an important emphasis (Kuratko, 2016; Stevenson & Jarillo, 1990). Entrepreneurial orientation is a key facet in an enterprise or firm (Anderson, Kreiser, Kuratko, Hornsby, & Eshima, 2015; Grand, 2008). Focus for entrepreneurial orientation includes proactiveness, innovation, and risk taking. "Entrepreneurship requires action" (McMullen & Shepherd, 2006, p. 132). This action does not happen in a vacuum or solely by the entrepreneur. The entrepreneur has to rally the resources, people, and systems in order to meet a market need or to create a market opportunity (Davidsson, 2015; Timmons,

1997; Timmons & Spinelli, 2009; Zacharakis et al., 2011) McMullen and Shepherd (2006) define this process as *entrepreneurial action,* and a lack of knowledge in these areas can suppress entrepreneurial action. "The primary reason for these failures is mismanagement, resulting from a lack of business know-how" (Pride, Hughes, & Kapoor, 2014, p. 136). Additionally, "lack of planning can be as deadly as lack of money to a new small business" (Pride, Hughes, & Kapoor, 2014, p. 144).

Innovation is important to a firm's strategy (Hitt & Ireland, 2000). An entrepreneur needs to create an internal entrepreneurial culture of innovation in a firm (Hitt & Reed, 2000). Both knowledge acquisition and knowledge sharing contribute to the process of innovation (Jain, 1998). "Organizational learning is defined as the development of new knowledge that has the potential to influence behavior and improve firm performance," (Hitt & Ireland, 2000, p. 53). Organizational learning includes evaluation of various contingencies and incorporating those most viable (Anand & Khanna, 2000; Argote, 2012). Organizational learning contributes to innovation thus leading to profitability.

Also at a firm level is the concept of corporate entrepreneurship, which exists in ongoing businesses and medium or larger companies and corporations. Corporate entrepreneurship is the function of innovation and creativity within a company (Carsrud et al., 1986; Kuratko, 2016). The main difference is that an entrepreneur takes on risk and responsibility personally, whereas corporate entrepreneurs are insulated from risk because they are safely functioning within a company that plans to be innovative. In other words, in corporate entrepreneurship, an employee is empowered to function entrepreneurially, but with the backing of management and the company's resources—not his or her own.

Macro-Level 1: The Community

At the macro-level 1, or *community level,* considerations relating to sociological dynamics, socio-culture, community as an organizational unit or institutional unit, and environmental or ecological framings arise (Aldrich, 1990; Aldrich & Fiol, 1994; Corno, Lal, & Colombo, 2014; Dana, 1997, 2008; Dana & Dana, 2007; Hindle, 2010; Julien, 2007; Karatas-Özkan et al., 2014; Landström, 2005; Mourdoukoutas & Papadimitriou, 2002; Ruef & Lounsbury, 2007; Sine & David, 2010; Thornton, 1999; Tolbert et al., 2011). A community unit in society can be viewed in the organizational or institutional frame just like a firm, but much larger and more complex.

"The idea of the American community is deceptively simple, as long as one does not require a rigid definition" (Warren, 1987, p. 1). Traditional consideration of "community" is defined as a geographical area with attributes relating to location, natural physical boundaries, or demographic patterns (Chaskin, Brown, Benkatesh, & Vidal, 2001; Smith, 2001). The term "community" may also identify a formal or informal group based on "social attributes and interests—such as language, custom, class, or ethnicity—shared by inhabitants and commonly used to designate them as a collective entity, regardless of geographic proximity" (Chaskin et al., 2001, p. 8).

In general, any "community" is about belonging or connectedness (Chaskin, 1997; Chaskin et al., 2001; Cohen, 1982, 1985; McMillan & Chavis, 1986; Putnam, 2000). This belonging creates a "collective," or community with shared beliefs, priorities, and relationships (Chaskin, 1997; Putnam, 2000). As a community, participants share a vision, values, and norms (McMillan Chavis, 1986). Beem (1999) said, "Interaction enables people to build communities, to commit themselves to each other, and to knit the social fabric" (p. 20). Any individual or organization is usually involved in many different "communities." Each community boils down to the culture of that given social network (Hofstede, 2001; Hustedde, 2007; Putnam, 2000). From America's early roots, the concept of community is the very society itself. However, communities are dynamic and constantly changing (Chaskin et al., 2001). Hindle (2010) defines community as

> Any context where a self-defined group of people see their mutual belonging to the community as distinguishing them (but not excluding them) from all other members of society at large and where continued membership of the community is valued highly enough to impose some constraints on behavior.
>
> (p. 608)

Entrepreneurship is strongest within a community when "the importance of flexibility, breadth or reach, and particularly, integration are emphasized" (Kanter, 2002, p. 267). This integration stems from the joint efforts of community stakeholders working together to create an entrepreneurial community. Thus an entrepreneurial culture is also needed at the community level (Huggins & Thompson, 2012).

Lichtenstein, Lyons, and Kutzhanova (2004) believe an entrepreneurial community supports new market opportunities and tolerance of entrepreneurs. Lichtenstein et al. believe an entrepreneurial community has "a group of entrepreneurs that constitute a distinct and recognizable community within the community" (2004, p. 6), or *place*. Entrepreneurs must have a place with a positive people climate with strong human capital, diversity, and support that is actively working to cultivate an entrepreneurial environment. This process is accomplished by investing in lots of great lifestyle amenities in a community to attract and retain innovative, optimistic, diverse, and creative people who value being entrepreneurial (Florida, 2002; Lichtenstein et al., 2004; Ruef & Lounsbury, 2007; Sine & David, 2010). Thus these sociological interactions constitute a macro-sociological concern (Young, 1971).

Boundaries

Discussion of community might evoke the question of boundaries. Where do communities start and stop? Each individual is engaged in many social networks, or communities. Cohen (1985) believes boundaries may be physical (i.e., geographic) or administrative (e.g., in law, linguistics, or religion). Boundaries also "may be thought of, rather, as existing in the minds of the beholders" (Cohen, 1985, p. 12). These boundaries are shared ideas with those in a community and those outside the community. Scott (2002) believes boundaries are "complex and subtle" (p. 185). He notes that social networks, organizations, and, thus, communities are "incomplete" systems and, therefore, "depend on exchanges with other systems" (p. 185). Laumann, Marsden, and Prensky (1983) note that three ideas enact boundaries: the actors, their relations, and their activities. Smith (2001) indicates each community "has its own symbols and markers of boundaries defining who is . . . 'in community,' and who is not" (p. 7). Communities function within three key concepts of: tolerance (Walzer, 1997), reciprocity (Putnam, 2000), and trust (Coleman, 1988; Putnam, 2000). Capacity and growth of these values enhance entrepreneurial community development.

Scott (2002) discusses boundary spanning, which widens systems, social networks, and communities. Entrepreneurs function best in open, diverse, flexible environments where role switching is commonplace. An entrepreneur, for instance, might open a business then move on to another one. That same entrepreneur serves as a mentor to someone else. Fluidity and organic activities are the norm. Difficulties arise in static, siloed, tight, or closed environments. Examples would include undercutting competition, unwillingness to share information, suppressed innovation, and lock-in. Community, on the other hand, is concerned with all facets for a successful society through improvements in collective well-being.

Barriers

Communities themselves build capacity or grow based on availability and access to resources including human, economic, physical, and political (Chaskin et al., 2001). Community context affects entrepreneurial process (Hindle, 2010). Difficulties and closed environments create barriers. Just as boundaries are understood to create a community, those same boundaries or a community may "become an exclusionary act" (Smith, 2001, p. 7). These boundaries create benefits for members just as well simultaneously creating barriers disallowing benefits to non-members.

Common social barriers to entrepreneurship include restricted access to resources and information, hyper-competitiveness, small-town mentalities, lack of understanding of entrepreneurship by leaders and the public, an unwillingness to support small business, and unproductive policies such as excessive taxation and regulations.

Macro-Level 2: The Macro Environment

The macro-level 2 constitutes the *larger environmental* levels such as the regional, state, national industry, and national key issues of culture, economic, and environmental (i.e., macro) concerns. These levels are framed as part of a country's unique national culture (Fayolle & Kyro, 2008; Hayton & Cacciotti, 2014; Hofstede, 1996, 2001; Trompenaars & Hampden-Turner, 2012). In the United States, these pluralistic ideas and concerns form civic society (Carroll & Buchholtz, 2015; McGuire, 1963).

Many find it difficult to isolate entrepreneurship to measure and report on it as part of the GDP (van Stel, Carree, & Thurik, 2005). Low, Henderson, and Wiler (2005) utilize self-employment to measure entrepreneurial breadth and depth, revenue, capital, human capacity, amenities, and infrastructure to explain entrepreneurial productivity and success. Additionally, the total entrepreneurial activity is a measurement (Liñán et al., 2013). Bell (1976) explored society, class, and the economy and provides an interesting compilation of emphases based on historic time period (see Table 2.2). Florida (2012) explains,

> Here's what leaders need to know: Jobs and GDP growth *do not* predictably follow innovation. Jobs and GDP growth *do* predictably follow entrepreneurship. Put another way: Entrepreneurs create customers. And customers, in turn, create jobs and economic growth. Almost no leader knows this.
>
> (p. 6)

Therefore, we need to place an emphasis on entrepreneurship.

Hofstede (1996, 2001) is best known for national culture variables of power distance, uncertainty avoidance, individuals versus collectivism, masculinity versus femininity, and long-term versus short-term orientation. Those individualistic cultures with low uncertainty avoidance are found to be the highest entrepreneurial settings (Thomas & Mueller, 2000).

Both Hofstede (2001) and Pinillos and Reyes (2011) found that a major shift in individualist versus collective cultures illustrate different entrepreneurial propensities. Entrepreneurship at the country level has been

Table 2.2 Consideration of Historic Emphases and Resource Determination

	Pre-industrial	*Industrial*	*Post-industrial*
Resource	Raw materials	Energy	Information
Mode	Extractive	Fabrication	Processing
Technology	Labor-intensive	Capital-intensive	Knowledge-intensive
Design	Game against nature	Game against fabricated nature	Game between persons

(Source: Bell, 1976, p. 198)

explored by Davidsson (1995) with an entrepreneurial values index, Davidsson and Wicklund's (1997) values and beliefs toward entrepreneur behaviors, Beugelsdijk and Noorderhaven's (2004) moral and social values focused on regional economic development, Beugelsdijk's (2007) entrepreneurial culture measures, and Basu and Altinay's (2002) family networks and entrepreneurial behavior relating to religion, language, and educational attainment.

Macro-Level 3: Worldwide

Finally, the worldwide level—addressing levels of national culture, economies, and environmental—promote Hofstede's (1996, 2001) variables. Meyer and Hepperd (2000) indicate, "Entrepreneurship has emerged as one of the most important forces in the world economy" (p. xi). The impact of globalization through a more cooperative multicultural industrialization and rapid communication has increased significantly (Hitt & Reed, 2000). In Chapter 4, Breazeale and Hustedde (2017) discuss the impact of culture on entrepreneurship with specific emphasis on community.

Again, the macro environments are concerned with objective structures, industry rules and procedures, competition, entrepreneurial networks, organizational history, culture, social regulations, legislation, labor market dynamics, and structures of resources and constraints. Wortman (1986) poses these questions in environmental-level concerns:

> What internal and external environmental factors have an impact on the effectiveness of an entrepreneur?
> What relationships exist between environmental factors and individual characteristics of an entrepreneur?
> What differences exist in internal environments for entrepreneurs in owner-managed companies versus large-scale companies?
> What environmental differences are there in business, governmental and nonprofit organizations for entrepreneurs? (p. 327)

These considerations lead us into a discussion about entrepreneurial community development and then entrepreneurial ecosystems.

Entrepreneurial Community Development

Lichtenstein and Lyons (2010) define an entrepreneurial community as "a critical mass of entrepreneurs that constitutes a distinct and recognizable community within a larger community or region" (p. 167). Entrepreneurial communities entail the for-profit sector: start-ups (true entrepreneurs), serialpreneurs, small business owners, family businesses, small and medium enterprises (SME), and corporations. Entrepreneurial communities also include a wide range of other individual and organizational actors.

A culture supportive of entrepreneurial ventures—including the ability and acceptability to fail—is needed to foster a complex, economic-enhancing phenomenon that is entrepreneurship. For example, "entrepreneurship is a process and must be viewed in dynamic terms rather than in cross-sectional snapshots" (Aldrich & Zimmer, 1986, p. 3). Hindle (2010) notes that there is a growing focus on entrepreneurial communities and related necessary support systems.

Entrepreneurs are not all the same. Some are market-fulfilling agents responding to demand economics. Others are more creative and provide the market with their own products and services with a supply-side view of attracting the right customers. To explain this diversity among entrepreneurs, Aldrich and Zimmer (1986) promote "the population perspective . . . of four evolutionary processes in entrepreneurial development: variation, selection, retention, and diffusion" (p. 9). *Variations* depend on a variety of comfort levels of entrepreneurs. Likewise, *selection* deals with acquiring resources and networks to execute on delivering goods and services, but external variables—outside the control of entrepreneurs—greatly impact the process, such as competition, market forces, and technological issues. *Retention* includes considerations of control by entrepreneurs for survival. Finally, *diffusion* occurs once competencies and functions are acted upon, ideally to positive ends. Diffusion creates adjustments to continue the entrepreneurial process.

Bhidé (2000) notes four other types of models that have been explored with focus on entrepreneurs—and none have ecosystems: mainstream economic theories, life-cycle models, evolutionary theories, and business strategy models. These models consider social attitudes, trust at varying levels, risk, feedback, technology, corporate beliefs, uncertainty, taxes, and regulatory policies (Bhidé, 2000; Mourdoukoutas & Papadimitriou, 2002). Given the lack of attention to ecosystems in exploring entrepreneurial communities and their complexities, more research and theory development are much needed.

Entrepreneurial Ecosystems

Aldrich (1990) began using the biological workings from ecology as a metaphor to understand the complex relationships in entrepreneurial communities. Ecosystems develop at various levels (Cain, 2012; Corno et al., 2014; Fortunato, 2017; Mazzucato, 2013). Aldrich and Wiedenmayer (1993) explored entrepreneurial activity at various levels including intrapopulation (i.e., firms and density) to inter-population (i.e., competition in an industry), and then societal-levels (e.g., cultural norms, governmental policies, macro considerations). Cain (2012) said,

> Cultivating a business environment is no different [than a biological ecosystem]—you are assessing and strengthening a system, loosely characterized by accessibility to mentors, knowledge centers, like-minded

> partners (leadership), capital, workforce (talent), and the desirability of the city, town, or place in which you operate.
>
> (p. 6)

Ecosystems differ from entrepreneurial communities. The key: ecosystems are dynamic, generative, and inhere in the relationship between actors and their environment. Like communities, ecosystems carry with them "system ethics," but like entrepreneurship, they also connote a degree of destruction and turnover to benefit the entire system. Communities are often viewed as an "ideal state," by contrast, that exists quite happily in perpetuity and does not focus on system change and evolution (central to ecosystems).

Conclusion

The contexts of entrepreneurship and community are complex and dynamic. This chapter provided an overview to understand better who entrepreneurs are and what they do. The field of entrepreneurship as both a practice of business and a field of study has been growing, and research in both areas continues to develop deeper concepts, convergence, and the understanding of these sophisticated inner workings that involve many other disciplines: psychology, sociology, economics, political science, and anthropology. The rich history of the American entrepreneur—as well as immigrants who become entrepreneurs—gave the United States a prominence in opportunity and the freedom to express creativity, innovation, and choice of livelihood.

Additionally, exploration and discussion of the framework of *levels of analysis* of entrepreneurship is useful to understand components at micro-, meso-, and macro-levels and their interrelated significance. Reviewing and relating all of these concepts provides the foundation to explore the deeper the entrepreneurial community unit of analysis in the development of entrepreneurial community ecosystems, which support entrepreneurs and the economic development function in the United States and globally.

Entrepreneurship continues to be very important to America's economy and economic development strategy (Sexton, 1997; Shane, 2004). Entrepreneurs—whether born or made—clearly have an important role in society (Cochran, 1949; Lichtenstein & Lyons, 2010). However, recent statistics from Gallup indicate, "Four hundred thousand new businesses are being born annually nationwide, while 470,000 per year are dying" (Clifton & Badal, 2014, p. 11). Obviously, as Florida (2012) notes, we "need to put entrepreneurialism front and center on the economic agenda" (p. 389).

Entrepreneurship education is vital. In America, highly intelligent, musically inclined, or athletically talented individuals are discovered in their youth. Such brilliance is difficult to hide. However, Florida (2012) points out: "if you have the rare, innate ability to create a customer, to build a company—if you have the talent for entrepreneurship—your early identification and subsequent development is left to chance" (p. 20). Therefore, one priority is additional emphasis as well as the necessary resources invested into an "education system that spurs, not squelches, creativity" (Florida, 2012, p. 390). Such support can promote being an entrepreneur as a lifestyle or career of choice. Additional programming at the K–12 levels in curriculum and after school programs can engrain a vision for children to understand business.

Another priority is continued tolerance and encouragement of entrepreneurs and openness in communities to foster an entrepreneurial environment. Reality television and other series programming are helping to create awareness. Further, local leaders, the governments at various levels, and industries need to continue to place entrepreneurs and entrepreneurial community development as a priority through formal and informal organizations.

A kaleidoscope is described as "a mixture of different things" or "a changing pattern or scene" (Merriam-Webster, 2016). The concept of an entrepreneurial community is dynamic and ever changing—a kaleidoscope of individuals, firms, communities, and all their related complexities. The rest of this book digs deeper into the various actors reflected in this kaleidoscope. Chapters 3, 7, and 8 illuminate real-world entrepreneurial communities with local leaders and entrepreneurs. Chapter 4 highlights the acceptability and supports for entrepreneurship through the lens of culture. Chapter 5 elaborates on the role of local leaders supporting an entrepreneurial community to help transform the community to new heights of functionality. Chapters 6 and 9 explore the psychology and sociology of people relationships with social networks and individual viewpoints in entrepreneurship. The success of the economy and American pursuit of happiness rely on all of these actors—whether individual or organizational—to create this beautiful kaleidoscope.

References

4-H Mall. (2016). *EntrepreneurShip investigation: Discover the e-scene series*. Retrieved from http://www.4-hmall.org/Category/4-hcurriculum-entrepreneurship.aspx?_ga=1.158263738.1060230187.1474217289

Acs, Z. J., & Audretsch, D. B. (Eds.). (2003). *Handbook of entrepreneurship research: An interdisciplinary survey and introduction*. Boston, MA: Kluwer Academic Publishers.

Acs, Z. J., & Audretsch, D. B. (Eds.). (2011). *Handbook of entrepreneurship research: An interdisciplinary survey and introduction* (2nd ed.). Boston, MA: Springer.

Adler, P. S., & Kwon, S. W. (2002). Social capital: Prospects for a new concept. *Academy of Management Review*, *27*, 17–40.

Aldrich, H. E. (1990). Using an ecological perspective to study organizational founding rates. *Entrepreneurship Theory and Practice*, *14*(3), 7–24.

Aldrich, H. E., & Fiol, C. M. (1994). Fools rush in? The institutional context of industry creation. *Academy of Management Review*, *19*(4), 645–670.

Aldrich, H. E., & Wiedenmayer, G. (1993). From traits to rates: An ecological perspective on organizational foundings. In J. A. Katz & R. H. Brockhaus (Eds.),

Research in organizational behavior, firm emergence, and growth (Vol. 1, pp. 145–195). Greenwich: JAI Press.
Aldrich, H. E., & Zimmer, C. (1986). Entrepreneurship through social networks. In D. L. Sexton & R. W. Smilor (Eds.), *The art and science of entrepreneurship* (pp. 3–23). Cambridge, MA: Ballinger Publishing Company.
Allen, C., & Lee, D. R. (1997). *The entrepreneur on the heroic journey*. Foundation for Economic Freedom. Retrieved from https://fee.org/articles/the-entrepreneur-on-the-heroic-journey/
Alvarez, S. A., Agarwal, R. R., & Sorenson, O. (Eds.). (2005). *Handbook of entrepreneurship research: Disciplinary perspectives*. New York, NY: Springer.
Alvarez, S. A., & Barney, J. (2000). Entrepreneurial capabilities. In G. D. Meyer & K. A. Hepperd (Eds.), *Entrepreneurship as strategy: Competing on the entrepreneurial edge* (pp. 63–81). Thousand Oaks, CA: Sage.
Anand, B. N., & Khanna, T. (2000). Do firms learn to create value? The case of alliances. *Strategic Management Journal, 21*(3), 295–315.
Anderson, B. S., Kreiser, P. M., Kuratko, D. F., Hornsby, J. S., & Eshima, Y. (2015). Reconceptualizing entrepreneurial orientation. *Strategic Management Journal, 36*, 1579–1596.
Argote, L. (2012). *Organizational learning: Creating, retaining, and transferring knowledge*. Boston, MA: Springer.
Astrachan, J. H. (2003). Commentary on the special issue: The emergence of a field. *Journal of Business Venturing, 18*(5), 567–573.
Avolio, B. J., & Bass, B. M. (1988). Transformational leadership, charisma and beyond. In J. G. Hunt, B. R. Baliga, H. P. Dachler, & C. A Schriesheim (Eds.), *Emerging leadership vistas* (pp. 29–50). Lexington, MA: Lexington.
Bae, T. J., Qian, S., Miao, C., & Fiet, J. O. (2014). The relationship between entrepreneurship education and entrepreneurial intentions: A meta-analytic review. *Entrepreneurship Theory and Practice, 38*, 217–254.
Baron, R. A., & Shane, S. A. (2007). *Entrepreneurship: A process perspective* (2nd ed.). Cincinnati, OH: Cengage Learning.
Basu, A., & Altinay, E. (2002). The interaction between culture and entrepreneurship in London's immigrant business. *International Small Business Journal, 20*, 271–293.
Baumol, W. J. (1990). Entrepreneurship: Productive, unproductive, and destructive. *Journal of Political Economy, 98*(5), 893–921.
Beem, C. (1999). *The necessity of politics. Reclaiming American public life*. Chicago, IL: University of Chicago Press.
Bell, D. (1976). *The cultural contradictions of capitalism*. New York, NY: Basic Books.
Beugelsdijk, S. (2007). Entrepreneurial culture, regional innovativeness and economic growth. *Journal of Evolutionary Economics, 17*, 187–210.
Beugelsdijk, S., & Noorderhaven, N. (2004). Entrepreneurial attitude and economic growth: A cross-section of 54 regions. *Annals of Regional Science, 38*, 199–218.
Bhidé, A. V. (2000). *The origin and evolution of new businesses*. Oxford, UK: Oxford University Press.
Bird, B., Schjoedt, L., & Hanke, R. (2014). Behavior of entrepreneurs—existing research and future directions. In E. Chell & M. Karatas-Özkan (Eds.), *Handbook of research on small business and entrepreneurship* (pp. 207–221). Northampton, MA: Edward Elgar.
Bolman, L. G., & Deal, T. E. (2013). *Reframing organizations: Artistry, choice and leadership* (5th ed.). Thousand Oaks, CA: Jossey-Bass.

Bourdieu, P. (1977). *Outline of theory of practice*. Cambridge, MA: Cambridge University Press.
Bourdieu, P. (1984). *Distinction: A social critique of the judgement of taste*. London: Routledge.
Bourdieu, P. (1987). What makes a social class? On the theoretical and practical existence of groups. *Berkeley Journal of Sociology*, *31*, 1–18.
Bourdieu, P. (1990). *The logic of practice*. Stanford, CA: Stanford University Press.
Bourdieu, P. (1998). *Practical reason: On the theory of action*. Cambridge, MA: Polity Press.
Bowser, J. (2016). *8 traits of successful entrepreneurs—do you have what it takes?* Minority Business Development Agency, U.S. Department of Commerce. Retrieved from http://www.mbda.gov/blogger/starting-business/8-traits-successful-entrepreneurs-do-you-have-what-it-takes
Breazeale, N. D., & Hustedde, R. J. (2017). Understanding the impact of culture in entrepreneurship. In M. W-P Fortunato & M. R. Clevenger (Eds.), *Toward entrepreneurial community development: Leaping cultural and leadership boundaries* (pp. 104–125). New York, NY: Routledge.
Brockhaus, R. H., & Horowitz, P. S. (1986). The psychology of the entrepreneur. In D. L. Sexton & R. W. Smilor (Eds.), *The art and science of entrepreneurship* (pp. 25–48). Cambridge, MA: Ballinger Publishing Company.
Burns, J. M. (1978). *Leadership*. New York, NY: Harper & Row.
Bygrave, W. D. (2007). The entrepreneurship paradigm (I) revisited. In H. Neergaard & J. P. Ulhøi (Eds.), *Handbook of qualitative research methods in entrepreneurship* (pp. 17–48). Northampton, MA: Edward Elgar.
Byrne, J., Fayolle, A., & Toutain, O. (2014). Entrepreneurship education: What we know and what we need to know. In E. Chell & M. Karatas-Özkan (Eds.), *Handbook of research on small business and entrepreneurship* (pp. 261–288). Northampton, MA: Edward Elgar.
Cain, C. (2012). The entrepreneurial ecosystem: Think biology 101. *The Small Business Advocate*, May–June 2012, 6.
Carraher, S. M., & Paridon, T. J. (2015). Entrepreneurship journal rankings across the discipline. *Journal of Small Business Strategy*, *19*(2), 89–98.
Carroll, A. B., & Buchholtz, A. K. (2015). *Business & society: Ethics, sustainability, and stakeholder management* (9th ed.). Stamford, CT: Cengage Learning.
Carsrud, A. L., Olm, K. W., & Eddy, G. G. (1986). Entrepreneurship research in quest of a paradigm. In D. L. Sexton & R. W. Smilor (Eds.), *The art and science of entrepreneurship* (pp. 367–387). Cambridge, MA: Ballinger Publishing Company.
Casson, M. (2003). Entrepreneurship, business culture, and the theory of the firm. In Z. J. Acs & D. B. Audretsch (Eds.), *Handbook of entrepreneurship research: An interdisciplinary survey and introduction* (pp. 223–246). Boston, MA: Kluwer Academic Publishers.
Casson, M., Yeung, B., Basu, A., & Wadeson, N. (2006). *The Oxford handbook of entrepreneurship*. Oxford, UK: Oxford University Press.
Chandler, G. N., & Lyon, D. W. (2001, Summer). Issues of research design and construct measurement in entrepreneurship: The past decade. *Entrepreneurship Theory and Practice*, 101–113.
Chaskin, R. J. (1997, December). Perspectives on neighborhood and community: A review of the literature. *Social Service Review*, 521–547.

Chaskin, R. J., Brown, P., Benkatesh, S., & Vidal, A. (2001). *Building community capacity*. New York, NY: Aldine De Gruyter.

Chell, E., & Karatas-Özkan, M. (Eds.). (2014). *Handbook of research on small business and entrepreneurship*. Northampton, MA: Edward Elgar.

Churchill, N. C., & Lewis, V. L. (1986). Entrepreneurship research: Directions and methods. In D. L. Sexton & R. W. Smilor (Eds.), *The art and science of entrepreneurship* (pp. 333–365). Cambridge, MA: Ballinger Publishing Company.

Clevenger, M. R., Fortunato, M. W-P, & Houlihan, K. (2017). The value and process of social networking for entrepreneurs. In M. W-P Fortunato & M. R. Clevenger (Eds.), *Toward entrepreneurial community development: Leaping cultural and leadership boundaries* (pp. 152–176). New York, NY: Routledge.

Clevenger, M. R., & Miao, C. (2017). Transformational leadership to build an entrepreneurial community. In M. W-P Fortunato & M. R. Clevenger (Eds.), *Toward entrepreneurial community development: Leaping cultural and leadership boundaries* (pp. 126–151). New York, NY: Routledge.

Clifton, J., & Badal, S. B. (2014). *Entrepreneurial strengthsfinder*. New York, NY: Gallup Press.

Cochran, T. C. (1949). Role and sanction in American entrepreneurial history. In A. H. Cole (Ed.), *Change and the entrepreneur: Postulates and patterns for entrepreneurial history* (pp. 153–175). Boston, MA: Harvard Business School Press.

Cohen, A. P. (Ed.). (1982). *Belonging: Identity and social organization in British rural cultures*. Manchester, UK: University of Manchester.

Cohen, A. P. (Ed.). (1985). *The symbolic construction of community*. London, UK: Routledge.

Coleman, J. S. (1988). Social capital in the creation of human capital. *American Journal of Sociology*, *94*, S95–S120.

Cooper, A. C., Markman, G. D., & Niss, G. (2000). The evolution of the field of entrepreneurship. In G. D. Meyer & K. A. Hepperd (Eds.), *Entrepreneurship as strategy: Competing on the entrepreneurial edge* (pp. 115–133). Thousand Oaks, CA: Sage.

Cornelius, B., Landström, H., & Persson, O. (2006). Entrepreneurial studies: The dynamic research front of a developing social science. *Entrepreneurship Theory & Practice*, May, 375–398.

Corno, F., Lal, R., & Colombo, S. (2014). "Entrepreneurship & new venture creation" key elements of the entrepreneurial ecosystem facilitating the growth of ICT entrepreneurs in Italy. *European Scientific Journal*, 2, 330–345.

Creswell, J. W. (2013). *Research design: Qualitative, quantitative, and mixed methods approaches* (4th ed.). Los Angeles, CA: Sage.

Creswell, J. W. (2014). *A concise introduction to mixed methods research (Sage mixed methods research)*. Los Angeles, CA: Sage.

Cuevas, J. G., & Carrasco, F. R. C. (2008). New elements for the analysis of entrepreneurial structure. In A. Fayolle & P. Kyro (Eds.), *The dynamics between entrepreneurship, environment and education* (pp. 15–27). Northampton, MA: Edward Elgar.

Cunningham, J. B., & Lischeron, J. (1991). Defining entrepreneurship. *Journal of Small Business Management*, *29*(1), 45–61.

Dana, L-P. (1997). The origins of self-employment in ethno-cultural communities: Distinguishing between orthodox entrepreneurship and reactionary enterprise. *Revue Canadienne des Sciences de l'Administration*, *14*(1), 52–68.

Dana, L-P. (2008). Community based entrepreneurship in Norway. *Entrepreneurship and Innovation*, *9*(2), 77–92.

Dana, L-P., & Dana, T. (2007). Collective entrepreneurship in a Mennonite community in Paraguay. *Latin American Business Review*, *8*(4), 82–96.

Davidsson, P. (1995). Culture, structure and regional levels of entrepreneurship. *Entrepreneurship and Regional Development*, *7*, 41–62.

Davidsson, P. (2008). *The entrepreneurship research challenge*. Cheltenham, UK: Edward Elgar.

Davidsson, P. (2015). Entrepreneurial opportunities and the entrepreneurship nexus: A re-conceptualization. *Journal of Business Venturing*, *30*, 674–695.

Davidsson, P., & Wiklund, J. (1997). Values, beliefs, and regional variations in new firm formation rates. *Journal of Economic Psychology*, *18*(2–3), 179–199.

Davidsson, P., & Wiklund, J. (2001, July). Levels of analysis in entrepreneurship research: Current research practice and suggestions for future. *Entrepreneurship Theory and Practice*, 601–618.

Dean, M. A., Shook, C. L., & Payne, G. T. (2007, Summer). The past, present, and future of entrepreneurship research: Data analytic trends and training. *Entrepreneurship Theory and Practice*, 81–99.

Della-Giusta, M., & King, Z. (2006). Enterprise culture. In M. Casson, B. Yeung, A. Basu, & N. Wadeson (Eds.), *The Oxford handbook of entrepreneurship* (pp. 629–670). Oxford, UK: Oxford University Press.

Evans, G. H. (1949). The entrepreneur and economic theory: A historical and analytical approach. *American Economic Review*, *39*(3), 336–348.

Fayolle, A. (2014). What we know and what we need to know in the field of entrepreneurship. In A. Fayolle (Ed.), *Handbook of research on entrepreneurship: What we know and what we need to know* (pp. 1–12). Northampton, MA: Edward Elgar.

Fayolle, A., & Kyro, P. (Eds.). (2008). *The dynamics between entrepreneurship, environment and education*. Northampton, MA: Edward Elgar.

Feld, B. (2012). *Startup communities: Building an entrepreneurial ecosystem in your city*. Hoboken, NJ: Wiley.

Florida, R. (2002). *The rise of the creative class and how it's transforming work, leisure, community and everyday life*. New York, NY: Basic Books.

Florida, R. (2012). *The rise of the creative class, revisited*. New York, NY: Basic Books.

Forson, C., Ozbilgin, M., Ozturk, M. B., & Tatli, A. (2014). Multi-level approaches to entrepreneurship and small business research—transcending dichotomies with Bourdieu. In E. Chell & M. Karatas-Özkan (Eds.), *Handbook of research on small business and entrepreneurship* (pp. 54–69). Northampton, MA: Edward Elgar.

Fortunato, M. W-P (2017). High- and low-entrepreneurial communities: A multiple case study. In M. W-P Fortunato & M. R. Clevenger (Eds.), *Toward entrepreneurial community development: Leaping cultural and leadership boundaries* (pp. 177–235). New York, NY: Routledge.

Gartner, W. B. (1988). "Who is an entrepreneur?" is the wrong question. *American Journal of Small Business*, *12*(4), 11–31.

Gartner, W. B. (1990). What are we talking about when we talk about entrepreneurship? *Journal of Business Venturing*, *5*(1), 15–28.

Gartner, W. B., Davidsson, P., & Zahra, S. A. (2006, May). Are you talking to me? The nature of community in entrepreneurship scholarship. *Entrepreneurship Theory and Practice*, 321–331.

Gasse, Y. (1986). The development of new entrepreneurs: A belief-based approach. In D. L. Sexton & R. W. Smilor (Eds.), *The art and science of entrepreneurship* (pp. 49–60). Cambridge, MA: Ballinger Publishing Company.

Gerber, M. E. (1995). *The myth revisited: Why most small businesses don't work and what to do about it*. New York, NY: Harper Collins.

Gompers, P. A. (1999). Resource allocation, incentives and control: The importance of venture capital in financing entrepreneurial firms. In Z. J. Acs, B. Carlsson, & C. Karlsson (Eds.), *Entrepreneurship, small and medium-sized enterprises and the macroeconomy* (pp. 206–235). New York, NY: Cambridge University Press.

Grand, J. (2008). Linking entrepreneurial orientation and dynamic capabilities: Research issues and alternative models. In A. Fayolle & P. Kyro (Eds.), *The dynamics between entrepreneurship, environment and education* (pp. 220–244). Northampton, MA: Edward Elgar.

Grégoire, D. A., Nöel, M. X., Déry, R., & Béchard, J-P. (2006, May). Is there conceptual convergence in entrepreneurship research? A co-citation analysis of Frontiers of Entrepreneurship Research, 1981–2004. *Entrepreneurship Theory and Practice*, 333–372.

Guo, X., Chen, W., & Yu, A. (2015). Is college education worth it? Evidence from its impacts on entrepreneurship in the United States. *Journal of Small Business and Entrepreneurship*, *28*(1), 1–26.

Haltiwanger, J. (2009). Entrepreneurship and job growth. In Z. J. Acs, D. B. Audretsch, & R. J. Strom (Eds.), *Entrepreneurship, growth, and public policy* (pp. 119–145). New York, NY: Cambridge University Press.

Hansemark, O. C. (2003). Need for achievement, locus of control and the prediction of business start-ups: A longitudinal study. *Journal of Economic Psychology*, *24*, 301–319.

Harrington, C., & Maysami, R. (2015). Entrepreneurship education and the role of the regional university. *Journal of Entrepreneurship*, *18*(2), 29–28.

Hayton, J. C., & Cacciotti, G. (2014). Culture and entrepreneurship: Empirical evidence for direct and indirect effects. In A. Fayolle (Ed.), *Handbook of research on entrepreneurship: What we know and what we need to know* (pp. 147–182). Northampton, MA: Edward Elgar.

Hayton, J. C., George, G., & Zahra, S. A. (2002). National culture and entrepreneurship: A review of behavioral research. *Entrepreneurship Theory and Practice*, 26(4), 33–52.

Hébert, R. F., & Link, A. N. (2009). *A history of entrepreneurship*. New York, NY: Routledge.

Hechavarria, D. M., & Ingram, A. (2014, Fall). A review of the entrepreneurial ecosystem and the entrepreneurial society in the United States: An exploration with the global entrepreneurship monitor dataset. *Journal of Business & Entrepreneurship*, Special Issue, 1–35.

Herron, L., Sapienza, H. J., & Smith-Cook, D. (1991, Winter). Entrepreneurship theory from an interdisciplinary perspective: Volume I. *Entrepreneurship Theory and Practice*, 7–12.

Hill, C. E. (2012). *Consensual qualitative research: A practical resource for investigating social science phenomena*. Washington, DC: American Psychological Association.

Hindle, K. (2010, November/December). How community context affects entrepreneurial process: A diagnostic framework. *Entrepreneurship and Regional Development*, 22(7/8), 599–647.

Hitt, M. A., & Ireland, R. D. (2000). The intersection of entrepreneurship and strategic management research. In D. L. Sexton & H. Landström (Eds.), *Handbook of entrepreneurship* (pp. 43–63). Malden, MA: Blackwell Publishers.

Hitt, M. A., & Reed, T. S. (2000). Entrepreneurship in the new competitive landscape. In G. D. Meyer & K. A. Hepperd (Eds.), *Entrepreneurship as strategy: Competing on the entrepreneurial edge* (pp. 23–47). Thousand Oaks, CA: Sage.

Hofstede, G. (1996). Riding the waves of commerce: A test of Trompenaars' model of national cultural differences. *International Journal of Intercultural Relations, 20*, 189–198.

Hofstede, G. (2001). *Culture's consequences* (2nd ed.). Thousand Oaks, CA: Sage.

Hollander, B. S., & Elman, N. S. (1988). Family-owned businesses: An emerging field of inquiry. *Family Business Review, 1*, 145–164.

Hornaday, J. A., & Aboud, J. (1971). Characteristics of successful entrepreneurs. *Personnel Psychology, 24*, 141–153.

Huggins, R., & Thompson, P. (2012). Entrepreneurship and community culture: A place-based study of their interdependency. *Entrepreneurship Research Journal, 2*(1), 1–34.

Hustedde, R. (2007). What's culture got to do with it? Strategies for strengthening an entrepreneurial culture. In N. Walzer (Ed.), *Entrepreneurship and local economic development* (pp. 39–58). Lanham, MD: Lexington Books.

Hwang, H., & Powell, W. W. (2005). Institutions and entrepreneurship. In S. A. Alvarez, R. Agarwal, & O. Sorenson (Eds.), *Handbook of entrepreneurship research: Disciplinary perspectives* (pp. 201–232). New York, NY: Springer.

INCubatoredu®. (2016). *Entrepreneurship curriculum*. Retrieved from http://incubatoredu.org

Ireland, R. D., & Webb, J. W. (2007). A cross-disciplinary exploration of entrepreneurship research. *Journal of Management, 33*(6), 891–927.

Isenberg, D. J. (2010). How to start an entrepreneurial revolution. *Harvard Business Review, 88*(6), 40–50.

Jain, P. C. (Ed.). (1998). *Handbook for new entrepreneurs*. New York, NY: Oxford University Press.

Julien, P-A. (2007). *A theory of local entrepreneurship in the knowledge economy*. Northampton, MA: Edward Elgar.

Junior Achievement. (2016). *JA Be Entrepreneurial®*. Retrieved from https://www.juniorachievement.org/web/ja-usa/ja-programs?p_p_id=56_INSTANCE_abcd&p_p_lifecycle=0&p_p_state=maximized&p_p_mode=view&p_p_col_id=ja-maincontent&p_p_col_count=1&_56_INSTANCE_abcd_groupId=14516&_56_INSTANCE_abcd_articleId=19466

Kanter, R. M. (1986, February). Creating the creative environment. *Management Review*, 11–12.

Kanter, R. M. (2002). When a thousand flowers bloom: Structural, collective, and social conditions for innovation in organization. In R. Swedberg (Ed.), *Entrepreneurship: The social science view* (pp. 167–210). New York, NY: Oxford University Press.

Karatas-Özkan, M., Yavuz, C., & Howells, J. (2014). Theorising entrepreneurship: An institutional theory perspective. In E. Chell & M. Karatas-Özkan (Eds.), *Handbook of research on small business and entrepreneurship* (pp. 70–80). Northampton, MA: Edward Elgar.

Katz, D., & Kahn, R. L. (1966). *Organizations and the system concept. The social psychology of organizations*. New York, NY: Wiley.

Kerr, S. P., & Kerr, W. R. (2016). *Immigrant entrepreneurship*. Working paper. Cambridge, MA: National Bureau of Economic Research. Retrieved from http://www.nber.org/papers/w22385

Kirzner, I. (1973). *Competition and entrepreneurship*. Chicago, IL: University of Chicago Press.

Krackhardt, D. (1995). Entrepreneurial opportunity in an entrepreneurial firm: A structural approach. *Entrepreneurship Theory and Practice*, *19*(3), 53–69.

Kuckertz, A. (2013). Entrepreneurship education: Status quo and prospective developments. *Journal of Entrepreneurship Education*, *16*, 59–71.

Kuratko, D. F. (2005). The emergence of entrepreneurship education: Development, trends, and challenges. *Entrepreneurship Theory and Practice*, *29*, 577–598.

Kuratko, D. F. (2007). Entrepreneurial leadership in the 21st Century. *Journal of Leadership and Organizational Studies*, *13*(4), 1–11.

Kuratko, D. F. (2016). *Entrepreneurship: Theory, process, and practice* (10th ed.). Cincinnati, OH: Southwestern College Pub.

Kuratko, D. F., Cornwall, J. R., & Morris, M. H. (2013). *Entrepreneurship programs and the modern university*. Northampton, MA: Edward Elgar.

Kuratko, D. F., Morris, M. H., & Schindehutte, M. (2015). Understanding the dynamics of entrepreneurship through framework approaches. *Small Business Economics*, *45*, 1–13.

Kutzhanova, N., Lyons, T. S., & Lichtenstein, G. A. (2009). Skill-based development of entrepreneurs and the role of personal and peer group coaching in enterprise development. *Economic Development Quarterly*, *23*(3), 193–210.

Landström, H. (2005). *Pioneers in entrepreneurship and small business research*. New York, NY: Springer.

Landström, H. (2014). A history of entrepreneurship research. In A. Fayolle (Ed.), *Handbook of research on entrepreneurship: What we know and what we need to know* (pp. 23–62). Northampton, MA: Edward Elgar.

Landström, H., Parhankangas, A., Fayolle, A., & Riot, P. (2017). *Challenging entrepreneurship research*. New York, NY: Routledge.

Lane, D., & Maxfield, R. (1996). Strategy under complexity: Fostering generative relationships. *Long Range Planning*, *29*, 215–231.

Lane, J. E., & Johnstone, D. B. (2012). *Universities and colleges as economic drivers: Measuring higher education's role in economic development*. Albany, NY: SUNY Press.

Laumann, E. O., Marsden, P., & Prensky, D. (1983). The boundary specification problem in network analysis. In R. S. Burt & M. Minor (Eds.), *Applied network analysis* (pp. 18–34). Beverly Hills, CA: Sage.

Li, Z., & Liu, Y. (2011). Entrepreneurship education and employment performance: An empirical study in Chinese University. *Journal of Chinese Entrepreneurship*, *3*(3), 195–203.

Lichtenstein, G. A., & Lyons, T. S. (2001). The entrepreneurial development system: Transforming business talent and community economies. *Economic Development Quarterly*, *15*(1), 3–20.

Lichtenstein, G. A., & Lyons, T. S. (2010). *Investing in entrepreneurs: A strategic approach for strengthening your regional and community economy*. Santa Barbara, CA: Praeger.

Lichtenstein, G. A., Lyons, T. S., & Kutzhanova, N. (2004). Building entrepreneurial communities: The appropriate role of enterprise development activities. *Journal of the Community Development Society*, *35*(1), 5–24.

Liñán, F., Fernández-Serrano, J., & Romero, I. (2013). Necessity and opportunity entrepreneurship: The mediating effect of culture. *Revista de Economia Mundial, 33*, 21–47.

Low, M. B. (2001, Summer). The adolescence of entrepreneurship research: Specification of purpose. *Entrepreneurship Theory and Practice*, 17–25.

Low, M. B., & MacMillan, I. C. (1988). Entrepreneurship: Past research and future challenges. *Journal of Management, 14*, 139–161.

Low, S., Henderson, J., & Wiler, S. (2005). Gauging a region's entrepreneurial potential. *Economic Review—Federal Reserve Bank of Kansas City, 90*(3), 61–90.

Macke, D., & Markley, D. (2003). *Civic entrepreneurs and entrepreneurship*. Lincoln, NE: RUPRI Center for Rural Entrepreneurship.

Marti, I., Courpasson, D., & Barbosa, S. D. (2013). "Living in the fishbowl." Generating an entrepreneurial culture in a local community in Argentina. *Journal of Business Venturing, 28*, 10–29.

Martin, B. C., McNally, J. J., & Kay, M. J. (2013). Examining the formation of human capital in entrepreneurship: A meta-analysis of entrepreneurship education outcomes. *Journal of Business Venturing, 28*, 211–224.

Martinelli, A. (2004). The social and institutional context of entrepreneurship. In G. Corbetta, M. Husc, & D. Ravasi (Eds.), *Crossroads of entrepreneurship* (pp. 53–73). New York, NY: Springer.

Mazzucato, M. (2013). *The entrepreneurial state: Debunking public vs. private sector myths*. New York, NY: Anthem Press.

McCann, J. E., III, Leon-Guerrero, A. Y., & Haley, J. D., Jr. (2001). Strategic goals and practices of innovative family businesses. *Journal of Small Business Management, 39*(1), 50–59.

McClelland, D. C. (1961). *The achieving society*. Princeton, NJ: Van Nostrand.

McDaniel, P. (2015). How immigrant entrepreneurs move the U.S. economy forward. *Business the Workforce, Entrepreneurship/Innovation*. Retrieved from http://immigrationimpact.com/2015/05/06/how-immigrant-entrepreneurs-move-the-u-s-economy-forward/

McGuire, J. W. (1963). *Business and society*. New York, NY: McGraw-Hill.

McKeever, E., Anderson, A., & Jack, S. (2014). Social embeddedness in entrepreneurship research: The importance of context and community. In E. Chell & M. Karatas-Özkan (Eds.), *Handbook of research on small business and entrepreneurship* (pp. 222–236). Northampton, MA: Edward Elgar.

McMillan, D. W., & Chavis, D. M. (1986). Sense of community: A definition and theory. *Journal of Community Psychology, 14*, 6–23.

McMullen, J. S., & Shepherd, D. A. (2006). Entrepreneurial action and the role of uncertainty in the theory of the entrepreneur. *Academy of Management Review, 31*(1), 132–152.

Merriam-Webster. (2016). *Kaleidoscope*. Retrieved from http://www.merriam-webster.com/dictionary/kaleidoscope

Meyer, G. D., & Hepperd, K. A. (Eds.). (2000). *Entrepreneurship as strategy: Competing on the entrepreneurial edge*. Thousand Oaks, CA: Sage.

Meyer, J. W., & Jepperson, R. L. (2000). The "actors" of modern society: The cultural construction of social agency. *Sociological Theory, 18*(1), 100–120.

Mitchell, R. K., Smith, J. B., Morse, E. A., Seawright, K. W., Peredo, A. M., & McKenzie, B. (2002). Are entrepreneurial cognitions universal? Assessing entrepreneurial cognitions across cultures. *Entrepreneurship: Theory and Practice, 26*(4), 9–32.

Mitra, J. (2012). *Entrepreneurship, innovation and regional development: An introduction*. New York, NY: Routledge.

Morgan, G. (2006). *Images of organization*. Thousand Oaks, CA: Sage.

Morris, M. H. (Ed.). (1998). *Entrepreneurial intensity: Sustainable advantages for individuals, organizations, and societies*. Westport, CT: Praeger.

Morris, M. H. (Ed.). (2014). *Annals of entrepreneurship education and pedagogy*. Northampton, MA: Edward Elgar.

Mourdoukoutas, P., & Papadimitriou, S. (2002). *Nurturing entrepreneurship: Institutions and policies*. Westport, CT: Praeger.

Nahapiet, J., & Ghoshal, S. (1998). Social capital, intellectual capital, and the organizational advantage. *Academy of Management Review*, *23*, 242–266.

Nandram, S. S., & Samson, K. J. (2006). *The spirit of entrepreneurship*. Berlin, Germany: Springer.

Narayan, B. (2015). Entrepreneurship education: Bridging the gap. *Journal of Asia Entrepreneurship and Sustainability*, *11*(4), 74–107.

National Governors Association. (2004). *A governor's guide to strengthening state entrepreneurship policy*. Retrieved from http://www.nga.org/files/live/sites/NGA/files/pdf/0402GOVGUIDEENTREPRENEUR.pdf

Neck, H. M., & Regele, M. D. (2012). The entrepreneurship education subecosystem in the United States: Opportunities to increase entrepreneurial activity. *Journal of Business & Entrepreneurship*, *23*(2), 25–44.

Neergaard, H. (2007). Sampling in entrepreneurial setting. In H. Neergaard & J. P. Ulhøi (Eds.), *Handbook of qualitative research methods in entrepreneurship* (pp. 253–278). Northampton, MA: Edward Elgar.

Neergaard, H. (2014). The landscape of qualitative methods in entrepreneurship: A European perspective. In A. Fayolle (Ed.), *Handbook of research on entrepreneurship: What we know and what we need to know* (pp. 86–105). Northampton, MA: Edward Elgar.

Neergaard, H., & Ulhøi, J. P. (2007). *Handbook of qualitative research methods in entrepreneurship*. Northampton, MA: Edward Elgar.

Norris, F., & Bockelmann, C. (2000). *The New York Times: Century of business*. New York, NY: McGraw-Hill.

Parker, S. C. (2005). The economics of entrepreneurship: What we know and what we don't. *Foundations and Trends in Entrepreneurship*, *1*(1), 1–54.

Phan, P. (2004). Entrepreneurship theory: Possibilities and future directions. *Journal of Business Venturing*, *19*(5), 617–620.

Pinillos, M. J., & Reyes, L. (2011). Relationship between individualist-collectivist culture and entrepreneurship activity: Evidence from global entrepreneurship monitor data. *Small Business Economics*, *37*, 23–37.

Pittaway, L., Holt, R., & Broad, J. (2014). Synthesizing knowledge in entrepreneurship research—the role of systematic literature reviews. In E. Chell & M. Karatas-Özkan (Eds.), *Handbook of research on small business and entrepreneurship* (pp. 83–105). Northampton, MA: Edward Elgar.

Portes, A. (1995). *The economic sociology of immigration: Essays on networks, ethnicity, and entrepreneurship*. New York, NY: Russell Sage Foundation.

Poza, E. J., & Daugherty, M. S. (2014). *Family business*. Mason, OH: Cengage Learning.

Pride, W. M., Hughes, R. J., & Kapoor, J. R. (2014). *Business* (12th ed.). Mason, OH: Cengage Learning.

Putnam, R. D. (2000). *Bowling alone: The collapse and revival of American community*. New York, NY: Simon & Schuster.

Rauch, A., & Frese, M. (2007). Let's put the person back into entrepreneurship research: A meta-analysis on the relationship between business owners' personality traits, business creation, and success. *European Journal of Work and Organizational Psychology*, *16*, 353–385.

Renski, H. (2009). New firm entry, survival, and growth in the United States: A comparison of urban, suburban, and rural areas. *Journal of the American Planning Association*, *75*(1), 60–77.

Reynolds, P. D. (2007). *Entrepreneurship in the United States: The future is now*. New York, NY: Springer.

Ruef, M., & Lounsbury, M. (2007). Introduction: The sociology of entrepreneurship. In M. Ruef & M. Lounsbury (Eds.), *The sociology of entrepreneurship* (pp. 1–29). Bingley, UK: Emerald Group Publishing.

Ryan, R. (2004, September). The next generation of entrepreneurs: How to attract, keep and grow them. *Journal of State Government*, *77*(4), 37.

Sandburn, J. (2012). Immigrants outpacing the rest of us in small business ownership. *Time*. Retrieved from http://business.time.com/2012/06/15/immigrants-outpacing-the-rest-of-us-in-small-business-ownership/

Schumpeter, J. A. (1934). *The theory of economic development: An inquiry into profits, capital, credit, interest, and the business cycle*. Cambridge, MA: Harvard University Press.

Scott, W. R. (2002). *Organizations: Rational, natural, and open systems* (5th ed.). Upper Saddle, NJ: Prentice Hall.

Sexton, D. L. (1997). Entrepreneurship research needs and issues. In D. L. Sexton & R. W. (Eds.), *Entrepreneurship 2000* (pp. 401–408). Chicago, IL: Upstart Publishing Co.

Sexton, D. L., & Smilor, R. W. (Eds.). (1986). *The art and science of entrepreneurship*. Cambridge, MA: Ballinger Publishing Company.

Sexton, D. L., & Smilor, R. W. (Eds.). (1997). *Entrepreneurship 2000*. Chicago, IL: Upstart Publishing Co.

Shane, A. S. (2004). *A general theory of entrepreneurship: The individual-opportunity nexus*. Cheltenham, UK: Edward Elgar.

Shane, A. S., & Venkataraman, S. (2000). The promise of entrepreneurship as a field of research. *The Academy of Management Review*, *25*(1), 217–226.

Sharma, P., Chrisman, J. J., & Gersick, K. E. (2012). 25 years of family business review: Reflections on the past and perspectives for the future. *Family Business Review*, *25*(1), 5–15.

Sharma, P., & Manikutty, S. (2005). Strategic divestments in family firms: Role of family structure and community culture. *Entrepreneurship: Theory and Practice*, *29*(3), 293–311.

Shuffstall, B. (2013). *Entrepreneurial community self-assessment*. State College, PA: Penn State University Extension.

Shuffstall, B., & Fortunato, M. (2013). *Part 2: Tools and techniques for creating an entrepreneurial community*. Retrieved from http://extension.psu.edu/community/ecd/courses/entrepreneurial-communities/webinars/creating-entrepreneurial-communities-session-ii/creating-entrepreneurial-communities-session-ii

Sine, W. D., & David, R. J. (2010). *Institutions and entrepreneurship*. Bingley, UK: Emerald Publishing Group.

Smith, M. K. (2001). *'Community' in the encyclopedia of informal education*. Retrieved from http://www.infed.org/mobi/community.htm
Solomon, G. (2007). An examination of entrepreneurship education in the United States. *Journal of Small Business and Enterprise Development*, *14*(2), 168–182.
Soltow, J. H. (1968). The entrepreneur in economic history. *American Economic Review*, *58*(2), 84–92.
Sorenson, R. L., Yu, A., Brigham, K. H., & Lumpkin, G. T. (2013). *The landscape of family business*. Northampton, MA: Edward Elgar.
Stam, W., Arzlanian, S., & Elfring, T. (2014). Social capital of entrepreneurs and small firm performance: A meta-analysis of contextual and methodological moderators. *Journal of Business Venturing*, *29*, 152–173.
Stevenson, H. H., & Jarillo, J. C. (1990). A paradigm of entrepreneurial management. *Strategic Management Journal*, *11*, 17–27.
Surie, G., & Hazy, J. K. (2006). Generative leadership: Nurturing innovation in complex systems. *E:CO*, *8*(4), 13–26.
Swedberg, R. (Ed.). (2000). *Entrepreneurship: The social science view*. New York, NY: Oxford University Press.
Tajfel, H. (1982). Social psychology of intergroup relations. *Annual Review of Psychology*, *33*, 1–39.
Tan, J. (2002). Culture, nation, and entrepreneurial strategic orientations: Implications for emerging economy. *Entrepreneurship: Theory and Practice*, *26*(4), 95–111.
Thomas, A. S., & Mueller, S. L. (2000). A case for comparative entrepreneurship: Assessing the relevance of culture. *Journal of International Business Studies*, *31*, 287–301.
Thornton, P. H. (1999). The sociology of entrepreneurship. *Annual Review of Sociology*, *25*, 19–46.
Thornton, P. H., & Flynn, K. H. (2003). Entrepreneurship, networks, and geographies. In Z. J. Acs & D. B. Audretsch (Eds.), *Handbook of entrepreneurship research: An interdisciplinary survey and introduction* (pp. 401–433). Boston, MA: Kluwer Academic Publishers.
Thurik, R. (2009). Entreprenomics entrepreneurship, economic growth, and policy. In Z. J. Acs, D. B. Audretsch, & R. J. Strom (Eds.), *Entrepreneurship, growth, and public policy* (pp. 219–249). New York, NY: Cambridge University Press.
Timmons, J. A. (1997). *New venture creation*. Homewood, IL: Irwin.
Timmons, J. A., & Spinelli, S. (2009). *New venture creation* (8th ed.). Boston, MA: McGraw-Hill.
Tolbert, P. S., David, R. J., & Sine, W. D. (2011). Studying choice and change: The intersection of institutional theory and entrepreneurship. *Organization Science*, *22*(5), 1332–1344.
Trompenaars, F., & Hampden-Turner, C. (2012). *Riding the waves of culture: Understanding diversity in global business* (3rd ed.). New York, NY: McGraw-Hill.
van Stel, A., Carree, M., & Thurik, R. (2005). The effect of entrepreneurial activity on national economic growth. *Small Business Economics*, *24*, 311–321.
Venkataraman, S. (1997). The distinctive domain of entrepreneurship research: An editor's perspective. In J. Katz & R. Brockhaus (Eds.), *Advances in entrepreneurship, firm emergence and growth* (Vol. 3, pp. 119–138). Greenwich, CT: JAI Press.
Walzer, M. (1997). *On tolerance*. New Haven, CT: Yale University Press.

Walzer, N. (2004). Introduction: Entrepreneurship in community development. *Journal of the Community Development Society*, *35*(1), 1–4.
Walzer, N. (Ed.). (2007). *Entrepreneurship and local economic development*. New York, NY: Lexington Books.
Walzer, N., & Athiyaman, A. (2007). Introduction and overview. In N. Walzer (Ed.), *Entrepreneurship and local economic development* (pp. 1–19). New York, NY: Lexington Books.
Warren, R. L. (1987). *The community in America* (3rd ed.). Lanham, MD: University Press of America.
Weber, M. (1930). *The protestant ethic and the spirit of capitalism*. New York, NY: Scribner.
Westhead, P., & Wright, M. (2013). *Entrepreneurship: A very short introduction*. Oxford, UK: Oxford University Press.
Wilken, P. H. (1979). *Entrepreneurship: A comparative and historical study*. Norwood, NJ: Ablex.
Wilkinson, K. P. (1991). *The community in rural America*. New York, NY: Greenwood Press.
Wortman, M. S., Jr. (1986). A unified framework, research typologies, and research prospectuses for the interface between entrepreneurship and small business. In D. L. Sexton & R. W. Smilor (Eds.), *The art and science of entrepreneurship* (pp. 273–331). Cambridge, MA: Ballinger Publishing Company.
Young, F. W. (1971). A macrosociological interpretation of entrepreneurship. In P. Kilby (Ed.), *Entrepreneurship and economic development* (pp. 139–149). New York, NY: Education Free Press.
Zacharakis, A., Spinelli, S., & Timmons, J. A. (2011). *Business plans that work: A guide for small business*. New York, NY: McGraw-Hill.
Zahra, S. A. (2005). Entrepreneurship and disciplinary scholarship: Return to the fountainhead. In S. A. Alvarez, R. Agarwal, & O. Sorenson (Eds.), *Handbook of entrepreneurship research: Disciplinary perspectives* (pp. 253–268). New York, NY: Springer.

Suggested Additional Reading

Aldrich, H. E. (2002). Entrepreneurial strategies in new organizational populations. In R. Swedberg (Ed.), *Entrepreneurship: The social science view* (pp. 212–228). New York, NY: Oxford University Press.
Audretsch, D. B. (2007). *The entrepreneurial society*. Oxford, UK: Oxford University Press.
Audretsch, D. B., & Keilbach, M. (2004). Entrepreneurship and regional growth: An evolutionary interpretation. *Journal of Evolutionary Economics*, *14*(5), 605–616.
Cole, A. H. (1949). *Change and the entrepreneur: Postulates and patterns for entrepreneurial history*. Boston, MA: Harvard Business School Press.
Congregado, E. (Ed.). (2008). *Measuring entrepreneurship: Building a statistical system*. New York, NY: Springer.
Cooper, A. C., & Daily, C. M. (1997). Entrepreneurial teams. In D. L. Sexton & R. W. (Eds.), *Entrepreneurship 2000* (pp. 127–150). Chicago, IL: Upstart Publishing Co.

Greenfield, S. M., Strickon, A., Aubey, R. T., & Rothstein, M. (1979). Studies in entrepreneurial behavior: A review and an introduction. In S. M. Greenfield, A. Strickon, & R. T. Aubey (Eds.), *Entrepreneurs in cultural context* (pp. 3–18). Albuquerque, NM: University of New Mexico Press.

Hitt, M. A., Ireland, R. D., Camp, S. M., & Sexton, D. L. (Eds.). (2002). *Strategic entrepreneurship: Creating a new mindset*. Malden, MA: Blackwell Publishers.

Jenks, L. H. (1949). Role structure of entrepreneurial personality. In A. H. Cole (Ed.), *Change and the entrepreneur: Postulates and patterns for entrepreneurial history* (pp. 108–152). Boston, MA: Harvard Business School Press.

Leviticus, J. (2016). What do entrepreneurs contribute to society? Small Business, *Houston Chronicle*. Retrieved from http://smallbusiness.chron.com/entrepreneurs-contribute-society-78923.html

Marquez-Lopez, J. C., Guzman, C., & Linan, F. (2013). Could the perception about entrepreneurial culture be explained by demographic variables? In A. Fayolle, P. Kyro, T. Mets, & U. Venesaar (Eds.), *Conceptual richness and methodological diversity in entrepreneurship research* (pp. 47–65). Northampton, MA: Edward Elgar.

Read, S., & Domans, S. (2014). A review on effectuation. In A. Fayolle (Ed.), *Handbook of research on entrepreneurship: What we know and what we need to know* (pp. 238–261). Northampton, MA: Edward Elgar.

Sarasvathy, S. D. (2009). *Effectuation: Elements of entrepreneurial expertise*. Cheltenham, UK: Edward Elgar.

Schumpeter, J. A. (1949). Economic theory and entrepreneurial history. In A. H. Cole (Ed.), *Change and the entrepreneur: Postulates and patterns for entrepreneurial history* (pp. 63–84). Boston, MA: Harvard Business School Press.

3 Models of Entrepreneurial Community and Ecosystem Development

Michael W-P Fortunato

The notion that entrepreneurs exist in communities, or can interact together to form a community of their own, is not revolutionary (Cornwall, 1998; Lyons, Alter, Audretsch, & Augustine, 2012; Peredo & Chrisman, 2006). Entrepreneurship does not occur in a vacuum, but is embedded deeply in a messy web of social relationships, spread across different economic, social, and geographic environments (Acs & Armington, 2006; Huggins & Thompson, 2012; Lyons et al., 2012; Peredo & Chrisman, 2006; Rupasingha & Goetz, 2013). These relationships impact the people who are (or may become) entrepreneurs, and their actions in turn impact the people and institutions around them (Kwon, Heflin, & Ruef, 2013; Van de Ven, 1993). People in an entrepreneurs' community may take the form of other entrepreneurs, or entrepreneurial supporters, buyers and suppliers, regulatory agents, local leaders, and lots of people who have nothing to do with the entrepreneur's business—but whose attitudes may profoundly impact the entrepreneur's own actions and beliefs. Whereas much of the early literature on entrepreneurship focused on the traits, behaviors, and strategic actions of entrepreneurs as individuals and firms (Gartner, 1990), modern insights recognize the fundamental role of the community not just as an environmental or framework condition for entrepreneurship, but as an active set of participants shaping, supporting, and even inhibiting entrepreneurial behavior both individually and collectively (Johannisson & Nilsson, 1989; Lyons et al., 2012; Peredo & Chrisman, 2006; Thornton, 1999).

The term "collectively" is important to understand entrepreneurship more holistically than a narrow focus on individual firm behavior. Even in the most individualistic of cultures, it is becoming increasingly clear that entrepreneurs almost never act alone (DeBresson, 1999; Vissa & Chacar, 2009; West, 2007). Entrepreneurial teams are common occurrences (and often consist of family members), and entrepreneurs may form friendships, alliances, and partnerships with other entrepreneurs (Blatt, 2009; Sirolli, 2012; Stuart & Sorenson, 2007; Zolin, Kuckertz, & Kautonen, 2011). Furthermore, supporting actors from across the community may step into the picture to support entrepreneurs through various formal and informal mechanisms (Feld, 2012; Flora & Flora, 1993). However, actors from within the community can also fail to support local entrepreneurship, or outright inhibit entrepreneurial action, sometimes in subtle and unintended ways (Fortunato & McLaughlin, 2012; Williams & Williams, 2011).

This chapter is intended to unpack the complex relationship between entrepreneurs and their communities and environments. It will examine a wide variety of existing models in the literature that each takes a different perspective on how entrepreneurs interact, and how entrepreneurship can best be supported locally. It should become clear to the reader that the community is far from an "environmental" or mere "ecological" factor affecting entrepreneurship, but often plays an active role in facilitating, inhibiting, or changing the course of entrepreneurial action in a particular place. Additionally, the roles of culture, leadership, policy, and the local environment profoundly affect the nature of the entrepreneurial community and support network, or *ecosystem*. It is our view in this book that the culture, leadership, policies, and environments supporting entrepreneurial action can be improved in communities desiring to support entrepreneurship more seriously. Prior research on supporting entrepreneurship at the community level, while widely scattered across the distinctive literatures of sociology, economics, business, community development, and psychology, will be integrated here to form a more holistic look at how entrepreneurial communities can and do emerge.

The chapter begins by looking at spatial variations in entrepreneurship and self-employment levels. While some spatial variations can be attributed to the presence of urban amenities, research institutions, or major infrastructure routes, it should become clear that much of the variation cannot be accounted for by factors typically associated with higher levels of entrepreneurship. Following this analysis, the chapter examines four levels of entrepreneurial community analysis, or four ways of "thinking about" entrepreneurial communities. Then the chapter moves into a meta-analysis of existing entrepreneurial community and ecosystem models, highlighting their similarities and differences, and how these models can inform the field's thinking about how the many individual, social, institutional, psychological, cultural, and community-based pieces of the entrepreneurship puzzle fit together. Finally, the chapter briefly summarizes and compares the strengths and weaknesses of each model, setting up a context for the examinations comprising the remainder of this book.

Spatial Variation in Local Entrepreneurship

Entrepreneurship is not the same everywhere. Multiple studies have found wide variation across geographic regions in levels of self-employment, new firm starts, profitability of the self-employed, and the duration of new firms (Acs & Armington, 2006; Goetz & Rupasingha, 2014; Henderson, Low, & Weiler, 2007). Differences in entrepreneurship across geographic space exist for many reasons. Some of the most commonly cited reasons for different levels of entrepreneurship include differences in local assets and infrastructure (Henderson et al., 2007), specialized knowledge and the presence of research institutions (Audretsch & Lehmann, 2005), regional economic conditions and social networks (Malecki, 1993), and different cultural milieus (Julien, 2007).

In the research literature, much of the historical focus has been on *framework conditions* as drivers of entrepreneurial action. *Framework conditions* are local conditions that facilitate the emergence of entrepreneurship and stimulate entrepreneurial action across the local population, including factors like good governance, positive attitudes toward entrepreneurship, access to resources, training options, entrepreneurial finance, and R&D transfer organizations (Bosma & Levie, 2009). However, new approaches have moved beyond the study of entrepreneurial environments to understand the human, technological, and institutional elements of place, as well as how they affect entrepreneurial behavior. Many of these approaches—from framework (or facilitating) conditions through to complex human interdependencies—will be the focus of this chapter.

To illustrate this point, a very brief analysis is presented to demonstrate how widely entrepreneurial action can vary, even across adjacent places. There are several reasons that entrepreneurship rates can vary from place to place that are expected. When factors comprising the expected variation are accounted for in a regression analysis, however, one would theoretically expect no further variation from place to place. One finds that entrepreneurship does indeed vary widely from place to place, even across directly adjacent places, for reasons not explained by common factors. This analysis will utilize county-level self-employment data from the Bureau of Economic Analysis Regional Economic Information System (REIS) for Texas in 2012. Based on explorations by Goetz and Rupasingha (2009) and Henderson, Low, and Weiler (2007), a regression model was created with the following common factors explaining entrepreneurial variation at the county level (see Figure 3.1).

$$
\begin{aligned}
Y = \alpha &+ \beta_1[MedianAge] + \beta_2[MedianHHI] + \beta_3[Unemployment] + \\
&\beta_4[PercentBachelors] + \beta_5[PresentForeignBorn] + \\
&\beta_6[ExtractionEstablishment] + \beta_7[RuralUrbanContinuum] + \\
&\beta_8[Population]^2 + \beta_9[Population] + \varepsilon
\end{aligned}
$$

Figure 3.1 Entrepreneurship Breadth/Depth OLS Regression Equations

In this equation, Y is the dependent variable, which can be self-employment *breadth* or *depth*. *Breadth* is the ratio of the share of self-employed persons to the total population, while *depth* is the average income of self-employed persons to total employed persons in the county. Areas of high breadth have many self-employed persons per capita, while areas of high depth have self-employed persons who earn more on average (see Henderson et al., 2007 for a complete methodology).

Control variables in Equation 1 include those found to be important in Goetz and Rupasingha (2009), and include median age, median household income (HHI), unemployment, percent of the population with a bachelor's degree, percent of the foreign born population, number of extraction-based establishments (an important industry variable in Texas), USDA rural-urban continuum category for the county (from central city to remote rural, a one-to-nine scale), and a squared term for population size. All population variables were taken from the U.S. Census American Community Survey 2012 (five-year data) (see Figure 3.2), while the number of extraction establishments was taken from the Census County Business Patterns survey (2012). The USDA rural-urban classification used 2010 county designations (see Figure 3.3). Non-significant control variables were dropped from the equation systematically until a final model was established.

$$0.208[RUCC] + 0.458[MedianAge] + 0.238[MedianHHI] \bullet R2 = 0.330, \quad Model\ F = 40.982,\ p < 0.001$$

Figure 3.2 OLS Regression Entrepreneurial Breadth Model Controlling for USDA Rural/Urban Continuum Code (RUCC), Median Age, and Median Household Income

$$—0.184[MedianAge] + 0.801[Extract] — 0.126[RUCC] — 0.375[Population] \bullet R2 = 0.402, Model\ F = 41.797,\ p < 0.001$$

Figure 3.3 OLS Regression Entrepreneurial Depth Model Controlling for Median Age, Density of Extraction Industry, USDA Rural/Urban Continuum Code (RUCC), and Population Size

Accounting for these independent variables affecting entrepreneurship, the residuals of the equation can be mapped county by county. A negative value indicates that the self-employment breadth or depth is lower than the predictive equation would expect. A positive value indicates that self-employment breadth or depth is higher than the predictive equation would expect. This analysis means that some counties in Texas "punch above their weight class" when it comes to self-employment, while others are weaker than expected. These mapped differences can be found in Figures 3.4 and 3.5:

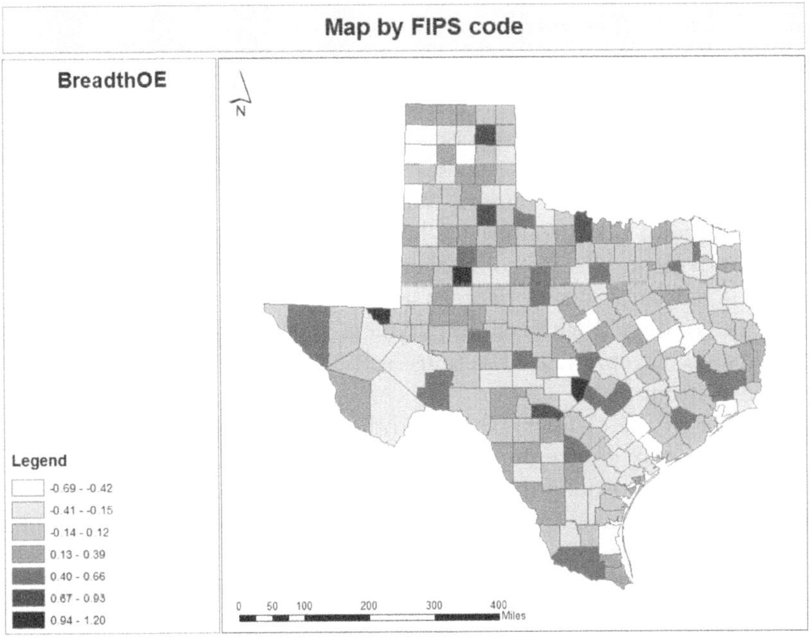

Figure 3.4 County Map of Texas Illustrating County-Level Deviance from OLS Regression Breadth Model in Figure 3.2

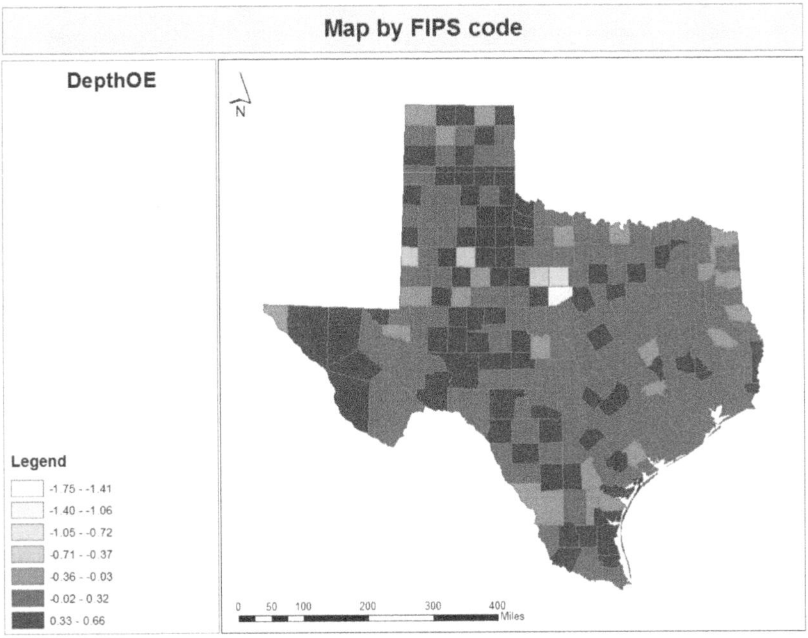

Figure 3.5 County Map of Texas Illustrating County-Level Deviance from OLS Regression Depth Model in Figure 3.3

It can be seen from these figures that areas of high self-employment performance (darker colors) and areas of low self-employment performance (lighter colors) do not follow a consistent or clustered pattern. They can be in rural or urban parts of the state, densely or sparsely populated, close to the highway or very remote. With these explanations removed, what is the source of this variation? When accounting for major predictors of self-employment, why do some counties seem to "out-perform" others in terms of self-employment breadth and depth? This analysis could just as easily be conducted with self-employment growth, new firm starts, or any measure of entrepreneurial action—self-employment is just an example for illustration.

The rest of the chapter examines other social, cultural, and leadership factors that may contribute to higher or lower levels of entrepreneurship that are harder to quantify, and do not fall into many predictive models. This data requires researchers to think beyond an input-output focus about what supports entrepreneurship, as we progress toward models that include complex and often unpredictable local action, bounded by culture, and stimulated or inhibited by local leadership. Could culture and leadership be factors influencing variations in entrepreneurial action? Before examining these factors, it is important to discuss the various levels of analysis through which we can think about entrepreneurial action: At the group level, the community level, and the ecosystem level.

Entrepreneurs as a Group

Sociologists have a keen interest in studying social groups, from social classes to minorities, religious groups to gang members, and the national culture straight down to the culture of the urban sidewalk. Sociology has examined so many different types of social groups that it is surprising that Thornton (1999) observed as recently as the late 1990s that entrepreneurs had essentially evaded being studied as a "social group" by sociologists. Historically, entrepreneurs have been seen as social actors and unusual outliers that disrupt economies and think differently about opportunities by a variety of fields (Mitra, 2012). Each field's definition of entrepreneurship captured a particular facet of what entrepreneurship is about (i.e., behavioral aspects, or risk aspects, or market aspects, or business strategy, or personal motivations, or especially traits predicting this socially deviant behavior), but no one definition seemed to capture entrepreneurship holistically (Low & MacMillan, 1988).

Lamenting the overarching fixation on traits-based research and firm-level examination of entrepreneurship until the late 20th Century, Thornton (1999) and later Ulhøi (2005) and others began to examine the social dimensions of entrepreneurship. Building on work by Granovetter (1985) that warned against thinking about economic actors as purely rational and unaffected by social forces, the sociological school of thinking began to see entrepreneurs as a cohesive group of economic actors playing a distinctive role in the economy rather than a ragtag group of individuals who deviate from mainstream behavioral models in different ways according to a variety of academic fields. Like any other social group, their actions are deeply embedded in social relations that enhance and constrain their behavior (Thornton, 1999; Ulhøi, 2005). Turning toward what Thornton (1999) termed the "demand side" of entrepreneurship analysis (i.e., that which does not inhere in the entrepreneur's personal characteristics and circumstances), she drew from Aldrich (1990) and others to suggest that the social context in which an entrepreneur operates matters as much as personal agency. From this argument, Thornton (1999) linked the microanalysis of entrepreneurial firms to the macro-analysis of start-up rates as a feature of economies, political regimes, and cultural zones, bringing a distinctive social geography component to the field.

Around the same time, Shane and Venkataraman (2000) wrote *The Promise of Entrepreneurship as a Field of Research* in the *Academy of Management Review,* one of the most widely cited entrepreneurship papers to this day. In it, Shane and Venkataraman cogently argue that entrepreneurship is distinct enough as an empirical social phenomenon that it warrants its own domain of inquiry, rather than a tertiary, "hodgepodge" collection of ideas by a variety of fields examining pieces of the entrepreneurial puzzle (Shane, 2012). This idea was a major advancement, as it outlined the defining features that unify the study of entrepreneurs and gave legitimacy to the idea that entrepreneurs did not belong in the residual of economic behavior models, but at the center of explained variance in a new kind of model accounting for opportunity identification and exploitation behavior under conditions of uncertainty and bounded by a supportive environment (Shane, 2003; Shane & Venkataraman, 2000).

Many scholars have since sought to examine entrepreneurs as a cohesive group—far too many to list here. The focus of the field has shifted distinctively from understanding entrepreneurs as wild and deviant individuals, toward a more holistic understanding of entrepreneurs as a social group with identifiable social and economic functions, deeply embedded in community and political relations that enhance and constrain their action. While entrepreneurs transform the markets around them, the local, regional, and national social and institutional climate in which they do their work frame their actions, right down to cultural supports or discouragements of whether to become an entrepreneur in the first place. Studies examining entrepreneurs at this level seek to understand which facilitating conditions enhance entrepreneurship, and which constraints can be removed to maximize entrepreneurial action in a given place—recognizing the massive geographic variation in start-up rates, and the nature of start-ups in different places (Acs & Armington, 2006; Amorós & Bosma, 2014).

Entrepreneurs in the Community ~ Entrepreneurs as a Community

Clevenger (2017) discussed the terms "entrepreneurship" and "community" in a mutualistic context. A step beyond the analysis of entrepreneurs as a sociologically and economically important group, entrepreneurs can also be studied *in* a community context, or *as* a community themselves. Each has different implications. First, returning to the definition of community advanced by Wilkinson (1991), a community has three essential components: a locality, a local society, and a set of locally oriented collective actions. Entrepreneurs *in* the community preserve the notion that entrepreneurs are relatively independent, autonomous actors, but their actions fundamentally affect their locality—and their locality affects their actions. Through this embeddedness, entrepreneurs are deeply influenced by place identities and the people around them, and through their creative endeavors, help to recreate, renew, revitalize, and reinvent those places (McKeever, Jack, & Anderson, 2015). As cultures transform to accept and respect entrepreneurs for their productive works, the community itself can take on an entrepreneurial flavor, where opportunistic action is celebrated and natural and human capital are commonly utilized to engage in community-based enterprise (Paredo & Chrisman, 2006). At this level of analysis, entrepreneurs must be viewed as more than a group. What is interesting to researchers are the relationships and social exchanges between entrepreneurs and the community, the cultural attitudes and legal frameworks surrounding entrepreneurship at a local level, and the community-level actions that arise out of local entrepreneurial action.

Most every entrepreneur does business *in* communities; however, can entrepreneurs *form* communities of their own? Research illustrates that entrepreneurs, despite their competitive reputation, frequently self-organize into communities. Beginning with the formation of networks (Aldrich & Zimmer, & Jones, 1986), entrepreneurs are often times drawn into networks to support the community around them (Johannisson & Nilsson, 1989). Not only is this an excellent source of opportunity based in the immediate needs of the community, but it also improves the local business climate for themselves and other entrepreneurs. Furthermore, entrepreneurs may even formalize their communities by creating formal organizations dedicated to supporting community-based entrepreneurship development (Fortunato & McLaughlin, 2012). An analysis of entrepreneurs *as* a community must go beyond the more common focus on venture teams to illustrate the linkages between firms that might otherwise consider themselves in competition with one another, instead collaborating to build a better local economy.

The Entrepreneurial Ecosystem

Ecosystem is a term borrowed from the field of natural ecology. The preeminent ecologist Charles Darwin largely viewed ecosystems as highly dynamic living systems through which evolution occurs, replacing some species with newer species that are better adapted to a changing environment. Studies of *entrepreneurial ecosystems* are just emerging (see Feld, 2012; Isenberg, 2010), and surprisingly, few deeply compare entrepreneurial ecosystems to the natural ecosystems that inspired the term in the first place. This section begins by discussing natural and human ecosystems in a general sense. It then compares these insights from natural ecosystems to the entrepreneurial ecosystem, demonstrating that entrepreneurial ecosystems decidedly follow many of the same principles.

Ecosystems in Nature and Human Ecology

Ecosystems are a curious way to describe the way entrepreneurs interact within a community. The term *ecosystem* comes from biology and environmental studies, and can be defined as "all of the organisms and the abiotic pools with which they interact" in a given geographical area (Chapin, Matson, & Vitousek, 2011, p. 5). The Oxford Dictionary relaxes the biological definition, defining ecosystems more generally as "A complex network or interconnected system" (Oxford Dictionary, 2016). The dictionary cites "Silicon Valley's entrepreneurial ecosystem" as a more general usage of the word, suggesting that the usage of "ecosystem" to describe entrepreneurs in an interactive environment is relatively commonplace. This insight relates more generally to complexity in social-ecological systems (SES). In any SES, the components that comprise the system are not the focus, but rather the *interactions* between components including resources, users, and governance systems, and the *outcomes* generated from these interactions (Ostrom, 2009). In an entrepreneurial ecosystem, this involves the complex interactions among entrepreneurs and between entrepreneurs and their governance and resource systems, with the recognition that some arrangements of these actors within an environment will lead to better outcomes for entrepreneurs than others.

Aldrich (1990) first examined entrepreneurship through an "ecological" lens examining spatial factors contributing to difference in firm formation rates. Other approaches, including Neck, Meyer, Cohen, and Corbett (2004) and Spilling (1996), used the term "entrepreneurial systems" to describe systems where entrepreneurs and their facilitating environment are in constant interaction, using as examples entrepreneurially minded action surrounding the 1994 Lillehammer Olympics (Spilling, 1996) and the density of high-tech spin-off activity in Boulder County, Colorado (Neck et al., 2004). Neck et al. (2004) is notable in that these authors began to use porto-ecosystem language to describe the interrelated system there, including the genealogy and taxonomy of local actors.

The term *entrepreneurial ecosystem* in its current form can be traced back to an article by Zacharakis, Shepherd, and Coombs (2003) titled, *The Development of Venture-backed Internet Companies: An Ecosystem Perspective* in the *Journal of Business Venturing*. While the biological definition of *ecosystem* may seem to be a questionable fit to describe entrepreneurs, Zacharakis et al. (2003) borrowed their insights directly from entrepreneurs who interacted very differently in different environments, questioning why different geographic regions seem to possess characteristics that benefit some types of Internet companies, but not others. These scholars examined several regions of Northern California, and found that some parts of the region excelled at creating Internet hardware, some at Internet software, and some at e-commerce companies. In addition to a variety of different "environmental" framework conditions, these micro-industries evolved around other companies, pioneering enterprises, and supportive knowledge networks that developed in those areas over time (Zacharakis et al., 2003).

In nature, ecosystems consist of a diversity of organisms (from microorganisms to macro-fauna) and a wide array of environmental conditions. Some organisms fare better under some conditions than others, as some organisms have adapted over time to heat or to cold, to humidity or extreme dryness, to salt or fresh water. Organisms have also co-evolved and adapted to one another, developing unique defenses against predators, or special hunting and predation techniques, or particularly effective camouflage. Each population of organisms lives in a state of ongoing dynamic equilibrium with each other, and with their environment. The ecosystem exists in a relative state of balance, but as soon as any change occurs (such as a food surplus or shortage, the emergence of a disease, a wildfire, or a slow change in the environment), the effects ripple through the ecosystem, rapidly creating a new set of framework conditions. This dynamic feeds back on populations of organisms, as some will find that their defenses are no longer useful, or that the habitat is no longer compatible, or perhaps that the environment has changed to their advantage. Booms and busts can happen in an ecosystem, but many well-regulated ecosystems (with a relatively consistent climate, low levels of disease, and few invasive species) can persist in a state of dynamic equilibrium for thousands of years.

There are a few features of natural ecosystems that are important to mention before bringing the discussion back to entrepreneurs. First, ecosystems constantly change. Even though some ecosystems are considered to be in a "steady state," new perspectives recognize that the inputs and outputs of ecosystems are often unbalanced, even if the change is difficult to observe (Chapin et al., 2011; Wessels, 2013). This constantly dynamic equilibrium is critical to the survival of ecosystems, as better-adapted species tend to persist in the environment as a result of change, while ill-adapted species fade away. This leads to the development of species with some extraordinary traits! Flying squirrels, angler fish with their own deep sea "lanterns," predator night vision, cheetah speed, exotic mating dances, bacteria that can grow in near-boiling water—these all arose from adaptations to the ecosystem environment, and typically as a response to environmental (or competitor) stressors. Through natural selection, those organisms possessing special advantageous traits persist. To paraphrase loosely Darwin, it is not the strongest that survive, or the smartest that survive: it is the organism most adapted to its environment that survives.

A second feature that is worth mentioning is that, in an ecosystem, everything is fundamentally connected. Even a small change in one part of the ecosystem can have a massive impact on an entire food chain. Sometimes called the "butterfly effect," a seemingly innocuous change to an ecosystem can balloon into massive system challenge—for better or for worse (see Adlard, Miller, & Smit, 2015). The sub-fields of parasitology, epidemiology, and invasive species management are focused on the dramatic effects and outcomes of an introduced species or vector owing to a combination of facilitating environmental conditions, an absence of control factors (such as natural predators), and the high interconnectedness of local ecosystems (see Pyšek & Richardson, 2010, for an invasive species example).

A third feature relates to symbiosis and competition. People often think of organisms as being in constant competition in an ecosystem. It seems natural to speak about businesses in this regard as well, as businesses tend to compete with one another in a free market economy. When talking about human ecosystems, many of the central ideas relating to competition and collaboration come from the human ecology school founded at the University of Chicago by Robert Park. Park was deeply influenced by Darwin, and at a time when Darwinian thinking was *en vogue* in the academy (especially because of social scientists such as Herbert Spencer, founder of social Darwinism), he began to apply the insights of natural selection to the nature of human organization. Park focused these insights on cities, observing that social organization exhibits two primary traits: competition and communication (Park, 1939). In his book, *The City* (1925), Park examined the tribalism of certain social groups that banded together for social advantage, much like species in an ecosystem. He also noted that these groups often clashed with one another, and he focused deeply on the competitive behavior that arose from the intergroup social unrest of the day. Park suggested that, in the city, the ultimate form of social competition was competition for space, particularly for central locations in the city where the best opportunities for economic advancement could be found (Park et al., 1925). While Park is widely regarded to be the founder of the human ecology school, and applied many of Darwin's own terms to human ecological systems such as symbiosis, invasion, and succession, some of his most widely cited ideas stemmed from this analysis of social and class conflict that arose out of competition for land and resources in the urban environment. Along with the term "survival of the fittest," the term "ecosystem" often conjures images of a constant battle for survival through both competition and communication, a war of all species against all others for competitive advantage with evanescent and dynamic alliances appearing when it benefits the involved social groups.

In natural ecosystems, this war of "all against all" is simply not true, and for one simple reason: The primary goal of species is to conserve scarce energy, and competing excessively takes a lot of energy (Wessels, 2013). If species are continually fighting for survival against other species and their environment, then they are burning calories that they must conserve to survive harsh seasons; or to hunt, gather, and find food and water; or to find a mate. Food is scarce in an ecosystem, as populations of organisms will continue to expand as long as there is a viable food source until reaching an upper limit that can no longer sustain growth—so when food surpluses occur, they are normally very short-lived as populations of eaters also swell. To truly be "the fittest," organisms spend very little time fighting and competing over scarce resources, and much more time adapting to highly specific niches in the ecosystem (Wessels, 2013). Wessels (2013) gives the examples of two birds: the black-capped chickadee and the white-breasted nuthatch. Both birds look very similar and occupy highly overlapping ecological niches, feeding on bugs from tree bark in the forest. Rather than compete directly, each species co-evolved different beak and claw morphologies suited to different parts of the tree. Nuthatches have very long "back toes," which allow them to slide up and down the trunks of trees, and long, slender beaks to get bugs the chickadees cannot access. Chickadees have rounded wings, allowing them to hover over the branches, and their rounded beaks allow them to extract bugs from leaves and bark that are out of range for nuthatches (Wessels, 2013).

Many of the same insights can be applied to the co-evolution of social groups within an economy, including entrepreneurs. Indeed, while Park spent much of his time examining capitalistic competition for advanced land uses—what he felt was the driving force causing cities to grow and develop—he mostly saw communication and symbiosis as the glue holding social groups together (Park et al., 1925). However, it is his insights about mutualism and the diversification of human activity across social groups and symbiotic collaboration between groups for collective benefit that may, in fact, bear the closest resemblance to an actual natural ecosystem.

Fourth, in an ecosystem, individual organisms must often perish to benefit and perpetuate the entire species. This is an important feature of Darwin's (1859) *natural selection*, which is a harsh, cruel reality of ecosystems, but it is fundamental to understanding how well-adapted, value-creating firms emerge. As ecosystem changes occur, organisms possessing ill-adapted characteristics may perish so that better-adapted members of the species can continue to live. An example might be a species of river otter—some of whom have webbed feet, and some who do not. Following the introduction of a fast predator (such as an alligator, for example), the webbed-footed otters will be able to out-swim their non-webbed counterparts. As more and more non-webbed otters meet their demise, the species will appear to "evolve" webbed feet, being the only members of the species left to procreate. This adaptation may have other advantages for the otters, such as an improved ability to catch fish, leading to further perpetuation of the species. Or ill-adapted organisms may serve as a warning to other organisms, taking risks that end in death or injury. Early hunter-gathering humans tried a wide variety of new foods, some of which are poisonous. Consumption of a poisonous berry or bark would quickly let others in the community know of the dangers of eating that particular plant, and then that information could be passed down as ancestral knowledge about which foods to avoid for the betterment of the wider species. This is fundamental not only to ecosystems but also in economic philosophies such as Taleb's (2012) *antifragility,* which posits that complex systems tend to benefit from occasional errors, stressors, and disorder, and actually need these things to develop. The sacrifice of the individual—be it an otter or a small business—creates a more informed, more resilient system for those who remain.

Entrepreneurial Ecosystems

All of the biological principles relate to entrepreneurial ecosystems as well, and differentiate a focus on entrepreneurial ecosystems from foci on framework conditions or simple social relations. First, entrepreneurial ecosystems are always changing. At the very heart of entrepreneurial action is novelty: new firm starts, new market entrants, new innovative ideas, new technologies, new business models. In Schumpeterian (1934) fashion, creative destruction represents this flux of new ideas replacing older ones, all with the intention of bringing more value to the overall economy. And, entrepreneurial environments can change rapidly, either because of rapidly changing market conditions (Kirzner, 1973), policy conditions (Baumol, 1968), and industrial and social conditions (Shane, 2003).

Second, everything is interconnected in an entrepreneurial community. If one feature of the local ecosystem changes, it can send a cascading ripple effect throughout the entire local economy, or what Isenberg (2010) calls the "law of small numbers" (p. 7). This interconnectedness can conceivably have a positive or negative effect, as small entrepreneurial successes can encourage hundreds of would-be entrepreneurs if promoted well, or the simple closure of a classic local business can equally discourage people. Third, entrepreneurs very rarely compete head-to-head with established businesses using the same business model without differentiating their offering in some way. Direct competition with a large, well-funded competitor would take far too many resources, and few companies (other than some well-known and well-funded examples, like Compaq; see Feld, 2012) are able to start incipient businesses through direct competition. Instead, much like species in an ecosystem, they find strategic niches they can fill more effectively, perhaps providing highly specialized products or services, or improving upon the value proposition of a major competitor through better service, lower prices, or faster processing times (Davidsson, 2009).

Finally, entrepreneurial ventures often fail. These failures were either not suited to the marketplace at the time they were launched or they made critical errors that were only evident in retrospect. As Knight (1921) argued, entrepreneurs are routinely subject to uncertainty, and those who succumb to uncertainty are—for the time being—destroyed by prevailing market conditions, opening the door for other firms to learn and succeed (Schumpeter, 1934). The creative destruction cycle of failure and rebirth not only allows better-adapted businesses to grow and proliferate, giving them more access to scarce resources, but also the innocuous errors of one firm can be a lesson to all other firms in the ecosystem not to follow suit, or to take a different approach.

The term "ecosystem" is beginning to appear more frequently in the literature, and it is not always clear if the systems being described truly exhibit ecosystem characteristics. To truly be considered an ecosystem approach to entrepreneurship, the approach must (a) favor dynamic models over static ones; (b) observe interconnectedness and interdependency well beyond the entrepreneurs themselves, incorporating entrepreneurs, their supporters, and the environment; (c) be a system of creative destruction through which a "natural selection" of firms can occur; and (d) recognize that individual firm failure serves to make the whole system stronger. The next section examines different models for examining entrepreneurship locally. These models appear to comprise a "sequence" from framework conditions toward more holistic ecosystems, but it will be demonstrated that each offers a unique and useful perspective on developing entrepreneurial economies.

A Meta-Analysis of Entrepreneurial Community and Ecosystem Models

A diverse cross-section of integrated models and frameworks that have been used to make sense of the messiness of entrepreneurship across geographic space, and the differential features that appear to drive entrepreneurship in some areas, while inhibiting it (or having a neutral effect) in others is discussed. For this analysis, some of the best-known frameworks for analyzing entrepreneurship in a geographic or community context will be chosen. There are certainly more frameworks in the world than can possibly be covered here, and there is no offense whatsoever by their omission. In fact, it is hoped that the presentation of different models here can touch on a discussion of which community elements *should* be part of a framework or theoretical model supporting entrepreneurial behavior. Moreover, the organization of these approaches is merely intended to be useful to entrepreneurship researchers and practitioners in the context of this book's focus on entrepreneurial communities, culture, and leadership. A future consideration is an examination of entrepreneurial drivers across multiple dimensions.

The models are clustered into four basic approaches, related to the four levels of analysis presented earlier. The four basic approaches to analyzing entrepreneurship spatially are (1) the facilitating conditions approach, (2) the national and regional policy approach, (3) the entrepreneurial communities approach, and (4) the entrepreneurial ecosystem approach. It should be noted that these four categories have fuzzy boundaries. Many studies that fall into one category or another may contain elements of another category. For example, a study that focuses on the conditions that facilitate entrepreneurship may also contain some regional and national policy elements, or an entrepreneurial communities' perspective may approach ecosystem thinking without quite including all the necessary elements to make it a true ecosystem. What matters here is that most frameworks fall primarily into one category based on assumptions about how entrepreneurs behave, or how they can best be supported and/or analyzed. This in turn affects the nature of the findings of any study using that framework, and it drastically affects the study implications—particularly how entrepreneurship can best be supported in an applied sense.

Also, it is easy to think of these four approaches as an evolutionary sequence flowing from entrepreneurs as an outcome of local environments toward the interconnected messiness and reinvention of an entrepreneurial ecosystem. While each approach appears to build sequentially in terms of complexity and new insights about entrepreneurial behavior, each approach also contributes something unique to our understanding of entrepreneurship. These unique contributions draw largely from the fact that each approach occurs at a different level of analysis, and factors at each level of analysis are constantly impacting on local entrepreneurial action in different ways and at different times. Sometimes the key inhibitor of entrepreneurial action is ecosystem-driven, dealing with the contentious and fractured nature of social relations across certain institutional boundaries in a place. Sometimes it's simpler: there's a bad ordinance in the community that makes it really tough for entrepreneurs to get access to local customers. Both levels are equally important, theoretically and in terms of their real impact on local entrepreneurship.

Facilitating Conditions Approach

This approach views entrepreneurs as a special, sociologically and economically important group of individuals, who generally act independently to launch new firms and ventures. Under the facilitating conditions approach, entrepreneurs are seen as an "output" of certain places, with high levels of local business starts, self-employment, proprietor earnings, and opportunity-driven venturing equated more or less with "success." High levels of output are facilitated by a variety of "inputs," or environmental conditions that appear to support "successful outcomes." This approach is often seen taking the form of OLS regression analysis, a spatial determinants approach, or spatial autocorrelation of facilitating factors in an attempt to understand which of those factors appear to impact entrepreneurship levels across place and time. Of course, the specific inputs and outputs of the equation can change somewhat (i.e., analyzing business starts versus self-employment levels as a dependent variable), but no matter the specific focus of the approach, facilitating conditions inheres in the idea that it is the environment which supports or inhibits entrepreneurial action.

To use a curious scientific example, one might expect a particular strain of bacteria to grow quickly and robustly in a variety of environments. However, the growth of those bacteria can also be severely enhanced or constrained by the substrate (i.e., physical medium containing food on which the bacteria grow, and its salinity, alkalinity, nourishing content) and the environmental conditions (i.e., temperature, humidity). In comparing entrepreneurs to bacteria, there is a similarity here: much of the literature focuses on the growth potential of entrepreneurs and fully expects entrepreneurial firms to grow rapidly in a variety of environments. And, like microbiologists examining the environments in which bacteria grow best, scientists using the facilitating conditions approach try to understand what environments and conditions facilitate entrepreneurship best—something they expect to occur naturally and freely when conditions are right and inhibiting factors are removed.

Key Models in the Facilitating Conditions Approach

Models from Bhidé's (2000), Gnyawali and Fogel (1994), Van de Ven (1993), special determinants models, and The Global Entrepreneurship Model are summarized.

GNYAWALI AND FOGEL

Gnyawali and Fogel (1994) were not the first to explore facilitating conditions. They themselves point to a diversity of scholars who pointed out various elements of a facilitating environment, including Bruno and Tyebjee (1982), Dana (1987), Gartner (1985), and others. Perhaps Gnyawali and Fogel's biggest contribution is the recognition that

> most of these studies have been fragmented, highly descriptive, and focused on only a few aspects of the environment . . . most of the literature has neither paid adequate attention to the needs of the entrepreneur—the main beneficiary of the environment—nor described the environmental conditions in terms of the process of new venture creation.
>
> (p. 43)

As a response, they systematically analyzed the literature, assembling diverse components into a coherent framework leading from the presence of opportunities toward new venture creation. According to these scholars, "A key role of the entrepreneurial environment is to help entrepreneurs develop both propensity to enterprise and ability to enterprise" (Gnyawali & Fogel, 1994, p. 54).

KEY COMPONENTS

In this framework, government policies (including restrictions on imports and exports, provision of bankruptcy laws, low barriers to entry, procedural requirements for registration and licensing, low number of institutions for entrepreneurs to report to, reasonable rules and regulations governing entrepreneurial activities, and laws to protect property rights) directly affect the "supply" of opportunities (Gnyawali & Fogel, 1994). The presence or absence of opportunity in turn affects both the entrepreneur's *ability to enterprise* and *propensity to enterprise*. The *ability to enterprise* relates to a person's physical ability to launch a new venture if one wants to. This is influenced by one's entrepreneurial and business skills, enhanced by the presence of technical and vocational education, business education, entrepreneurial training programs, technical and vocational training programs, and high availability of information (Gnyawali & Fogel, 1994). *Propensity to enterprise* relates to the likelihood that a person will actually launch a business if they possess the skills, and the opportunity to do so is there. This concept is influenced by socioeconomic factors including the public's attitude toward entrepreneurship, presence of experienced entrepreneurs, presence of successful role models, existence of persons with entrepreneurial characteristics, recognition of exemplary entrepreneurial performance, high proportion of small firms in the population of total firms, a high diversity of economic activities, and high overall economic growth (Gnyawali & Fogel, 1994). When both *propensity to enterprise* and *ability to enterprise* are high, facilitated by the environmental factors mentioned here, it increases the overall *likelihood to enterprise* for entrepreneurs. The only resources standing between the potential entrepreneur and a new venture are the presence of both *financial assistance* (e.g., venture capital, alternative sources of financing, low-cost loans, willingness of financial institutions to finance small entrepreneurs, credit guarantee program for start-up enterprises, and high competition among financial institutions) and *nonfinancial assistance* (e.g., mentoring, counseling and support services for entrepreneurs; entrepreneurial networks, incubator facilities, government procurement programs for small businesses, government support for research and development, tax incentives and exemptions, local and international information networks, and modern transport and communication facilities) (Gnyawali & Fogel, 1994).

Van de Ven

While predating Gnyawali and Fogel (1994) by a year with a less-comprehensive model, Van de Ven (1993) made an important conceptual advancement, the relics of which can be found throughout the entrepreneurship literature to this day. Van de Ven named his *Journal of Business Venturing* article, *The Development of an Infrastructure for Entrepreneurship*. This manner of discussing entrepreneurship immediately connected the field of entrepreneurship research to the worlds of community and economic development, urban planning, and local government policy at a time when those fields were keenly exploring asset-based community development (see Kretzmann & McKnight, 1993) and the role of infrastructure in everything from sustainable development (see Ostrom, Schroeder, & Wynne, 1993) to agriculture (see Binswanger, Khandker, & Rosenzweig, 1993) to economic development (see Kessides, 1993). The idea that entrepreneurship had an infrastructure was novel. Van de Ven (1993) was referring to little more than facilitating conditions, but framing these conditions as infrastructure—on par with roads, airports, and telecommunications infrastructure—that could be built progressively by a variety of public, nonprofit, and public-sector entrepreneurs. The idea that entrepreneurship benefits from favorable policies was not new (see Baumol, 1968), but the idea that local and regional infrastructure policy could be built was a young one.

It should be noted, too, that Van de Ven (1993) did not see infrastructure building as a government enterprise. These infrastructures, which include policy, social, and institutional components, are accretive over time and largely arise because of the leadership of entrepreneurs themselves. This theme of an entrepreneur-led economy will arise again in the upcoming discussion of ecosystems, and it is challenged by policy-driven views of entrepreneurship development.

KEY COMPONENTS

Van de Ven's (1993) original model has three central components: (1) institutional arrangements to legitimate, regulate, and standardize a new technology; (2) public resource endowments of basic scientific knowledge, financing mechanisms, and a pool of competent labor; and (3) proprietary R&D, manufacturing, marketing, and distribution functions by private entrepreneurial firms to commercialize the innovation for profit (p. 211). While it is evident in Van de Ven's (1993) writing that *the community* as a collective of entrepreneurs from multiple sectors, public leaders, and supportive citizens would give rise to such an infrastructure over time, there is a distinct focus on the conditions facilitating entrepreneurship, and that are likely to continue the cycle. The focus on community, but lesser focus on social ties, provided an opening for Flora and Flora (1993) to discuss entrepreneurial *social* infrastructure specifically. That article will be discussed under the entrepreneurial communities section.

Bhidé

Bhidé's (2000) *The Origin and Evolution of New Business* is a deep and penetrating examination into how and why businesses are launched, why some places launch more businesses than others, and why some firms grow and mature while others remain small in perpetuity, or fail entirely. With a title that conjures Darwin's *Origin of Species,* Bhidé's treatise focuses more on firms and less on the remainder of a Darwinian-style ecosystem, examining in great detail how and why firms evolve over time. Bhidé (2000) recognizes that the environment is critical to supporting entrepreneurship (what he calls *facilitating conditions)*, but his greatest contribution may be a recognition that the factors contributing to an abundance of promising start-ups differs from those conditions favoring firm growth. In other words, different fertilizer is needed for seeds than for young plants.

KEY COMPONENTS

To stimulate an abundance of start-ups, a local or regional environment should meet four facilitating conditions: (1) It should have positive social attitudes toward entrepreneurship, (2) adequate access to technology, (3) pro-entrepreneurial corporate beliefs among larger companies in the environment, and (4) unrestrictive tax and regulatory policies (Bhidé, 2000). In terms of positive social attitudes, people in the environment should be openly supportive of small business venturing, and the media can play a role in touting and promoting new business ventures. Also, high levels of trust are essential for any kind of economic development, especially in the world of entrepreneurship, as this entails risk. Trust ensures that local actors can "get over it" if a business failure occurs, and move on knowing the entrepreneur tried his/her best. Also, high trust and promotion of new businesses can create a feedback effect, where latent (i.e., potential) entrepreneurs see the success of others, and a sense that success is possible and widespread may be sufficient for those individuals to overcome sensations of risk aversion holding them back. Access to technology, especially to broadband Internet, is not only important for reaching customers, suppliers, and information on a global scale but also removes constraints to competition with larger entities and otherwise inaccessible markets. Corporate attitudes, especially if they see the emergence of small firms as advantageous, can be a fundamental source of synergistic relationships in the community. Rather than seeing new entrants as competitors, companies may see them as strategic partners, able to undertake important and highly customized tasks that are a poor fit for a large organization. Finally, beneficial tax policies such as investment tax credits, double-taxation of dividends, and low capital gains rates can incentivize larger corporations to spend more money on R&D and new incentives, indirectly supporting roles for small business to play; and low personal income taxes can bolster the savings necessary to start a business. Smart regulations, including variable compliance costs (lower for smaller businesses) and small business exemptions keep regulation costs manageable for small businesses and remove barriers to entry; while increased compliance on corporations and new policy shifts provide opportunities for small businesses to provide critical services to larger corporations.

Many of the elements that support and stimulate the presence of start-ups are mirrored by those factors contributing to growth, with some slight differences. According to Bhidé (2000), conditions favoring firm growth still include social attitudes, but with an emphasis on cultural celebration of winners and acceptance of a "winner-take-all" attitude to firm growth (i.e., if you're winning, keep going for it!). Corporate beliefs still matter, but embedded corporate pessimism can be excellent for small firm growth, as small firms can often recruit top employees (and seek discarded opportunities) from corporations in a state of contraction. Tax and regulatory policies are always important, but, naturally, tax and regulatory regimes that become less daunting as a company grows are favored over those that are universally stringent. Different from the conditions favoring promising start-ups is a focus on capital and labor markets, with high capital and labor mobility, as well as limited personal liability during bankruptcy, supporting the growth of young businesses.

Spatial Determinants Models

Models for analyzing the differences in firm creation rates, self-employment rates, self-employment earnings, and other entrepreneurial activity were discussed earlier in the chapter. These approaches take as a basic assumption that measurable, quantitative factors impact entrepreneurship rates across geographic space, leading to wide variation in the number and nature of start-ups. Additionally, geographies may be analyzed for spillover effects from their adjacency to areas with important characteristics, like a research institution or major city. Spatial determinants models have been used to identify industry clusters, examine the extent of influence of major cities on entrepreneurship, and determine whether infrastructure plays a role in self-employment rates—and much more. Spatial determinants models are increasingly common and often found intertwined with the field of regional studies. By analyzing the factors affecting entrepreneurship geographically, it is therefore assumed that these factors, if reproduced elsewhere, will have a similar positive effect on the type of entrepreneurial action being measured.

KEY COMPONENTS

There are simply too many spatial determinants studies to summarize here, but the following examples are well known. Acs and Armington (2006) used Census micro data to examine labor market areas across the United States to understand which population-oriented factors affected firm formation and employment growth rates. Looking at the mid-1990s specifically, they found that high sector specialization, the percentage of the population with college degrees, population growth, and income growth had a significant, positive relationship with firm formation rates, while the presence of large establishments and a high population with a high school diploma had a negative effect. Similarly, Henderson et al. (2007) found that factors like share of the population with a college degree, percent foreign born population, presence of information and arts infrastructure, scenic topography, number of bank deposits, and interstate highways and broadband infrastructure affect a region's share of self-employment, and the amount of money self-employed individuals earn, differently. These findings were often interactive with an urban/rural variable, showing that these relationships differ depending on whether or not one is in a city. Other studies, such as Goetz and Rupasingha (2009), looked at lagged rates of self-employment growth, while Ghani, Kerr, and O'Connell (2014), Mason (2015), and Naudé, Gries, Wood, and Meintjies (2008), examine self-employment and new firm formation in a variety of global contexts.

The Global Entrepreneurship Monitor (2015/2016)

The Global Entrepreneurship Monitor (GEM) is a widely known annual report on the state of entrepreneurship across national boundaries, examining the effects of a wide variety of national-level framework conditions on rates of entrepreneurship, and on the prosperity of entrepreneurs. While national policy is an obvious focus, the GEM has historically placed profound emphasis on the role that culture plays in suppressing or enhancing entrepreneurial behavior, including the propensity of national citizens to see entrepreneurship as an honorable lifestyle, cultural tendency to see opportunities, and overall optimism and/or fear about venturing (Kelley, Singer, & Herrington, 2016). The strong focus on the social and cultural features of nations points to the importance of social relations supporting (or inhibiting) entrepreneurship, and the incorporation of a variety of different policies affecting entrepreneurship might suggest that the GEM belongs in the national and regional policy approach described in this chapter. However, the GEM sees both culture and policy as critical framework conditions that, in the end, either support or inhibit entrepreneurship environmentally. The GEM directly mentions the quality of the national entrepreneurship ecosystem, and makes room for the idea that robust entrepreneurial communities can exist at the local level (Kelley et al., 2016). While it may be compelling to call the GEM an ecosystem approach for this reason, the GEM's listing of key components making up an entrepreneurial ecosystem, rather than a focus on nascent and evolutionary complexity that is central to ecosystem thinking, places the GEM under the facilitating conditions approach—albeit one that accounts for a great deal of complexity. Put differently, the GEM sees the ecosystem as essential human and non-human *inputs* to high-quality entrepreneurship, rather than viewing it as a complex and stochastic *process* with multiple uncertain outcomes.

KEY COMPONENTS

The GEM (Kelley et al., 2016) measures national-level entrepreneurship using four categories of indicators: (1) perception of local values related to entrepreneurship, (2) individual self-perceptions about entrepreneurship, (3) entrepreneurial activity indicators, and (4) perceived quality of the entrepreneurship ecosystem. Local values relate to the national culture, and involve beliefs about whether or not entrepreneurship is a good career choice, whether or not successful entrepreneurs enjoy high status in their society, and whether or not the media promotes and gives attention to entrepreneurs. Self-perceptions about entrepreneurship are largely psychological and individualistic, but may be embedded in cultural values as well. These include one's perception of opportunities, perception of one's own entrepreneurial capabilities, personal entrepreneurial intentions, and fear of failure. Entrepreneurial activity is a *post hoc* measure of actual entrepreneurship activity and includes total early stage entrepreneurial activity, the ratio of self-reported opportunistic versus necessity-driven entrepreneurial activity (i.e., starting a business because one wants to, not because one has no other option for economic survival), the established business ownership rate, the business discontinuation rate, and entrepreneurial employee activity (i.e., job creation). Finally, perceived quality of the entrepreneurship ecosystem includes environmental, policy, and cultural factors affecting entrepreneurship. These include the presence of entrepreneurial finance, supportive and relevant government policies, low taxes and reasonable bureaucracy, the presence of government entrepreneurship programs, entrepreneurship education at a variety of school ages, R&D transfer institutions, commercial and legal infrastructure, internal market dynamics, burdens, and entry regulation, physical infrastructure, and cultural and social norms bounding entrepreneurial activity (Kelley et al., 2016).

These elements exist in a number of feedback loops. National (government and culture) and entrepreneurial (relating directly to entrepreneurs) framework conditions can influence both individual capabilities and attitudes related to venturing, as well as social attitudes. This, in turn, can have an effect on the start-up process at various stages of the venture. As with Bhidé (2000), the GEM recognizes that some nations may support very small businesses but discourage firm growth, or support small business but with little regard for those businesses that create a large impact in terms of jobs and revenues. Regardless, these factors create entrepreneurial outputs, which in turn have macro-economic outcomes in the aggregate (i.e., job creation, GDP growth), which then creates a feedback loop with national framework conditions (Kelley et al., 2016). On a macro scale, the GEM recognizes the need for feedback loops to exist suggested by Bhidé (2000), the importance of a healthy industrial and cultural environment suggested by Shane (2003), and the momentum of entrepreneurial infrastructure development suggested originally by Van de Ven (1993).

Shane

In 2003, Scott Shane wrote *A General Theory of Entrepreneurship: The Individual-Opportunity Nexus*. The book was landmark in the field of entrepreneurship, as it (a) built on previous work by Shane and Venkataraman (2000) clarifying entrepreneurship as a field of research, and (b) centralizing the relationship between entrepreneurs and sources of opportunity as fundamental to entrepreneurial action. While other scholars like Kirzner (1973) understood this, Shane's opportunity brought new life to the relationship between entrepreneurs, who have agency, and opportunities, that have no agency and the presence of which is governed by a variety of contextual factors. Upon being criticized for placing too much emphasis on the agency of entrepreneurs in discovering and exploiting opportunity and not enough to the contextual environment, Shane (2012) retorted by stating that this was not the case: emphasis was only given to entrepreneurs to focus conceptually on their agency, but was in no way intended to give the impression that such agency is context-free. Personal factors like psychology and propensity interact with environmental factors like industrial and cultural conditions to structure the relationship between entrepreneurs and sources of opportunity.

KEY COMPONENTS

Shane (2003) is mentioned here not only because of the impact his work has had on the field of entrepreneurship research but also to note that Shane's contextual factors primarily focus on conditions rather than on examining the social processes within them. Shane accounts for two categories of facilitating conditions that facilitate the ability and propensity of potential entrepreneurs to exploit an opportunity: Industry effects and environmental factors. Under industry effects, he lists (a) knowledge conditions (R&D intensity, locus of innovation, size of the innovating entities, and uncertainty of the industry), (b) demand conditions (market size, growth, and segmentation), (c) industry life cycles (industry age, dominant design, and presence of a density of firms), (d) appropriability conditions (strength of patents and importance of contemporary assets), and (e) industry structure (profitability of the industry, cost of inputs, capital intensity, advertising intensity, industry concentration, and average firm size) (Shane, 2003, pp. 118–144). More mature industries that are capital and marketing intensive tend to suppress new firm formation, while newer industries with a density of firms, lack of a dominant industry design, and whose firms compete in more segmented market spaces all lead to greater firm formation, for example. Environmental factors affecting the entrepreneur-opportunity nexus include (a) the economic environment (income, capital gains, and property taxes; economic growth and societal wealth; low rates of inflation and stable economic conditions), (b) the political environment (freedom, strong rule of law and property rights, decentralization of power), and (c) the sociocultural environment (social desirability of entrepreneurship, presence of entrepreneurial role models, specific cultural beliefs) (Shane, 2003, pp. 145–160). Free, open societies with low regulatory barriers and taxes in which entrepreneurship is viewed as a respectable means of economic action will spawn more entrepreneurs, for example. While Shane (2003) points to the presence of social and community processes in this last part of his framework, he accounts for their presence or absence rather than a deeper understanding of how social and cultural factors influence processes over time.

What is missing from these models?

Facilitating conditions models have progressed over time to incorporate not only services and "infrastructures" (typically institutional and financial ones) to support entrepreneurs but also social and community support structures as well. However, one large difference remains between these types of approaches and the "entrepreneurial communities" approaches we will discuss shortly: culture, community support, and effective leadership are viewed as either being *present* or *absent* to some degree, and part of a broader set of measurable *place characteristics* necessary for entrepreneurs to emerge. This consideration contrasts with the entrepreneurial community or ecosystem idea that culture, leadership, and community social relations—among entrepreneurs and between entrepreneurs and other important actors—are the *focus* of development efforts.

Facilitating conditions approaches are not blind to this idea. Going back to Van de Ven (1993) through the GEM (Kelley et al., 2016), studies using this framework recognize the generative nature of support structure as being accretive over time, and this is largely the result of positive feedback loops that are driven by successful entrepreneurs and supportive local actors. Acknowledging *social processes* as a mechanism of change, *facilitating conditions* approaches are most concerned with analyzing and measuring environmental attributes and identifying strengths, weaknesses, and gaps without necessarily getting into the messy details of the social relations producing such conditions. The facilitating conditions approach should therefore not be seen as somehow "subordinate" or "archetypical" to other approaches; in fact, a good facilitating conditions approach can be an excellent way to determine the specific entrepreneurial advantages of place and identify spots where there is more work to be done. The question that facilitating conditions approaches leave mostly unanswered is, "How does one fill the gaps?" This reflection provides a transition into our next set of approaches: the national and regional policy approach, where governments and institutions have primacy over creating a favorable climate for business, and the entrepreneurial communities and ecosystem approaches, where entrepreneurs have primacy in creating a better working environment for their own community.

National and Regional Policy Approach

This approach recognizes a strong role for governments and major quasi-governmental and nonprofit institutions to play in supporting entrepreneurship and facilitating the development of entrepreneurial communities. While some thinkers discourage the government from playing any sort of leading role in the creation of an entrepreneurial ecosystem (see Feld, 2012; Isenberg, 2010), others see the government as playing a central and pivotal role in supporting entrepreneurial communities through effective policies and regulation (see Mason & Brown, 2014). Others take a more moderate approach, stating that government may not always be central in creating entrepreneurial communities, but they clearly have a nontrivial role to play that can benefit entrepreneurship development efforts (Lyons, 2002).

Regardless of the level of involvement, a national and regional policy approach takes as a basic assumption that entrepreneurship is critically important to economic growth. This position is often taken in the wake of failed industrial recruitment strategies with lackluster outcomes (Mason & Brown, 2014), and the realization that all net job creation in the United States between 1980 and 2005 was from firms less than five years old (Kauffman Foundation, 2009). Similarly, in the United Kingdom, 54 percent of all net jobs created between 2002 and 2008 came from only 6 percent of companies, most of which employed under 50 people (but were over 5 years old) (Anyadike-Danes, Bonner, Hart, & Mason, 2009). Since governments care about job growth as the central cornerstone to an empowered economy (Coad, Daunfeldt, Johansson, & Wennberg, 2014), creating a regulatory environment that supports entrepreneurship has become a priority for many governments across the world. There is often a focus on developing clusters of entrepreneurial action, which are partially related to both entrepreneurial communities and ecosystems. In addition, there is plenty of debate about what the appropriate role of government should be. Should governments actively incentives small business, or simply remove rigid barriers to firm entry? Should leadership come from enlightened government agencies, or from entrepreneurs themselves? Is a hands-on approach to policy appropriate, or will it backfire? These and other questions remain to be seen, but there are two things most entrepreneurial community thinkers can agree upon: rigid, oppressive, and excessive government policies tailored to larger industries have a chilling effect on entrepreneurship, and blindly investing in all start-ups with little regard to their quality and likelihood of success is a disastrous strategy.

It should be noted here that the link between government policy and entrepreneurship is an old one (Baumol, 1968; Kirzner, 1973). The aim of this section is not to review the classics in this space, but rather to review those documents focusing on how government policy can stimulate the creation of *entrepreneurial communities* and *ecosystems* specifically. This consideration goes well beyond a flat focus on policy supporting new business starts, young company growth, and job growth, and instead focuses on the role government plays in creating and enhancing human interaction and excitement around entrepreneurship. It also focuses heavily on the high-growth outcomes that many governments seek to foster through this strategy.

Key Models in the National and Regional Policy Approach

Several models are important to review in the policy approach: Mason and Brown's (2014), The Small Enterprise Association of Australia and New Zealand (SEAANZ) (2014), and Lyons (2002).

Mason and Brown

Mason and Brown's (2014) approach seeks to remedy a common problem for governments: that creating favorable framework conditions for entrepreneurship is insufficient for the generation of high-growth firms (HGFs). The solution is that governments can engineer a vibrant ecosystem through policy interventions that are more holistic, focusing on "entrepreneurial actors within ecosystems, entrepreneurial resource providers within ecosystems, entrepreneurial connectors within ecosystems, and entrepreneurial orientation within ecosystems" (pp. 1, 20). Fundamental to their approach is the assumption that it is a few, elite, "blockbuster" entrepreneurs that create most of the job growth in most economies. Policies that simply support entrepreneurship more generally are inefficient, as they spend vital public resources on new companies, the majority of which will be unsuccessful or will not grow into major job creating businesses. A tailored policy approach is necessary to target the special needs of blockbuster entrepreneurs who have an outsized impact on the total economy (Mason & Brown, 2014).

What is interesting about Mason and Brown's (2014) model is that it views policy's role not so much as a provider of resources, but as a catalyst of highly interdependent ecosystems that transcend specific actors. Very much aware of the importance of ecosystems, the authors synthesize their own definition of *entrepreneurial ecosystem* as

> a set of interconnected entrepreneurial actors (both potential and existing), entrepreneurial organizations (e.g. firms, venture capitalists, business angels, banks), institutions (universities, public-sector agencies, financial bodies), and entrepreneurial processes (e.g. the business birth rate, numbers of high-growth firms, levels of 'blockbuster entrepreneurship,' number of serial entrepreneurs, degree of sell-out mentality within firms and levels of entrepreneurial ambition) which formally and informally coalesce to connect, mediate and govern the performance within the local entrepreneurial environment.
>
> (Mason & Brown, 2014, p. 5)

This highly robust definition pivots around the idea of the entrepreneurship *process* as a fundamental component of ecosystems, with important roles to be played by multiple entrepreneurial, organizational, and institutional actors. Mason and Brown (2014) separate this interconnected action into six domains of the entrepreneurship ecosystem: policy, finance, culture, supports, human capital, and markets. The authors suggest that high performance in all six are necessary to produce the sustained effects of an entrepreneurship ecosystem that produces many HGFs. Interestingly, while the authors specify a strong role for government to play, they also acknowledge that government makes for a poor incubator, as young businesses need maximum exposure to the marketplace to test the market worthiness of their products and services (Mason & Brown, 2014).

KEY COMPONENTS

The authors recognize that entrepreneurial ecosystems do not, and probably cannot, emerge just anywhere. Governments can take an active role in stimulating HGF development, not by providing resources, but by developing the ecosystems that spawn HGFs in perpetuity. The four-pronged approach of holistic policy intervention of supporting entrepreneurial actors, resource providers, connectors, and the overall cultural orientation, is expected to create a more vibrant entrepreneurial ecosystem over time. Specifically, supporting entrepreneurial actors involves the provision of assistance to entrepreneurs during the pre-start-up, start-up, and early post-start-up phases of business with mentoring and support (Roper & Hart, 2013; in Mason & Brown, 2014), and business incubation providing advice, networking, shared resources, and financial opportunities (Miller & Bound, 2011; in Mason & Brown, 2014). Policy action regarding resource providers involves underwriting the operating costs of angel investments, and creating "dating networks" to match potential funders to like-minded entrepreneurs. Third, policy makers can support, promote, and even fund entrepreneurial connector organizations that sponsor meet-ups, start-up weekends, competitions, and co-learning events. These organizations are powerful not only for existing entrepreneurs but also for attracting potential entrepreneurs to the ecosystem. Finally, governments can improve the entrepreneurial orientation of the culture by providing public access to entrepreneurial education, supporting place-based development strategies in select geographic locations as an entrepreneurial attraction or "hub" strategy, and promoting events that showcase entrepreneurs and the small business scene. All of these approaches can be evaluated using a wide range of indices at both the individual (culture, satisfaction, and performance) and community (market, job creation, innovation, and economic health) levels (Mason & Brown, 2014).

While the Mason and Brown (2014) approach is decisive and deliberate, these authors agree with critics of entrepreneurship policy that a "one size fits all" approach that is too prescriptive and not flexible enough is likely to be disastrous. Additionally, government action without the fundamental inclusion of entrepreneurs is divisive and unlikely to gain necessary support from the entrepreneurship community. They set out seven general principles of government policy in entrepreneurial ecosystems: (1) you cannot create something from nothing, (2) policy approaches need to evolve over time,

(3) no one size fits all, (4) government initiatives are likely to be ineffective in isolation, (5) entrepreneurial ecosystems require a "top-down" and "bottom-up" approach, (6) distinguish between small business (i.e., low growth) and entrepreneurship (i.e., high growth) policy, and (7) policies for high-growth enterprises should reflect the diversity of such firms (Mason & Brown, 2014; compiled by Mazzarol, 2014, p. 10).

SEAANZ

The Small Enterprise Association of Australia and New Zealand (SEAANZ) (2014) wrote a white paper integrating across multiple strands of both the national and regional policy approach, and the entrepreneurial ecosystems approach. Their synthesis was framed within the G20 Challenge for Small Enterprise and Entrepreneurship (G20 SME), that presented 12 ways that G20 governments could better support small- and medium-sized enterprises, and entrepreneurship more broadly (Mazzarol, 2014). The approach is unquestionably policy forward, with national policy makers playing a leading role in catalyzing entrepreneurial ecosystem development. However, by incorporating more ideas from the entrepreneurial ecosystem approach, the white paper takes a much more *laissez-faire* stance toward ecosystem development than Mason and Brown (2014), although that paper is cited often, too. The SEAANZ model attempts to balance the holistic, exclusive, and government-driven approach presented by Mason and Brown (2014), with more open-ended and entrepreneur-driven approaches (like Isenberg, 2010) that allow virtuous cycles of entrepreneurial support and reinforcement to appear naturally (see Venkataraman, 2004 to learn more about virtuous vs. vicious cycles). The result is a moderate, blended, more inclusive approach that begins with a definitive call for government to act as a catalyst to change attitudes about supporting SMEs among decision makers. Furthermore, it positions some government and institutional actors as "institutional entrepreneurs" capable of taking action to change the cultural climate of their organization. After this initial action, the government can let much of the process drive itself organically (Mazzarol, 2014).

KEY COMPONENTS

Integrating across approaches, SEAANZ offers the following key recommendations for government policy: (1) the formulation of effective policy for entrepreneurial ecosystems requires the active involvement of government ministers, working with senior public servants, who act as 'institutional entrepreneurs' to shape and empower policies and programs; (2) policy should be developed that is holistic and encompasses all components of the ecosystem rather than seeking to 'cherry pick' areas of special interest; (3) build from existing industries that have formed naturally within the region or country rather than seeking to generate new industries from green field sites; (4) encourage growth across all industry sectors including low-, mid-, and high-tech firms; (5) adopt a 'top-down' and 'bottom-up' approach, devolving responsibility to local and regional authorities; and (6) recognize that small business policy is 'transactional,' while entrepreneurship policy is 'relational' in nature (Mazzarol, 2014, p. 14).

The approach borrows the holism and top-down/bottom-up approach of Mason and Brown (2014), but is broadly inclusive and encouraging of entrepreneurs from across the spectrum. Rather than trying to pick winners, this policy approach puts more stock in building effective relationships and letting them evolve naturally, and working with the local entrepreneurial climate rather than inducing an entrepreneurship strategy *de novo*. Unique to this approach is the goal of eventually devolving responsibility over the ecosystem to more localized authorities, although the tendency to call them "authorities" creates a power relationship that would likely be rejected by ecosystem thinkers.

Lyons[1]

A scholar and practitioner whose ideas also appear in the section on entrepreneurial ecosystems, Lyons (2002) also sets out a policy agenda for building entrepreneurship development systems (EDS) (Lichtenstein & Lyons, 2001). Of the three models covered here, Lyons (2002) is the least prescriptive. However, it also represents a very early attempt at aiming policy at the development of an entire ecosystem, rather than using policy to stimulate entrepreneurship numbers through standard support and assistance mechanisms. Lyons focuses on the importance of building multiple partnerships across many institutions, conceding that visionary leadership can come from anywhere—government, nonprofits, big business, or entrepreneurs themselves. Rather than focusing on roles and policy mechanisms, policy works best when co-created among actors who share the same vision for the region. Since his focus was primarily on rural areas, where HGFs are comparatively rare, Lyons (2002) purports that entrepreneurship policy must be considerate of all entrepreneurs with all types of growth profiles, as this diversity is critical to creating a robust community environment.

KEY COMPONENTS

While having very few formal "components," Lyons (2002) mentions that policy approaches to date provide ingredients for supporting entrepreneurship, but no recipe or guidelines about the process. However, this approach begins with a multilateral partnership including entrepreneurs, governments, local institutions, and nonprofits. A "champion" is needed to get the initiative going, and this champion can come from any sector of the community. However, what gives this approach continuity is a co-created organization with a charter, aimed directly at supporting the local ecosystem.

The charter not only sets forth a strategic vision of the organization but also provides a means for building membership, resolving disputes, and working across regional boundaries. The organization is expressly dedicated to entrepreneurship development, and should also seek to build linkages to other regions, states, and even nations. In this way, Lyons's (2002) approach can be quite localized, and is even appropriate for very small communities and regions as it inheres in the creation of an organization dedicated to entrepreneurial thinking and action. Once this organization has been created, then a formal entrepreneurship development system (EDS) can be put into place. The EDS model will be reviewed in the section on entrepreneurial ecosystems. Before developing an ecosystem, however, Lyons (2002) believes that an organization upholding the vision of the community should exist prior to ecosystem development, as this ensures that the ecosystem is a reflection of community and regional values more broadly and therefore more likely to sustain in perpetuity.

What is missing from the models?

The national and regional policy approach is decidedly interventionist, following the belief that governments can, and should, take meaningful action to improve the entrepreneurial climate of their nation and/or region. These policies will likely do little to hurt the entrepreneurial environment. However, this approach also raises several important questions. First, the approach diverges widely from other ecosystem thinkers, who see the development of an entrepreneurial ecosystem as a job solely to be led by entrepreneurs themselves (Feld, 2012; Isenberg, 2010). If a push for entrepreneurship is viewed as a "government initiative," will this crowd out the unique flavor of an ecosystem designed from the bottom up *by* entrepreneurs *for* entrepreneurs? Or, as Lyons (2002) has suggested, is there a role for both types of leadership? Second, many of the policy approaches presented in this style focus on stimulating HGFs. If HGFs only represent about 6 percent of enterprises in the United Kingdom, for example (Anyadike-Danes et al., 2009), what about the other 94 percent? Are firms that are not identified as "blockbuster" also unworthy of the kinds of support laid out in this approach? To the extent that national and regional policy efforts attempt to "pick winners," or even support an environment that "produces lots of winners," such an approach says little about what happens to entrepreneurs who fall short of this mark. Such an approach runs the risk of becoming highly elitist and exclusionary, and even less efficient than blanket entrepreneurship approaches that liberate resources for all entrepreneurs, regardless of their prospects. Third, this exclusion could easily migrate to how different geographic places, and their component institutions, are treated under this policy. Mason and Brown (2014) concede that, "since successful entrepreneurial systems are likely to have had some pre-existing economic advantages, this approach will involve governments supporting locations that are already favoured over those that are not" (p. 27). If left unchallenged, could such policies actually become *anti*-developmental in nature by making successful places even more successful, and eschewing those places that struggle to support an entrepreneurial ecosystem?

This discussion is not to discourage the potential positive effects of the national and regional policy approach. Indeed, the GEM notes that some nations have policies that are more favorable to entrepreneurship than others (Kelley et al., 2016), and governments can lead the charge in removing barriers to entrepreneurship, providing supports, and also—as Lyons (2002) suggests—being an active partner in the creation of an entrepreneurial ecosystem. Governments can also choose to be exclusive or inclusive in terms of their approach toward entrepreneurial ecosystem; the latter is more effective, and less likely to turn away would-be entrepreneurs. While there is some debate over the matter, it may be that the real question is not whether government leadership should be top down or bottom up, but rather finding the appropriate ways, and timings, for government to engage to maximize the benefit for all parties. This view is likely to look different across entrepreneurial ecosystems because of their unique characteristics and circumstances.

Entrepreneurial Communities Approach

The entrepreneurial community approach stems from the idea that entrepreneurs never act alone. All entrepreneurial action is inherently embedded in dense social networks (Clevenger, Houlihan, & Fortunato, 2017). While many of these connections are "vertical," leading out of the community, many more are "horizontal," or found within and across the community. Even though it is ultimately up to the entrepreneur to launch and sustain a business, the entrepreneurial communities approach accepts the premise that social networks not only make entrepreneurship possible but also limit what is possible through local attitudes, customs, rules, and norms (Julien, 2007). Identities matter as well, as the local culture can deeply affect whether or not local residents grow up to see entrepreneurship as a respectable and viable lifestyle option in the first place (Julien, 2007; Kelley et al., 2016), or whether potential entrepreneurs have the perceived self-efficacy to launch a venture (Kourilsky & Walstad, 1998). National, regional, and local culture carry considerable weight in this approach, as local culture can in turn affect the structure of local networks, which can in turn affect who has access to resources and information locally (Hayton, George, & Zahra, 2002; Kelley et al., 2016). This dimension, in turn, can have a supportive or constraining effect, depending on how far-reaching (or siloed) these networks are across the community, and the nature of the relationships that fill those networks.

Environmental factors, local leadership, and government policy all play an important role in the entrepreneurial communities approach—most thinkers supporting this approach are fully aware of the dangers of presenting an "oversocialized" view of entrepreneurial action (see Granovetter, 1985, for a discussion of under- and oversocialized views of the economy). However, when it comes to supporting entrepreneurship, proponents of this approach see wider, broader, better community relations as antecedent to other forms of entrepreneurship development. The first step would involve building the social infrastructure of the place (Flora & Flora, 1993) by creating networks, building local alliances, creating "third places," formalizing support pathways, and finding some kind of common vision that entrepreneurs and local leaders alike can contribute to. An ideal entrepreneurial community would feature lots of interaction among entrepreneurs, and plenty of involvement by supporting organizations. What appears to differentiate this approach most sharply from an ecosystem approach is that entrepreneurial communities seek to create a well-connected, supportive community with a great culture in perpetuity—an ideal state. Ecosystem approaches give more weight to environmental factors affecting entrepreneurial start-ups, and seem to have a greater acceptance of the "unpleasant" side of entrepreneurship, including a "winner-take-all" mentality and creative destruction through routine business failure. While entrepreneurial communities appear to connect actors as they currently appear, ecosystems account more for the evolution of actors over time, including their skill levels and the role they play in the ecosystem. In short, entrepreneurial communities appear to be slightly more static, but both entrepreneurial communities and the ecosystem approach rely heavily on the ascendance and ubiquity of social relations as a driving force behind entrepreneurship development.

Key Models in the Entrepreneurial Communities Approach

There are several views on the entrepreneurial communities approach, which has been a growing area of interest: Van de Ven's (1993) article on entrepreneurial infrastructure, Flora and Flora (1993) wrote about entrepreneurial social infrastructure, (or ESI); E^2 by Macke, Markley, and Fulwider (2014); and the University of Nebraska-Lincoln Extension Entrepreneurial Communities Activation Process (ECAP).

Entrepreneurial Social Infrastructure (ESI)

Seemingly, in response to Van de Ven's (1993) article on entrepreneurial infrastructure, Flora and Flora (1993) wrote about entrepreneurial social infrastructure, or ESI, publishing at about the same time as Van de Ven. The focus of Flora and Flora's (1993) work is to address a major shortcoming overlooked by scholars in the facilitating conditions approach: that physical infrastructures are insufficient to support entrepreneurship development, especially in times of scarce resources. As rural community developers, Flora and Flora (1993) recognized that effective community networks were essential to cultivating strategies for community development and entrepreneurship, as rural areas were likely to be "left behind" in terms of resource allocation during the economic recession at the time. Better networks could in turn translate into better resource mobilization—but more importantly, it could also create the social conditions through which local organizations and citizens alike could identify and act upon opportunities. Interestingly, this model does not address entrepreneurship directly, but rather aims to build a more entrepreneurial mind-set among members of the community to solve critical resource issues (Flora & Flora, 1993). It symbolizes a guide for getting beyond "small-town politics" and opening the culture to diverse perspectives. It does not take much imagination to understand how this fundamental base could translate into an increase in entrepreneurial action among citizens. While among the first articles to propose entrepreneurial thinking as a community-spanning activity, the model does little to translate these ideas into actual firm creation.

KEY COMPONENTS

Flora and Flora (1993) build upon Swanson's (1992) definition of social infrastructure, which has three components: social institutions (like governments, and social and professional organizations), human resources (community inhabitants and their special skills and capabilities), and characteristics of social networks (including the innovativeness, connectedness, and resourcefulness of the local culture, although the opposite could be true). These elements describe *what* constitutes social infrastructure, but it does not describe *how* this infrastructure might operate.

Fundamentally, Flora and Flora (1993) set out three components of effective ESI, each based in a broader context of successful community relations. First is symbolic diversity, which is an inclusive acceptance of people and ideas that differ across the community. The density of relationships (communities that are too tight-knit can become exclusive) and role homogeneity (communities where the same people play most of the leadership roles) can be major barriers to symbolic diversity. An acceptance of controversy, paired with the depersonalization of political matters, is also essential. Finally, symbolic diversity is enhanced when there is a focus on local processes (not people), and when community identity is defined broadly and with permeable boundaries, and not tightly focused on one group that is "in control." The second dimension of ESI is resource mobilization, which can be defined in terms of relative equality in the distribution of resources, a willingness to invest collectively, and a willingness to invest private capital locally. Resource mobilization has the effect of freeing capital, and directing it more broadly toward community-led projects that do not normally receive sufficient funding. The third dimension of ESI is the quality of networks, including the density of networks (how many people participate), the presence of horizontal networks (networks spanning boundaries within the community), and the presence of vertical networks (networks connecting the community to other communities, and state, federal, and regional agencies, companies, and organizations).

E2

In their book *Energizing Entrepreneurial Communities* (or E^2), Macke, Markley, and Fulwider (2014) present a detailed method for boosting entrepreneurship, grounded strongly in community development-oriented techniques for local capacity building. Aimed primarily at community leaders, the book takes cues from ESI that strong communities can cultivate a social environment for strong entrepreneurs. However, E^2 is more deliberate about supporting entrepreneurship and not just resource mobilization. As a result, entrepreneurship development is a community-driven activity involving many actors, even though the book is tailored for non-entrepreneurs, with sections describing how to understand entrepreneurs, and occasional use of the term "your entrepreneurs," as in "understanding your entrepreneurs." The book does not draw from the literature very much, but represents reflexive practice from the long careers of the books' authors. It is also highly comprehensive, covering many aspects of entrepreneurial community development. While egalitarian in terms of its engagement strategies, E^2 is deliberate about focusing on growth-oriented entrepreneurs and growth-oriented entrepreneurial coaching to maximize impact (Macke et al., 2014).

KEY COMPONENTS

The E^2 approach is embodied in ten "keys," or steps to catalyzing entrepreneurial community development. These keys are (1) embrace local responsibility, (2) design a smart game plan, (3) commit to robust investment, (4) build an entrepreneurial development system (see the following section on ecosystems), (5) sustain your effort and renew leadership, (6) focus on growth entrepreneurs, (7) develop the attributes of an entrepreneurial community, (8) incorporate immigrants and new residents, (9) practice genuine regional collaboration, and (10) cultivate civic and social entrepreneurs (Macke et al., 2014, p. 25).

The seven keys can be divided into five sub-points: entrepreneurial talent, entrepreneurial culture, entrepreneurial infrastructure, human development focus, and youth engagement. Throughout the E^2 process, there is a focus on simultaneously welcoming people into the community, improving skill levels through coaching, and building capacity as a collective.

University of Nebraska-Lincoln Extension Entrepreneurial Communities Activation Process (ECAP)

Practitioners and governments from around the world are becoming interested in implementing entrepreneurial community models in a variety of settings. This attention has led to the creation of a variety of entrepreneurial development programs, some led by universities (i.e., Cooperative Extension, as in Nebraska and Michigan), and some by the private sector (including the Certified Entrepreneurial Community program, information available at www.creativecec.com). The University of Nebraska-Lincoln was among the first extension programs to publicize its framework for entrepreneurial community development. While the model reads like a typical "facilitating conditions" framework, it overwhelmingly focuses on the social infrastructure of place much like ESI does, emphasizing the connections between elements in the model.

KEY COMPONENTS

ECAP uses engaged community development techniques to bring people together across boundaries, much as ESI suggests. Unlike ESI, the ECAP model focuses on a few different areas. The interrelated elements of ECAP are leadership, sense of place, infrastructure, digitally connected, education/ workforce IQ, entrepreneurial support systems, community vision, and culture of change. It is recognized that each of these is not a "facilitating condition," but rather a set of processes that must be cultivated. Since processes change over time, ECAP begins to approximate an ecosystem approach, although the program appears to be directed at community leaders who wish to develop a good environment *for* entrepreneurship, rather than at entrepreneurs themselves who may take their own, divergent, stochastic route forward. It should be noted in this model that there is more emphasis on basic community-building processes like local leadership, sense of place, and visioning than there is on entrepreneurship and workforce education. This prioritization is commonplace in entrepreneurial community models that see a strong entrepreneurial sector as a natural outcropping of a strong community.

What is missing from the models?

The entrepreneurial communities approach is a grassroots, bottom-up, highly egalitarian and inclusive set of models intended to maximize participation in entrepreneurial thinking within and across the community. These approaches place community matters first and make the tacit assumption (suggested in the ESI model) that those attributes making a community stronger would also make entrepreneurs within that community stronger. Unlike the facilitating conditions approach, this often means that addressing issues of social inclusion, cultural change, strategic visioning, and conflict resolution are antecedent to (and eventually concurrent with) the provision of an environment that is suitable for entrepreneurship. Building an exemplary human-centered support system beyond traditional financial and business support is fundamental to these models. In addition, unlike policy-driven approaches, the entrepreneurial communities approach envisions a high degree of participation from entrepreneurs and policy makers alike, who are equal partners in entrepreneurship development.

However, there are some shortcomings to this model. Even though the entrepreneurial communities model is dynamic and process-driven (rather than output-driven), it still assumes that the entrepreneurial community, when built, will continue in perpetuity. As such, it lacks the sometimes harsh realities of ecosystem thinking, including a consistent turnover of firms, unexpected structural changes to the local economy, and preferential treatment given to higher growth firms over lower growth firms (except in the E^2 model). The egalitarian nature of entrepreneurial communities models may therefore downplay the fact that some entrepreneurs have an outsized impact on the community over others, and the models may inadvertently value inclusiveness and high participation over market robustness. While models like ESI address openness to controversy, is it possible for a culture to be "too" harmonious to accept truly contrarian thinking? Second, many of these approaches are directed as much at local leaders as they are at entrepreneurs—perhaps even more so, but not to the extent of the national and regional policy approach. Entrepreneurial communities models are well suited for local and some regional governments that would like to simultaneously bolster their economy *and* address social fracturing in their communities. This framing diverges from the ecosystem approach as well, which sees entrepreneurs as the only group truly capable of leading an entrepreneurial revolution. Finally, entrepreneurs are of course fundamental to the entrepreneurial communities model, but often find themselves occupying only one small portion of these models, in which other community and government organizations can play an outsized role. This runs the risk of taking an "oversocialized" view of entrepreneurship (see Granovetter, 1985), and overlooking the importance of individualistic action, risk taking, and personal agency. While a strong community can provide an ideal setting for entrepreneurs, it is still individuals who must launch the business and—even more importantly—bear the majority of the risk if something goes wrong.

The Entrepreneurial Ecosystem Approach

The entrepreneurial ecosystem approach captures much of the discussion of ecosystems found earlier in this chapter, recognizing entrepreneurs as deeply embedded in and inseparable from their environment, and from the human community surrounding them. This approach is distant from approaches that merely view entrepreneurs as part of "an economy," or even just part of "a community," as ecosystems not only account for the local economy but also the social, cultural, natural, and policy environments that helped to shape the local economy in the first place. In an ecosystem approach, *everything* is profoundly interdependent, and a change in one feature of the entrepreneurial ecosystem may have important effects (positive, negative, or neutral) elsewhere in the ecosystem. As change occurs across the ecosystem, so do the nature and types of firms that emerge, which impacts the types of support systems available, and local policy and the legal framework, and other organizations in the ecosystem, and so on. As the last sentence demonstrates, a litmus test of an ecosystem approach is that it can be difficult to talk about one part of an ecosystem without acknowledging the myriad other parts of the ecosystem supporting and affecting it.

This complexity may seem to make the ecosystem approach rather daunting and impractical, but it does not have to be. Just as it is possible to set a tea kettle to boil and then turn one's attention to chopping tomatoes for the evening's caprese salad, it is necessary to recognize that, when speaking about any component part of an ecosystem, all other parts are still hard at work in the background. Practically, this means we can list the component "parts" of an ecosystem, but we must simultaneously recognize that all of these parts are constantly interacting with one another via social networks. So one can speak about an ecosystem's great incubator spaces: their "start-up weekend" events, loads of entrepreneurial mentors, local craft beer scene that serves as a gathering place, and enlightened venture capitalists hanging around town—not to mention a few hundred entrepreneurs. As the following models demonstrate, much more focus is given to meta-level processes of entrepreneurial action than prescriptive conditions and environments. What we must realize is that, in an ecosystem, roles, relationships, and spaces overlap constantly and seamlessly, evolve quickly, and are always directed toward one meta-level goal: Launching great ventures that make a difference.

Key Models in the Entrepreneurial Ecosystem Approach

The most recent decade has shown a stronger understanding of the complexities in entrepreneurship through the ecosystem lens: Feld's (2012) *The Boulder Thesis;* Isenberg's (2010), and Lichtenstein and Lyons's (2001) promotion of EDS.

Isenberg

Isenberg's (2010) article in the *Harvard Business Review, How to Start an Entrepreneurial Revolution*, was a major step forward in understanding how some places effectively developed a culture and habits of spawning new, promising entrepreneurs. Isenberg's work was a major departure from other approaches, such as the national and regional policy approach, and the facilitating conditions approach. He criticized governments who seek to recreate unattainable ecosystems (especially famous ones, like the Silicon Valley) in places where they cannot possibly occur, and mentions that some of the healthiest ecosystems are currently appearing in the remote corners of the world, away from the attention of decision makers, where funding, democracy, and legal protections are scarce. While previous approaches had focused on ways that local leaders could prescriptively build a more entrepreneurial culture, Isenberg espoused only meta-level steps that embrace a relative *lack* of total control by local leaders, and instead empower *entrepreneurs* to lead their own revolution. This does not amount to inaction by local leaders—quite the opposite—but his model implies that any attempt to nail down the secret recipe of entrepreneurial ecosystem development flies in the face of what makes an ecosystem an ecosystem: constant evolution and change. Eschewing an overly prescriptive approach, Isenberg (2010) states,

> [Leaders] must follow an incomplete and ever-changing set of prescriptions and relentlessly review and refine them. The alternatives—taking decades to devise a model set of guidelines, acting randomly, or doing nothing—all are unacceptable . . . To make progress, leaders need practical if imperfect maps and navigational guidelines.
>
> (p. 3)

Put plainly, Isenberg lays bare a critique of any approach taking the form "that created jobs for [community X], so we want it too," and instead charts a path to ecosystem development that is far more *laissez-faire* than its predecessors.

KEY COMPONENTS

Isenberg (2010) presents nine "prescriptions" for creating an entrepreneurship ecosystem. "Prescriptions" is presented in quotations, because, by his own admission, these are really rough guidelines and suggestions more than prescriptions, and should be subject to ongoing reflexive analysis and critique: (1) Stop emulating Silicon Valley. Ecosystems arise from unique assets, leaders, and ideas. Even the Silicon Valley could not become itself today, as those conditions that gave rise to it have changed. (2) Shape the ecosystem around local conditions. Do not try to create someone else's economy, but rather work with what "works" in your area. (3) Engage the private sector. An entrepreneurial ecosystem is, in the end, a private-sector endeavor, not a government project. Effective development begins with a candid conversation with private-sector actors and entrepreneurs right from the beginning, and self-liquidation built right into the design of early projects. (4) Favor the high potentials. Do not be exclusive, but do take time to nurture those entrepreneurs that can give the ecosystem continuity—and they are not necessarily in the tech sector. (5) Get a big win on the board. Early, visible success stories help to build the critical mass needed to attract others to the ecosystem. (6) Tackle cultural change head-on. One of the things government truly can do to be helpful is to promote a public understanding of entrepreneurship, and to lift up success stories of all types as role models. (7) Stress the roots. Do not over-incubate businesses or flood the market with incentives. Real-world, hard-market exposure is necessary to test the long-term viability of new businesses. (8) Don't overengineer clusters: help them grow organically. Do not incentivize certain industries just because some other community has been successful in doing so—build upon what works locally. (9) Reform legal, bureaucratic, and regulatory frameworks.

Simply put, if you are a government, do less. Remove legislation that creates barriers for entrepreneurs, and focus instead on building cultural awareness, and educational and support programs (Isenberg, 2010, pp. 3–10).

What constitutes an effective ecosystem, according to Isenberg (2010)? According to him, the presence and effectiveness of an ecosystem can be assessed using the following questions. (1) Do public leaders act as strong public advocates of entrepreneurs and entrepreneurship? Open their doors to entrepreneurs and those promoting entrepreneurship? (2) Do governments create effective institutions directly associated with entrepreneurship (research institutes, overseas liaisons, forums for public-private dialogue)? Remove structural barriers to entrepreneurship, such as onerous bankruptcy legislation and poor contract enforcement? (3) Does the culture at large tolerate honest mistakes, honorable failure, risk taking, and contrarian thinking? Respect entrepreneurship as a worthy occupation? (4) Are there visible success stories that inspire youth and would-be entrepreneurs? Show ordinary people that they too can become entrepreneurs? (5) Are there enough knowledgeable people who have experience in creating organizations, hiring, and building structures, systems, and controls? Have experience as professional board members and advisers? (6) Are there capital sources that provide equity capital for companies at a pre-sales stage? Add non-monetary value, such as mentorship and contacts? (7) Are there nonprofits and industry associations that help investors and entrepreneurs network and learn from one another? Promote and ally themselves with entrepreneurship (such as software and biotechnology associations)? (8) Are there educational institutions that teach financial literacy and entrepreneurship to high school and college students? Allow faculty to take sabbaticals to join start-ups? (9) Does the public infrastructure provide sufficient transportation (roads, airports, railways, container shipping) and communication (digital, broadband, mobile)? (10) Are there geographic locations that have concentrations of high-potential and high-growth ventures? Proximity to universities, standards agencies, think tanks, vocational training, suppliers, consulting firms, and professional associations? (11) Are there formal or informal groups that link entrepreneurs in the country or region and diaspora networks—in particular, high-achieving expatriates—and new ventures and local offices of multinationals? (12) Are there venture-oriented professionals, such as lawyers, accountants, and market and technical consultants, who will work on a contingency basis or for stock? (13) Are there local potential customers who are willing to give advice, particularly on new products and services? Willing to be flexible with payment terms to accommodate the cash flow needs of young, rapidly growing suppliers? (Isenberg, 2010, p. 5).

Notice that Isenberg (2010) does not merely ask about the *presence* of these elements, but about their *orientation*, as many communities (especially urban communities) contain these elements but lack the orientation toward entrepreneurial support. A major advantage of Isenberg's (2010) work is that it moves beyond measuring facilitating conditions, assuming the "ingredients" are all that matters, toward measuring their orientation toward entrepreneurship, and the processes that interconnect these elements. At the center is a true support system for entrepreneurs that does not take the form of a program or certification, but rather a genuine cultural orientation toward understanding the fundamentals and challenges of entrepreneurial action.

The Boulder Thesis

Feld's (2012) book, *Startup Communities* moved the entrepreneurial ecosystems approach into uncharted territory. While scholars and practitioners had constructed models of entrepreneurial action from their own diverse experiences, or a widely scattered literature, or both, Feld (2012) used a single case study in Boulder, Colorado, to describe, in detail, how entrepreneurial ecosystems arise in the first place. The case study only examines one city under one set of circumstances at one point in time, so the external generalizability is relatively low. However, where prior approaches presented pieces, components, and elements of what comprises an effective ecosystem, Feld's (2012) case study reflexively examined the generative processes of ecosystem development from multiple perspectives within the ecosystem. Since Feld lived and worked in Boulder during the years of rapid ecosystem expansion and occupied a central position in the ecosystem while playing many roles, his observations from inside the system are thorough and multifaceted. When Feld could not describe a phenomenon, he relied on his very dense networks of well-known local entrepreneurs and entrepreneurial supporters to tell their stories. The case study is a tapestry of narratives, but meta-analyzed so that the reader can take away the key features of Boulder's story that led to the creation of a robust ecosystem. Feld (2012) is sage enough to recognize that Boulder's story is idiosyncratic, but also that certain lessons from Boulder's development could be helpful to other places as well, no matter how diverse.

One central theme emerges throughout the book: any ecosystem has *leaders* and *feeders*. *Leaders* are nearly always entrepreneurs, as only entrepreneurs truly and instinctively know what is needed to support entrepreneurial action. All other supporters, including government, larger business, nonprofit organizations, and institutions, are *feeders*. The goal of feeders is to understand entrepreneurs, and provide and foster a supportive environment any way they can. Beyond this, it is the job of feeders *not to lead*, and to get out of the way of entrepreneurs who are trying to create their own ecosystem. This insight is a major departure from other approaches that view governments, organizations, and institutions as equal and ongoing partners in stimulating entrepreneurial action—or in some cases, even seeing them as the primary catalysts of entrepreneurship development. Feld (2012) envisions a more servile and subordinate role for feeders, at least in the realm of entrepreneurship development, stating:

> Historically, many of the feeders thought of themselves as leaders. This has been one of the primary inhibitors of the long-term growth and evolution of many startup communities. These feeders run on different time cycles (e.g., the two- or four-year cycle of government) or have different motivations (i.e., service providers grow by generating increasing revenue from clients) than the entrepreneurs in the startup community. Although this misalignment may seem minor, it has a huge negative impact on the evolution of the startup community when in a leadership role . . . the absence of entrepreneurs as leaders, or the overwhelming leadership by feeders, will doom a startup community.
>
> (pp. 32–33)

As a result, Feld (2012) downplays the roles of most entrepreneurial assistance programs that do not arise from the entrepreneurs themselves, and no matter what the source. Entrepreneurial ecosystems start small, with only a few leaders, and grow stochastically according to the unique strengths, leadership, and talent of the entrepreneurs in the ecosystem. The ecosystem is inclusive, but especially supports entrepreneurs who are deeply involved, as this familiarity among members of the ecosystem mitigates the idea of start-up risk. Additionally, failure is not only tolerated but also celebrated as honorable. Failed businesses can educate the entire community, and their founders often quickly get snapped up by other businesses in the ecosystem, and with them their extensive knowledge. Altruism is also a central theme, not only for feeders who support entrepreneurs (but relinquish their claim to leadership) but also for leaders and feeders who become mentors, giving their knowledge to others with no expectation of return. As knowledge and mentorship ripple throughout the system in an unplanned, deeply holistic fashion involving both leaders and feeders, a culture of mutual help and care emerge overlaid on a spirit of venturing, innovating, and developing cunning business strategies collectively (Feld, 2012).

KEY COMPONENTS

Feld (2012) titles his framework for entrepreneurial ecosystem development "The Boulder Thesis." It is very simple, and focuses on process within the ecosystem, not components that comprise it. Beneath its simplicity are important assumptions about the behaviors, culture, knowledge, and style of both leaders and feeders. The Boulder Thesis contains four elements: (1) entrepreneurs must lead the start-up community, (2) the leaders must have a long-term commitment, (3) the start-up community must be inclusive of anyone who wants to participate in it, and (4) the start-up community must have continual activities that engage the entire entrepreneurial stack (Feld, 2012, p. 25). Beyond these general process suggestions, Feld (2012) offers no definitive recipe for how to launch an ecosystem. This framing is done purposefully, as Feld criticizes overly prescriptive approaches.

However, each step contains ethical rules about how participants should behave to maximize effectiveness. First, leaders should be entrepreneurs, as only entrepreneurs understand, first-hand, what it means to launch a business, bear risk, face financial constraints, build a customer base, and to struggle with uncertainty and instability at the early stages of venture formation. In cases where feeders attempt to lead, they often do not face the same constraints, and design programs in a fashion that suits the ways that larger organizations evaluate themselves. Long-term commitment is critical, as the ecosystem must outlast political cycles. While inclusiveness is important to entrepreneurial community advocates as well, what is important here is an entrepreneur's *desire* to take part in the ecosystem serving as the litmus test for entry. Unlike policy-driven approaches, intention matters more than performance. This consideration brings Feld (2012) to point four, that the entire "entrepreneurial stack" of high- to low-tech businesses, new entrepreneurs and older veterans, and venture ideas spanning all industries, should be engaged simultaneously. The reason: Entrepreneurs tend to learn from one another, and through one another's mentorship. While it is tempting to pick winners, the Boulder experience demonstrates that it is sometimes the most unlikely company in an industry that is not "hot" that eventually becomes extremely successful. If an entrepreneur becomes successful, it is his or her turn to mentor others, or to become an investor, or to switch roles entirely in the ecosystem so that others may have a chance to thrive. This dynamism of roles, engagement of all strategic niches, and recycling of knowledge through a mentorship "pipeline" sets the ecosystem approach apart from the entrepreneurial communities approach that views an active community as being relatively static in its role assignments.

Feeders also play a key role, and Feld (2012) certainly does not mean to diminish them. While playing a more supporting role, effective feeders are often the gatekeepers of local opportunity, and actively seek out entrepreneurs for important contracts. In an ecosystem, it is well recognized that entrepreneurs, government, universities, investors, and large companies all can benefit from one another, with entrepreneurs often taking on useful roles that are beyond the mission of governments and corporations. Rather than taking deliberate leadership, often the best thing that feeders can do is to simply open the door to opportunity for local entrepreneurs, interact regularly, provide spaces for them to meet, and rely on them for tasks they would otherwise outsource. This matters more to an entrepreneur's bottom line than an assistance program, and it occurs within the marketplace rather than being insulated from it (Feld, 2012). Finally, Feld (2012) lays out several attributes of effective leadership in an entrepreneurial ecosystem. Leaders should be inclusive, play a non-zero-sum game (i.e., do not strive to take market share from others in the community, but work together to grow the overall market), be mentorship driven, have porous boundaries (i.e., break down institutional silos that divide people and information), give people assignments (often a good litmus test to gauge their interest in the community), and experiment and fail fast (and honor and respect failure as essential to the process) (Feld, 2012, pp. 47–57).

Entrepreneurial Development Systems (EDS) (2001; 2010)

In their 2001 article entitled *The Entrepreneurial Development System: Transforming Business Talent and Community Economies* in *Economic Development Quarterly*, Lichtenstein and Lyons (2001) turn away from the elements that make up a successful community environment for a moment, and instead focus on the core processes through which a robust, sustaining, and self-perpetuating entrepreneurial "pipeline" emerges. They term this pipeline and its environment the entrepreneurial development system (EDS) These ideas were refined over time, eventually being combined in their 2010 book, *Investing in Entrepreneurs: A Strategic Approach for Strengthening Your Regional and Community Economy*. Rather than view entrepreneurs unidimensionally, Lichtenstein and Lyons (2010) recognize that small businesses are wildly diverse—and so are their founders. Perhaps the most important aspect of that diversity for business success is the experience of the entrepreneur, and also the phase of the business, as latent ideas are likely to take different types of support than businesses that are well along the path to maturity.

Lichtenstein and Lyons (2010) cross over into the ecosystem perspective through the recognition that assistance programs often have disappointing outcomes because they often try to address this diversity of entrepreneurial needs through one set of program activities. However, entrepreneurs—especially more experienced entrepreneurs—understand the needs of new entrepreneurs better than anyone. Rather than create an assistance program requiring constant energy inputs (funding and resources to keep the program going), more experienced entrepreneurs in more mature businesses could be tapped as mentors to support and educate less experienced entrepreneurs, thus closing the knowledge loop. Called a "pipeline," this micro-ecosystem of entrepreneurs eventually grows as entrepreneurs within the pipeline help each other to mature new businesses, and launch more ventures. Entrepreneurs have absolute primacy in this model as leaders, facilitators, and mentors, but Lichtenstein and Lyons (2010) also recognize the importance of strategic leaders and the community environment, and key economic development partners, as well as the regulatory regime to facilitating or constraining the development of an EDS.

KEY COMPONENTS

Lichtenstein and Lyons (2010) really enjoy baseball, so it is fitting that some baseball analogies are used when describing EDS. According to Lichtenstein and Lyons (2010), entrepreneurs can be categorized across two dimensions: Skill level (as an entrepreneur), and life-cycle stage of the entrepreneur's current venture. On the first dimension, EDS categorizes skill levels into five leagues: Rookie, A, AA, AAA, and Major League. Each skill level represents an experiential "rung," also identifiable by different behavior sets. A Major League entrepreneur, for example, will have launched multiple businesses, probably received substantial funding for at least one business at some point, and has taken a few companies to maturity. This classic serialpreneur will behave differently than a Rookie launching a small-scale business for the first time, learning the ropes, and overcoming common beginners' errors in the process. On the second dimension, EDS categorizes the entrepreneur's current venture into one of six life-cycle categories: Pre-Venture, Existence, Early Growth, Expansion, Maturity, and Decline. The goal is for entrepreneurs to advance in their skill level over time, while also advancing the life-cycle stage of their business (ideally stopping short of decline). Community leaders (who can be entrepreneurs themselves) can analyze this pipeline by examining the current entrepreneurs across the community, and determining at which stage they seem to be getting "stuck," which can be remedied with a strategic intervention. So if a community has a glut of AA entrepreneurs who are stuck at the early growth stage, then mentorship, consulting, education, and support can be directed at building the skills and strategies *collectively* to advance to the next business stage and skill level. The energy and "buzz" of the pipeline will, in turn, attract more novice and interested entrepreneurs, thus completing the cycle (Lichtenstein & Lyons, 2010).

Instead of thinking about a pipeline's components, Lichtenstein and Lyons (2010) keep their focus on process the entire time. The pipeline process has five stages. (1) Segment the market. By differentiating between entrepreneurs in terms of their skills, experience, aspirations, and stage of development, entrepreneurs can be organized into a pipeline. (2) Sort the entrepreneurs. This places entrepreneurs into the pipeline according to the two dimensions mentioned earlier. (3) Map the assets. This not only includes human assets within the pipeline but also community assets as well. (4) Evaluate options for managing the pipeline. This process involves the creation of a portfolio and a collective management strategy of how the entire portfolio of entrepreneurs can be promoted and supported over time. (5) Choose an investment strategy. This dynamic involves determining how the broader community will invest in the pipeline. It should be noted that these stages would involve both entrepreneurs within the pipeline and key community partners.

Other Ecosystem Models

Several other scholars have made important contribution to the relatively narrow research literature on entrepreneurship ecosystems. Cohen (2006) produced an early effort to understand the interaction between entrepreneurs and their environment via their formal and informal networks. Drawing heavily from the entrepreneurial systems literature and focusing on several facilitating conditions like access to capital and the talent pool, Cohen (2006) was early to point out that entrepreneur-environment interaction can generatively create a "sustainable valley" through a combination of resources and network connections.

Soon after in the business literature, Bloom and Dees (2008) outlined strategies for cultivating an entrepreneurial ecosystem from the perspective of a social entrepreneurial venture offering affordable home and business loans to low-income individuals. A major step forward from the facilitating conditions approach, Bloom and Dees (2008) illustrated several facilitating conditions in the environment, but then diagrammed how these pieces interacted over time to create ongoing, dynamic relationships. Environmental conditions were political, economic, and social structural features, but the real ecosystem evolved from interactions between resource providers, the firm, competitors, allies, bystanders, beneficiaries, and opponents. It should be noted that these groups represent *both* facilitating and inhibiting components, which is a major advancement over other models that view all elements in the ecosystem as potentially facilitating and helpful. Even resistance from competitors (i.e., traditional financial lenders) "problem makers" (i.e., private companies who are impacted by the social entrepreneur's innovation) are helpful to strengthening the company's position. Bloom and Dees (2008) broke ground by showing the unevenness of ecosystems, the process through which different types of interactions occur generatively, and the diversity of sub-processes, both facilitating and inhibiting, that are required to create a viable ecosystem. Remarkably, the environment surrounding the ecosystem has a far lesser focus than *actors* within the ecosystem, which is a stark departure from the facilitating conditions approach. Similar ideas about the primacy of entrepreneurial agency are appearing in new theories about self-regulation and organization within entrepreneurial ecosystems (Nambisan & Baron, 2013).

What is missing from the models?

Ecosystem models are highly comprehensive and, since they tend to be less prescriptive in terms of what should comprise an ecosystem, they are often times missing *details*. Ecosystem thinkers anticipate that entrepreneurial leaders and feeders will themselves fill in the blanks according to their specific circumstances, their unique local needs, and their imaginations. This dilemma can be challenging for governments and local organizations who are seeking a more specific set of guidelines to follow, or clean metrics for evaluation. Additionally, ecosystem approaches tend to strongly downplay the role of governments, universities, and larger companies and organizations in the creation of the ecosystem. This situation, too, can be frustrating for public servants whose goal it is to boost the local economy. One of the key themes here is a relinquishing of control by larger organizations who may otherwise be used to having greater control over decisions, and more bargaining power over outcomes. However, some ecosystem models, like EDS, do emphasize a stronger, partnering role of other community actors beyond the entrepreneurs themselves.

Conclusion: Culture and Leadership in the Four Types Models

Along with developing entrepreneurial communities, the theme of this book is to leap cultural and leadership boundaries. In a practical sense, each model has slightly different implications for applied inquiry and real-world practice beyond the realm of research. This chapter concludes by reviewing the role of culture and leadership in each model, and examining the barriers inherent in each.

Facilitating Conditions

This approach examines the environments in which entrepreneurs launch new firms, and suggests that a fertile environment is what is most needed for entrepreneurship to flourish naturally. As a result, culture and leadership can be thought of as "environmental factors" under this model. Those places with a pro-venturing culture supporting local entrepreneurs, and entrepreneurially minded leadership promoting entrepreneurs, will be hypothesized to support more firm launches. Conversely, the presence of fractured leadership that primarily supports industrial recruitment, large corporate incentives, or even the status quo in terms of their economic development strategy could establish barriers to entrepreneurs, who may feel ignored or neglected by their leadership. Entrepreneurs may see local leaders as comprising an "elite" complicit with larger and older local firms. Similarly, local citizens may see entrepreneurs as social outcasts, or they may themselves prefer to see more large firms in their community. They may also lack a "buy local" ethic, instead eating at chain restaurants, shopping at chain stores, and going out of town to meet most of their needs. These are facilitating conditions for "disentrepreneurship" (see Honig & Dana, 2008) that create social and cultural disincentives for new ventures. The local mood around such ventures may be pessimistic, and locals may predict the failures of firms publicly before they even launch. Without strong leadership to counter such ideas, such negativity can have adverse effects on the psychology of local entrepreneurs, and suppress the dreams of would-be entrepreneurs.

National and Regional Policy

This approach assumes it is the government's responsibility to create policies that stimulate entrepreneurship, thus boosting growth and economic development. Any national or regional policy that levies high taxes or places restrictive regulatory burdens on young businesses can be a major barrier. Additionally, an "election cycle culture" of pursuing short-term victories can suppress the longer-term goal of building an entrepreneurial economy. For this reason, governments may incentivize larger companies that can create 5,000 jobs quickly over several dozen new businesses that primarily create jobs for the proprietor. If government leaders incentivize large industry through tax benefits, regulatory loopholes, and large-scale contracts—but do not include entrepreneurs, which presents a major barrier to entrepreneurship development.

Entrepreneurial Communities

Entrepreneurial communities arise from the belief that strong communities are antecedent to strong entrepreneurial economies, that entrepreneurship inheres in inclusive social relationships emblematic in the local community, and that techniques to bolster entrepreneurs can be used to bolster the community at large. Any highly fractured community, therefore, will present major challenges to the entrepreneurial communities approach. A community may contain many institutions that do not communicate or deep-rooted conflicts across race, class, or religious lines. When there is local tension, this can lead to local unrest, which can create an unpleasant environment for entrepreneurs. Furthermore, conflict can disrupt entrepreneurial support networks, especially if the entrepreneur is perceived to belong to one "faction" within the community. Entrepreneurs in fractured communities may see each other as vicious competitors, suppressing collaboration and cooperation for fear of giving away important knowledge, or giving a rival an advantage. Leaders can contribute to these problems by failing to address local conflict directly, or by isolating themselves from entrepreneurs. They may also provide incentives to entrepreneurs with little understanding of their needs, and inadvertently enact policies that divide entrepreneurs, such as competitive grants in a very small town.

Entrepreneurial Ecosystems

Entrepreneurs typically lead ecosystems, which evolve holistically as a result of the unique circumstances and talents found in each community. This approach focuses more on process than specific inputs and outputs. One immediate leadership barrier is leaders who insist on running, overplanning, overengineering, or otherwise enforcing an ecosystem for the sake of economic development. Leaders that favor a higher degree of control may, with good intentions, implement programs and processes that are more appropriate for larger institutions, or lack the flexibility needed for early stage ventures to thrive. Culturally, this thinking may present challenges as well, as not all cultures value the openness, inclusiveness, and shared leadership required to sustain an ecosystem. There also may not be enough entrepreneurs locally who are interested in interacting in that manner, if the local culture has always been more structured and incentives have been input/output-oriented.

In closing, these boundaries are all surmountable, and the following chapters will address culture and leadership issues separately. In any community, region, or nation, it is possible to analyze entrepreneurial community development using any of these frameworks to understand what makes entrepreneurship in that place unique. Each can also be used as a method for cultivating a more entrepreneurial community. In Chapter 8, these frameworks for understanding entrepreneurship development will return, and they will be used to analyze case study data presented in Chapter 7. Across the models presented here, researchers and practitioners are challenged to think deeply about the role of the entrepreneur, and of the surrounding community; of static conditions, and of dynamic processes; of inclusivity and camaraderie, and of competition, failure, and rebirth; of the role of local policy, and policies of nations and states. It should become clear that no one perspective provides a complete understanding of entrepreneurial action at the community level, but rather contributes an important facet that may be particularly salient depending on the research question.

Note

1 It should be noted that this paper appears publicly on the Federal Reserve Bank of Kansas City's website as a "preliminary" paper at https://www.kansascityfed.org/publicat/research/regionaleconomy/03prelim/Lyons_paper.pdf. While bearing the words "Not For Quote," the paper has been cited 37 times as of this writing by prominent scholars. It is included here without direct quotes, and with the intention of providing Lyons's highly valuable perspective on policy, but echo the caveat that the paper should not be quoted directly.

References

Acs, Z. J., & Armington, C. (2006). *Entrepreneurship, geography, and American economic growth*. Cambridge, UK: Cambridge University Press.

Adlard, R. D., Miller, T. L., & Smit, N. J. (2015). The butterfly effect: Parasite diversity, environment, and emerging disease in aquatic wildlife. *Trends in Parasitology*, *31*(4), 160–166.

Aldrich, H. E. (1990). Using an ecological perspective to study organizational founding rates. *Entrepreneurship Theory and Practice*, *14*(3), 7–24.

Aldrich, H. E., Zimmer, C., & Jones, T. (1986). Small business still speaks with the same voice: A replication of 'the voice of small business and the politics of survival.' *The Sociological Review*, *34*(2), 335–356.

Amorós, J. E., & Bosma, N. (Eds.). (2014). *Global Entrepreneurship Monitor 2013 Global Report. Global Entrepreneurship Research Association (GERA)*. Retrieved from http://www.babson.edu/Academics/centers/blank-center/global-research/gem/Documents/GEM%202013%20Global%20Report.pdf

Anyadike-Danes, M., Bonner, K., Hart, M., & Mason, C. (2009). *Measuring business growth: High growth firms and their contribution to employment in the UK*. London, UK: Nesta.

Audretsch, D. B., & Lehmann, E. E. (2005). Does the knowledge spillover theory of entrepreneurship hold for regions? *Research Policy*, *34*(8), 1191–1202.

Baumol, W. J. (1968). Entrepreneurship in economic theory. *The American Economic Review*, *58*(2), 64–71.

Bhidé, A. (2000). *The origin and evolution of new businesses*. New York, NY: Oxford University Press.

Binswanger, H. P., Khandker, S. R., & Rosenzweig, M. R. (1993). How infrastructure and financial institutions affect agricultural output and investment in India. *Journal of Development Economics*, *41*(2), 337–366.

Blatt, R. (2009). Tough love: How communal schemas and contracting practices build relational capital in entrepreneurial teams. *Academy of Management Review*, *34*(3), 533–551.

Bloom, P. N., & Dees, G. (2008). Cultivate your ecosystem. *Stanford Social Innovation Review*, *6*(1), 47–53.

Bosma, N., & Levie, J. (2009). *Global entrepreneurship monitor 2008 global report*. Boston, MA: Babson College.

Bruno, A. V., & Tyebjee, T. T. (1982). The environment for entrepreneurship. *Encyclopedia of Entrepreneurship*, *2*(4), 288–315.

Chapin, F. S., III, Matson, P. A., & Vitousek, P. (2011). *Principles of terrestrial ecosystem ecology*. Berlin, Germany: Springer.

Clevenger, M. R. (2017). Perceptions of entrepreneurs and community: From historical roots to a contemporary kaleidoscope. In M. W-P Fortunato & M. R. Clevenger (Eds.), *Toward entrepreneurial community development: Leaping cultural and leadership boundaries* (pp. 10–50). New York, NY: Routledge.

Clevenger, M. R., Houlihan, K., & Fortunato, M. W-P (2017). The value and process of entrepreneur social networking. In M. W-P Fortunato & M. R. Clevenger (Eds.), *Toward entrepreneurial community development: Leaping cultural and leadership boundaries* (pp.). New York, NY: Routledge.

Coad, A., Daunfeldt, S. O., Johansson, D., & Wennberg, K. (2014). Whom do high-growth firms hire? *Industrial and Corporate Change*, *23*(1), 293–327.

Cohen, B. (2006). Sustainable valley entrepreneurial ecosystems. *Business Strategy and the Environment*, *15*(1), 1–14.

Cornwall, J. R. (1998). The entrepreneur as a building block for community. *Journal of Developmental Entrepreneurship*, *3*(2), 141.

Dana, L. P. (1987). Entrepreneurship and venture creation—an international comparison of five commonwealth nations. In N. C. Churchill, J. A. Hornaday, B. A. Kirchhoff, O. J. Krasner, & K. H. Vesper (Eds.), *Frontiers of entrepreneurship research* (pp. 573–583). Wellesley, MA: Babson College.

Darwin, C. (1859). *On the origins of species by means of natural selection*. London, UK: Murray.

Davidsson, P. (2009). *The entrepreneurship research challenge*. Cheltenham, UK: Edward Elgar.

DeBresson, C. (1999, June). An entrepreneur cannot innovate alone: Networks of enterprises are required. *DRUID Summer Conference Proceedings*, 9–12.

Ecosystem. (2016). *In Oxford dictionaries online*. Retrieved from http://www.oxforddictionaries.com/us/definition/american_english/ecosystem

Feld, B. (2012). *Startup communities: Building an entrepreneurial ecosystem in your city*. Hoboken, NJ: Wiley.

Flora, C. B., & J. L. Flora. (1993). Entrepreneurial social infrastructure: A necessary ingredient. *The Annals of the American Academy of Political and Social Science*, *529*, 48–58.

Fortunato, M. W., & McLaughlin, D. K. (2012). Interaction and purpose in highly entrepreneurial communities. *Entrepreneurship Research Journal*, *2*(1), 1–36, Article 6.

Gartner, W. B. (1985). A conceptual framework for describing the phenomenon of new venture creation. *Academy of Management Review*, *10*(4), 696–706.

Gartner, W. B. (1990). What are we talking about when we talk about entrepreneurship? *Journal of Business Venturing*, *5*(1), 15–28.

Ghani, E., Kerr, W. R., & O'Connell, S. (2014). Spatial determinants of entrepreneurship in India. *Regional Studies*, *48*(6), 1071–1089.

Gnyawali, D. R., & Fogel, D. S. (1994). Environments for entrepreneurship development: Key dimensions and research implications. *Entrepreneurship Theory and Practice*, *18*, 43–43.

Goetz, S. J., & Rupasingha, A. (2009). Determinants of growth in non-farm proprietor densities in the US, 1990–2000. *Small Business Economics*, *32*(4), 425–438.

Goetz, S. J., & Rupasingha, A. (2014). The determinants of self-employment growth insights from county-level data, 2000–2009. *Economic Development Quarterly*, *28*(1), 42–60.

Granovetter, M. (1985). Economic action and social structure: The problem of embeddedness. *American Journal of Sociology*, *91*(3), 481–510.

Hayton, J. C., George, G., & Zahra, S. A. (2002). National culture and entrepreneurship: A review of behavioral research. *Entrepreneurship Theory and Practice*, *26*(4), 33.

Henderson, J., Low, S., & Weiler, S. (2007). The drivers of regional entrepreneurship in rural and metro areas. In N. Walzer (Ed.). *Entrepreneurship and local economic development* (pp. 81–102). New York, NY: Lexington Books.

Honig, B., & Dana, L. (2008). Communities of disentrepreneurship: A comparative cross-national examination of entrepreneurial demise. *Journal of Enterprising Communities: People and Places in the Global Economy*, *2*(1), 5–20.

Huggins, R., & Thompson, P. (2012). Entrepreneurship and community culture: A place-based study of their interdependency. *Entrepreneurship Research Journal*, *2*(1), 1–34.

Isenberg, D. J. (2010). How to start an entrepreneurial revolution. *Harvard Business Review*, *88*(6), 40–50.

Johannisson, B., & Nilsson, A. (1989). Community entrepreneurs: Networking for local development. *Entrepreneurship & Regional Development*, *1*(1), 3–19.

Julien, P. A. (2007). Le réseautage riche: une condition de croissance pour les PME. *Vème Congrès International de l'Académie de l'Entrepreneuriat.*

Kauffman Foundation. (2009). *Business dynamics statistics briefing: Jobs created from business startups in the United States.* Kansas City, MO: The Ewring Marion Kauffman Foundation.

Kelley, D. J., Singer, S., & Herrington, M. (2016). *Global entrepreneurship monitor 2016 global report.* London, UK: Global Entrepreneurship Research Association, London Business School.

Kessides, C. (1993). *The contributions of infrastructure to economic development: A review of experience and policy implications* (Vol. 213). Washington, DC: World Bank Publications.

Kirzner, I. (1973). *Competition and entrepreneurship.* Chicago, IL: University of Chicago Press.

Knight, F. H. (1921). *Risk, uncertainty, and profit.* Mineola, NY: Dover Publications.

Kourilsky, M. L., & Walstad, W. B. (1998). Entrepreneurship and female youth: Knowledge, attitudes, gender differences, and educational practices. *Journal of Business Venturing*, *13*(1), 77–88.

Kretzmann, J. P., & McKnight, J. L. (1993). *Building community from the inside out: A path toward finding and mobilizing a community's assets*. Evanston, IL: Northwestern University Press.

Kwon, S. W., Heflin, C., & Ruef, M. (2013). Community social capital and entrepreneurship. *American Sociological Review*, *78*(6), 980–1008.

Lichtenstein, G. A., & Lyons, T. S. (2001). The entrepreneurial development system: Transforming business talent and community economies. *Economic Development Quarterly*, *15*(1), 3–20.

Lichtenstein, G. A., & Lyons, T. S. (2010). *Investing in entrepreneurs: A strategic approach for strengthening your regional and community economy*. Santa Barbara, CA: Praeger.

Low, M. B., & MacMillan, I. C. (1988). Entrepreneurship: Past research and future challenges. *Journal of Management*, *14*(2), 139–161.

Lyons, T. S. (2002). *Policies for creating an entrepreneurial region*. Kansas City, MO: Federal Reserve Bank of Kansas City. Retrieved from http://www.kansascityfed.org/publicat/research/regionaleconomy/03prelim/Lyons_paper.pdf

Lyons, T. S., Alter, T. R., Audretsch, D., & Augustine, D. (2012). Entrepreneurship and community: The next frontier of entrepreneurship inquiry. *Entrepreneurship Research Journal*, *2*(1), Article 1, doi: 10.2202/2157-5665.

Macke, D. W., Markley, D. M., & Fulwider, J. M. (2014). *Energizing entrepreneurial communities: A pathway to prosperity*. Lincoln, NE: Center for Rural Entrepreneurship.

Malecki, E. J. (1993). Entrepreneurship in regional and local development. *International Regional Science Review*, *16*(1–2), 119–153.

Mason, C. M. (2015). Spatial variations in enterprise: The geography of new firm formation. In Burrows, R. (Ed.), *Deciphering the enterprise culture: Entrepreneurship, petty capitalism, and the restructuring of Britain* (pp. 74–106). New York, NY: Routledge.

Mason, C. M., & Brown, R. (2014). *Entrepreneurial ecosystems and growth oriented entrepreneurship*. Paris, France: OECD.

Mazzarol, T. (2014). *Growing and sustaining entrepreneurial ecosystems: What they are and the role of government policy*. White Paper WP01–2014. Small Enterprise Association of Australia and New Zealand (SEAANZ).

McKeever, E., Jack, S., & Anderson, A. (2015). Embedded entrepreneurship in the creative re-construction of place. *Journal of Business Venturing*, *30*(1), 50–65.

Miller, P., & Bound, K. (2011). *The startup factories: The rise of accelerator programmes to support new technology ventures*. London, UK: Nesta. Retrieved from http://businessincubation.com.au/wp-content/uploads/StartupFactories-Accelerators-Evaluation-NESTA-June-2011.pdf

Mitra, D. (2012). The role of crowdfunding in entrepreneurial finance. *Delhi Business Review*, *13*(2), 67.

Nambisan, S., & Baron, R. A. (2013). Entrepreneurship in innovation ecosystems: Entrepreneurs' self-regulatory processes and their implications for new venture success. *Entrepreneurship Theory and Practice*, *37*(5), 1071–1097.

Naudé, W., Gries, T., Wood, E., & Meintjies, A. (2008). Regional determinants of entrepreneurial start-ups in a developing country. *Entrepreneurship and Regional Development*, *20*(2), 111–124.

Neck, H. M., Meyer, G. D., Cohen, B., & Corbett, A. C. (2004). An entrepreneurial system view of new venture creation. *Journal of Small Business Management, 42*(2), 190–208.

Ostrom, E. (2009). A general framework for analyzing sustainability of social-ecological systems. *Science, 325*(5939), 419–422.

Ostrom, E., Schroeder, L., & Wynne, S. (1993). *Institutional incentives and sustainable development: Infrastructure policies in perspective.* Boulder, CO: Westview Press.

Park, R. E. (1939). Symbiosis and socialization: A frame of reference for the study of society. *American Journal of Sociology, 45*(1), 1–25.

Park, R. E., Burgess, E. W., & McKenzie, R. D. (1925). *The city.* Chicago, IL: University of Chicago Press.

Peredo, A. M., & Chrisman, J. J. (2006). Toward a theory of community-based enterprise. *Academy of Management Review, 31*(2), 309–328.

Pyšek, P., & Richardson, D. M. (2010). Invasive species, environmental change and management, and health. *Annual Review of Environment and Resources, 35*, 25–55.

Roper, S., & Hart, M. (2013). *Supporting sustained growth among SMEs—policy models and guidelines.* Coventry, UK: Enterprise Research Centre.

Rupasingha, A., & Goetz, S. J. (2013). Self-employment and local economic performance: Evidence from US counties. *Papers in Regional Science, 92*(1), 141–161.

Schumpeter, J. A. (1934). *The theory of economic development: An inquiry into profits, capital, credit, interest, and the business cycle.* New York, NY: Transaction Publishers.

Shane, S. A. (2003). *A general theory of entrepreneurship: The individual-opportunity nexus.* Cheltenham, UK: Edward Elgar.

Shane, S. A. (2012). Reflections on the 2010 AMR decade award: Delivering on the promise of entrepreneurship as a field of research. *Academy of Management Review, 37*(1), 10–20.

Shane, S. A., & Venkataraman, S. (2000). The promise of entrepreneurship as a field of research. *Academy of Management Review, 25*(1), 217–226.

Sirolli, E. (2012). *How to start a business and ignite your life: A simple guide to combining business wisdom with passion.* Garden City Park, NY: Square One Publishers.

Spilling, O. R. (1996). The entrepreneurial system: On entrepreneurship in the context of a mega-event. *Journal of Business Research, 36*(1), 91–103.

Stuart, T. E., & Sorenson, O. (2007). Strategic networks and entrepreneurial ventures. *Strategic Entrepreneurship Journal, 1*(34), 211–227.

Swanson, L. (1992). Rural social infrastructure. In J. N. Reid (Ed.), *Foundations of rural development policy.* Boulder, CO: Westview Press.

Taleb, N. N. (2012). *Antifragile: Things that gain from disorder.* New York, NY: Random House.

Thornton, P. H. (1999). The sociology of entrepreneurship. *Annual Review of Sociology, 25*, 19–46.

Ulhøi, J. P. (2005). The social dimensions of entrepreneurship. *Technovation, 25*(8), 939–946.

Van de Ven, H. (1993). The development of an infrastructure for entrepreneurship. *Journal of Business Venturing, 8*(3), 211–230.

Venkataraman, S. (2004). Regional transformation through technological entrepreneurship. *Journal of Business Venturing*, *19*(1), 153–167.

Vissa, B., & Chacar, A. S. (2009). Leveraging ties: The contingent value of entrepreneurial teams' external advice networks on Indian software venture performance. *Strategic Management Journal*, *30*(11), 1179–1191.

Wessels, T. (2013). *The myth of progress: Toward a sustainable future*. Lebanon, NH: University Press of New England.

West, G. P. (2007). Collective cognition: When entrepreneurial teams, not individuals, make decisions. *Entrepreneurship Theory and Practice*, *31*(1), 77–102.

Wilkinson, K. P. (1991). *The community in rural America*. Appleton, WI: Social Ecology Press.

Williams, N., & Williams, C. C. (2011). Tackling barriers to entrepreneurship in a deprived urban neighbourhood. *Local Economy*, *26*(1), 30–42.

Zacharakis, A. L., Shepherd, D. A., & Coombs, J. E. (2003). The development of venture-capital-backed internet companies: An ecosystem perspective. *Journal of Business Venturing*, *18*(2), 217–231.

Zolin, R., Kuckertz, A., & Kautonen, T. (2011). Human resource flexibility and strong ties in entrepreneurial teams. *Journal of Business Research*, *64*(10), 1097–1103.

4 Understanding the Impact of Culture in Entrepreneurship

Nicole D. Breazeale and Ronald J. Hustedde

In *Ripples from the Zambezi*, Sirolli (1999) crafts an engaging story about the human drive to pursue personal growth and unleash one's creative talents. His story reveals how even in poor, forgotten places, there are people who dream of building enterprises. This natural entrepreneurial spirit means that one will find an occasional tree growing in the most unlikely of places, such as in and around solid rock. Yet some places are brimming with entrepreneurial activity, while others are not. Sirolli's approach to local economic development, which he terms "enterprise facilitation," is but one example of how the *entrepreneurial context* matters. Through strategic efforts, he demonstrates how we can transform a foundation of rock into soil that is fertile for plants and trees to grow and thrive, and in doing so, we can liberate a great deal of creative potential in many forgotten places.

In recent years, community economic developers around the world have succeeded in putting entrepreneurship on the map as an important goal for revitalizing communities (Markley, Lyons, & Macke, 2015). This recognition has increased the need for social science research to explain why rates of entrepreneurship vary substantially across locations and societal groups. This line of research bursts the myth of the independent risk taker, the "heroic economic superman," who operates in a vacuum and needs little, other than perhaps some money and technical advice, in order to create a successful venture (Schumpeter, 1934). Rather, many important scholars have noted that economic behavior is best understood within its many contexts (Granovetter, 1985; Polanyi, 1957; Weber, 1930), since external variables provide openings, but also set boundaries for individual actions and desires. As such, contextualizing entrepreneurship helps explain who gets involved in entrepreneurship and where and how it happens (Julien, 2007; Welter, 2011).

Current research on entrepreneurship and place is just beginning to examine an important, but often hidden aspect of this contextual dimension: namely the *culture of a locality*. According to Welter (2011), the "where" dimension of context "refers to the manifold locations in which entrepreneurship happens . . . It includes both distal contexts, for example, countries, political systems, or society, as well as more proximate contexts such as the social environment or the local neighborhood of entrepreneurs" (p. 167). The majority of empirical research in this vein focuses on national and regional level variables, despite the fact that small firms tend to be deeply embedded in specific localities, where they are highly dependent on local networks, norms, assets, policies, etc. (Julien, 2007; Spigel, 2013). It is also important to differentiate between the *structure* and *culture* of society and to ensure that analyses consider place-specific variables above and beyond what Julien (2007) refers to as "classical location factors (infrastructures, workforce, and so on)" (p. 120). In other words, it is crucial to consider the "local culture" of a place and its role in the entrepreneurial development process—particularly in more isolated and marginalized regions, such as rural communities, the forgotten rustbelt, abandoned production towns and cities, or declining environments in the United States.

As social scientists, we are also interested in the extent to which our empirical research is grounded in theory that provides a guidepost for understanding the complexity of social life and how social change occurs. In *Seven Theories for Seven Community Developers*, Hustedde (2008) makes a compelling case for the value of theory in conducting relevant research and creating tools for effective practice. Often a strong and consistent theoretical framework does not guide empirical research on entrepreneurship and place (Julien, 2007). Specifically, theories about how culture affects the entrepreneurship process are particularly underdeveloped (Spigel, 2013). An emerging body of scholarship on entrepreneurial cultures builds from a Boudieuian (1977, 1986) framework and has real potential to enhance and explain several observations and case studies regarding the diverse geography of entrepreneurship (de Clercq & Voronov, 2009a, 2009b; Spigel, 2013; Terjesen & Elam, 2009).

Finally, in the end of this chapter, it is vital to stand back and ask the following questions. *What does this exciting theoretical framework combined with what we currently know about entrepreneurial culture mean for practitioners? How can we go about fostering a local culture for innovation, creativity, and entrepreneurship?* There are at least five approaches to creating new possibilities for entrepreneurship within the framework outlined by Bourdieu (1977, 1986). These approaches are discussed in detail, incorporating direct experience from entrepreneurial support programs such as the Kentucky Entrepreneurial Coaches Institute. In conclusion, there is ample opportunity for future research to investigate how culture (at various levels, units of analysis, and contexts) impacts entrepreneurial community development as part of the larger entrepreneurial community ecosystem.

A Discussion of the Relevance of Culture to Entrepreneurship Studies

In his extensive literature review, Welter (2011) takes stock of the multitude of ways in which external factors can influence entrepreneurship, expressing the need to fully contextualize entrepreneurship, and to understand economic behavior within historical, temporal, institutional, geographic, and social contexts that set opportunities and boundaries for action. Drawing on examples from former Soviet countries, he highlights various types of *entrepreneurial contexts* that impact upon entrepreneurship: the business, social, spatial, institutional, and societal contexts. He explores each of these contexts in turn (minus the business context) and then offers some suggestions for how researchers can do a better job of contextualizing entrepreneurship research. Finally, despite his attempts to describe distinct contexts, Welter (2011) notes that in reality, entrepreneurship is happening "in intertwined social, societal, and geographic contexts, thus indicating the difficulties in developing a clear-cut distinction between the contexts" (p. 170). Nonetheless, his is a very useful assessment of how we might better theorize and study entrepreneurial contexts.

One of the most important contexts for entrepreneurship research is the spatial, or geographic context—particularly the community context (Julien, 2007). Spigel (2013) notes,

> Entrepreneurs largely draw on local resources as they start and grow their firms, be it venture capital, mentorship, or knowledge and support obtained through their social networks. Therefore, the provision of all these resources will be affected by local cultural norms, such as how 'respectable' entrepreneurship is compared to traditional employment or the social consequences of business failure.
>
> (p. 807)

Research that explores *entrepreneurial geographies* or *environments* examines a wide range of structural and cultural factors that seek to explain the variation in economic activity between localities, regions, and nations. Much of this research highlights the importance of government policies, access to infrastructure, and network structures, among other social structural variables (Thornton & Flynn, 2003). For example, Malecki (1997) reviews some of the major explanations for geographic variations in the rates of entrepreneurship. One variable he highlights is the importance of "institutional embeddedness" for catalyzing entrepreneurial communities. Institutional embeddedness refers to networks of entrepreneurial support institutions that "provide know-how to a region in the form of educational programs, technical support programs, capable local advisers, and professionals support organizations, as well as incubator organizations and business networks," (Malecki, 2006, p. 15), and which are deeply embedded within the local socioeconomic structures.

While considerable evidence underscores the importance of external structural variables in explaining geographic variations in the rates of entrepreneurship, the role of *culture* is often underappreciated and understudied in this line of entrepreneurship research (Hayden & Cacciotti, 2013;

Marquez-Lopez, Guzman, & Linan, 2013). Although structure and culture are related to each other in a continuous feedback loop, it can be helpful to separate out what is meant by each so that analyses do not focus on one to the exclusion of the other. In his study of racial inequality, Wilson (2009) provides one helpful distinction. Social structure refers to "social positions, social roles and networks of social relations that configure people into particular positions and relationships" (Roithmayr, 2011, para 4). In Wilson's analysis, structural forces include social acts (individual behavior) and social processes (the "machinery" of society, such as laws, policies, and institutional practices). Culture, on the other hand, refers to (1) national views and beliefs and (2) "cultural traits—shared outlooks, modes of behavior, traditions, belief systems, worldviews, values, skills, preferences, styles of self-presentation, etiquette, and linguistic patterns—that emerge from patterns of intra-group interaction" (Wilson, 2009, p. 12). In other words, there are specific cultural frameworks of meaning that guide human action and interaction.

The pervasiveness and importance of culture has been recognized by many anthropologists and cultural sociologists since the time of Durkheim (1984) and Weber (1930). All groups have a culture. Children are taught the basics of a group's culture early in their lives, causing values to appear natural and incontrovertible and behaviors to become routinized. As a consequence, cultural pathways develop a permanence, including what is considered good, desirable, and important in a society (Giddens, 1991). Once set in motion, some cultural traits are very persistent and difficult to change. Thus the culture of certain groups and places still bear the imprint of their ancestors in many surprising ways, as is underscored by studies of cultural permanence in societies (Gaventa, 1982) or institutional memory within institutions and organizational structures (Berger & Udell, 2004). This idea of cultural permanence applies to entrepreneurship as well.

Culture and Its Effects on Entrepreneurial Activity

Definitional Issues and Data Sources

How, then, does the culture of a place impact upon our economic behavior? The entrepreneurial culture of a place can be defined and measured in a wide variety of ways. One clear definition comes from Julien (2007),

> An entrepreneurial culture is, fundamentally, the attitude or aptitude of a society in a given territory for recognizing and stimulating the personal values and management skills of entrepreneurs, allowing them to benefit in various ways from their initiative, sense of risk and ability to innovate and manage their relations with the milieu in an effective way. (p. 120)

Because of the complexity of studying culture, there are many other terms in the literature that encompass and/or appear to be related to this concept of entrepreneurial culture, including community social capital (Besser & Miller, 2013; Kwon, Heflin, & Ruef, 2013; Roxas & Azmat, 2014), community entrepreneurial climate (Chatman, Altman, & Johnson, 2008; Goetz & Freshwater, 2001), and the institutional environment (Fortunanto & McLaughlin, 2012; Frazier, Stoel, Niehm, & Eckerson, 2013; Kibler, 2013). Some of the relevant research focuses on specific cultural values, such as whether or not a society values individualism (Hofstede, 2001) or if the culture perceives entrepreneurship as desirable (Klyver & Thornton, 2010). Other research measures perceptions of the entrepreneurial culture and whether it fosters innovation (Breazeale, Fortunato, Allen, Hustedde, & Pushkarskaya, 2015). Taken together, these studies paint a general picture of some of the most important aspects of culture as it relates to entrepreneurship, although there is still much research to be done.

The research on entrepreneurial culture to date largely focuses on the impact of *national* characteristics on entrepreneurship. The nation state is a convenient level of analysis. Many countries have some degree of cultural insularity, relatively homogeneous policy regimes, and a historical identity of nationhood (Nakata & Sivakumar, 1996). There is also a plethora of available data.

One important source of data is collected annually by the Global Entrepreneurship Monitor (GEM), which fosters scholarship on the legal, social, and cultural frameworks supporting or inhibiting entrepreneurship across the globe (Amorós & Bosma, 2014; GEM, 2016). Of particular interest here, GEM tracks "entrepreneurial attitudes and perceptions" across 70 participating nations at various levels of development. It includes measures of perceived opportunities, perceived capabilities, fear of failure, entrepreneurial intentions, entrepreneurship as a good career choice, high status to successful entrepreneurs, and media attention to successful entrepreneurs as indicators of the importance and viability of entrepreneurship in the national culture.

The Global Entrepreneurship and Development Institute (Acs, Szerb, & Autio, 2016) provides another important source of national-level data. GEDI collects data on cultural attitudes, abilities, and aspirations as well as infrastructural variables such as broadband connectivity to construct the Global Entrepreneurship Index, which is then used to rank countries (GEDI, 2016). The index is an attempt to measure the entrepreneurship "ecosystem" of a region, accounting for the importance of attitudes, resources, *and* infrastructure that jointly foster entrepreneurial activity (GEDI).

Finally, it is important to note that much of the research on entrepreneurial culture is based, at least partly, on Hofstede's (2001) work, which focuses on five dimensions: power distance, uncertainty avoidance, individualism versus collectivism, masculinity versus femininity, and long- versus short-term orientation. According to Hofstede, cultures with high power distance tend to have more top-down control that inhibits spontaneous and entrepreneurial behavior, while cultures with low power differences encourage self-employment. Cultures with uncertainty avoidance will have strict contracts and structured work places. In such cultures, the certainties of a dependable paycheck and a job are more accepted than the uncertainty of being self-employed. Hofstede also argues that those cultures that value individualism will foster self-reliant people who can set independent goals, resulting in higher levels of self-employment, such as entrepreneurship. He notes that high levels of masculinity are associated with ego-boosters such as higher-earning levels and recognitions. On the other hand, femininity is associated with pleasing the boss and peers. From Hofstede's perspective, societies with more masculinity will create more entrepreneurs. Finally, he contends that societies with long-term orientations are more concerned about investments that will yield gradual returns and economic efficiencies. Consequently, delayed gratification and the resulting competitive environment will positively impact on entrepreneurial activity. In contrast, those countries that focus on the short run will be more concerned with consumption and lower investment strategies and will see minimal entrepreneurship.

Empirical Research on Entrepreneurial Culture

An interesting body of literature explores these and other national-level cultural variables and their effects on entrepreneurship. For example, Huggins & Thompson (2012) examined entrepreneurship in Wales, investigating a range of attitudes and activities associated with new firm start-ups and ownership. They discovered that caring and more feminine attitudes and activities were negatively associated with entrepreneurship while the embracement of work and education and observance of social rules and cohesion were more positively associated with an entrepreneurial culture. In another empirical study, Hofstede et al. (2004) found that dissatisfaction with society is one of the most important determinants of the level of entrepreneurship. In other words, countries where people are less satisfied typically have more self-employed individuals. This concept is the "dissatisfaction hypothesis."

Cross-national research has also interrogated the relationship between entrepreneurial culture and individual-level variables. For example, a random sample research study in 51 countries combined the cognitive concept of self-efficacy with institutional theory that people are pulled into entrepreneurship by a supportive culture (Klyver & Thornton, 2010). The concept of self-efficacy is about the ability of individuals to discover and act on opportunities in the process of starting a new business while institutional pressures can affirm or discourage entrepreneurship participation. They discovered that self-efficacy plays a larger role in explaining entrepreneurial intentions in societies where entrepreneurship status is relatively low. In contrast, supportive societies create the conditions for self-efficacy as an antecedent of intention. Policy makers need to be aware that self-efficacy is not a competence but it merely reflects the individual's perception of entrepreneurial abilities. Klyver and Thornton (2010) contend that there is a danger that incompetent individuals may enter the entrepreneurial process and will be a higher risk in societies where entrepreneurship is highly valued.

In a similar vein, Wennberg, Pathak, and Autio (2013) studied 42 countries to investigate the effects of attitudes toward institutional collectivism, assertiveness, performance orientation, and uncertainty avoidance on individual self-efficacy and fear of entrepreneurial failure. One of their surprising conclusions was that if a country's culture is inclined toward uncertainty avoidance, this cultural attribute does not discourage individuals with high entrepreneurial self-efficacy. They also found that many cultures with a high emphasis on results, continuous improvement, and a high work ethic exhibited low rates of entrepreneurship because the economic framework was more oriented toward large firms. Their study concluded that societies with low institutional collectivism should promote an image of entrepreneurship as an act that celebrates individuals and minimizes the risks associated with investments in entrepreneurial growth. Wennberg et al. (2013) also supported that societies with low performance orientation should highlight entrepreneurship as a lifestyle choice rather than merely as a way to gain wealth.

It is important to recall that scholars define entrepreneurial culture differently and attempt to measure and study it using a wide range of objective and subjective indicators. For example, Dimitratos, Voudouris, Plakoyiannaki, and Nakos (2012) designed a six-dimensional scale of international entrepreneurial culture that included measures for motivation, networking, and entrepreneurial, market, and learning orientation that explained some international variation in entrepreneurship across the U.S. and U.K. context. By comparing entrepreneurs and non-entrepreneurs, Beugelsdijk (2007) also constructed a measure of entrepreneurial culture that incorporated views on individual effort, government ownership, state responsibility, unemployment, and long-term success. The measure was then found to have a significant correlation with economic growth in 54 European regions.

Overall, this group of international, cross-cultural studies provides useful insights about some of the central cultural elements influencing entrepreneurship, but provides less information about how *local dynamics* can influence small business behavior. In large, heterogeneous countries like the United States, policies affecting trade as well as cultural histories vary substantially by state, and even by locality. For instance, both socioeconomic circumstances and societal norms are profoundly different in Silicon Valley, rural Kentucky, and Native American communities. National approaches for examining entrepreneurial culture can ignore the complexities of diverse regions, especially the economic and cultural distinctions between rural and urban settings (Fortunato, 2014).

Understanding why entrepreneurship rates and successes vary from place to place at the sub-national level, especially across areas that might be expected to be similar in terms of their economic policies, is important not only from a pure academic point of view but also from the entrepreneurial educational and support programs perspective. In fact, studies have found substantial variation in rates of entrepreneurship across counties (Acs & Armington, 2006; Low, Henderson, & Weiler, 2005) and county types (Rapasingha & Goetz, 2013). These findings suggest that important factors influence entrepreneurship at the local level as well.

Much like the international literature, these US-based scholars have attempted to pinpoint more localized determinants of entrepreneurship, including demographic, infrastructural, and policy factors, but there is a growing recognition that local culture (e.g., shared beliefs and values) must be systematically considered alongside elements of social structure (e.g., local institutions, structural pathways). There is strong evidence that local cultures exist[1] and matter a great deal. For example, studies have found that entrepreneurial regions often remain entrepreneurial even after a major political shift (Fritsch & Wyrwich, 2012). On the other hand, research has shown that some "company towns" exhibit a strong cultural preference for wage employment over self-employment long after the primary industry declined (Fortunato & McLaughlin, 2012), resulting in a legacy of economic disempowerment (Gaventa, 1982; Luloff & Bridger, 2003). These kinds of cultural influences can have a long-lasting effect on small businesses, especially innovators, in a community or region.

What, then, do we know about localized entrepreneurial cultures, how to measure them, and what impacts they have on entrepreneurial behavior and success? In one study, Frazier et al. (2013) used responses from a community-wide attitudes survey of 1,161 residents and business owners in 32 rural U.S. communities. Their measure of institutional norms, which included openness to change, community performance actions, community symbolic actions, retailer symbolic actions, and retailer performance actions, was positively related to both resident and business owner optimism about the success of a start-up. Community innovativeness, largely stemming from openness to and acceptance of productive change, was identified as being critical to building a more entrepreneurial culture (Hustedde, 2007).

Openness to change is a recurring theme among the studies presented in this literature review, either explicitly or implicitly: for example, the GEM pairing of perceived opportunities and perceived capabilities suggests that not all cultures and policy structures enable entrepreneurs to take advantage of novel situations with equal ease. For example, Canada ranked higher than the United States in terms of perceived opportunity (an index of 57.4 to 47.2, respectively), but the United States outranked Canada in terms of perceived capabilities to take advantage of those opportunities (55.7 to 48.5, respectively) (Amorós & Bosma, 2014, p. 27). Fortunato and McLaughlin (2012) similarly discovered in qualitative research that a history of industrial change (in Rockland, Maine), openness to diversity and newcomers (in Alma, Wisconsin), and a history of bootstrap agriculture rather than industrial development (in McConnellsburg, Pennsylvania) led to higher levels of entrepreneurship in these places compared to rural communities with very low levels of entrepreneurship. In those low-entrepreneurship communities, a preference for wage employment over self-employment paired with institutional fragmentation inhibited entrepreneurship in pervasive ways.

Sub-national research in Japan also confirms the importance of local culture on entrepreneurship in cities as well. While Japan's national budget for small business assistance reached historic highs in the early 2000s, the impact was mixed. Aoyama (2009) explored the cultural differences between two communities in Japan: Hamamatsu and Kyoto. He focused on information technologies. The former has a regional legacy for automation and mass production. They are more transparent, value information sharing, and welcome outsiders from the region—including entrepreneurs. Their colleges and universities are a breeding ground for new ideas. On the other hand, Kyoto is known for its handcrafts, and it tends to give higher social status to fiber producers than entrepreneurs. They tend to view openness with suspicion. Consequently, Hamamatsu tends to generate more information technology entrepreneurs than Kyoto.

Community economic developers have also weighed in on this topic, drawing from case studies and their experiences out in the field. For example, Hustedde (2007) suggests that communities can view themselves as an entrepreneurial venture that questions the status quo and sees opportunities where others only see obstacles. He contends that an entrepreneurial culture can take several forms and could include informal counter-cultures that question the dominant culture of aversion to risk taking or starting a new enterprise. He uses case studies to argue that an entrepreneurial culture can be fostered through seven venues: (1) creating openness to new ideas, (2) welcoming fresh voices and embracing diversity, (3) mobilizing resources for entrepreneurs, (4) cultivating informal networks for entrepreneurs to thrive, (5) focusing on community assets rather than deficits, (6) building a collective vision about entrepreneurship, and (7) fostering entrepreneurial leaders and advocates. Similarly, Lyons, Alter, Audretsch, and Augustine (2012) explain that the entrepreneurial capacity of a community should not focus exclusively on supporting entrepreneurs *within* the community, but rather should foster a sense of support *for* an entrepreneurial community.

Social Capital

Strong cultures of trust, support, and interaction are another important theme in this literature. In the aforementioned study by Fortunato and McLaughlin (2012), the researchers describe the policy implications of their work on entrepreneurship and social capital: top-down programs or other entrepreneurial assistance programs are institutionally driven and expensive while high level entrepreneurship communities have cultures with strong interaction among existing entrepreneurs and institutions. They contend that local institutions can create a sense of purpose and interaction among businesses and other groups that will foster entrepreneurial success. In a similar vein, Besser and Miller (2013), in their empirical study of remote rural areas in the United States, discovered that those entrepreneurs who perceived themselves as successful were influenced by community bridging social capital, which is associated with higher levels of civic engagement. Bridging capital refers to links among diverse groups to build a culture for general community betterment and economic vibrancy. Civic engagement involves a greater tendency for community and business input into local government decisions to advance business success. They conclude that remote rural communities can foster more perceived entrepreneurial successes through policies that foster high bridging social capital.

These lessons are not just applicable to rural communities, however. Social capital is important in all localities. Entrepreneurs depend on social trust because it facilitates a free flow of information across social boundaries. Social trust and connected organization membership and individual memberships help independent entrepreneurs who lack a widely diffused reputation to secure financing or partnerships. Although individual effects of social trust are important, communities that have a higher level of social trust are more likely to make it easier for suppliers, investors, and partners to work with new and small businesses. A community's level of social trust increases the probability that marginal members of a community—recent immigrants, ethnic minorities, and physically or mentally challenged individuals for instance—can become self-employed. However, a community's dominant members are more likely to have more individual-level social capital than those with limited education or greater poverty and are more likely to have more entrepreneurial success than marginal members (Kwon et al., 2013).

In general, however, the research on local culture, communities, and entrepreneurship is in its infancy, in part because of the difficulty of measuring and studying these concepts. In an attempt to move this line of inquiry forward, Breazeale et al. (2015) developed a multifaceted measure of local entrepreneurial culture based on residents' perceptions. The scale was developed through in-depth interviews with entrepreneurs and non-entrepreneurs, and it was included in a large-scale survey of rural and urban Kentuckians. Factor analysis resulted in a 17-item scale with four major components that was validated by correlating the survey results with county-level rates of entrepreneurship obtained from an independent data set. The analysis confirmed that perceptions of the local entrepreneurial culture as measured by this scale do correlate with entrepreneurial activity. The research also found that the correlation between perceived entrepreneurial culture and actual entrepreneurship rates was much stronger in rural than in urban areas. Furthermore, the sub-scale that the researchers called DCC ("Diversity and Change") was the strongest predictor of entrepreneurial activity. Items loaded in this sub-scale included perceptions on whether the community is forward looking and open to change. Other cultural subscales that emerged focused on business discouragements, business promotion, and a focus on local.

Dana and Dana (2005) offer a different way forward, arguing for the need to expand the scope of methodologies used in entrepreneurship research and move away from the current reliance on quantitative methods. They argue that the best way to contextualize entrepreneurship properly is to examine a particular place in great detail in order to discern the key aspects of the local culture and structure that impact upon the entrepreneurial process. They argue for a qualitative, inductive case study approach to studying entrepreneurial culture and point out that it is difficult to understand culture and its role in influencing entrepreneurship through surveys alone. They reference the few studies that have proceeded in this direction, and have thus been particularly sensitive to a consideration of local culture. For example, Dana (1995) applied current theories of entrepreneurship to his anthropological investigation of entrepreneurship in a remote Alaskan village. He finds that few entrepreneurs in the region are opportunity seeking (by culture or by personality), but rather are reactive, responding to opportunities that fall in their laps or lack of other opportunities (primarily the former). Eskimos are also far less likely to seek out opportunities than are their non-native counterparts, which is explained based on their culture that does not value competitive, profit-seeking behavior. Dana argues that entrepreneurship programs should start by seeking to build an entrepreneurial spirit rather than just providing assistance to those who are opportunity seeking, thus hopefully increasing the volume, quality, and success of entrepreneurial ventures. In his view, entrepreneurship should not just be viewed as a function of the opportunities that exist in a region, but rather in terms of how these opportunities are culturally perceived (in other words, what entrepreneurship means to people from different backgrounds and cultures).

Theorizing the Relationship Between Local Culture and Entrepreneurship

In the emerging entrepreneurship literature on culture, there is a paucity of theoretical work that elucidates the processes through which culture affects the local entrepreneurial process. Consequently, researchers rely on a wide range of proxies as they seek to identify the most salient attributes of culture that impact upon entrepreneurship in the context of their study. Without a theoretical framework, they are also unable to identify how this influence occurs (Spigel, 2013).

One notable exception is the work of Julien (2007). In his book, *A Theory of Local Entrepreneurship in the Knowledge Economy*, Julien develops a general theory about why some localities have a thriving small business sector, while others do not. He challenges conventional economic theory that business actors are purely self-interested rational beings, and puts forth a theory of entrepreneurship that builds on insights from a variety of disciplines, including sociology, anthropology, geography, and economics. One of his central concepts is the "entrepreneurial milieu," which he explains is both a key condition for entrepreneurship to flourish, but something that can also impede entrepreneurship. For Julien, an entrepreneurial milieu is

> the social market construction that can facilitate multiple links between resources, on one hand, and purchasers, on the other. It is a context of territorial production measured by know-how, technical culture and learning capacity, placing more or less value on the proximity of key players to create synergy with the environment. In other words, it is the socio-economic environment surrounding the entrepreneur and the small business, that facilitates, or fails to facilitate, the commercial and non-commercial links that distinguish one territory from another . . . It is therefore at the heart of the local dynamism when it systematically provides rich relationships that bring ideas and change.
>
> (pp. 119–120)

The regional milieu includes local resources (such as an educated workforce) and good infrastructure, but also open conventions and an entrepreneurial culture. Together these aspects of the milieu generate social capital, facilitate rich knowledge exchanges, and promote innovative business activity. This book is an important contribution to the field, but it tells us less about how and why specific individuals might decide to move forward with their entrepreneurial dreams given their particular social and cultural context.

The work of Bourdieu (1977, 1986), on the other hand, may provide a promising conceptual approach for understanding how individual entrepreneurial actions seem sensible within the broader societal context (Spigel, 2013). Spigel (2013), in his article, "Bourdieuian approaches to the geography of entrepreneurial cultures" lays out a framework to connect culture with everyday entrepreneurial practices. Bourdieu (1977, 1986) utilizes three conceptual tools: field, habitus, and capital. Practices such as entrepreneurship take place within *fields*. A field includes the "rules of the game" in which social action occurs. Bourdieu asserts that the fields are so embedded in our lives that they are often invisible. These unwritten rules are termed *doxa* because they appear to be so natural and unquestionable.

Fields may have obvious and unwritten rules and structures, but entrepreneurs and other actors do not interpret them uniformly. Each actor has an internalized set of intentions and dispositions that are referred to as *habitus*. It could be interpreted as an internalized understanding of rules, structures, and hierarchies along with a knowledge of one's position in the field and its applicability to oneself. An actor may be successful by adapting to the rules. In other cases, the actor may unconsciously or consciously violate the rules because the rewards outweigh potential sanctions.

Bourdieu (1977, 1986) also claims that the power of an actor is influenced by at least four forms of *capital*: the traditional economic form, social capital (e.g., the resources available through one's social network), cultural capital (e.g., knowledge of particular cultural roles and norms), and symbolic capital (e.g., respect and trust of various professions or brands). Power is about controlling the various forms of capital in a field. Entrepreneurs may use economic capital or symbolic capital to strengthen their influence.

Bourdieu would view *culture* as the dominant understanding of a particular field that emerges within a group or region. Power within an entrepreneurial field is influenced by the ability to define the practices that are seen as legitimate forms of entrepreneurship that deserve support. In essence, start-up or expansion decisions are influenced by the visible and invisible rules of the field, and how one understands those rules. For example, an entrepreneur may use the symbolic capital of creating a firm because of its perceived value and will share risk with outside investors (traditional economic power) and draw upon social capital with friends and other supporters. Collective understanding of a field produces a culture that becomes the context for entrepreneurial actions.

The entrepreneur's *habitus* is an internalized form of understanding of local and non-local fields (such as the "industry" field). A field can be described as a discipline, domain, or culture in which one can specialize. Fields may involve education, economic development, community development, psychology, sports, mystery writing, or painting. Each individual is likely to be associated with a variety of fields. Some fields in various regions are interpreted differently by entrepreneurs as risk averse or closed, while others are perceived as creative and open. These habits or actions affect reflexive and relational connections.

It should be noted that part of a field's *doxa*, its unquestionable logic, changes as new practices and entrepreneurial practices emerge. Routinized and habitual thinking can stifle the innovation and creativity that is associated with entrepreneurship. However, entrepreneurial advocates can work with organizations and communities to find cracks in *doxa* and to influence *habitus*.

Five Approaches for Supporting an Entrepreneurial Culture Using a Bourdieuian Framework

Local culture, or the collective understanding of the "rules of the game," provides the social context within which individuals make sense of their options and determine what actions seem reasonable; as such, it can foster or inhibit a foundation of fertile soil for entrepreneurial activity. A Bourdieuian perspective on entrepreneurial culture offers practitioners a different way to think about entrepreneurship, with implications for how we might go about establishing a local culture for innovation, creativity, and entrepreneurship. There are at least five directions that community developers might consider in line with this framework, including: developing an intersection of fields, empowering regional and local entrepreneurs, enhancing symbolic capital, busting myths, and integrating the aforementioned approaches.

Developing an Intersection of Fields

The first approach is about developing an intersection of *fields*. It involves welcoming fresh voices and embracing diversity. Johansson (2004) contends that fields have concepts about knowledge and practice. To develop an expertise in a field, one must understand many concepts about that field. At the same time, that expertise can lead to a mind-set that may neglect to see new opportunities. When fields are intersected, they lead to leaps in new directions and can open up entirely new fields. For example, musicians cross the boundaries of classical, pop, Latino, and Anglo music to create new genres. Disciplinary sciences have given way to multiple sub-categorizations. Increasingly, university students are adding hyphens to their majors: biology music, economic-sociology, and mathematics-economics. These intersections are leading to new ways to look at problems. For example, hospitals are hiring musical therapists to complement the healing arts.

As immigrants enter more homogeneous countries, they bring different kinds of knowledge and practice that intersect with conventional *doxa* to create new concepts and knowledge that leads to new ventures. The same holds true for women, various ethnic groups, and those who are disabled. When organizations and communities intersect different fields with each other, there is a greater likelihood that new ideas and innovation will take place. The intersection of fields must involve a climate for brainstorming and questioning, weighing consequences of various alternatives, choosing an approach and finding resources for implementation and frequent reflections on what is working or not working. When communities and organizations see the value of intersections and intentionally create climates for an intersection of fields, there is a greater chance of innovation and entrepreneurship to blossom.

Empowering Regional and Local Entrepreneurs

The second approach focuses on strengthening the power of entrepreneurship at the regional or local level. Gruidl and Markley (2015) and Markley and Dabson (2008) believe that too many states, communities, and regions focus almost exclusively on policies geared toward the attraction of businesses to bring wealth and jobs and improve the quality of life while giving scant attention to creating a support system for entrepreneurs and small businesses, who are creators of the bulk of new jobs and wealth. From a Bourdieuian (1977, 1986) perspective, we argue that power is integral for building community capacity for entrepreneurship. Bourdieu asserts that power is achieved through four forms of capital: traditional economics, social capital, cultural capital, and symbolic capital. Isenberg (2010) purports that such power emerges when a community, organization, or government takes a more holistic approach toward the integration of these capitals. It is known as an entrepreneurial ecosystem. Communities and groups that only focus on individual components—such as financial and technical assistance—are not as likely to stimulate entrepreneurship because they are enacted in isolation. In contrast, an entrepreneurial ecosystem is holistic (Isenberg, 2010; Markley et al., 2015). There are a variety of principles involved. It involves an exploration and identification of local assets such as cultural capital, natural resources capital, built capital, financial capital, political capital, social capital, and human capital to identify opportunities to address complex problems and needs. It is also about building an entrepreneurial vision around those assets, and mobilizing resources to help entrepreneurs emerge or expand. An entrepreneurial ecosystem might include evaluation of legal and regulatory frameworks that might impede or provide opportunities for innovation.

A healthy ecosystem is a place-based strategy that calls for community partnerships to build the capacity for entrepreneurs. It is not a short-term endeavor but requires long-term commitments to be sustainable. For example, Kansas used a community engagement process to build the community capacity for entrepreneurship through community coaching and an assessment process that targeted five focus areas for strengthening entrepreneurship: ascertaining development opportunities, identifying entrepreneurial talent, identifying relevant resources, setting local development goals for entrepreneurship, and engaging stakeholders in the community or region who have a self-interest in entrepreneurship. The primary shift is from providing services to entrepreneurs to developing aspiring or existing entrepreneurs. This paradigm shift involves the transformation of a local community to improve the network of entrepreneurs and to connect different sets of stakeholders. It may involve field experiments to create entrepreneurial communities and to develop policy changes for more holistic approaches as well as new forms of measuring impact and research to document the long-term community change that takes place through an ecosystem framework.

Enhancing Symbolic Capital

The third approach builds on Bourdieu's (1977, 1986) framework about the role of *symbolic capital* as an aspect of power. Symbolic capital is a value that involves prestige and social obligations within a historical or cultural context. For example, a well-known clergy leader might have significant political or social influence because of her role within the context of a local historic culture. Symbolic capital is not boundless; what matters in one cultural context may not transfer to another culture or locality.

Stories regarding how entrepreneurs emerge or thrive influence symbolic capital. People are not *Homo sapiens* but *homo narrans*—the only species that tell stories (Fischer, 1987). Stories are how we organize our thoughts. They inform and influence us about what is essential. There are stories that dominate the culture, while others are seldom heard. Entrepreneurs come in a variety of forms. The stories of survival entrepreneurs will differ from aspiring and lifestyle entrepreneurs, and slow growth and high-growth entrepreneurs. However, their stories can awaken dormant dreams about addressing problems, needs, and wants through profit or nonprofit approaches to entrepreneurship. They can raise questions about the *status quo* and create a healthy soil for entrepreneurial growth.

The stories also create a kind of temporal solidarity to inspire people to support entrepreneurs or to awaken dormant dreams. There are a variety of fields that can create climates for the entrepreneurial stories to be told. They include venues to overcome perceived and real social barriers through schools, faith-based communities, economic organizations, arts groups, and venues such as the arts for the written and spoken word. For communities to thrive there must be opportunities to hear the stories from those with diverse racial, ethnic, geographic, and marginalized backgrounds—including those who are disabled. To be authentic, these stories must not be limited to 'successes' but should explore barriers, untapped opportunities, and lessons learned from failures. Some places such as Fairfield, Iowa, create venues for entrepreneurs of various levels to tell their stories to investors, community people, and youth. There are also rewards and recognition programs as well as a Buy Local ethic. As a consequence, Fairfield is a place in which entrepreneurship is a pronounced part of the everyday narrative in which individual and collective dreams can take root (Gruidl & Markley, 2015).

Busting Myths

The fourth approach is myth busting. It's about discovering cracks in some of the economic development assumptions and behaviors associated with *doxa* and *habitus*, and stimulating critical thinking.

Sirolli (2012) argues against the popular myth of the entrepreneur as a single individual. He contends that the most successful entrepreneurs consist of teams who are skilled in three areas: the development of a product or service, marketing or sales, and finance, including anticipated sales, overhead, and potential profits. While some individuals may be talented or drawn to two of these areas, they are seldom accomplished in all three. The team concept makes it easier for individuals to focus on their strengths rather than perceived limitations.

There's the myth that entrepreneurship is about mindless consumerism or the dead-end futures of hyper-industrial capitalism. These assumptions can be challenged by the emergence of civic or social entrepreneurs who are driven by the need to bring about some form of social change. Communities are dotted with civic ventures that focus on issues such as affordable and safe housing, alternative health care, asset-based economic development, arts and artisans, environmental conservation, disability rights, youth development, and community-based philanthropic organizations. Capital access has been a problem for these entrepreneurs but web-based intermediaries, socially conscious investors and the growth of local philanthropies are minimizing some of these obstacles (Bornstein, 2007; Bornstein & Davis, 2010; Shapiro, 2012). Social entrepreneurs are also being nurtured through business schools and other institutions that integrate social issues with business concepts. For example, Berea College in Kentucky has a multi-year undergraduate program, *Entrepreneurship for the Public Good*. Its intent is to help rural communities in Central Appalachia. It focuses on "a process when one person or a group of people in a community originate an idea or innovation for a needed change and influence others in that community to commit to realizing that change, despite the presence of risk, ambiguity, or uncertainty" (*Entrepreneurship for the Public Good*, 2016, para 2).

Integrating Approaches

The fifth approach is practical; it's about integrating the other four approaches—an intersection of fields, building a healthy entrepreneurial ecosystem, storytelling, and myth busting. An entrepreneurial culture is not characterized by centralized or decentralized leadership but by interrelated leadership. An entrepreneurial community is fostered through linking leaders in finance, the arts, local government, social services, youth, and other groups to develop a shared vision. It goes beyond team building and focuses more on developing a healthy ecosystem and critical thinking and shared learning. For example, the Kentucky Entrepreneurial Coaches Institute (KECI) is a unique leadership development program that was founded to create an entrepreneurial culture in rural areas that are making the painful transition from tobacco dependent economies. KECI exhibits all four of the Bordieuian approaches in an integrated fashion. KECI recruits grassroots and traditional leaders of varying ages and backgrounds and provides them with the conceptual tools and skills to build entrepreneurial friendly communities. They work in teams to create youth entrepreneurship projects, other forms of innovation, and raise tough questions about conventional economic development strategies such as industrial recruitment. Those interrelated leaders are changing the entrepreneurial climate in the region (Hustedde, 2007).

Conclusion

This chapter explored the impact of culture on entrepreneurship. Culture can be viewed as a kind of collective mind programming. It includes shared beliefs, value judgments, and behavior about what is acceptable and what is not. Culture is influenced by external and internal factors such as settlement patterns, religion, economics, media, shared stories, art, and entertainment. Some cultures encourage the traits associated with entrepreneurship: critical thinking, creativity, risk taking, and openness toward change. They may welcome innovative approaches toward problems and needs. Other cultures may place a greater emphasis on conformity and may be less open to change or the risks associated with creativity. Some cultures may have less tolerance of the independent streak of entrepreneurs who question the *status quo*. Cultures are not fixed but shift over time because of external and internal influences.

A significant part of the research on entrepreneurial culture focuses at the national level. While this may be valuable, it does not take into account the cultures at the sub-national level. In recent years, more scholars are concentrating on the localized determinants of entrepreneurship. Some subnational cultures have a regional legacy for transparency and value information sharing and welcome outsiders. Their colleges and universities can be a breeding ground for entrepreneurs. In contrast, communities that view openness with suspicion will give less status to entrepreneurs. For the most part, the research about local cultures and entrepreneurship is in its infancy.

The work of Bourdieu (1977, 1986) and Spigel (2013) provide a promising conceptual framework for understanding how entrepreneurship might thrive or be deemphasized within a local or regional culture. Based on Bourdieu's framework, five approaches for supporting an entrepreneurial culture are offered. First, foster an intersection of fields that welcomes fresh voices and ideas. When fields are intersected, they can lead to innovation and open up entirely new fields. Second, empower regional and local entrepreneurs through the development of an entrepreneurial ecosystem that simultaneously enhances all forms of power. Third, enhance the symbolic capital of established and aspiring entrepreneurs by creating space for public storytelling and creating a 'buzz' around innovation. Fourth, bust common myths about entrepreneurship and find cracks in a field's *doxa* and *habitus* in order to stimulate critical thinking. Fifth, integrate these four approaches through decentralized and diverse, grassroots leadership to create entrepreneurial advocates and leaders.

Note

1 "Local culture" is considered, of course, to be those people in a particular place who view themselves as a collective and who share common experiences, traits, values, attitudes, traditions, and institutions that distinguish them from other people.

References

Acs, Z., & Armington, C. (2006). *Entrepreneurship, geography, and American economic growth*. Cambridge, UK: Cambridge University Press.

Acs, Z., Szerb, L., & Autio, E. (2016). *Global entrepreneurship index*. Washington, DC: Global Entrepreneurship and Development Institute.

Amorós, J. E., & Bosma, N. (2014). *Global entrepreneurship monitor 2013 global report*. Washington, DC: Global Entrepreneurship Research Association.
Aoyama, Y. (2009). Entrepreneurship and regional culture: The case of Hamamatsu and Kyoto, Japan. *Regional Studies*, *43*(3), 495–512.
Berger, A., & Udell, G. (2004). The institutional memory hypothesis and the procyclicality of bank lending. *Journal of Financial Intermediation*, *13*(4), 458–495.
Besser, T., & Miller, N. J. (2013). Community matters: Successful entrepreneurship in remote rural US locations. *Entrepreneurship and Innovation*, *14*(1), 15–27.
Beugelsdijk, S. (2007). Entrepreneurial culture, regional innovativeness and economic growth. *Journal of Evolutionary Economics*, *17*, 187–210.
Bornstein, D. (2007). *How to change the world: Social entrepreneurs and the power of new ideas*. Oxford, UK: Oxford University Press.
Bornstein, D., & Davis, S. (2010). *Social entrepreneurship: What everyone needs to know?* Oxford, UK: Oxford University Press.
Bourdieu, P. (1977). *Outline of a theory of practice*. Cambridge, UK: Cambridge University Press.
Bourdieu, P. (1986). The forms of capital. In J. Richardson (Ed.), *Handbook of theory and research for the sociology of education* (pp. 241–258). New York, NY: Greenwood Press.
Breazeale, N., Fortunato, M., Allen, J., Hustedde, R., & Pushkarskaya, H. (2015). Constructing a multi-dimensional measure of local entrepreneurial culture. *Community Development*, *46*(5), 516–540.
Chatman, D., Altman, I., & Johnson, T. (2008). Community entrepreneurial climate: An analysis of small business owners' perspectives in 12 small towns in Missouri, USA. *Journal of Rural and Community Development*, *3*, 60–77.
Dana, L. (1995). Entrepreneurship in a remote sub-arctic community. *Entrepreneurship Theory & Practice*, *20*, 57–71.
Dana, L., & Dana, T. (2005). Expanding the scope of methodologies used in entrepreneurship research. *International Journal of Entrepreneurship and Small Business*, *2*(1), 79–88.
de Clercq, D., & Voronov, M. (2009a). Towards a practice perspective of entrepreneurship: Entrepreneurial legitimacy as habitus. *International Small Business Journal*, *27*(4), 395–419.
de Clercq, D., & Voronov, M. (2009b). The role of cultural and symbolic capital in entrepreneurs' ability to meet expectations about conformity and innovation. *Journal of Small Business Management*, *47*(3), 398–420.
Dimitratos, P., Voudouris, I., Plakoyiannaki, E., & Nakos, G. (2012). International entrepreneurial culture—toward a comprehensive opportunity-based operationalization of international entrepreneurship. *International Business Review*, *21*, 708–721.
Durkheim, E. (1984). *The division of labor in society*. New York, NY: Free Press.
Entrepreneurship for the public good. (2016). Berea, Kentucky: Berea College. Retrieved on July 27, 2016 from http://104.131.44.191/en/about-us/about/
Fischer, W. (1987). *Human communication as narration*. Columbia, SC: University of South Carolina Press.
Fortunato, M. W-P (2014). Supporting rural entrepreneurship: A review of conceptual developments from research to practice. *Community Development*, *45*, 387–408.

Fortunato, M. W-P, & McLaughlin, D. K. (2012). Interaction and purpose in highly entrepreneurial communities. *Entrepreneurship Research Journal*, *2*(1), 1–34.

Frazier, B., Stoel, L., Niehm, L., & Eckerson, N. (2013). Optimism for new business survival in rural communities: An institutional perspective. *Journal of Small Business & Entrepreneurship*, *26*(5), 443–462.

Fritsch, M., & Wyrwich, M. (2012). *The long persistence of regional entrepreneurship culture: Germany 1925–2005*. Discussion papers. Berlin: German Institute for Economic Research. Retrieved on July 27, 2016 from https://www.diw.de/documents/publikationen/73/diw_01.c.405874.de/dp1224.pdf

Gaventa, J. (1982). *Power and powerlessness: Quiescence and rebellion in an Appalachian valley*. Champaign, IL: University of Illinois Press.

Giddens, A. (1991). *Modernity and self-identity: Self and society in the late modern age*. Stanford, CA: Stanford University Press.

The Global Entrepreneurship and Development Institute (GEDI). (2016). Retrieved from https://thegedi.org/

Global Entrepreneurship Monitor (GEM). (2016). Retrieved from http://www.gemconsortium.org/

Goetz, S., & Freshwater, D. (2001). State-level determinants of entrepreneurship and a preliminary measure of entrepreneurial climate. *Economic Development Quarterly*, *15*, 58–70.

Granovetter, M. (1985). Economic action and social structure: The problem of embeddedness. *American Journal of Sociology*, *91*, 481–510.

Gruidl, J., & Markley, D. (2015). Entrepreneurship as a community development strategy. In R. Phillips & R. Pittman (Eds.), *An introduction to community development* (pp. 278–294). New York, NY: Routledge.

Hayden, J. C., & Cacciotti, G. (2013). Is there an entrepreneurial culture? A review of empirical research. *Entrepreneurship & Regional Development*, *25*(9–10), 708–731.

Hofstede, G. (2001). *Culture's consequences: Comparing values, behaviors, institutions and organizations across nations* (2nd ed.). Thousand Oaks, CA: Sage.

Hofstede, G., Noorderhaven, G., Thurik, A., Uhlaner, L., Wennekers, A., & Wilderman, R. (2004.) Culture's role in entrepreneurship: Self-employment out of dissatisfaction. In *Innovation, entrepreneurship and culture: The interaction between technology, progress and economic* (pp. 162–203). SSRN. Retrieved on July 27, 2016 from http://ssrn.com/abstract=1496783http://ssrn.com/abstract=1496783

Huggins, R., & Thompson, P. (2012). Entrepreneurship and community culture: A place-based study of their interdependency. *Entrepreneurship Research Journal*, *2*(1), 1–34.

Hustedde, R. (2007). What's culture got to do with it? Strategies for strengthening entrepreneurial culture. In N. Walzer (Ed.), *Entrepreneurship and local economic development* (pp. 39–58). Lanham, MD: Lexington Books.

Hustedde, R. (2008). Seven theories for seven community developers, In R. Phillips & R. Pittman (Eds.), *An introduction to community development* (1st ed., pp. 20–37). New York, NY: Taylor & Francis.

Isenberg, D. J. (2010, June). How to start an entrepreneurial revolution, *Harvard Business Review*, 41–50.

Johansson, F. (2004). *The Medici effect: Breakthrough insights at the intersection of ideas, concepts and cultures*. Boston, MA: Harvard Business School Press.

Julien, P-A. (2007). *A theory of local entrepreneurship in the knowledge economy*. Northampton, MA: Edward Elgar.

Kibler, E. (2013). Formation of entrepreneurial intentions in a regional context. *Entrepreneurship & Regional Development, 25*, 293–323.

Klyver, K., & Thornton, P. (2010). *The cultural embeddedness of entrepreneurial self-efficacy and intentions: A cross-national comparison*. Paper presented at Fourth Global Entrepreneurship Monitor Research Conference, London, United Kingdom.

Kwon, S-W., Heflin, C., & Ruef, M. (2013). Community social capital and entrepreneurship. *American Sociological Review, 78*(6), 980–1008.

Low, S., Henderson, J., & Weiler, S. (2005). Gauging a region's entrepreneurial potential. *Economic Review—Federal Reserve Bank of Kansas, 90*, 61–89.

Luloff, A., & Bridger, J. (2003). Community agency and local development. In D. Brown & L. Swanson (Eds.), *Challenges for rural America in the twenty-first century* (pp. 203–213). University Park, PA: Pennsylvania State University Press.

Lyons, T., Alter, T., Audretsch, D., & Augustine, D. (2012). Entrepreneurship and community: The next frontier of entrepreneurship inquiry. *Entrepreneurship Research Journal, 2*(1), 1–24.

Malecki, E. J. (1997). Entrepreneurs, networks, and economic development: A review of recent research. In J. A. Katz (Ed.), *Advances in entrepreneurship, firm emergence and growth* (Vol. 3, pp. 57–118). Greenwich, CT: JAI Press.

Malecki, E. J. (2006). How development occurs: Local knowledge, social capital, and institutional embeddedness. *Urbana, 8*, 1–25.

Markley, D. M., & Dabson, B. (2008). *Creating a system of support for entrepreneurs and small businesses in Kentucky: Insights and policy recommendations*. Berea, KY: Mountain Association for Community Economic Development.

Markley, D. M., Lyons, T. S., & Macke, D. W. (2015). Creating entrepreneurial communities: Building community capacity for ecosystem development. *Community Development, 46*(5), 580–598.

Marquez-Lopez, J. C., Guzman, C., & Linan, F. (2013). Could the perception about entrepreneurial culture be explained by demographic variables? In A. Fayolle, P. Kyro, T. Mets, & U. Venesaar (Eds.), *Conceptual richness and methodological diversity in entrepreneurship research* (pp. 47–65). Northampton, MA: Edward Elgar.

Nakata, C., & Sivakumar, K. (1996). National culture and new product development: An integrative review. *Journal of Marketing, 60*, 61–72.

Polanyi, K. (1957). *The great transformation: The political and economic origin of our time*. Boston, MA: Beacon Hill.

Rapasingha, A., & Goetz, S. (2013). Self-employment and local economic performance: Evidence from US counties. *Papers in Regional Science, 92*, 141–161.

Roithmayr, D. (2011). Structure and/or culture. *JOTWELL*. (reviewing Wilson, W. J. (2009). Toward a framework for understanding forces that contribute to or reinforce racial inequality. *Race and Social Problems, 1*(1), 1–33. Retrieved on July 27, 2016 from http://juris.jotwell.com/structure-andor-culture/

Roxas, H. B., & Azmat, F. (2014). Community social capital and entrepreneurship: Analyzing the links. *Community Development, 45*, 134–149.

Schumpeter, J. (1934). *The theory of economic development: An inquiry into profits, capital, credit, interest, and the business cycle*. New York, NY: Transaction Publishers.

Shapiro, R. (Ed.). (2012). *The real problem solvers: Social entrepreneurs in America.* Stanford, CA: Stanford University Press.

Sirolli, E. (1999). *Ripples from the Zambezi.* Vancouver, Canada: New Society Publishers.

Sirolli, E. (2012). *How to start a business and ignite your life: A simple guide to combining business wisdom with passion.* New York, NY: Square One Publishers.

Spigel, B. (2013). Bourdieuian approaches to the geography of entrepreneurial cultures. *Entrepreneurship & Development: An International Journal, 25*(9), 804–818.

Terjesen, S., & Elam, A. (2009). Transnational entrepreneurs' venture internationalization strategies: A practice theory approach. *Entrepreneurship Theory and Practice, 33*(5), 1093–1120.

Thornton, P., & Flynn, K. (2003). Entrepreneurship, networks, and geographies. In Z. Acs & D. Audretsch (Eds.), *Handbook of entrepreneurship research* (pp. 401–433). Leiden, The Netherlands: Kluwer Law International.

Weber, M. (1930). *The protestant ethic and the spirit of capitalism.* New York, NY: Routledge.

Welter, F. (2011). Contextualizing entrepreneurship—conceptual challenges and ways forward. *Entrepreneurship, Theory, and Practice, 35*(1), 165–184.

Wennberg, K., Pathak, S., & Autio, E. (2013). How culture moulds the effects of self-efficacy and fear of failure on entrepreneurship. *Entrepreneurship & Regional Development: An International Journal, 25*(9–10), 756–780.

Wilson, W. J. (2009). Toward a framework for understanding forces that contribute to or reinforce racial inequality. *Race and Social Problems, 1*(1), 1–33.

5 Transformational Leadership to Build an Entrepreneurial Community

Morgan R. Clevenger and Chao Miao

Leadership is a critical topic for both researchers and practitioners (Barling, Christie, & Hoption, 2011; Bonjean & Olson, 1964; Bradberry & Greaves, 2012; Hackman & Johnson, 2009; Morris & Seeman, 1950; Pierce & Newstrom, 2008a, 2008b; Smilor & Sexton, 1996). The concept of leadership takes on various forms and meanings depending upon the context and application (Bolman & Deal, 1996; Pierce & Newstrom, 2008b). Researchers typically define leadership according to their particular discipline, background, or field of interest, and definitions may illuminate a range of attributes, styles, or actions including traits, behavior, interaction patterns, and roles (Hackman & Johnson, 2009; Northouse, 2015; Pierce & Newstrom, 2008a). Dimensions of leadership include persuasion, influence, goals, followers, structure, and power relationships. Leadership is a key contributing variable in entrepreneurial community ecosystems because leaders shape and improve organizational functionality and influence change (Antonakis & Autio, 2007; Bolman & Deal, 1996; Feld, 2012; Wilkinson, 1991). While a great deal of theory and practice has been developed regarding leadership, its application in communities continues to be explored and expanded (Banyai, 2009). Some researchers are hesitant to dig deep into community relations, leadership, and entrepreneurship because it is often perceived that the community takes more from the academy than they return to it (Churchill & Lewis, 1986). Feld (2012) and Isenberg (2010) believe entrepreneurs themselves are leaders in start-up communities. All of the rest of the actors are followers, who should not try to lead because they typically "mess things up" by implementing programs that are better suited for governments and larger institutions—not entrepreneurs. While entrepreneurs can be leaders, non-entrepreneurs abound, and they play vital roles in the community to support entrepreneurial communities and help to create acceptability for the culture and resources necessary to facilitate a process. This chapter explores a conceptual idea of the process of transformational leadership in supporting entrepreneurs and the entrepreneurial culture.

The Importance of Leadership in Entrepreneurial Community Development

Banyai (2009) said, "Leadership is the driving force behind development and the channel through which the characteristics to improve community capacity flow" (p. 241). Such leadership is the starting point for entrepreneurial community development. The development of an entrepreneurial community may depend heavily on entrepreneurially minded leaders, as each leader's capacity and preference for innovation and risk may also encourage new ventures of teams to surmount riskiness of newness (Antonakis & Autio, 2007; Banyai, 2009; Nambisan & Baron, 2013; Singh, Tucker, & House, 1986).

Most current scholars believe leadership skills can be developed (George, 2004; Northouse, 2015; Yukl, 2012). Developing core leadership skills for use in the community and specifically the entrepreneurial community include conceptual, administrative, and interpersonal skills (Northouse, 2015). However, only recently have leadership constructs begun to be examined in the entrepreneurship literature and contexts (Engelen, Gupta, Strenger, & Brettel, 2015). The study of leadership itself grew greatly after World War II in the United States (Morris & Seeman, 1950). For community leadership, a key question was "who has responsibility to govern," and the key issue was defining power and span of control (Bonjean & Olson, 1964; Hunter, 1953). Hunter's (1953) *Community Power Structure* leaned toward government and other elected or paid professionals as decision-making leaders—including business, but overlooked private organizational positions. Evolving from Hunter's positional approach, other ideas emerged including the reputational approach, the decisional approach, the *Covert Power Elite* view, and finally the leadership model (Bonjean & Olson, 1964). In 1978, Doolittle and MacDonald created the *Sense of Community Scale* with a 40-item evaluation tool to assess attitudes and behaviors in communities and neighborhoods. Concerns of safety, interaction, privacy, neighbor perception, and commitment to locality were considered. Emerging from those various theories were four characteristics of community leadership: legitimacy, visibility, scope of influence, and cohesiveness (Bonjean & Olson, 1964).

Kirk and Shutte (2004) and Yukl (2012) indicate community leadership is sociocultural leadership and serves the collective environment found in communities. Transformational leaders serving community development possess all of those important facets necessary for community leadership. Additionally, these transformational leaders serve as change agents (Avolio & Bass, 1988; Pierce & Newstrom, 2008b). This form of leadership is also as a member of the community of practice and is not seen as a hierarchical dynamic (Horner, 1997).

"Community leadership enables members of the community to take initiative to pursue the vision of the community, as well as realise community objectives" (Banyai, 2009, p. 241). Leadership has increasingly been shown to be an important integrating and aligning mechanism that shapes environment and culture (Banyai, 2009; Engelen et al., 2015; Panagopoulos & Avlonitis, 2010). Leaders also help to form a culture where the interests of its members are aligned (Bass & Steidlmeier, 1999). Under the influence of a strong culture where all entities share a set of common norms, values, and beliefs, leaders are able to foster an entrepreneurial community where interconnected entities' knowledge, skills, and abilities may co-evolve and work collaboratively to develop new products and services (Eggers & Smilor, 1996; Moore, 1993; Nambisan & Baron, 2013).

Feld (2012) provides four basic attributes for leadership: be inclusive, play a non-zero-sum game, be mentorship driven, and have porous boundaries. Feld's actions are to give people assignments, experiment, and fail fast. These actions are cyclical in nature.

Katz (1955, 1974) and Northouse (2015), on the other hand, elaborate on developing core leadership skills for use in the community to include conceptual, administrative, and interpersonal skills. First, *conceptual skills* are the foundation of leadership development and include creative visioning, problem solving, and strategic planning (Northouse, 2015). Second, *administrative skills*—while not glamorous—create a platform for actions including managing resources, managing people, and utilizing technical skills (Northouse, 2015). Finally, *interpersonal skills* aid in managing people, accomplishing goals, fostering the transformative environment. Interpersonal skills include being socially perceptive, showing *emotional intelligence*, and managing expectations and interpersonal conflict (Bradberry & Greaves, 2012; Northouse, 2015). Specifically, emotional intelligence is likely the most important consideration in transformational leadership: knowing one's own intent and motives, and being sensitive to others' intent, motives, and timing (Bradberry & Greaves, 2012). Emotional intelligence includes self-awareness, self-management, social awareness, and relationship management (Bradberry & Greaves, 2012) and is shown to impact leader effectiveness (Miao, Humphrey, & Qian, 2016).

The Concept and Shaping of Community

Warren (1987) said, "The idea of the American community is deceptively simple, as long as one does not require a rigid definition" (p. 1). In a traditional sense, a community is defined by geographic location or social ties (Banyai, 2009; Bowman, 1932; Gusfield, 1975; McMillan & Chavis, 1986). Examples of geographic boundaries include concepts such as towns, boroughs, counties, utility zones, voting precincts, or school districts. Durkheim (1964) observed that modern communities share interests and skills and not necessarily locality (e.g., professional, spiritual, economic, etc.). Finally, Aldrich and Zimmer (1986) and Feld (2012) indicate the geographic concentration creates a *network effect*, which are systems where other participants enhance value for other users. Unification of a community may rally around common issues, which are social concepts congregated to focus on a character of human relationships. Simple forms such as a prairie school house doubling for politics and church is an example. Today, however, a community involves a pluralistic group of organizations as actors of various sizes—for-profit and nonprofit, public and private, large and small, etc.—that interact with supplemental and complementary capacities. A more modern definition of community explained by Banyai (2009) would be

> [an] area, such as an administrative unit, and all of the relevant stakeholders in that area including, but not limited to residents, local administration, institutions, private enterprises with interest or activities in the area, and the civil society organisations with membership or activities within the area.
>
> (p. 242)

A community is complex with "competing and complementary needs, desires, and perceptions among the stakeholders" (Banyai, p. 243). Community members are most successful when they learn to contribute or give before taking (Feld, 2012).

While individual actors participate in the community, leaders take on the role to facilitate the process and ultimately pursue goals. One might conceive the establishment of a community by picturing the creation of a mosaic, stained glass window, tapestry, or quilt. Depending on the economic utility, the actors, leaders, and community form various arrangements to prepare and produce the form or relationships or community interactions. However, communities are not static such as the mosaic, stained glass, tapestry, or quilt; rather communities are dynamic, emergent, and iterative in their processes. A basis for developing communities stems from three key elements with contextual influences: community capacity attributes, community agents, and community actions (Banyai, 2009). *Community capacity* would be the rudiments of creation, establishment, goals, and participants. *Community agents* are all actors and leaders—the participants, which can be individuals, organizations, or networks. "Community agents are the mechanisms through which community actions are performed and through which development subsequently occurs" (Banyai, 2009, p. 241). *Community actions*, then, are the purposeful engagement and continual process of acting to further the interests and affairs of the community. Therefore, "community leadership connects people and empowers them to pursue their individual and collective goals, thus allowing community members to take ownership of collective goals" (Banyai, 2009, p. 246).

Of the various considerations of leadership, *transformational leadership* tends to be the emphasis for the greatest impact to contribute to entrepreneurial community development because of its ability to shift paradigms, create new directions, and unify constituents. Additionally, entrepreneurial community culture is a vital component transcending and yet binding coalitions, individual entrepreneurial agents, and both formal and informal voices. Transformational leaders shape entrepreneurial community culture and serve as change agents. While the ultimate goal is inclusiveness, the entrepreneurial community culture may serve as a funnel to screen in and out entrepreneurial firms. The conceptual model of this process is illustrated in Figure 5.1, and it creates a visual representation of an ongoing, dynamic process that will be discussed later in this chapter. The process includes three propositions regarding the actors that impact the entrepreneurial community development process with an emphasis of transformational leadership, community amenities, and cyclical manifestation to develop and sustain entrepreneurial culture formation.

A Backdrop to Various Approaches of Leadership

Leadership exists at various dimensions and levels of analysis within a community: formal and informal, elected officials, key citizens, entrepreneurs, industry representatives, and businesses and nonprofits of various sizes. Important considerations of community leaders' styles include such concepts as traits, abilities, skills, behaviors, relationships, and processes that are manifested in psychological, behavioral, and actionable behaviors with labels such as transactional, transformational, servant, shared, authentic, distributed, leader-member exchange, etc. The implications of leadership responsibilities on fostering both community cultures and entrepreneurial community development create an important function to facilitate the iterative development and redevelopment cycle. There are three major theoretical approaches to leadership: trait-based approach, behavioral approach, and situational approach (Northouse, 2015).

Trait-Based Approach

The trait-based approach, also known as the "great man" approach to leadership, supports that stable and inheritable traits differentiate leaders from non-leaders (Kirkpatrick & Locke, 1996). Nineteenth and early 20th Century thought postulated that leaders were born, not made. Some of these inheritable traits may include but not are not limited to cognitive ability, personality, physical appearance, and gender (Barling et al., 2011; Kirkpatrick & Locke, 1996; Miao & Qian, 2016; Miao, Qian, & Ma, 2017).

The trait-based approaches to leadership have received an abundant amount of coverage in the literature through meta-analytic reviews (Derue, Nahrgang, Wellman, & Humphrey, 2011; Hoffman, Woehr, Maldagen-Youngjohn, & Lyons, 2011; Judge, Bono, Ilies, & Gerhardt, 2002; Judge, Colbert, & Ilies, 2004). These reviews are important for understanding various dimensions, but research is inconclusive on any single trait or variable leading to success (Northouse, 2015). However, evidence suggests the

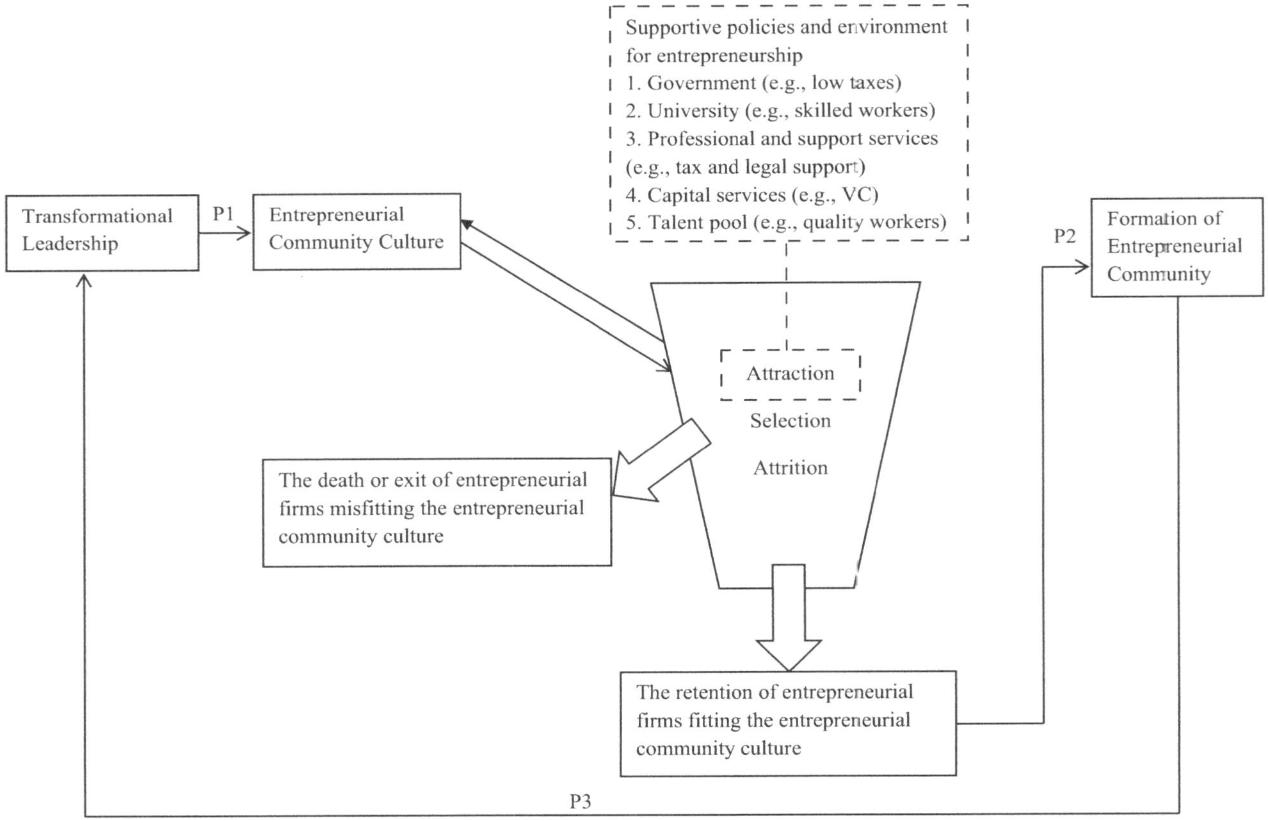

Figure 5.1 Transformational Leadership Process in the Entrepreneurial Community Development Process diagram to develop an entrepreneurial community. Variables include transformational leadership, community amenities attracting entrepreneurs or raising up entrepreneurs, creating a community culture, and dynamic emergence of new leaders.

traits roll up into categories, and various categories of traits—not individual traits—have been proved to matter. Such categories include strategy, ethics, action, cognitive ability, and problem solving (Bradberry & Greaves, 2012; Hackman & Johnson, 2009; Kirkpatrick & Locke, 1996; Pierce & Newstrom, 2008a). Strategy includes vision, acumen, planning, and drive to lead (Bradberry & Greaves, 2012). Ethics includes personal character mastery of integrity, credibility, and diversity as well as application through fairness, information sharing, and concern of well-being of others. Cognitive abilities include lifelong learning, emotional intelligence, and communication. Problem solving includes risk taking, agility, and goal attainment.

The Behavioral Approach

The behavioral approach to leadership has tried to identify universally effective leadership behaviors. Behavioral approaches allow leaders to choose actions and leverage relationships. Three of the most positively discussed behavioral approach leadership styles for effective local leadership are *authentic*, *shared*, and *transformational*. Heifitz (1994) referred to these approaches as adaptive leadership. Additionally, Bradberry and Greaves (2012) identify character, emotional intelligence, organizational justice, and ongoing development of self and others as adaptive leadership. All of these styles emphasize both the leader's core beliefs and behaviors as well as their approach to building and maintaining strong leader-follower relationships between the leader and others.

Authentic leadership emphasizes the authentic self (Avolio & Gardner, 2005; Avolio, Walumbwa, & Weber, 2009; Feld, 2012; Gardner, Cogliser, Davis, & Dickens, 2011; Walumbwa, Avolio, Gardner, Wernsing, & Peterson, 2008). This characterization is one reflecting a harmony within a leader's personality, makeup, and character and is rooted in a genuine desire to serve others (George, 2004). George (2004) highlights five dimensions of this authentic focus: passion, values, heart, emphasis on relationships, and self-discipline, and promotes that these are the qualities that make authentic leaders. In a similar vein, Shamir and Eilam (2005) summarize a set of key defining characteristics of authentic leaders into four aspects, suggesting that authentic leaders (1) do not fake their leadership; (2) do not just undertake leadership roles for honor, status, or other personal rewards; (3) are originals, not duplicates; and (4) are leaders whose actions originate from their values and convictions. Akin to this concept are also servant leadership and spiritual leadership. *Servant leadership* considers followers and community goals greater than the actual leader and emphasizes care of people as most important (Robert K. Greenleaf Center for Servant Leadership, 2016). Characteristics of servant leaders include such ideas as empowering and developing people, authenticity, humility, providing direction, interpersonal acceptance, and stewardship (Van Dierendonck, 2011). *Spiritual leadership* includes values reflecting a higher power (Northouse, 2015). Spiritual leaders form a vision wherein organizational members experience a sense of calling and create a social culture based on altruistic love (Fry, 2003). Both authentic leadership and spiritual leadership may be found in communities, nonprofit organizations or causes, religious entities, and organizations based on deep ethical commitments.

Many different types of work—such as knowledge-based work—is increasingly team-based; as such, it becomes a daunting challenge for any one person to be an expert on every aspect of the work across a variety of different contexts (Pearce, 2004). This structural change in the design of modern work challenges the conventional model of vertical leadership where one person (i.e., a leader) dictates all other persons (i.e., followers) in a given unit. Recent research advocates that when a work task requires a high level of interdependence, creativity, and complexity, leadership should be shared by leaders and followers to unleash the fullest potential of the team (Ensley, Hmieleski, & Pearce, 2006; Pearce, 2004; Pearce & Sims, 2002). This concept of leadership is known as *shared leadership* (or also called distributive or collective leadership), which refers to a willingness to have joint ownership of authority to lead or manage (Yukl, 2012). The successes of co-sharing responsibilities centralizes shared goals, creating ongoing mutual support, and *voice*, the concept that each member has equal involvement and/or input into decision making (Avolio et al., 2009; Carson, Tesluk, & Marrone, 2007; Pearce & Conger, 2002; Yukl, 2012). A recent meta-analysis confirmed a positive relationship between shared leadership and team effectiveness (Wang, Waldman, & Zhang, 2014). Shared leadership is likely the key for community leaders to create shared purpose effectively (Avolio et al., 2009).

Dynamic entrepreneurial communities emphasize creativity, change, growth, accessibility, and improvement, making *transformational* leadership a potential key emphasis. Transformational leadership is coordinating people, causes, organizations, or communities to a higher performance or quality level (Avolio & Bass, 1988; Burns, 1978). These goals meet "more universal needs and purposes" (Bolman & Deal, 2008, p. 368). Transformational leaders lead others by co-creating a purpose that transcends short-term goals and concentrates on their followers' higher order intrinsic needs rather than just focusing on the efficient exchange of resources (Wofford, Goodwin, & Whittington, 1998). Leaders who focus exclusively on the exchange of resources, whose leadership can be measured by the completion of tasks, can be called transactional leaders (Judge & Piccolo, 2004). Burns (1978) indicates transactional leaders "approach followers with an eye to exchanging one thing for another" (p. 3). In comparison to transactional leaders—often viewed as a negative behavioral approach—transformational leaders are more likely to produce dramatic and systematic changes in the organizations they lead because of their unconventional leadership methods (Judge & Piccolo, 2004). Burns (1978) described transformational leaders as raising "one another to higher levels of motivation and morality" (p. 20).

Many of these needs considerations tied heavily to the work of Maslow (1954). Transformational leadership has been shown through research to be a predictor of important individual, team, and organizational-level outcomes, such as job satisfaction, motivation, task performance, contextual performance (i.e., organizational citizenship behavior), creative performance, team performance, and organization performance (Avolio & Bass, 1988; Derue et al., 2011; Judge & Piccolo, 2004; Wang, Oh, Courtright, & Colbert, 2011; Wofford et al., 1998). Among the different leadership styles, transformational leadership is also the one that is most relevant to entrepreneurship because empirical evidence has demonstrated that transformational leadership positively impacts product innovation, organizational revitalization, business venturing, and encouraging an entrepreneurial orientation (Baum, Locke, & Kirkpatrick, 1998; Gumusluoğlu & Ilsev, 2009; Hackman & Johnson, 2009; Ling, Simsek, Lubatkin, & Veiga, 2008; Wofford et al., 1998; Zahra, 1996). Part of the transformational leadership role is often a supporting role of entrepreneurs (Feld, 2012). Leaders can serve as a conduit of network resources and other people in the entrepreneurial ecosystem. This type of behavior is the essence of transformational leadership.

A key attribute of transformational leaders is their creative capacity to be innovative and forward thinking (Hackman & Johnson, 2009). Additionally, transformational leaders are interactive, visionary, empowering, passionate, and ethical (Hackman & Johnson, 2009). These attributes are often described separately as charismatic leadership (Pierce & Newstrom, 2008a; Weber, 2012). Charisma is considered a relational component. Scholars differ in relating or distinguishing charismatic leadership from transformational leadership. Shamir, House, and Arthur (1993) couched charismatic leadership in self-concept based theory and argued that charismatic leaders produce transformational effects via implicating the self-concept of followers by increasing the intrinsic value of efforts and goals. More specifically, charismatic leaders tried to connect followers' efforts and goals to valued aspects of followers' self-concept, therefore harvesting the motivational effects of self-consistency, self-esteem, self-expression, and self-worth. These effects are successful with positive charismatic leadership.

Situational Approaches

In contrast to the trait-based and behavioral based approaches, the situational or contingent approach to leadership suggests that leader emergence and effectiveness is contingent on situational characteristics, including characteristics of an organization, workplace, and followers (Barling et al., 2011). Stogdill (1974) said, "The qualities, characteristics, and skills required in a leader are determined to a large extent by the demands of the situation in which [s]he is to function as a leader" (p. 63). Compared to the trait-based and behavioral approaches to leadership, this stream of leadership research allows leaders to select from all leadership styles to apply as needed. Some scholars and practitioners find this option incongruent and manipulative. Others believe having the option to act allows greater flexibility. Such options based on situation include path-goal theory, contingency theory, and situational theory (Pierce & Newstrom, 2008a).

The first situational behavior option is House's (1971) path-goal theory. *Path-goal theory* is rooted in expectancy theory based on attitude and behavior predicted from expectancy and valences (Vroom, 1964). Motivation is influenced for subordinates' productivity and goal attainment. Concerns include a combination of support, intrinsic and extrinsic influence, job satisfaction, and leader directiveness. The combination of subordinate demeanor and environmental factors yields a variety of options for goal attainment by combining various path options.

The second method of situational behavior is Fiedler's (1972) *contingency theory*. This theory includes leader-member relations, positional power, the leader's motivation, and a leader's influence with subordinates. While individuals' behaviors can be measured and plotted, the challenge becomes providing the right leader for the right follower for the right task(s). Changing the circumstances, goal, or participants creates a challenging dynamic here. However, Fiedler's efforts concluded that there is not one best leadership style, but any given leader is not always effective in all circumstances. Additionally, leadership can be conditioned or learned.

The third example of *situational theory behavior* is Hersey and Blanchard's (1988) Situational Leadership® based on task behavior and relationship behavior to accomplish goals. Three factors interplay: (1) guidance or direction from a leader, (2) socio-emotional support from a leader, and (3) readiness level of the follower (Hersey & Blanchard, 1988). From the three variables, styles emerge to best predict performance. This model has been used successfully for decades in many U.S. companies to evaluate workers and match appropriate tasks to achieve goals.

From an entrepreneur standpoint, these traditional situational models are used as needed based on the actors and situations presented. Entrepreneurs are more likely to be transformational leaders yet act and react based on other peoples' and other organizations' actions and reactions.

Leadership: A Process Model

Figure 5.1 illustrates the dynamic impact of leadership, community amenities for entrepreneurs, entrepreneurial creation, and reinvestment into the entrepreneurial ecosystem. Three propositions create the explanation of the flow of this process: (P1) the relevance of transformational leadership, (P2) the formation of the entrepreneurial community, and (P3) entrepreneurial leadership. This process is a dynamic engagement of all community actors, the support network, and each entrepreneur.

Proposition 1: The Relevance of Transformational Leadership

The concept of transformational leadership has slowly come to light over the past few decades, and it has been shown to be an effective leadership style that positively influences outcomes in various settings including business and entrepreneurship (Avolio, 2011; Avolio & Bass, 2004; Bass, 1985, 1998; Bass & Riggio, 2005; Bono & Judge, 2004; Bradberry & Greaves, 2012; Hackman & Johnson, 2009; Pierce & Newstrom, 2008a; Rafferty & Griffin, 2008). Transformational leaders often see the leadership potential in every member of an organization or community and are typically good at co-establishing goals and at helping organization members to agree on common goals through supportive leadership (Avolio, 2011; Humphrey, 2013; Rafferty & Griffin, 2008). Additionally, transformational leaders are effective communicators of goals and visions so that they can cultivate high goal congruence among their followers to let them cooperatively work well together (Colbert, Kristof-Brown, Bradley, & Barrick, 2008; Rafferty & Griffin, 2008).

The Four 'I's of Transformational Leadership

Transformational leadership consists of four major components, known as the four "I"s of transformational leadership: idealized influence, inspirational motivation, intellectual stimulation, and individualized consideration (Humphrey, 2013). The first "I" of transformational leadership is *idealized influence* by which leaders act as role models who demonstrate high standards of ethical conduct and inspire loyalty, respect, trust, and identification from followers (Bass & Riggio, 2005; Bono & Judge, 2004).

The second "I" refers to *inspirational motivation* by which leaders inspire their followers by shaping a strong vision for the future, offering challenge and meaning to their followers, and instilling enthusiasm, confidence, and optimism in their followers (Bass & Riggio, 2005; Bono & Judge, 2004). The followers who work with leaders using inspirational motivation are more likely to have high goal commitment (Piccolo & Colquitt, 2006). This joint ownership creates combined attention for positive engagement.

The third "I" dimension of transformational leadership is *intellectual stimulation* by which leaders encourage innovation, creativity, divergent thinking, and norm-breaking (Bass & Riggio, 2005; Bono & Judge, 2004). Entrepreneurs often initiate newness through invention, extension, imitation, or synthesis of innovation (Clevenger, 2017).

The last "I" component of transformational leadership is *individualized consideration* by which leaders become mentors to their followers by coaching and consulting with their followers and by providing help to their followers to satisfy their needs for growth and accomplishment (Bass & Riggio, 2005; Bono & Judge, 2004). This concept is empowerment (Kirk & Shutte, 2004). Empowerment is appreciating others' competence, being open and honest on all accounts, being reliable with joint ownership, and trust (Hackman & Johnson, 2009). These relationship ties and behaviors create an environment to allow for trial-and-error, exploration, failure, and ultimately success.

Transformational leadership is particularly relevant for fostering the formation of entrepreneurial community culture (Engelen et al., 2015; Gumusluoğlu & Ilsev, 2009; Jaskyte, 2004; Sarros, Cooper, & Santora, 2008). Leaders are the ones who maintain responsibility for unifying objectives shared among community members, supporting community members to overcome the liabilities of newness and smallness, and facilitating the construction of a platform where community members can thrive and collaborate together via resource exchanges (Nambisan & Baron, 2013; Singh, Tucker, & House, 1986). Existing leaders may be considered or known as "definers" and "givers" of culture, as they are the antecedents of existing culture. Transformational leaders link the past culture and history while understanding, cultivating, and building the values, beliefs, and assumptions shared across community members (Jaskyte, 2004). A purposeful process creates an ongoing dynamic among actors of both individuals and entrepreneurial firms. "Transformational leaders can help supply long-term vision to entrepreneurial endeavors by bringing meaning to otherwise disconnected activities" (Ensley, Pearce, & Hmieleski, 2006, p. 250). Such a long-term vision may include big-picture and abstract ideas (Wofford et al., 1998).

Culture

Culture refers to "the collective programming of the mind that distinguishes the members of one group or category of people from another" (Hofstede, 2001, p. 9). Culture is the only factor unanimously agreed to be beneficial and important to the development of entrepreneurial community (Cohen, 2006). Theories from the fields of organizational behavior and management and apply to this context. Entrepreneurial community culture refers to cultural norms that allows and encourage people within in that culture to act entrepreneurially by providing a supportive environment that breeds entrepreneurial activities and fosters collective beliefs, values, and minds about entrepreneurship (Coleman & Kariv, 2014; Fortunato & Clevenger, 2015; Huggins & Thompson, 2012; Marti, Courpasson, & Barbosa, 2013). Oftentimes an entrepreneurial environment is enriched when innovative or creative people are attracted with their ideas (Florida, 2002, 2012). Entrepreneurial community culture provides an incubating, entrepreneurial social infrastructure that will produce, cultivate, and maintain the social relationships among like-minded members, thus improving members' entrepreneurial capacity and entrepreneurial potential (Flora & Flora, 1993; Huggins & Thompson, 2012; Woolcock, 1998). This culture boosts community members' willingness and confidence to participate in activities related to the development of new business ventures (Huggins & Thompson, 2012). In light of the significant influence of entrepreneurial community culture on entrepreneurial activities, an entrepreneurial community culture serves as an important context for the cultivation of an entrepreneurial community.

Transformational leaders are the architects of entrepreneurial community culture because transformational leaders advocate and foster entrepreneurship by motivating community members to constantly experiment with new ideas, reframe problems, and challenge existing situations, and they have enormous amount of energy and commitment dedicated to entrepreneurship (Eisenbeiss, van Knippenberg, & Boerner, 2008; Engelen et al., 2015; Sarros et al., 2008). To produce entrepreneurial community culture, transformational leaders integrate creative thoughts and energy and create a sense of purpose and a feeling of family based on long-term commitment so that leaders and community members share a sense of shared fates toward entrepreneurship (Bass & Avolio, 1993; Wofford et al., 1998). Transformational leaders become conduits by supporting entrepreneurial actions for community members, setting compelling and attractive visions for them, empowering them to be entrepreneurial, and constantly coaching and nurturing community members (Chen, Lin, Lin, & McDonough III, 2012). Over time, community members are likely to develop shared beliefs and collective interests, spirits, and actions toward entrepreneurship, which are the essential building blocks of entrepreneurial community culture.

Proposition 2: The Formation and Process of Entrepreneurial Community Development

Proposition 2 engenders three interrelated processes—attraction, selection, and attrition (ASA)—that over time retain the entrepreneurial firms fitting the entrepreneurial community culture and weed out the entrepreneurial firms misfitting the entrepreneurial community culture. The homogeneous pool of entrepreneurial firms created as a result of ASA ultimately results in the formation of an entrepreneurial community.

Schneider's (1987) attraction-selection-attrition (ASA) model suggests that culture is essentially a reflection of collective characteristics of its participating members; over time, an entity, such as an organization, will become homogeneous in its members' characteristics (Ployhart, Weekley, & Baughman, 2006; Schneider, Ehrhart, & Macey, 2013). There are three related processes as proposed in ASA model. The first process is *attraction* that refers to the fit between participating members' characteristics and an organization's characteristics. The second process is *selection*, which means an organization or potential member are more likely to choose the other because they are able to meet each other's needs. The third process is *attrition*, meaning that the participating members who do not ultimately fit with the community are likely to leave. Taken altogether, the ASA model functions like a funnel by retaining the persons who fit the environment and weeding out the entities that are misfits. As such, these processes generate a group of participants (i.e., businesses or entrepreneurial firms) that tend to be compatible with each other in various aspects; thus, they have shared vital commonalities, needs, and supports, thus ultimately creating culture that is formed and shaped because of the norms, values, and beliefs across participants.

The ASA model is a useful theoretical framework to explicate the formation of entrepreneurial community development. First, in order for an entrepreneurial firm to be attracted to a community or for the creation of a firm, a community must have supportive policies, various entrepreneurial amenities, and an open environment that are available to entrepreneurship (Cohen, 2006; Neck, Meyer, Cohen, & Corbett, 2004; Prevezer, 2001; Siegel, Wessner, Binks, & Lockett, 2003). For example, regional or local governments may play a decisive role in attracting entrepreneurial firms because they can implement policies to foster entrepreneurial activities by eliminating bureaucratic "red tape" (e.g., reduce tax rates and increase incentives and grants). Research universities may help to create, disseminate, and promote knowledge about entrepreneurship and also serve to educate and produce skilled workers that are the cornerstone of successful entrepreneurship, thus raising community members' awareness of entrepreneurship and attracting them toward entrepreneurship. The availability of professional and support services, including entrepreneurial tax and legal support and consultants, attract entrepreneurial firms because they help entrepreneurial firms to understand the nature and essence of entrepreneurship and to overcome barriers hindering successful entrepreneurship. Attracting or growing entrepreneurs may also be contingent on the access to capital services, such as venture capitalists and angel investors who are of paramount importance to entrepreneurs, because start-up capital is a strong determinant of successful entrepreneurship. Finally, access to talent pool (e.g., qualified workers) influences the attraction of entrepreneurs because qualified workers having critical knowledge, skills, and abilities are necessary for successful entrepreneurship.

Second, entrepreneurial firms and a community are likely to select each other when they share commonalities. "In order to function in our daily activities we [community members] rely upon one another to complement and supplement our activities to reach our full potential" (Banyai, 2009, p. 242). For example, if a community provides some or all of the aforementioned conducive amenities for entrepreneurship, and if entrepreneurial firms really enhance the environment (e.g., job opportunities, tax base, etc.), they mutually select each other.

Third, ASA functions like a funnel that constantly filters out the entrepreneurial firms that are incompatible with entrepreneurial community culture and keeps the entrepreneurial firms embracing and fitting with the entrepreneurial community culture. Incompatibility can result from relevance to being edged out by competition or self-elimination for a host of reasons including financial, personal or organizational goals, exit strategy, or lack of needed resources.

Over time, this process cycle maintains its formation and renewal of an entrepreneurial community. An entrepreneurial community has three defining characteristics: the dependencies among members, a unifying set of goals, and a shared set of knowledge and skills (Nambisan & Baron, 2013). Dependencies among members means that the performance and survival of the firms embedded in an entrepreneurial community should be closely tied to the community itself. Second, a unifying set of goals, means that the objectives of the firms reside in a community should be shaped by community-level objectives or focuses. Finally, a shared set of knowledge and skills refers to the complementary set of knowledge shared across community members in a network. ASA will ultimately produce a pool of community members that are interdependent on each other and share similar values, beliefs, and assumptions (Ployhart et al., 2006; Schneider, 1987).

Proposition 3: Entrepreneurial Community Changes May Cause Changes in Leadership

An entrepreneurial community constantly evolves because of changes in the environment where an entrepreneurial community resides (Audia, Locke, & Smith, 2000). Leaders must be flexible (Hackman & Johnson, 2009; Schneider, 1987). In order to be change agents, transformational leaders must create fresh approaches and let go of unsuccessful patterns (Hackman & Johnson, 2009). Adaptability and change allow leaders to be open to possibilities and opportunity—the very definition of entrepreneurship. Transformational leaders—who are important constituents of an entrepreneurial community—navigate and facilitate the changes in an entrepreneurial community. These supporting behaviors result in environmental change so that their leadership behaviors remain effective. Note, however, that new transformational leaders are also created in the process and contribute to the overall process. The goal is creating a fertile entrepreneurial community ecosystem to perpetuate positive impact for the whole community.

Interestingly enough, jobs and creation of work follow entrepreneurial environments (Clifton & Badal, 2014). These indicators highlight success of the entrepreneur(s) and the entrepreneurial community development process. This dynamic process is cyclical in nature.

The main emphasis in an entrepreneurial community is people (Feld, 2012; Florida, 2002, 2012; Hackman & Johnson, 2009). Although Florida (2002) said he is "yet to find an American community whose leaders and citizens have sat down and written out an explicit strategy for building a people climate" (p. 294), it is the relationships of all actors that perpetuate a healthy entrepreneurial community ecosystem. In today's economy, this entrepreneurial community ecosystem is not stand-alone or operational in a vacuum, but rather a more complex landscape and complicated overlap through many organizational systems including—but not limited to—local geography (e.g., downtowns), accessibility to customers, competition, and extents of uniqueness in the market.

As a whole, a community has to be willing to engage in entrepreneurial community development. Each actor must be involved in the creation and ownership of the process. Chapter 6 discusses networking, which is a vital component of entrepreneurial community development. The process model provided here creates an illustration to understand the cyclical nature of entrepreneurial community development.

Myths

There are a number of myths that inhibit transformational leadership and entrepreneurial community development. Transformational leaders likely learn from experiences and improve their performance over time. Additionally, transformational leaders serve in a supporting role to the entrepreneurs and an entrepreneurial ecosystem that is created and dynamically maintained. Provided here are concerns challenging real transformational leadership.

One Best Leadership Style

The age-old argument of leaders being born and not made suggests that there is one leadership style that fits all circumstances. Frankly, that is not true. As noted earlier, communities are dynamic, emergent, and iterative in their processes. Given the number of actors, resources, and situations, other leadership styles may be needed to navigate certain situations, people, or other parts of the process.

Leadership Is Innate, Not Learned

Many current scholars believe leadership skills can be developed (George, 2004; Northouse, 2015; Yukl, 2012). Developing core leadership skills can be identified, understood, and practiced with effort and opportunity. Many local communities provide "Leadership Programs" specifically tailored to the needs of a local area relating to public, nonprofit, and volunteer leadership roles. Some of these programs are free; others charge a fee. However, given time and effort, individuals can learn and hone their leadership prowess for use in the community and specifically the entrepreneurial community. Some colleges and universities also provide opportunities for leadership development and even entrepreneurship development.

The Next Silicon Valley

Replicating other successful initiatives may not be attainable. Each community needs to evaluate its goals, culture, and potential for development. While Silicon Valley is a hotbed of ideas in technology and innovation, it is unwise to correlate goals and markets based on their model. The efforts may or may not pay off to replicate their success. Instead, collating and inventorying community assets, identifying stakeholders and actors, creating goals—both short-term and long-term, and establishing an inclusive culture of openness, creativity, and innovation will allow an entrepreneurial community development process to blossom and grow. This process takes conscientious effort, planning, and purposeful execution.

Waiting for a White Knight

A *White Knight* is a business term used to describe a resource hero who appears on the scene to save a company from downfall or financial ruin (Rutherford, 2013). Some towns or communities are often awaiting a White Knight. The community is waiting for and relies on generous benefactors, long-time named families, government agencies, or large billionaires, politicians, or philanthropists to change a community or underwrite its purpose and existence. While such resources may contribute to the development and maintenance of an entrepreneurial community, such resources should not impede the contribution by individuals, entrepreneurs, and new thinkers in creating a healthy entrepreneurial ecosystem. While appreciating a legacy or robust past, some communities need to forge a new future.

The Economy

While the economy has its effect on supply and demand, availability of financing, and creation of markets, it is only a backdrop and variable in the process. A community cannot stand still because of the economy. Actually, it is tough economic times that push creativity and efficiency. Tough economics also allow a fresh look at a community's resources, directions, and capacity. Therefore, the economy should not dictate the process, investment, or outcomes in purposeful entrepreneurial community development.

Negative Leadership

While the goal of leadership is execution to achieve goals through a shared vision with others, negative drawbacks exist with extremes or abuse of a leader's role(s) or power (Conger, 2008; Hackman & Johnson, 2009; Kets de Vries & Miller, 2008). Such problems or failures arise from a wide range of issues: narcissism, neglect, forcefulness, bad or premature timing, manipulation, poor use of networks, excessive dependence, or superficiality. Regardless of the root of the problem, leaders can spin negatively and harm oneself, organizations, followers, colleagues, and the community at large. Such disasters require re-establishing trust and reliability for forgivable offenses or transition to a more stable and functioning leader.

Kets de Vries and Miller (2008) indicate that narcissism is often a driving force behind an individual seeking a leadership role. Some narcissistic tendencies may permit an individual to self-select into a leadership capacity, but only the long list of attributes and behaviors previously discussed in this chapter would mitigate the negative attributes of narcissism for one to be effective. There are three main types of narcissism: constructive, self-deceptive, and reactive—ranging from least to most destructive (Kets de Vries & Miller, 2008). Typically, *constructive narcissism* includes pride, confidence, assertiveness, energy, creativity, humor, and patience. Kept in productive vanes, these behaviors can yield positive impact and do support transformational leadership. The other two domains of being self-deceptive or reactive are negative. *Self-deceptive* leaders are pre-occupied with self, have an unhealthy need or utilization of power, lack of feeling or empathy for others or situations, become exploitative, may be risk averse, or are controlling. Individuals with self-deceptive behaviors manifest negative impact in their relationships with others. Finally, *reactive* narcissism includes self-aggrandizement, ruthlessness, entitlement, domination, or win-lose mentality. Unfortunately, both reactive narcissism and self-deceptive leaders use negative charisma and typically derail.

Leaders may also produce negative results based on strategic vision, communications, public relations, or management abilities (Conger, 2008). Leaders with bad timing, or who press too hard to achieve their vision, can alienate people, fail to adjust to circumstances, misread or exaggerate information, or mismatch opportunities. The remaining categories deal with manipulation through inattention to administration, abuse of relationships, overstating or omitting key information, and creation of illusions.

Good leaders can face challenges that spin their behavior into unhealthy, hurtful, abusive, and unproductive directions. It's important to maintain a checks-and-balance of stakeholders to safeguard these unfortunate situations. Neglect, abuse, or manipulation of a leader's role(s) or power will lead to a derailing and potentially disastrous result (Conger, 2008; Hackman & Johnson, 2009; Kets de Vries & Miller, 2008).

Summary

Entrepreneurial communities seem to navigate divergent strands of thinking with the ASA model and transformational leadership successfully. How do the stabilizing tendencies of the ASA model interact with the destabilizing tendencies of transformational leadership? What eventually results is a continuously dynamic culture that respects and seeks out change, and therefore attracts other change-seekers on a regular basis. Whereas some cultures may isolate these individuals as "weirdos" or "deviants" for wanting to try something new, these "deviants" may find solace in a community of people who share their values of embracing novelty and diversity. How a community gets to be that way in the first place is the story or role of transformational leadership. Feld (2012) promotes *The Power of Community* by embracing weirdness, seeing everyone as a mentor, being open to any idea, being honest, networking, planning, and contributing before taking. Leadership and culture combine—or collide—to form an entrepreneurial community. Transformational leaders shape entrepreneurial community culture. Through ASA processes, entrepreneurial firms become cooperative and the firms which misfit an entrepreneurial community culture will leave the community. The pool of entrepreneurial firms are interdependent with each other, share common goals, beliefs, and values, and possess a shared set of knowledge and skills, which ultimately lead to the creation of an entrepreneurial community.

References

Aldrich, H., & Zimmer, C. (1986). Entrepreneurship through social networks. In D. L. Sexton & R. W. Smilor (Eds.), *The art and science of entrepreneurship* (pp. 3–23). Cambridge, MA: Ballinger Publishing Company.

Antonakis, J., & Autio, E. (2007). Entrepreneurship and leadership. In J. R. Baum, M. Frese, & R. Baron (Eds.), *The psychology of entrepreneurship* (pp. 189–208). Mahway, NJ: Lawrence Erlbaum Associates.

Audia, P. G., Locke, E. A., & Smith, K. G. (2000). The paradox of success: An archival and a laboratory study of strategic persistence following radical environmental change. *Academy of Management Journal*, *43*, 837–853.

Avolio, B. J. (2011). *Full range leadership development* (2nd ed.). Thousand Oaks, CA: Sage.

Avolio, B. J., & Bass, B. M. (1988). Transformational leadership, charisma, and beyond. In J. G. Hunt, B. R. Baliga, H. P. Dachler, & C. A. Schriesheim (Eds.), *Emerging leadership vistas* (pp. 29–50). Boston, MA: Lexington Books.

Avolio, B. J., & Bass, B. M. (2004). *Multifactor leadership questionnaire: Manual and sampler set* (3rd ed.). Menlo Park, CA: Mind Garden.

Avolio, B. J., & Gardner, W. L. (2005). Authentic leadership development: Getting to the root of positive forms of leadership. *The Leadership Quarterly*, *16*, 315–338.

Avolio, B. J., Walumbwa, F. O., & Weber, T. J. (2009). Leadership: Current theories, research, and future directions. *Annual Review of Psychology*, *60*, 421–429.

Banyai, C. (2009). Community leadership: Development and evolution of leadership in Himeshima. *Rural Society*, *19*(3), 241–261.

Barling, J., Christie, A., & Hoption, A. (2011). Leadership. In S. Zedeck (Ed.), *Handbook of industrial and organizational psychology* (pp. 183–240). Washington, DC: American Psychological Association.

Bass, B. M. (1985). *Leadership and performance beyond expectations*. New York, NY: Free Press.

Bass, B. M. (1998). *Transformational leadership: Industrial, military, and educational impact*. Mahwah, NJ: Lawrence Erlbaum Associates.

Bass, B. M., & Avolio, B. J. (1993). Transformational leadership and organizational culture. *Public Administration Quarterly*, 17(1), 112–121.

Bass, B. M., & Riggio, R. E. (2005). *Transformational leadership* (2nd ed.). Mahwah, NJ: Lawrence Erlbaum Associates.

Bass, B. M., & Steidlmeier, P. (1999). Ethics, character, and authentic transformational leadership behavior. *The Leadership Quarterly*, *10*, 181–217.

Baum, J. R., Locke, E. A., & Kirkpatrick, S. A. (1998). A longitudinal study of the relation of vision and vision communication to venture growth in entrepreneurial firms. *Journal of Applied Psychology*, *83*, 43–54.

Bolman, L. G., & Deal, T. D. (1996). Making the entrepreneurial team work. In R. W. Smilor & D. L. Sexton (Eds.), *Leadership and entrepreneurship: Personal and organizational development in entrepreneurial ventures* (pp. 114–125). Westport, CT: Quorum Books.

Bolman, L. G., & Deal, T. D. (2008). *Reframing organizations: Artistry, choice, and leadership* (4th ed.). San Francisco, CA: Wiley.

Bonjean, C. M., & Olson, D. M. (1964). Community leadership: Directions of research. *Administrative Science Quarterly*, *9*(3), 278–300.

Bono, J. E., & Judge, T. A. (2004). Personality and transformational and transactional leadership: A meta-analysis. *Journal of Applied Psychology*, *89*, 901–910.

Bowman, L. E. (1932). Community organization. *The American Journal of Sociology*, *37*(6), 924–929.

Bradberry, T., & Greaves, J. (2012). *Leadership 2.0: Learn the secrets of adaptive leadership*. San Diego, CA: TalentSmart.

Burns, J. M. (1978). *Leadership*. New York, NY: Harper Collins.

Carson, J. B., Tesluk, P. E., & Marrone, J. A. (2007). Shared leadership in teams: An investigation of antecedent conditions and performance. *The Academy of Management Journal*, *50*(5), 1217–1234.

Chen, M. Y. C., Lin, C. Y. Y., Lin, H. E., & McDonough, E. F., III. (2012). Does transformational leadership facilitate technological innovation? The moderating roles of innovative culture and incentive compensation. *Asia Pacific Journal of Management*, *29*, 239–264.

Churchill, N. C., & Lewis, V. L. (1986). Entrepreneurship research: Directions and methods. In D. L. Sexton & R. W. Smilor (Eds.), *The art and science of entrepreneurship* (pp. 333–365). Cambridge, MA: Ballinger Publishing Company.

Clevenger, M. R. (2017). Perceptions of entrepreneurs and community: From historical roots to a contemporary kaleidoscope. In M. W-P Fortunato & M. R. Clevenger (Eds.), *Toward entrepreneurial community development: Leaping cultural and leadership boundaries* (pp. 10–50). New York, NY: Routledge.

Clifton, J., & Badal, S. B. (2014). *Entrepreneurial strengthsfinder*. New York, NY: Gallup Press.

Cohen, B. (2006). Sustainable valley entrepreneurial ecosystems. *Business Strategy and the Environment*, *15*, 1–14.

Colbert, A. E., Kristof-Brown, A. L., Bradley, B. H., & Barrick, M. R. (2008). CEO transformational leadership: The role of goal importance congruence in top management teams. *Academy of Management Journal*, *51*, 81–96.

Coleman, S., & Kariv, D. (2014). 'Deconstructing' entrepreneurial self-efficacy: A gendered perspective on the impact of ESE and community entrepreneurial culture on the financial strategies and performance of new firms. *Venture Capital, 16*, 157–181.

Conger, J. A. (2008). The dark side of leadership. In J. L. Pierce & J. W. Newstrom (Eds.), *Leaders & the leadership process: Readings, self-assessments & applications* (5th ed., pp. 437–442). Boston, MA: McGraw-Hill.

Derue, D. S., Nahrgang, J. D., Wellman, N. E. D., & Humphrey, S. E. (2011). Trait and behavioral theories of leadership: An integration and meta-analytic test of their relative validity. *Personnel Psychology, 64*, 7–52.

Doolittle, R. J., & MacDonald, D. (1978). Communication and a sense of community in a metropolitan neighborhood: A factor analytic examination. *Communication Quarterly, 26*, 2–7.

Durkheim, E. (1964). *The division of labor in society*. New York, NY: Free Press of Glencoe.

Eggers, J. H., & Smilor, R. W. (1996). Leadership skills of entrepreneurs: Resolving the paradoxes and enhancing the practices of entrepreneurial growth. In R. W. Smilor & D. L. Sexton (Eds.), *Leadership and entrepreneurship: Personal and organizational development in entrepreneurial ventures* (pp. 15–38). Westport, CT: Quorum Books.

Eisenbeiss, S. A., van Knippenberg, D., & Boerner, S. (2008). Transformational leadership and team innovation: Integrating team climate principles. *Journal of Applied Psychology, 93*, 1438–1446.

Engelen, A., Gupta, V., Strenger, L., & Brettel, M. (2015). Entrepreneurial orientation, firm performance, and the moderating role of transformational leadership behaviors. *Journal of Management, 41*, 1069–1097.

Ensley, M. D., Hmieleski, K. M., & Pearce, C. L. (2006). The importance of vertical and shared leadership within new venture top management teams: Implications for the performance or startups. *The Leadership Quarterly, 17*, 217–231.

Ensley, M. D., Pearce, C. L., & Hmieleski, K. M. (2006). The moderating effect of environmental dynamism on the relationship between entrepreneur leadership behavior and new venture performance. *Journal of Business Venturing, 21*, 243–263.

Feld, B. (2012). *Startup communities: Building an entrepreneurial ecosystem in your city*. Hoboken, NJ: Wiley.

Fiedler, F. E. (1972). How do you make leaders more effective? New answers to an old puzzle. *Organizational Dynamics, 1*(2), 3–18.

Flora, C. B., & Flora, J. L. (1993). Entrepreneurial social infrastructure: A necessary ingredient. *The Annals of the American Academy of Political and Social Science, 529*, 48–58.

Florida, R. (2002). *The rise of the creative class and how it's transforming work, leisure, community and everyday life*. New York, NY: Basic Books.

Florida, R. (2012). *The rise of the creative class, revisited*. New York, NY: Basic Books.

Fortunato, M. W-P, & Clevenger, M. (2015). Developing baseline measures for the study of entrepreneurial community leadership and culture. *United States Association for Small Business and Entrepreneurship Conference Proceedings*.

Fry, L. W. (2003). Toward a theory of spiritual leadership. *The Leadership Quarterly, 14*, 693–727.

Gardner, W. L., Cogliser, C. C., Davis, K. M., & Dickens, M. P. (2011). Authentic leadership: A review of the literature and research agenda. *The Leadership Quarterly, 22*, 1120–1145.

George, B. (2004). *Authentic leadership: Rediscovering the secrets to creating lasting value*. San Francisco, CA: Jossey-Bass.

Gumusluoğlu, L., & Ilsev, A. (2009). Transformational leadership and organizational innovation: The roles of internal and external support for innovation. *Journal of Product Innovation Management*, *26*, 264–277.

Gusfield, J. R. (1975). *The community: A critical response*. New York, NY: Harper Colophon.

Hackman, M. Z., & Johnson, C. E. (2009). *Leadership: A communication perspective* (5th ed.). Long Grove, IL: Waveland Press, Inc.

Heifitz, R. (1994). *Leadership without easy answers*. Cambridge, MA: Harvard Press.

Hersey, P., & Blanchard, K. H. (1988). *Management of organizational behavior: Utilizing human resources*. Englewood Cliffs, NJ: Prentice Hall.

Hoffman, B. J., Woehr, D. J., Maldagen-Youngjohn, R., & Lyons, B. D. (2011). Great man or great myth? A quantitative review of the relationship between individual differences and leader effectiveness. *Journal of Occupational and Organizational Psychology*, *84*, 347–381.

Hofstede, G. (2001). *Culture's consequences: Comparing values, behaviors, institutions and organizations across nations* (2nd ed.). Los Angeles, CA: Sage.

Horner, M. (1997). Leadership theory: Past, present, and future. *Team Performance Management*, *3*(4), 270–287.

House, R. J. (1971). A path-goal theory of leader effectiveness. *Administrative Science Quarterly*, *16*, 321–338.

Huggins, R., & Thompson, P. (2012). Entrepreneurship and community culture: A place-based study of their interdependency. *Entrepreneurship Research Journal*, *2*, 1–34.

Humphrey, R. H. (2013). *Effective leadership: Theory, cases, and applications*. Los Angeles, CA: Sage.

Hunter, F. (1953). *Community power structure: A study of decision makers*. Chapel Hill, NC: University of North Carolina Press.

Jaskyte, K. (2004). Transformational leadership, organizational culture, and innovativenesss in nonprofit organizations. *Nonprofit Management and Leadership*, *15*, 153–168.

Judge, T. A., Bono, J. E., Ilies, R., & Gerhardt, M. W. (2002). Personality and leadership: A qualitative and quantitative review. *Journal of Applied Psychology*, *87*, 765–780.

Judge, T. A., Colbert, A. E., & Ilies, R. (2004). Intelligence and leadership: A quantitative review and test of theoretical propositions. *Journal of Applied Psychology*, *89*, 542–552.

Judge, T. A., & Piccolo, R. F. (2004). Transformational and transactional leadership: A meta-analytic test of their relative validity. *Journal of Applied Psychology*, *89*, 755–768.

Isenberg, D. (2010, June). The big idea: How to start an entrepreneurial revolution. *Harvard Business Review*, 1–10.

Katz, R. L. (1955). Skills of an effective administrator. *Harvard Business Review*, *33*(1), 33–42.

Katz, R. L. (1974). Skills of an effective administrator. *Harvard Business Review*, *52*(5), 90–102.

Kets de Vries, M. F. R., & Miller, D. (2008). Narcissism and leadership: An object relations perspective. In J. L. Pierce & J. W. Newstrom (Eds.), *Leaders & the leadership process: Readings, self-assessments & applications* (5th ed., pp. 443–453). Boston, MA: McGraw-Hill.

Kirk, P., & Shutte, A. M. (2004). Community leadership development. *Community Development Journal*, *39*(3), 234–251.

Kirkpatrick, S., & Locke, E. (1996). Direct and indirect effects of three core charismatic leadership components on performance and attitudes. *Journal of Applied Psychology*, *81*, 36–51.

Ling, Y. A. N., Simsek, Z., Lubatkin, M. H., & Veiga, J. F. (2008). Transformational leadership's role in promoting corporate entrepreneurship: Examining the CEO-TMT interface. *Academy of Management Journal*, *51*, 557–576.

Marti, I., Courpasson, D., & Barbosa, S. D. (2013). "Living in the fishbowl": Generating an entrepreneurial culture in a local community in Argentina. *Journal of Business Venturing*, *28*, 10–29.

Maslow, A. H. (1954). *Motivation and personality*. New York, NY: Harper.

McMillan, D. W., & Chavis, D. M. (1986). Sense of community: A definition and theory. *Journal of Community Psychology*, *14*, 6–23.

Miao, C., Humphrey, R. H., & Qian, S. (2016). Leader emotional intelligence and subordinate job satisfaction: A meta-analysis of main, mediator, and moderator effects. *Personality and Individual Differences*, *102*, 13–24.

Miao, C., & Qian, S. (2016). Does leadership matter? A multilevel investigation of the moderators for the relationship between openness and change-oriented behavior. *Journal of Leadership, Accountability and Ethics*, *13*, 77–89.

Miao, C., Qian, S., & Ma, D. (2017). The relationship between entrepreneurial self-efficacy and firm performance: A meta-analysis of main and moderator effects. *Journal of Small Business Management*, *55*, 87–107.

Moore, J. F. (1993). Predators and prey: A new ecology of competition. *Harvard Business Review*, *71*, 75–83.

Morris, R. T., & Seeman, M. (1950). The problem of leadership: An interdisciplinary approach. *American Journal of Sociology*, *56*(2), 149–155.

Nambisan, S., & Baron, R. A. (2013). Entrepreneurship in innovation ecosystems: Entrepreneurs' self-regulatory processes and their implications for new venture success. *Entrepreneurship Theory and Practice*, *37*, 1071–1097.

Neck, H. M., Meyer, G. D., Cohen, B., & Corbett, A. C. (2004). An entrepreneurial system view of new venture creation. *Journal of Small Business Management*, *42*, 190–208.

Northouse, P. G. (2015). *Introduction to leadership: Concepts and practice* (3rd ed.). Los Angeles, CA: Sage.

Panagopoulos, N. G., & Avlonitis, G. J. (2010). Performance implications of sales strategy: The moderating effects of leadership and environment. *International Journal of Research in Marketing*, *27*, 46–57.

Pearce, C. L. (2004). The future of leadership: Combining vertical and shared leadership to transform knowledge work. *The Academy of Management Executive*, *18*, 47–57.

Pearce, C. L., & Conger, J. A. (2002). *Shared leadership: Reframing the hows and whys of leadership*. Los Angeles, CA: Sage.

Pearce, C. L., & Sims, H. P., Jr. (2002). Vertical versus shared leadership as predictors of the effectiveness of change management teams: An examination of aversive, directive, transactional, transformational, and empowering leader behaviors. *Group Dynamics: Theory, Research, and Practice*, *6*, 172–197.

Piccolo, R. F., & Colquitt, J. A. (2006). Transformational leadership and job behaviors: The mediating role of core job characteristics. *Academy of Management Journal*, *49*, 327–340.

Pierce, J. L., & Newstrom, J. W. (2008a). *Leaders & the leadership process: Readings, self-assessments & applications* (5th ed.). Boston, MA: McGraw-Hill.

Pierce, J. L., & Newstrom, J. W. (2008b). On the meaning of leadership. In J. L. Pierce & J. W. Newstrom (Eds.), *Leaders & the leadership process: Readings, self-assessments & applications* (5th ed., pp. 7–11). Boston, MA: McGraw-Hill.

Ployhart, R. E., Weekley, J. A., & Baughman, K. (2006). The structure and function of human capital emergence: A multilevel examination of the attraction-selection-attrition model. *Academy of Management Journal, 49*, 661–677.

Prevezer, M. (2001). Ingredients in the early development of the US biotechnology industry. *Small Business Economics, 17*, 17–29.

Rafferty, A. E., & Griffin, M. A. (2008). Dimensions of transformational leadership: Conceptual and empirical extensions. In J. L. Pierce & J. W. Newstrom (Eds.), *Leaders & the leadership process: Readings, self-assessments & applications* (5th ed., pp. 394–403). Boston, MA: McGraw-Hill.

Robert K. Greenleaf Center for Servant Leadership. (2016). Retrieved from https://www.greenleaf.org/what-is-servant-leadership/

Rutherford, D. (2013). *Routledge dictionary of economics*. London, UK: Routledge.

Sarros, J. C., Cooper, B. K., & Santora, J. C. (2008). Building a climate for innovation through transformational leadership and organizational culture. *Journal of Leadership & Organizational Studies, 15*, 145–158.

Schneider, B. (1987). The people make the place. *Personnel Psychology, 40*, 437–453.

Schneider, B., Ehrhart, M. G., & Macey, W. H. (2013). Organizational climate and culture. *Annual Review of Psychology, 64*, 361–388.

Shamir, B., & Eilam, G. (2005). "What's your story?" A life-stories approach to authentic leadership development. *The Leadership Quarterly, 16*, 395–417.

Shamir, B., House, R. J., & Arthur, M. B. (1993). The motivational effects of charismatic leadership: A self-concept based theory. *Organization Science, 4*, 577–594.

Siegel, D. S., Wessner, C., Binks, M., & Lockett, A. (2003). Policies promoting innovation in small firms: Evidence from the US and UK. *Small Business Economics, 20*, 121–127.

Singh, J. V., Tucker, D. J., & House, R. J. (1986). Organizational legitimacy and the liability of newness. *Administrative Science Quarterly*, 31, 171–193.

Smilor, R. W., & Sexton, D. L. (1996). *Leadership and entrepreneurship: Personal and organizational development in entrepreneurial ventures*. Westport, CT: Quorum Books.

Stogdill, R. M. (1974). *Handbook of leadership: A survey of the literature*. New York, NY: Free Press.

Van Dierendonck, D. (2011). Servant leadership: A review and synthesis. *Journal of Management, 37*, 1228–1261.

Vroom, V. (1964). *Work and motivation*. New York, NY: Wiley.

Walumbwa, F. O., Avolio, B. J., Gardner, W. L., Wernsing, T. S., & Peterson, S. J. (2008). Authentic leadership: Development and validation of a theory-based measure. *Journal of Management, 34*, 89–126.

Wang, D., Waldman, D. A., & Zhang, Z. (2014). A meta-analysis of shared leadership and team effectiveness. *Journal of Applied Psychology, 99*, 181–198.

Wang, G., Oh, I. S., Courtright, S. H., & Colbert, A. E. (2011). Transformational leadership and performance across criteria and levels: A meta-analytic review of 25 years of research. *Group & Organization Management, 36*, 223–270.

Warren, R. L. (1987). *The community in America* (3rd ed.). Lanham, MD: University Press of America.

Weber, M. (2012). *The theory of social and economic organization*. New York, NY: Free Press.

Wilkinson, K. P. (1991). *The community in rural America*. New York, NY: Greenwood Press.

Wofford, J. C., Goodwin, V. L., & Whittington, J. L. (1998). A field study of a cognitive approach to understanding transformational and transactional leadership. *Leadership Quarterly*, 9(1), 55–85.

Woolcock, M. (1998). Social capital and economic development: Toward a theoretical synthesis and policy framework. *Theory and Society*, 27, 151–208.

Yukl, G. A. (2012). *Leadership in organizations*. New York, NY: Prentice Hall.

Zahra, S. A. (1996). Governance, ownership, and corporate entrepreneurship: The moderating impact of industry technological opportunities. *Academy of Management Journal*, 39, 1713–1735.

Suggested Additional Reading

The authors highly recommend Pierce and Newstrom's (2008a) *Leaders & the leadership process: Readings, self-assessments & applications*. The book is the most practical material available with self-assessments to build understanding and skill development in leadership. Additionally, we propose the following recommended reading list:

Badaracco, J. L., Jr. (2002). *Leading quietly: An unorthodox guide to doing the right thing*. Boston, MA: Harvard Business School Press.

Bennis, W. G. (2009). *On becoming a leader*. Philadelphia, PA: Basic Books.

Bennis, W. G., & Goldsmith, J. (2010). *Learning to lead: A workbook on becoming a leader*. New York, NY: Basic Books.

Bennis, W. G., & Thomas, R. J. (2002). *Geeks and geezers: How era, values, and defining moments shape leaders*. Boston, MA: Harvard Business School Press.

Blanchard, K. (2007). *The heart of a leader: Insights on the art of influence*. Colorado Springs, CO: David C. Cook.

Blanchard, K., & Hodges, P. (2003). *The servant leader: Transforming your heart, head, hands & habits*. Nashville, TN: Thomas Nelson.

Charan, R., Drotter, S., & Noel, J. (2011). *The leadership pipeline: How to build the leadership powered company* (2nd ed.). San Francisco, CA: Jossey-Bass.

Cottrell, D., & Adams, A. (2002). *Monday morning leadership: mentoring sessions you can't afford to miss*. Dallas, TX: CornerStone Leadership Institute.

Gardner, H. (1995). *Leading minds: Anatomy of leadership*. New York, NY: Perseus.

George, B., & Gergen, D. (2015). *Discover your true north: Becoming an authentic leader*. Hoboken, NJ: Wiley.

Giuliani, R. W., & Kurson, K. (2002). *Leadership*. Los Angeles, CA: Miramax.

Goleman, D., Boyatzis, R., & McKee, A. (2013). *Primal leadership: Unleashing the power of emotional intelligence*. Boston, MA: Harvard Business School Press.

Greenleaf, R. K., & Spears, L. C. (2002). *Servant leadership: A journey into the nature of legitimate power and greatness*. Mahwah, NJ: Paulist Press.

Heifitz, R. (1984). *Leadership without easy answers*. Cambridge, MA: Harvard Press.

Hybels, B. (2012). *Courageous leadership: Field-tested strategy for the 360° leader*. Grand Rapids, MI: Zondervan.

Iaococca, L. (2008). *Where have all the leaders gone?* New York, NY: Scribner.

Kellerman, B. (2004). *Bad leadership: What it is, how it happens, why it matters.* Boston, MA: Harvard Business School Press.

Kellerman, B. (2012). *The end of leadership*. New York, NY: Harper Collins.

Kotter, J. P. (1996). *Leading change.* Boston, MA: Harvard Business School Press.

Kouzes, J. M., & Posner, B. Z. (2012). *The leadership challenge: How to make extraordinary things happen in organizations* (5th ed.). San Francisco, CA: Jossey-Bass.

Kriegbaum, R. (1998). *Leadership prayers.* Carol Stream, IL: Tyndale House Publishers, Inc.

Lipman-Blumen, J. (2006). *The allure of toxic leaders: Why we follow destructive bosses and corrupt politicians—and how we can survive them.* New York, NY: Oxford University Press.

Maccoby, M. (2003). *The productive narcissist: The promise and peril of visionary leadership*. New York, NY: Random House.

Macintosh, G. L., & Rima, S. D. (2007). *Overcoming the dark side of leadership: How to become an effective leader by confronting potential failures.* Grand Rapids, MI: Baker Books.

Nielsen, J. S. (2011). *Myth of leadership: Creating leaderless organizations.* Boston, MA: Nicholas Brealey Publishing.

Sowcik, M., Andenoro, A. C., McNutt, M., & Murphy, S. E. (2015). *Leadership 2050: Critical challenges, key contexts and emerging trends.* Bingley, UK: Emerald Group Publishing.

Tichy, N. M., & Cardwell, N. (2004). *The cycle of leadership: How great leaders teach their companies to win.* New York, NY: HarperCollins Publishers, Inc.

Ulrich, D., Zenger, J., & Smallwood, N. (1999). *Results-based leadership.* Boston, MA: Harvard Business School Press.

Useem, M., & Bennis, W. (1999). *The leadership moment: Nine true stories of triumph and disaster and their lessons for us all.* New York, NY: Random House.

6 The Value and Process of Social Networking for Entrepreneurs

Morgan R. Clevenger,
Michael W-P Fortunato,
and Kathleen Houlihan

Building interpersonal and interorganizational social networks and alliances provides information, influence, and resources for entrepreneurs (Aldrich & Zimmer, 1986; Atterton, 2007; Birley, 1985; Burt, 2002; Cooper, 2002; Cropper, Ebers, Huxham, & Ring, 2008; Dutta, 2010; Hoang & Antoncic, 2003; Hoang & Yi, 2015; Johannisson, 2000; Lin, 2001; McQuaid, 1996; Mönstead, 1993; Nielsen, Klyver, Evald, & Bager, 2012; Scott, 1985; Scott & Carrington, 2011; Szarka, 1990; Thornton & Flynn, 2003). Social networking, coalition building, and establishing public-private partnerships maximizes efforts and builds a sense of community (Chaskin, Brown, Benkatesh, & Vidal, 2001; Goldsmith, 1946; Kanter, 2002; Pages, 2006; Wellman, Carrington, & Hall, 1988). Hindle (2010) said, "The community is the garden of entrepreneurship. No entrepreneurial venture can flower in isolation" (p. 639). Community agents include all actors and leaders—the participants, which can be individuals, organizations, entrepreneurs, businesses, or governments—who create social networks (Alter & Hage, 1993; Banyai, 2009; Chaskin et al., 2001; Coe, 1987; Powell & Smith-Doerr, 1994; Scott & Carrington, 2011; Smith-Doerr & Powell, 2005; Wellman & Berkowitz, 1988; Wellman et al., 1988). "Networks are a central component of an entrepreneurial climate—a cultural, social, and economic milieu that encourages and nurtures the creation of new business ventures" (Pages & Garmise, 2003, p. 20). Three key elements of social networks include network content, mechanisms to organize and regulate exchanges, and network structure (Hoang & Antoncic, 2003).

This chapter will focus on how information can be useful to build lasting alliances through social networking, coalition building, and public-private partnerships. Building alliances and coalitions within entrepreneurial communities are important along two dimensions: physical, face-to-face social networks within the community and virtual coalitions using social media. Social networks are the basic building blocks of an entrepreneurial community upon which collective action can be built (Aldrich & Zimmer, 1986; Shuffstall, 2013; Shuffstall & Fortunato, 2013). It is not the networks themselves, but the nature of the *relationships* that flow over these networks that matter. This chapter will discuss how well-networked communities maximize information flow, build trust and reciprocity, enhance social capital, link diverse knowledge silos, attract customers, build momentum, and "buzz," and even attract others into the community.

The Importance of Social Networks

Why are social networks important? Nielsen, Klyver, Evald, and Bager (2012) said,

> An entrepreneur without a [social] network is like a fisherman without a fishing rod. In order to be successful, the entrepreneurial process requires the involvement of more than just the entrepreneur. Entrepreneurs involve a number of different people through the entrepreneurial process. These may be people closely connected to the organization, including customers, suppliers, investors, auditors, etc. However, it might also include people who have a less visible, but equally crucial role in the entrepreneur's success. Here we might consider the significance of receiving free help and advice from experienced friends and family members along with the importance of emotional support and having the "right backing on the home front." So, the social environment, of which they are a part, including the network they possess, influences entrepreneurs. Entrepreneurial decisions are made not in a vacuum, but rather in social contexts.
>
> (p. 133)

Mackay (1990) promotes 10 reasons for having a strong social network: (1) knowing there is strength in numbers, (2) having a reflection or review of what one is doing with a sounding board is helpful, (3) knowing enemies or competition, (4) helping to expand others' networks, (5) educating oneself in other places—particularly in other countries, (6) gaining new experiences and new knowledge, (7) providing opportunities to help others, (8) insuring opportunities or a job down the road, (9) creating positive information, and (10) expanding connectivity to resources. All of these reasons create opportunities to leverage a social network or to contribute to a network. Social networking necessitates a "sincere desire to help others" (Colon, n.d., p. 5). This sincerity likely stems from an authentic self, concerned with a genuine desire to help others, which is based on *trust* (Aldrich, 2002; Cook, Levi, & Hardin, 2009; Feld, 2012; George, 2004; Hardin, 2002; Putnam, 2000; Uslaner, 1999).

Aldrich and Zimmer (1986) said, "A network is defined as the totality of all persons connected by a certain type of relationship and is constructed by finding the ties between all persons in a population" (p. 12). Mönstead (1993), Pages (2006), Smith-Doerr and Powell (2005), and Thornton and Flynn (2003) elaborate that social networks for economic productivity are formal and create opportunities for exchange of resources and information or exist as a governance function. Either way, the development of social networks for entrepreneurial activity creates interdependence and ideally long-term relationships. Further, Aldrich (2002) identifies three types of *trust* for social action: categorical, network, and institution-based. *Categorical* trust is created by "similarities based in sharing membership in some nominal group" (p. 218). *Social network* trust is "produced by social relationships in which the trusted and trusting parties are implicated" (p. 218) based on the nature of the relationship. *Institution-based* trust is supported by organizations' performance and trustworthiness (Alter & Hage, 1993; Cook et al., 2009).

Regardless of the purpose, the critical dimensions of social networks are density, reachability, and centrality (Aldrich & Zimmer, 1986; Carsrud, Gaglio, & Olm, 1987). *Density* considers the number of ties and strength of actors involved. *Reachability* considers the capacity to reach individuals in a social network as well as connectivity to each new actor's network. Finally, the reachability compounds to become *centrality*, or the total number of actors able to be reached. Nielsen et al. (2012) indicate that a social network is "situation-dependent" (p. 145). Relationships, activities, behaviors, and exchanges are reliant upon motive, purpose, and timing of interactions.

Social networks exist in both close relationships as well as second-degree and beyond acquaintance levels. Relationships contribute to social network building. Evald, Klyver, and Svendsen (2006), Scott and Davis (2007), and Shane and Cable (2002) explain that contacts in a network create ties. These ties are likely based on "social obligation and access to private information" (Shane & Cable, 2002, p. 367). Ties may be direct or indirect. Relationships and connecting in social networks is based on identity and reputation (Lin, 2001; Shane & Cable, 2002). The foundational component is *trust* (Ajzen & Fishbein, 1980; Aldrich, 2002; Blois, 1999; Currall & Judge, 1995; Hardin, 2002; Reese & Aldrich, 1995; Schurr & Ozanne, 1985; Uslaner, 1999). *Trust* is the concept of relying on another to fulfill responsibilities or actions (Ajzen & Fishbein, 1980; Blau, 1964; Rotter, 1967; Schurr & Ozanne, 1985). Trust from strong ties are found as an ongoing phenomenon with close actors such as family, friends, and co-workers (Atterton, 2007; Granovetter, 1973; Lin, Ensel, & Vaughn, 1981). Strong ties are reliable and trustworthy (Aldrich & Zimmer, 1986). Weak ties may or may not play a key role in response, but can create an education or marketing networking opportunity (Granovetter, 1973; Putnam, 2000; White, 1988). Atterton (2007) defines weak ties as those of "dispersed, less well-known individuals . . . of short duration and low frequency . . . [that are] broken more easily" (p. 231). A wide range of variables create strong or weak relationships including attitude, behavioral performance, trustworthiness, trust, and strength of a social network relation over time (Currall & Judge, 1995). MacKinnon, Chapman, and Cumbers (2004) indicate that short-term, weak ties provide much needed outside injection of ideas, information, or expertise to eliminate local introversion or closure that limits growth and development. Thus weak ties—in addition to strong ties—are important in building social network capacity for entrepreneurs.

Businesses need access to information more than ever before to stay relevant and to continue to be profitable (Lin, 2001). Entrepreneurs' success is facilitated or inhibited by the strength of their network (Aldrich & Zimmer, 1986). Mackay (1990) said, "A network never sleeps" (p. 7). Pages and Garmise (2003) encourage one to start small and think long term.

Dealing with Social Network Constituents

"Entrepreneurship is embedded in a social content, channeled and facilitated or constrained and inhibited by people's positions in social networks" (Aldrich & Zimmer, 1986, p. 4). These contacts are called *linkages*, or "patterns of social interaction" (Carsrud et al., 1987, p. 15). Aldrich and Zimmer (1986) indicate, "Entrepreneurship requires linkages or relations between key components of the process" (p. 3). Individuals, organizations, businesses, entrepreneurs, or governments may make connections. These network actors create a dynamic set of relationships for varying purposes, and these relationships create embeddedness (McKeever, Anderson, & Jack, 2014; Portes, 1995).

Hoang and Yi's (2015) *Network-Based Research in Entrepreneurship: A Decade in Review*, Powell and Smith-Doerr's (1994) Net*works and Economic Life*, Scott and Carrington's (2011) *Social Network Analysis*, and Wellman and Berkowitz (1988) *Social Structures: A Network Approach* are the most comprehensive collections of approaches to the study of social networks. Their reviews capture access and opportunity, power, organizations, and economic production. These comprehensive articles elaborate on the various types and purposes of networks including network content, governance, network structure, culture, industry, and both dependent and independent variables (Hoang & Yi, 2015; Huggins, 2000).

Two important concepts of social networking must be considered here: maximization of local networks and positionality in a network. Having as many people as possible in a local network is beneficial because it maximizes what Granovetter (1973) calls "weak ties." These are informal ties over which people receive most novel information about opportunities in the world around them (i.e., lots of informal connections are better for economies than lots of family connections, or "strong ties"). Second, where one is in the network matters. So it's not just about centrality, but bridging between actors that are central to a variety of siloed social networks. This phenomenon is what Burt (1995) calls "structural holes." Thus it is not only important to create lots of social networks but also to be strategic about where those social network linkages point to in order to maximize "nonredundant information" in the total knowledge system. Vissa and Chacar (2009) found positive performance in a recent study on structural holes.

Building Effective Social Networks for Entrepreneurial Communities

The process of building effective social networks takes time (Mackay, 1990). These alliances, partnerships, coalitions, and social networks are based on understanding network actors, being strategic with mindful social networking, marketing, leveraging social media, and managing resistance. Recognizing and leveraging these key concerns will provide a strong basis for entrepreneurial social networking.

Network Actors

Economic actors that work with the history, the culture, and the other actors of an area or industry are more likely to spawn new creative products and services that will benefit all parties. This deep understanding of community needs and historical facts can inspire cultural change. Entrepreneurs who understand the needs of the community may create a symbiotic relationship between their business and the broader community. The following is a description of common network actors in an entrepreneurial community, with a description of roles and strategies for incorporating these actors into the entrepreneurial community.

Understanding Community History

One of the first steps to building a more entrepreneurial community is to understand the history of the community, and that of its people and culture (Breazeale & Hustedde, 2017). Understanding any community's historical context can help to explain the current structure of social and institutional relations in that place, which is useful in leveraging actors to participate in the entrepreneurial network. Networks are more easily formed when actors have something in common to share, whether it be information or just a common perspective.

To bolster involvement first requires an understanding of which perspectives are most likely to resonate with prospective participants. This task can be difficult because local history is often manifested in subtle ways in the local culture, and many communities do not have a wealth of public or historical records on public display. Many communities may not have archives that are accessible let alone electronic. Going to a local senior center or history center, when available, might help to build an understanding of both the struggles and the successes of an area. These places often have the incentive to tell stories from their past, which are oftentimes from the first person point of view. Other options are to go to the local library and skim the local newspaper clippings. Too often, community development professionals and economic development practitioners—and entrepreneurs too—may begin to engage in community affairs without first understanding the unique cultural, economic, and political history shaping that place. Taking the time to understand this history not only provides strategic advantages about what is likely to work in that community but also prevents embarrassing and destructive gaffes and behaviors that could be perceived as insensitive or ignorant.

Engaging Entrepreneurs and Nascent Entrepreneurs

Feld (2012) notes that entrepreneurs are the most suited individuals to launch a start-up community, and there is little doubt that entrepreneurs play the central role in the community's leadership (Clevenger & Miao, 2017). However, it can be hard to find people who are interested in entrepreneurship, but may not yet have the confidence, financial or personal ability, or business skill to launch. One strategy for attracting both current and potential entrepreneurs to the same venue is through education and networking events (Clevenger, 2017). Co-learning gives current and would-be entrepreneurs the chance to network with one another while all learning something new. This offering is especially salient if the educational event, speaker, or workshop is geared toward pre-launch *and* newly launched entrepreneurs. Often times, the very presence of such events will bring together people who are interested in entrepreneurship, and the door should be kept open for other community members who can provide support. Small business networking evenings (e.g., business "after-hours" events), start-up weekends, boot camps, and maker fairs are all ways to bring together people who are interested in entrepreneurship in communities of any size. These events also create a local "buzz" that the community cares about and promotes entrepreneurial endeavors.

Engaging Gatekeepers and Brokers

Gatekeepers and brokers are individuals that have the power to grant or promote access (Brewer, 2000; Landström, 2005). In social networking, making connections to people who can provide actionable support to an entrepreneurial community is a major task in network development (Aldrich & Zimmer, 1986). Gatekeepers can be loyal assistants, secretaries, spouses or partners, relatives, accountant, lawyer, or anyone who can grant or inhibit access to another person of interest. These gatekeepers may be trained to eliminate certain people or opportunities automatically; likewise, they might be authorized to keep an eye out for certain people or opportunities. The deliberate inclusion of gatekeepers in the community, and rapport building, can create relationships that eventually open other doors. Similar to Burt's (1995) "structural holes," while it is important to be inclusive, it is also important to be deliberate about social networking with individuals who are connected to multiple social groups within a community. This tact broadens the network, maximizes inclusiveness, and improves information flow.

Involving Economic Development

Chambers of commerce, economic development authorities, and city or town councils are often elected or appointed. To assist with community development, these official economic development entities plan for the future, allocate or find resources, and link key stakeholders together (see Walzer, 2007). Accessing these official organizations may take formal requests, details to be included on an agenda, or establishing relationship contact to entertain an audience to explain and explore an objective or opportunity. However, they can be among the biggest supporters and partners in creating an environment that is suitable for entrepreneurs, and can be an integral part of entrepreneurial networks, providing assistance, access to resources, and mentorship as needed (Hoselitz, 1960; Kent, 1982). Ironically, economic development boards and related entities often know little about entrepreneurship. These "organizations are filled with CEOs of hospitals, utilities, banks, insurance companies, universities, accountants, and law firms, and with individuals who have inherited their businesses" (Lichtenstein & Lyons, 2010, p. 168).

Partnering with Higher Education

Colleges and universities are a wonderful source of new ideas, potential entrepreneurs, and another important element—workers who will become the first employees of a new business (Feld, 2012). Many colleges and universities operate in silos and are somewhat removed from their communities, and it will take the initiative of entrepreneurial community leaders to reach out to the universities to open the lines of communication to collaborate and strategize. Other colleges and universities have degrees in entrepreneurship, business incubators, house a Small Business Development Center (SBDC), research centers, or support other entrepreneur or economic development that could be used for support (Clevenger, 2017; Schultz, 2012). Some governments are also working to create policies to monitor and report on higher education value, such as the *College Scorecard*, which promotes environments where colleges and universities connect with the community and businesses to provide job opportunities for graduates.

Incorporating Policy Makers

National, state, and local governments support entrepreneurship (Goldsmith, 1946). Governments often offer incentives and tax breaks to entrepreneurs and businesses (Blanchflower & Oswald, 1998). Elected officials determine policies that can support or inhibit entrepreneurial activities. Communicating needs and opportunities with government official and their agencies can help to promote positive infrastructure to support entrepreneurs and business in general.

Bridging to Larger Organizations

Levels of social networking vary across industries or sectors (Chaskin et al., 2001; Steiner & Cleary, 2014). Aldrich and Zimmer (1986) describe the importance of "connections to resources and niches in an opportunity structure" within established actors in networks (p. 3). Alter and Hage (1993) and Gulati and Gargiulo (1999) describe how organizations create interorganizational alliances. Key factors—just like with individuals—stem from *trust* (Alter & Hage, 1993; Bromiley & Cummings, 1995; Currall & Judge, 1995; Granovetter, 1973, 1992; Powell, 1990). Building an alliance or coalition with organizational support is built organically through ongoing trust, performance of actions creating trustworthiness, and reputation of individuals and organizations.

Organizational networks can form important alliances with the community of entrepreneurs to provide information, employees, and resources. These interorganizational networks rely on individual linkages with large organizations that provide synergistic opportunities for small business as well (Cook et al., 2009; Granovetter, 1973; Hitt & Ireland, 2000; Johannisson, 2000; Powell & Smith-Doerr, 1994; Swedberg, 1994). For example, Feld (2012) and Isenberg (2010) illustrate several partnerships that can occur, including a willingness to hire small businesses to address regulatory issues, to take on riskier work than the larger organization can conduct, and to undertake ancillary tasks that are beyond the scope of the larger organization's mission.

Involving Customers

"Working together can sometimes attract new customers" (Steiner & Cleary, 2014, p. 13), and customers also rely on trust to establish relationships and establish an ongoing connection or relationship, in much the same way entrepreneurs do (Aldrich & Zimmer, 1986; Schurr & Ozanne, 1985; Zacharakis, Spinelli, & Timmons, 2011). Potential customers can be individuals within the broader community, but they can also be business-to-business, governments, or other local and regional organizations. This idea is suggestive of using a LEAN strategy (Reis, 2011), whereby involving potential customers in the entrepreneurial community from the beginning and understanding their needs and frustrations can lead to massive opportunities for local and regional entrepreneurs. This strategy builds trust, and gives the sense that the entrepreneurial community is as much about serving customers with excellence as it is about supporting entrepreneurs.

Reaching out to the Competition

Within a given community or industry, one might collaborate with competitors to advance the profession or field as a whole. This concept is called *co-opetition*, coined by Nalebuff and Brandenburger (1997), and it is becoming more acceptable as a way to conduct business in the digital age. Alter and Hage (1993) called this same concern "competitive cooperation" (p. 50). Because information is so readily available, companies are moving away from existing in a vacuum to more holistic ways of doing business. For example, companies can benefit greatly by finding ways to reduce the costs of their supply chain. Entrepreneurs can work collectively to find opportunities to pool resources and bargain jointly through their industry networks (Zacharakis et al., 2011). This process also improves information sharing, which can help to craft better strategies across firms. Instead of viewing other entrepreneurs as competitors, the entrepreneurial community can create a culture right from the beginning of *co-opetition* where former competitors now work to compete as a community or region. An example might be a local coffee shop. When a new entrant into the local marketplace appears (i.e., another coffee shop), it may form a rivalry. When a third appears, the rivalry is diffused somewhat. When a fourth, fifth, and sixth appear—now the community has a café *scene* that drives more customers into the community who are interested in good coffee. In this scenario, everyone benefits from a bigger economic pie.

Another example could look like this: it is possible that two companies in a rural area could be serviced by the same transportation vehicle for both companies, which could provide the opportunity for cost savings for each organization and less carbon emissions in the community. The opportunities for co-opetition are virtually limitless, provided that local entrepreneurs have the opportunity to network to improve operations together while focusing on mission and the customer experience. This mentality brings a community out of a "net sum" mentality where businesses or entrepreneurs compete for a fixed-size pie, toward a "bigger pie for everyone" mentality.

Mindful Social Networking

Effective networking takes time, and as an entrepreneur, this should be the fun part of the job. One never knows where each opportunity will arise, so it is important to stay open minded and respectful of everyone. Each interaction could be an opportunity to expand upon one's business. Colon (n.d.) defines social networking as "the process of developing and nurturing relationships with people" (p. 1). The process of networking leads to information and access as a personal success strategy. Pages and Garmise (2003) promote the following 10 steps to developing and maintaining networks: (1) exploring a territory to identify potential network constituents, (2) defining roles and target markets, (3) identifying and approaching key leaders, (4) making contact, (5) marketing, (6) linking common partners together to build an alliance, (7) creating sub-groups or alliances for additional specialization, (8) allowing time for relationships to develop, (9) promoting the success of networks and alliances, and (10) organically maintaining networks for additions or departures from a network. These steps create a process cycle. Some points in the process take strategic planning and action, while other steps take time and incubation for relationships to develop. Most ecosystem approaches, including Feld (2012) and Lichtenstein and Lyons (2010) propose some variation of network effects, or systems where participants enhance value for other users, whose value then feeds back onto participants.

Another way to think about network effects and mindful networking is through the development of *social capital* (Portes, 1995; Putnam, 2000). Unlike human capital, social capital inheres in human relationships, and is only expressed when individuals interact with one another (Coleman, 1988; Putnam, 2000). The social status, power structure, and capabilities of one individual can help or impede the progress of others (Loury, 1977). Social capital typically takes three forms: obligations and expectations, information flow capability, and norms accompanied by sanctions (Coleman, 1988). For positive social capital to exist, norms of mutual trust, reciprocity, and reasonable social expectations must be present (Coleman, 1988; Putnam, 2000). Networking is critical to building social capital, as social capital cannot exist or accumulate without networks. As networks develop and network actors establish a track record of positive interactions, a bond of trust forms that can be called upon in times of need. As networks form between different actors in a community environment—also known as *bridging* social capital—a sense of institutionalized trust emerges facilitating cooperation (Woolcock & Narayan, 2000). Social capital–rich networks help to build entrepreneurial communities in this way, by creating a platform for meaningful exchange, supporting a culture of collaboration, and ensuring that individualistic interests do not undermine information flow.

One might also consider a network as a team (Beckman, Schoonhoven, Rottner, & Kim, 2014; Brinckmann & Hoegl, 2011; Cooper & Daily, 1997; Grandi & Grimaldi, 2003; Hoang & Yi, 2015; Li, 2013; Neergaard, 2005; Nicolaou & Birley, 2003; Witt, 2004). Teams are developed through process formation, functionality, and reliable performance. Process formation includes developing a relationship. From the relationship, benefits and emotional psychological variables attach and roles are created. Interactions, then, create a give-and-take reciprocity toward goals (Colon, n.d.; Vissa & Chacar, 2009). This thinking can contribute to the "net sum" attitude and once again have entrepreneurs, businesses, and local leaders competing together as a community or region to drive business for everyone.

Marketing

Reaching the right individuals to support a business venture is a challenging process. Marketing and social networking efforts involve maximizing and targeting social network connections to deliver a message to a select group of individuals. Additionally, social networking may be needed to find resources or to open a door to opportunities or various marketing modalities (e.g., traditional, new media, social media). For better or worse, messages can spread very quickly because, "There's a chain of no more than six people that links every person on this planet to every other person" (Mackay, 1990, p. 8). Strategizing appropriate venues, planning key messages, determining best timing, and maximizing distribution channels will leverage marketing of ideas, opportunities, or initiatives.

A key component of collaboration and social networking is information exchange (Lin, 2001; Steiner & Cleary, 2014). Information could be one-way, such as a blog, press release to various mediums, or newsletters, or two-way such as e-mail or social networking events. The goal of marketing—and thus social networking—is increasing reachability, creating connections, facilitating the spread of information, and leveraging resources (Aldrich & Zimmer, 1986; Lin, 2001). A market is itself a social network based on the norms and values of economic exchange (White, 1988).

Companies and local groups that tell the story about what makes a community great can also help to spread an idea as an alliance or collective. Personal stories are effective ways to move and inspire others into action (Clow & Baack, 2010). Finding a few connectors in the community who can effectively use social media or can use the local media can be important to disseminate information. The local media can involve a blog, or a press release in the local newspaper, and then copies of this correspondence can be circulated through social media. Building a relationship within the market is important and engagement is key to the success of any venture.

In the past, companies were successful because they controlled the information customers received; messages were pushed onto the customers and the society in a one-way dialogue (Raff & Summers, 1987). Society accepted the message, customers made purchases based on perceived needs, and businesses spent little time looking for opportunities to deeply understand the needs of the customer. Henry Ford's famous quote illustrates the issue: "You can have a car in any color as long as it's black." Customers were very happy to have a new mode of transportation; they were not particularly interested in the aesthetic look and feel of this new technology. The new innovation changed the world for them, and the idea of options was, at that time, superfluous. The offering met a deep need in a way that was never available before—personal transportation that was fast and convenient. Today, however, digital age consumers are sophisticated and selective, which makes timing and an appropriate call to action important when using traditional and new marketing tools.

Social Media

Long before social media, social networks were analyzed and used for strategic communications. The three variables that are most important include communication, exchange content, and expectations behavior (Aldrich &

Zimmer, 1986). The goal of social networking is communicating opportunities with the intent of a call to action (Szarka, 1990).

Social media—through apps, e-networking, or blogs—help to build relationships with the customers and the community. The messages should be specific and based on the needs of the reader. Messaging that is too general and not directly engaging to the target audience will have little chance of being shared. Social media can be used to build relationships through relevant messaging, and to collect data about the tastes, preferences, and relevant interests of the community. Creating a two-way offering provides a call to action for the receiver. The goal is to develop an ongoing dialog, which in turn creates a relationship.

Social media is useful for learning, then engaging, and then developing a brand (Dutta, 2010). Organizations that use social media will be better positioned to prosper, because the company will understand the history and the culture. The listening first concept then applied through Search Engine Optimization, which will allow the organization to know which key words will be most effective in branding the concept or idea (Volcic & Andrejevic, 2011). If an organization tries to develop a message before it understands the culture, it will fall on deaf ears, and time and valuable resources may be lost. Engagement through social media should only occur after a targeted message is developed that defines the brand in relation to the community needs and fits the nature of a business.

Most communities need to look at the cumulative effort of projects. The plan needs to be well thought out in advance and cover an entire range of issues regarding economic development (Kulcsar & Yum, 2011). The conversations are "embedded in networks of continuing social relations" which create a deep understanding of the needs of the community (Aldrich & Zimmer, 1986, p. 8). This process will allow communities to get the correct message to the correct customer at the optimal time. When this process is aligned, marketing has served the intended purpose.

Managing Resistance

Organizational resistance is a "complex, dynamic, and interconnected nature of resistance practices" (Putnam, Grant, Michelson, & Cutcher, 2005, p. 5) by resisting or stonewalling individuals or organizations to deny assistance. The process can be overt or covert in communities (Putnam et al., 2005). Within the entrepreneurial community environment, the individuals or organizations who are likely to produce the most resistance are those who do not like change or may feel threatened by the success of others. When resistance occurs, it is often better not to become directly engaged in conflict, or any negative reputation that emerges from the conflict could spread contagiously to the entrepreneurial community. In the spirit of inclusion, it is important to politely avoid areas of social resistance, but always keep the door open. Just as innovation, adoption, and diffusion provides for both leaders and laggards (see Rogers, 2003), something as novel as an entrepreneurial community may make some individuals uncomfortable, at least at first. Many of these initial resistors may eventually see the benefits of the participation of others, and eventually want to join in themselves. Despite their initial skepticism, these individuals may still bring substantive benefits to the table, including a strong sense of local tradition, history, culture, and their own network connections.

Alliances, Local Initiatives, and Public-Private Partnerships

"Entrepreneurs can prosper without networks, but places with strong networks tend to have more entrepreneurs and more successful entrepreneurs" (Pages & Garmise, 2003, p. 20). As entrepreneurs are pressured to do more with less and find additional stakeholders to engage, alliances, local initiatives with various businesses and nonprofits, and public-private partnership become more and more important (Alter & Hage, 1993; Burt, 2002; Coe, 1987; Cooper, 2002; Jarillo, 1988). Samans (2005) promotes seven key traits that will lead to effective partnerships: honesty and trust, clear determination of roles and responsibilities, defining core organizational competencies, professional conduct, mutual respect, attention to win-win goals, and capacity building. Chaskin, Brown, Benkatesh, and Vidal (2001) provide three strategies for developing organizational collaboration:

> (1) establishing or supporting broker organizations that can foster and convene partnerships and networks among existing organizations; (2) creating mechanisms of direct, ongoing communication and collective planning and action among organizations; and (3) supporting or engaging in particular partnerships focused on specific goals and objectives.
>
> (pp. 125–126)

Clark (2014) and Corkindale (2009) note several mistakes to avoid when building an alliance. Corkindale (2009) encourages individuals not to underestimate existing relationships by creating an inventory. Writing down names of contacts, their purpose, and a goal of utilization in one's social network contact help to develop a sense of purpose. Clark (2014) advises entrepreneurs to understand "the pecking order" (para 5). This concern notes that power dynamics based on roles, responsibilities, and status matter. Some people are blind to this situation; however, using humility and rapport can help navigate these dynamics. Corkindale (2009) encourages being assertive to initiate contact. In interactions, Clark (2014) also promotes stating your value proposition clearly and being willing to create reciprocity as a foundational offering. Finally, Corkindale (2009) promoted follow-up and appreciation for taking time to discuss opportunities. This process adds to one's reputation and personal brand building.

Building Institutional Support

Institutional support begins when entrepreneurs and local leaders work together to create a sense of culture, support, and routines that embrace innovation. The format needs to be engaging, collaborative, and transparent. Local leadership that understands the interconnectedness of businesses will have created the best environment for supportive relationships and generative innovations (Lane & Maxfield, 1996; Surie & Hazy, 2006). Generative processes—relationships, leadership, or innovations—are those allowing cross-pollination of ideas, social network contacts, and resources to foster innovative environments (Lane & Maxfield, 1996; Surie & Hazy, 2006). These transformative processes are complex and the dynamics are complicated but if the mission is clear then individuals within the organization know how to act and react in each situation. When the business understands the complexity and the culture, this allows each individual to feel safe, even during times of change, allowing for full support of the project or innovation (Houlihan, 2015).

Interorganizational networks often create a platform for effective economic exchange (Currall & Judge, 1995). Organizations function in many, many different networks such as vendor relationships, supplier networks, distribution and marketing channels, trade associations, and even research capacities (Gulati & Gargiulo, 1999; White, 1988). There are roles for entrepreneurs to play in each of these, as well as serving as "connectors" between larger organizations and new opportunities.

"Inter-organizational relationships are subject to inherent development dynamics" (Ebers, 1999, p. 31), whose four key dynamics include "the parties' motives . . . the pre-conditions and contingencies of forming inter-organizational relationships . . . the content and . . . the outcomes" (Ebers, 1999, p. 31). Organizations constantly act and react to other organizations (Ebers, 1999; Meyer & Rowan, 1977; Morgan, 2006; Pfeffer & Salancik, 2003). Morgan (2006) said, "Organizations must develop cultures that support change and risk taking" (p. 91). The three processes for organizational learning and respective interorganizational engagement include understanding, revaluation, and adjustment (Ebers, 1999; Ring & Van de Ven, 1994). Ebers indicated,

> In the course of an ongoing inter-organizational relationship, the parties may for instance learn more about the environmental challenges and opportunities that affect the contents and outcomes of their relationship; they may learn more about one another, for example, about their goals, capabilities, or trustworthiness; and they may learn how they could perhaps better design their relationship in order to achieve desired outcomes.
>
> (p. 38)

Ebers said these dynamics and processes push interorganizational relationships "to evolve over time" (p. 38). This process allows organizations to grow in interdependence and create an alliance for strength as a network. This consideration is especially important for public-private partnerships with entrepreneurs and public or government agencies.

Public-Private Partnerships

Public-private partnerships are valuable and important (Mazzucato, 2013). Historically in the United States, attention to competitive markets and social issues have created key opportunities for "government, universities, and industry working together to create new knowledge" (Johnson, 2006, p. 100). Entrepreneurs play a key role in this environment as well, as privatization and devolution in government affairs have caused governments to turn increasingly toward the private sector as partners in the implementation of government policy (Savas, 2000). This situation is especially true in the provision of services for urban and rural development, including the development of infrastructure, public works, and public services (McQuaid, 1996). The history of public-private partnerships (PPPs) is somewhat checkered, as not every partnership has ended in success, or in better value for all parties involved. However, the devolution of economic activities that was formerly the exclusive domain of government to the private sector also has many benefits (Osborne, 2000).

PPPs involve a collaborative effort between at least one public entity (a government or quasi-governmental agency) and at least one private entity (a company, nonprofit, or business of any size) (Schultz, 2012). The term PPP is itself malleable, and can refer to a wide range of activities (Savas, 2000). Typically, a set of goals is established by a government for the public good, as well as policies providing a strategic vision (Blakely, 1989; Schultz, 2012). Partnerships typically occur for three reasons: (1) when there is a synergy between the public- and private-sector actor that can produce a higher value outcome, (2) when the strategic outcomes involve a range of activities where each actor is not equally involved at all times, and (3) when the goals of the project are not entirely commercial in nature (i.e., providing infrastructure). After a resource assessment, both public and private entities vested in the outcomes of the goals become active participants in public-private partnerships. These participants are assigned roles and are given responsibilities and deliverables to work toward the goals. The broad interest of society, or community, is always the mediating focus (Blakely, 1989). Ongoing communication and transparency must take place in order for all parties to contribute and adjust toward the goals.

The Four-Sector Model (Schramm, 2010) highlights the importance of partnerships among entrepreneurs, corporations, governments, and higher education. Corporations seek out entrepreneurs from every age group and from every corner of the world to harness their ideas. These corporations offer opportunities to submit ideas, offer competitions for new innovations, and listen to the feedback from customers. Entrepreneurs who are thinking about how to capture the most information are the businesses that will continue to evolve and provide the entrepreneurial spirit to the communities they serve locally, regionally, nationally, and worldwide. Likewise, universities and governments partner with entrepreneurs and corporations for developing new ideas and innovations (Schramm, 2010).

When turning to the idea of "innovation," we re-enter the realm of the entrepreneur. Mindful networking enables public and private actors to meet, discuss, and brainstorm new ideas for co-development in a structured environment. An entrepreneurial community can facilitate this type of routine interaction. When community leaders place an explicit focus on building PPPs, this can take the community into new intellectual territory for innovation. Since PPPs can be local and regional as well as state and federal, there are a broad range of projects that can be undertaken.

Formalizing a "Home" for Generative Innovations

Generative relationships and generative leadership revolve around the capacity, ability, and attention to innovation (Lane & Maxfield, 1996). Generative emergence for innovation requires two things, according to Bushe (2013). The first is a change in the way one thinks about a subject; which creates new options for decision or actions and second, there needs to be something that compels them to act upon it. It is the responsibility of community leaders to create a culture that allows for the sharing of ideas and this is involves the ability of the organizations to balance connectivity and interaction within the organization and within the community (Surie & Hazy, 2006). The leaders in a community need to create opportunities for generative innovation, including providing resources for incubators and for engagement between industries to share ideas and solve problems. When individuals feel safe to explain their perspective, then the organization, the community and society will have the opportunity to flourish. The initial success will impact other businesses and this will provide more success that will eventually lead to a productive and innovative home for generative innovations.

Marketing Coalitions Socially

Coalition building is selling ideas and growing mass support for an initiative, idea, or product (Kanter, 2002). All members of a social network build a coalition structure. These relationships are interdependent.

Being socially responsible and a community supporter will enhance opportunities for business. For example, nonprofit organizations can be supported by the for-profit organizations in the community. For-profit businesses benefit from a positive brand image when they create the impression of being socially responsible. Customers are more interested than ever in businesses that represent a positive image to society. For example, Abercrombie & Fitch publicly stated they did not want to market to larger size customers, and because this was seen by consumers as being elitist, profits declined. In August 2016, A&F decided to stop using shirtless models and move toward a more wholesome image to help the sinking brand (La Monica, 2016). Companies that attack individuals or groups tend to damage their brand, and because of social media, companies that do the wrong thing are quickly identified. Therefore, it is prudent for businesses and companies—including entrepreneurs—to consider collaborative socially responsible solutions whenever possible.

Walmart is often selected as a target for destroying communities and small businesses; however, the results indicate that the retail giant creates many benefits to counter the strains it causes in communities. Walmart supports the local economies by selling local products and by contributing to nonprofit organizations in the region (Carden, Courtemanch, & Meiners, 2009; Goetz & Swaminathan, 2006). Through this community outreach Walmart appears to be more socially responsible which helps the brand when the press wants to discuss negative impacts like low wages for workers. Interestingly enough, the presence of Walmart in a community can create a spillover effect. There is often a density of small, independent businesses co-located with Walmart, offering products and services one cannot find there (Carden et al., 2009). This symbiosis is enhanced when corporate-entrepreneur relationships remain strong and local communication lines remain open.

Establishing a community brand that is collaborative and socially responsible creates an ecosystem of shared responsibly and leads to prosperity. Silicon Valley in California and the Hsinchu-Taipei region in Taiwan have been able to create brand equity for the community through technology incubation focusing on transference of "capital, skills and know-how" (Saxenian, 2001). The ability to share resources has led to advances that have changed the world through their impact on a range of technology-related industries. These communities are prosperous when they have ability to be flexible and adapt to market shifts resulting incremental sustainable innovations. This community could not be developed without the clear tech focused mission, transparency and above all else collaboration.

Limitations to Social Networks

Note that some scholars believe social networks provide a backdrop for business purposes, but many more variables exist that minimize the real power of social networking whether with individuals (Reese & Aldrich, 1995) or organizations (Alter & Hage, 1993). Scott and Davis (2007) cautioned that "the playing field is not level: important differences exist in opportunity structures as well as in the capacity of individuals to take advantage of them" (p. 248). Hoang and Yi (2015) indicate that "initiating and maintaining" social networks "requires considerable resource input," which could be costly and time consuming (p. 28). Additionally, Alter and Hage (1993) and Watson (2007) explain that different types of social networks perform differently depending on purpose as performance indicators, such as survival, growth, or resources. So social networking must be used and monitored for various purposes at different stages and levels.

Brüderl and Preisendörfer (1998) and Littunen (2000) argue that social networks and social networking are not to be replacements for entrepreneurial skills, competence, or even experience. Chell and Baines (2000) believe social networks can be used to exclude—as well as include—key stakeholders but might reinforce barriers that promote discord, division, or exclusivity. Atterton (2007) said, "Over time, networks can also become restricting, conservative and stifling if they involve no new players or information, and thus can result in negative impacts" (p. 231). Atterton also noted that while strong ties create common knowledge and commitment, they may be "impediment to change," which would obviously stifle innovation and entrepreneurship (p. 231). Finally, Putnam (2000) believes that the social capital created in social networks may be "economically unproductive" because strong ties limit growth and may be taken for granted, and highly successful entrepreneurs can be taken advantage of based on obligations to their social networks (p. 322).

Conclusion

The old adage of "it's not what you know, it's whom you know" still holds true. Social networking is about creating an ongoing system that shares knowledge, cultural norms, and social capital related to the development of entrepreneurs and entrepreneurial opportunities. Open, targeted, constructive information exchange—built on trust—is the central pillar on which effective relationships are built. As these relationships branch out to become more inclusive of other community actors, the amount of information in the network and knowledge about opportunity increases.

When these knowledge-sharing relationships are supported by positive outcomes and a culture of creativity and helpfulness, trust and social capital are built and can be called upon again and again. The more habitual the interaction and the more visible the outcomes, the more likely other entrepreneurial thinkers will be likely to join the community, creating a virtuous cycle of entrepreneurship development (see Shane & Venkataraman, 2000). When entrepreneurs lead communities, then the incentives of entrepreneurs typically become central in how the community conducts its affairs, which can look quite different from how larger organizations do business. This action may differentiate the community somewhat, but such communities stand alone as attractors for like-minded thinkers who wish to create, venture, and launch. This process, in turn, supports the broader community by creating a mechanism for innovation that can lead to important partnerships with larger business, governments, and other organizations. Regardless of individual or organizational interactions, productivity stems from clear roles and responsibilities.

The strategies discussed in this chapter, including partnership, mindful networking, broad-based engagement, effective marketing, and social media, are all strategies for building the networks that eventually create an entrepreneurial community. Once networks are formed, it is up to community leaders (likely entrepreneurs, but sometimes other local leaders as well) to set the tone of exchange, and establish mutual cultural norms that support and enhance the will to venture, to take constructive risks, to fail gracefully, and to try again.

References

Ajzen, I., & Fishbein, M. (1980). *Understanding attitudes and predicting social behavior*. Englewood Cliffs, NJ: Prentice Hall.

Aldrich, H. (2002). Entrepreneurial strategies in new organizational populations. In R. Swedberg (Ed.), *Entrepreneurship: The social science view* (pp. 212–228). New York, NY: Oxford University Press.

Aldrich, H., & Zimmer, C. (1986). Entrepreneurship through social networks. In D. L. Sexton & R. W. Smilor (Eds.), *The art and science of entrepreneurship* (pp. 3–23). Cambridge, MA: Ballinger Publishing Company.

Alter, C., & Hage, J. (1993). *Organizations working together*. Newbury Park, CA: Sage.

Atterton, J. (2007). The 'strength of weak ties': Social networking by business owners in the Highlands and Islands of Scotland. *Sociologia Ruralis*, *47*(3), 228–245.

Banyai, C. (2009). Community leadership: Development and evolution of leadership in Himeshima. *Rural Society*, *19*(3), 241–261.

Beckman, C., Schoonhoven, C., Rottner, R., & Kim, S-J. (2014). Relational pluralism in de novo organizations: Board of directors as bridges or barriers? *Academy of Management Journal*, *57*(2), 267–294.

Birley, S. (1985). The role of networks in the entrepreneurial process. *Journal of Business Venturing*, *1*, 107–117.

Blakely, E. J. (1989). *Planning local economic development: Theory and practice*. Newbury Park, CA: Sage.

Blanchflower, D. G., & Oswald, A. J. (1998). What makes an entrepreneur? *Journal of Labor Economics*, *16*(1), 26–60.

Blau, P. M. (1964). *Exchange in power in social life*. New York, NY: Wiley.

Blois, K. J. (1999). Trust in business to business relationships: An evaluation of its status. *Journal of Management Studies*, *36*(2), 197–215.

Breazeale, N. D., & Hustedde, R. J. (2017). Understanding the impact of culture on entrepreneurship. In M. W-P Fortunato & M. R. Clevenger (Eds.), *Toward entrepreneurial community development: Leaping cultural and leadership boundaries* (pp. 104–125). New York, NY: Routledge.

Brewer, J. D. (2000). *Ethnography*. Philadelphia, PA: Open University Press.

Brinckmann, J., & Hoegl, M. (2011). Effects of initial teamwork capability and initial relational capability on the development of new technology-based firms. *Strategic Entrepreneurship Journal*, *5*(1), 37–57.

Bromiley, P., & Cummings, L. L. (1995). Transaction costs in organizations with trust. In R. Bies, R. Lewici, & B. Sheppard (Eds.), *Research in negotiations in organizations* (pp. 219–250). Bingley, UK: Emerald Group Publishing.

Brüderl, J., & Preisendörfer, P. (1998). Network support and the success of newly found business. *Small Business Economics*, *10*(3), 213–225.

Burt, R. S. (1995). *Structural holes: The social structure of competition*. Boston, MA: Harvard University Press.

Burt, R. S. (2002). The network entrepreneur. In R. Swedberg (Ed.), *Entrepreneurship: The social science view* (pp. 281–307). New York, NY: Oxford University Press.

Bushe, G. R. (2013). Generative process, generative outcome: The transformational potential of appreciative inquiry. In D. L. Cooperrider, D. P. Zandee, L. N. Godwin, M. Avital, & B. Boland (Eds.), *Organizational generativity: The appreciative inquiry summit and a scholarship of transformation*. Advances in appreciative inquiry (Vol. 4, pp. 89–113). Bingley, UK: Emerald Group Publishing.

Carden, A., Courtemanche, C., & Meiners, J. (2009). Does Wal-Mart reduce social capital? *Public Choice*, *138*(1), 109–136.

Carsrud, A. L., Gaglio, C. M., & Olm, K. W. (1987). Entrepreneurs—mentors, networks, and successful new venture development: An exploratory study. *American Journal of Small Business*, *12*(2), 13–18.

Chaskin, R. J., Brown, P., Benkatesh, S., & Vidal, A. (2001). *Building community capacity*. New York, NY: Aldine de Gruyter.

Chell, E., & Baines, S. (2000). Networking, entrepreneurship and micro-business behaviour. *Entrepreneurship and Regional Development*, *12*(3), 195–215.

Clark, D. (2014). *Three mistakes to avoid when networking*. Retrieved from http://blogs.hbr.org/2014/02/three-mistakes-to-avoid-when-networking/

Clevenger, M. R. (2017). Perceptions of entrepreneurs and community: From historical roots to a contemporary kaleidoscope. In M. W-P Fortunato & M. R. Clevenger (Eds.), *Toward entrepreneurial community development: Leaping cultural and leadership boundaries* (pp. 10–50). New York, NY: Routledge.

Clevenger, M. R., & Miao, C. (2017). Transformational leadership to build an entrepreneurial community. In M. W-P Fortunato & M. R. Clevenger (Eds.), *Toward entrepreneurial community development: Leaping cultural and leadership boundaries* (pp. 152–176). New York, NY: Routledge.

Clow, K. E., & Baack, D. (2010). *Marketing management: A customer-oriented approach* (3rd ed.). Thousand Oaks, CA: Sage.

Coe, B. A. (1987). *Public-private cooperation*. Jefferson, NC: McFarland & Co.

Coleman, J. S. (1988). Social capital in the creation of human capital. *American Journal of Sociology*, *94*, S95–S120.

Colon, R. (n.d.). *Professional networking 101: "Developing the known network"©*. Retrieved from http://www.medtalents.com/images/101.pdf

Cook, K. S., Levi, M., & Hardin, R. (2009). *Whom can we trust? How groups, networks, and institutions make trust possible*. New York, NY: Russell Sage Foundation.

Cooper, A. C. (2002). Networks, alliances, and entrepreneurship. In M. A. Hitt, R. D. Ireland, S. M. Camp, & D. L. Sexton (Eds.), *Strategic entrepreneurship: Creating a new mindset* (pp. 203–222). Malden, MA: Blackwell Publishers.

Cooper, A. C., & Daily, C. M. (1997). Entrepreneurial teams. In D. L. Sexton & R. W. Smilor (Eds.), *Entrepreneurship 2000* (pp. 127–150). Chicago, IL: Upstart Publishing Co.

Corkindale, G. (2009). *6 networking mistakes and how to avoid them*. Retrieved from http://blogs.hbr.org/2009/04/6-networking-mistakes-and-how/

Cropper, S., Ebers, M., Huxham, C., & Ring, P. S. (Eds.). (2008). *The Oxford handbook of inter-organizational relations*. New York, NY: Oxford University Press.

Currall, S. C., & Judge, T. A. (1995). Measuring trust between organizational boundary role persons. *Organizational Behavior and Human Decision Processes*, *64*(2), 151–170.

Dutta, S. (2010). Managing yourself: What's your personal social media strategy? *Harvard Business Review*. Retrieved on July 10, 2015 from https://hbr.org/2010/11/managing-yourself-whats-your-personal-social-media-strategy

Ebers, M. (1999). The dynamics of inter-organizational relationships. *Sociology of Organizations*, *16*, 31–56.

Evald, M. R., Klyver, K., & Svendsen, S. G. (2006). The changing importance of the strength of ties throughout the entrepreneurial process. *Journal of Enterprising Culture*, *14*, 1–26.

Feld, B. (2012). *Startup communities: Building an entrepreneurial ecosystem in your city*. Hoboken, NJ: Wiley.

George, B. (2004). *Authentic leadership: Rediscovering the secrets to creating lasting value*. San Francisco, CA: Jossey-Bass.

Goetz, S. J., & Swaminathan, H. (2006). Wal-Mart and county-wide poverty. *Social Science Quarterly*, *87*(2), 211–226.

Goldsmith, S. (1946). *The power of social innovation: How civic entrepreneurs ignite community networks for good*. San Francisco, CA: Jossey-Bass.

Grandi, A., & Grimaldi, R. (2003). Exploring the networking characteristics of new venture founding teams: A study of Italian academic spin-off. *Small Business Economics*, *21*(4), 329–341.

Granovetter, M. (1973). The strength of weak ties. *American Journal of Sociology*, *78*(6), 1360–1380.

Granovetter, M. (1992). Problems of explanation in economic sociology. In N. Nohria & R. Eccles (Eds.), *Networks and organizations: Structure* (pp. 25–56). Boston, MA: Harvard Business School Press.

Gulati, R., & Gargiulo, M. (1999). Where do interorganizational networks come from? The *American Journal of Sociology*, *104*(5), 1439–1493.

Hardin, R. (2002). *Trust and trustworthiness*. New York, NY: Russell Sage Foundation.

Hindle, K. (2010). How community context affects entrepreneurial process: A diagnostic framework. *Entrepreneurship & Regional Development*, *22*(7), 599–647.

Hitt, M., & Ireland, R. D. (2000). The intersection of entrepreneurship and strategic management research. In D. L. Sexton & H. Landström (Eds.), *Handbook of entrepreneurship* (pp. 43–63). Malden, MA: Blackwell Publishers.

Hoang, H., & Antoncic, B. (2003). Network-based research in entrepreneurship: A critical review. *Journal of Business Venturing*, *18*, 165–187. Retrieved from http://dx.doi:10.1016/S0883-9026(02)00081-2

Hoang, H., & Yi, A. (2015). Network-based research in entrepreneurship: A decade in review. *Foundations and Trends® in Entrepreneurship*, *11*(1), 1–54. Retrieved from http://dx.doi.org/10.1561/0300000052

Hoselitz, B. F. (1960). *Sociological aspects of economic growth*. Glencoe, IL: Free Press.

Houlihan, K. (2015). Business 2030: Enabling innovation, changing the workplace. Business Section. *Times Leader*. Retrieved from http://timesleader.com/news/business/2384/enabling-innovation-changing-the-workplace

Huggins, R. (2000). The success and failure of policy-implanted inter-firm network initiatives: Motivations, processes and structure. *Entrepreneurship and Regional Development*, *12*(2), 111–135.

Isenberg, D. J. (2010). How to start an entrepreneurial revolution. *Harvard Business Review*. Retrieved from https://hbr.org/2010/06/the-big-idea-how-to-start-an-entrepreneurial-revolution

Jarillo, J. C. (1988). On strategic networks. *Strategic Management Journal*, *9*, 31–41.

Johannisson, B. (2000). Networking and entrepreneurial growth. In D. L. Sexton & H. Landström (Eds.), *Handbook of entrepreneurship* (pp. 368–386). Malden, MA: Blackwell Publishers.

Johnson, W. C. (2006). The collaboration imperative. In L. E. Weber & J. J. Duderstadt (Eds.), *Universities and business: Partnering for the knowledge society* (pp. 99–110). London, UK: Economica Ltd.

Kanter, R. M. (2002). When a thousand flowers bloom: Structural, collective, and social conditions for innovation in organization. In R. Swedberg (Ed.), *Entrepreneurship: The social science view* (pp. 167–210). New York, NY: Oxford University Press.

Kent, C. A. (1982). Entrepreneurship in economic development. In D. L. Sexton & K. H. Vesper (Eds.), *Encyclopedia of entrepreneurship* (pp. 237–256). Englewood Cliffs, NJ: Prentice Hall.

Kulcsar, L. J., & Yum, Y. (2011). One nation, one brand? Nation branding and identity reconstruction in post-communist Hungary. In N. Kaneva (Ed.), *Branding post-communist nations: Marketizing national identities in the "new" Europe* (pp. 65–78). London, UK: Routledge.

La Monica, P. R. (2016). Summer girls no longer shop at Abercrombie & Fitch. *CNN Money*. Retrieved on August 30, 2016 from http://money.cnn.com/2016/08/30/investing/abercrombie-fitch-hollister-sales-earnings/

Landström, H. (2005). *Pioneers in entrepreneurship and small business research*. New York, NY: Springer.

Lane, D., & Maxfield, R. (1996, April). Strategy under complexity: Fostering generative relationships. *Long Range Planning*, *29*, 215–231.

Li, D. (2013). Multilateral R and D alliances by new ventures. *Journal of Business Venturing*, *28*(2), 241–260.

Lichtenstein, G. A., & Lyons, T. S. (2010). *Investing in entrepreneurs: A strategic approach for strengthening your regional and community economy*. Santa Barbara, CA: Praeger.

Lin, N. (2001). *Social capital: A theory of social structure and action*. New York, NY: Cambridge University Press.

Lin, N., Ensel, W. M., & Vaughn, J. C. (1981, August). Social resources and strength of ties: Structural factors in occupational status attainment. *American Sociological Review*, *46*, 393–405.

Littunen, H. (2000). Entrepreneurship and the characteristics of the entrepreneurial personality. *International Journal of Entrepreneurial Behavior & Research*, *6*(6), 295–310. Retrieved from http://dx.doi.org/10.1108/13552550010362741

Loury, G. (1977). A dynamic theory of racial income differences. In P. Wallace & A. LaMond (Eds.), *Women, minorities, and employment discrimination* (pp. 153–188). Lexington, MA: Lexington Books.

Mackay, H. (1990). *Dig your well before you're thirsty: The only networking book you'll ever need*. New York, NY: Doubleday.

MacKinnon, D., Chapman, K., & Cumbers, A. (2004). Networks, trust and embeddedness amongst SMEs in the Aberdeen oil complex. *Entrepreneurship and Regional Development*, *16*(2), 87–106.

Mazzucato, M. (2013). *The entrepreneurial state: Debunking public vs. private sector myths*. New York, NY: Anthem Press.

McKeever, E., Anderson, A., & Jack, S. (2014). Social embeddedness in entrepreneurship research: The importance of context and community. In E. Chell & M. Karatas-Ozkan (Eds.), *Handbook of research on small business and entrepreneurship* (pp. 222–236). Northampton, MA: Edward Elgar.

McQuaid, R. (1996). Social networks, entrepreneurship and regional development. In M. Danson (Ed.), *Small firm formation and regional economic development* (pp. 118–131). New York, NY: Routledge.

Meyer, J. W., & Rowan, B. (1977). Institutionalized organizations: Formal structure as myth and ceremony. *American Journal of Sociology*, *83*, 340–363.

Mönstead, M. (1993). Regional network processes: Networks for the service sector or development of entrepreneurs? In C. Karlsson, B. Johannisson, & D. Storey (Eds.), *Small business dynamics* (pp. 204–222). London, UK: Routledge.

Morgan, G. (2006). *Images of organization*. Thousand Oaks, CA: Sage.

Nalebuff, B. J., & Brandenburger, A. M. (1997). Co-opetition: Competitive and cooperative business strategies for the digital economy. *Strategy & Leadership*, *25*(6), 28–33.

Neergaard, H. (2005). Networking activities in technology-based entrepreneurial teams. *International Small Business Journal*, *23*(3), 257–278.

Nicolaou, N., & Birley, S. (2003). Social networks in organizational emergence: The university spinout phenomenon. *Management Science*, *49*(12), 1702–1725.

Nielsen, S. L., Klyver, K., Evald, M. R., & Bager, T. (2012). *Entrepreneurship in theory and practice: Paradoxes in play*. Northampton, MA: Edward Elgar.

Osborne, P. L. (2000). *Tropical ecosystems and ecological concepts*. New York, NY: Cambridge University Press.

Pages, E. R. (2006). *Hello, my business name is . . . a guide to building entrepreneurial networks in North Carolina*. Durham, NC: The Council for Entrepreneurial Development.

Pages, E. R., & Garmise, S. (2003, Summer). The power of entrepreneurial networking. *Economic Development Journal*, 20–30.

Pfeffer, J., & Salancik, G. R. (2003). *The external control of organizations: A resource dependence perspective*. Stanford, CA: Stanford University Press.

Portes, A. (1995). *The economic sociology of immigration: Essays on networks, ethnicity, and entrepreneurship*. New York, NY: Russell Sage Foundation.

Powell, W. W. (1990). Neither market nor hierarchy: Network forms of organization. In B. Shaw & L. Cummings (Eds.), *Research in organizational behavior* (pp. 295–336). Greenwich, CT: JAI Press.

Powell, W. W., & Smith-Doerr, L. (1994). Networks and economic life. In N. J. Smelser & R. Swedberg (Eds.), *The handbook of economic sociology* (pp. 368–402). New York, NY: Russell Sage Foundation; Princeton, NJ: Princeton University Press.

Putnam, L. L., Grant, D., Michelson, G., & Cutcher, L. (2005). Discourse and resistance: Targets, practices and consequences. *Management Communication Quarterly*, *19*(1), 5–19.

Putnam, R. D. (2000). *Bowling alone: The collapse and revival of American community*. New York, NY: Simon & Schuster.

Raff, D. M. G., & Summers, L. H. (1987). Did Henry Ford pay efficiency wages? *Journal of Labor Economics*, *5*(4), S57–S86, Part 2: The New Economics of Personnel.

Reese, P. R., & Aldrich, H. E. (1995). Entrepreneurial networks and business performance: A panel of small and medium-sized firms in the research triangle. In S. Birley & I. C. MacMillan (Eds.), *International entrepreneurship* (pp. 124–144). New York, NY: Routledge.

Reis, E. (2011). *The lean startup: How today's entrepreneurs use continuous innovation to create radically successful businesses*. Denvers, MA: Crown Business.

Ring, P. S., & Van de Ven, A. H. (1994). Developmental processes of cooperative interorganizational relationships. *Academy of Management Review*, *19*(1), 90–118.

Rogers, E. M. (2003). *Diffusion of innovations* (5th ed.). New York, NY: Free Press.

Rotter, J. B. (1967). A new scale for the measurement of interpersonal trust. *Journal of Personality*, *35*(4), 651–665.

Samans, R. (2005). *Partnering for success: Business perspectives on multistakeholder partnerships*. Boston, MA: Harvard University Press.

Savas, E. S. (2000). *Privatization and public-private partnerships*. London, UK: Chatham House.

Saxenian, A. L. (2001). The Silicon Valley-Hsinchu connection: Technical communities and industrial upgrading. *Berkeley Planning Journal*, *15*(1), 3–31. Retrieved from https://escholarship.org/uc/item/0v02k7kd

Schramm, C. J. (2010). Building entrepreneurial economies. In R. W. Price (Ed.), *Entrepreneurship* (Annual Editions, 6th ed., pp. 25–29). New York, NY: McGraw-Hill.

Schultz, L. I. (2012). University industry government collaboration for economic growth. In J. E. Lane & D. B. Johnstone (Eds.), *Universities and colleges as economic drivers* (pp. 129–162). Albany, NY: SUNY Press.

Schurr, P. H., & Ozanne, J. L. (1985). Influences on exchange processes: Buyers' preconceptions of a seller's trustworthiness and bargaining toughness. *Journal of Consumer Research*, *11*(4), 939–953.

Scott, A. (1985). *New industrial space: Flexible production organisation and regional development in North America and Western Europe*. London, UK: Pion.

Scott, J., & Carrington, P. C. (2011). *The SAGE handbook of social network analysis*. Los Angeles, CA: Sage.

Scott, W. R., & Davis, G. F. (2007). *Organizations and organizing: Rational, natural, and open system perspectives*. Upper Saddle River, NJ: Pearson/Prentice Hall.

Shane, S., & Cable, D. (2002). Network ties, reputation, and the financing of new ventures. *Management Science*, *48*(3), 364–381.

Shane, S., & Venkataraman, S. (2000). The promise of entrepreneurship as a field of research. *Academy of Management Review*, *25*(1), 217–226.

Shuffstall, B. (2013). *Entrepreneurial community self-assessment*. State College, PA: Penn State University Extension.

Shuffstall, B., & Fortunato, M. (2013). *Part 2: Tools and techniques for creating an entrepreneurial community*. Retrieved from http://extension.psu.edu/community/ecd/courses/entrepreneurial-communities/webinars/creating-entrepreneurial-communities-session-ii/creating-entrepreneurial-communities-session-ii

Smith-Doerr, L., & Powell, W. W. (2005). Networks and economic life. In N. J. Smelser & R. Swedberg (Eds.), *The handbook of economic sociology* (pp. 379–402). Princeton, NJ: Princeton University Press.

Steiner, A., & Cleary, J. (2014). What are the features of resilient businesses? Exploring the perception of rural entrepreneurs. *The Journal of Rural and Community Development*, *9*(3), 1–20.

Surie, G., & Hazy, J. K. (2006). Generative leadership: Nurturing innovation in complex systems. *E:CO*, *8*(4), 13–26.
Swedberg, R. (1994). Markets as social structures. In N. Smelser & R. Swedberg (Eds.), *The handbook of economic sociology* (pp. 255–282). Princeton, NJ: Princeton University Press.
Szarka, J. (1990). Networking and small firms. *International Small Business Journal*, *8*(2), 10–22.
Thornton, P. H., & Flynn, K. H. (2003). Entrepreneurship, networks, and geographies. In Z. J. Acs & D. B. Audretsch (Eds.), *Handbook of entrepreneurship research: An interdisciplinary survey and introduction* (pp. 401–433). Boston, MA: Kluwer Academic Publishers.
Uslaner, E. M. (1999). Trust but verify: Social capital and moral behavior. *Social Science Information Sur Les Sciences Sociales*, *38*, 29–155.
Vissa, B., & Chacar, A. S. (2009). Leveraging ties: The contingent value of entrepreneurial teams' external advice networks on Indian software venture performance. *Strategic Management Journal*, *30*(11), 1179–1191.
Volcic, Z., & Andrejevic, M. (2011). Nation branding in the era of commercial nationalism, *International Journal of Communications*, *5*, 598–618.
Walzer, N. (Ed.). (2007). *Entrepreneurship and local economic development*. New York, NY: Lexington Books.
Watson, J. (2007). Modeling the relationship between networking and firm performance. *Journal of Business Venturing*, *22*(6), 852–874.
Wellman, B., & Berkowitz, S. D. (1988). *Social structures: A network approach*. Cambridge, MA: Cambridge University Press.
Wellman, B., Carrington, P. J., & Hall, A. (1988). Networks as personal communities. In B. Wellman & S. D. Berkowitz (Eds.), *Social structures: A network approach* (pp. 130–184). New York, NY: Cambridge University Press.
White, H. C. (1988). Varieties of markets. In B. Wellman & S. D. Berkowitz (Eds.), *Social structures: A network approach* (pp. 226–260). New York, NY: Cambridge University Press.
Witt, P. (2004). Entrepreneurs' networks and the success of start-ups. *Entrepreneurship and Regional Development*, *16*(5), 391–412.
Woolcock, M., & Narayan, D. (2000). Social capital: Implications for development theory, research, and policy. *World Bank Research Observer*, *15*(2), 225–249. doi:10.1093/wbro/15.2.225.
Zacharakis, A., Spinelli, S., & Timmons, J. A. (2011). *Business plans that work: A guide for small business*. New York, NY: McGraw-Hill.

7 High- and Low-Entrepreneurial Communities

A Multiple Case Study[1]

Michael W-P Fortunato

Many communities—maybe even your own—exhibit a strong sense of support for entrepreneurs. The conceptual treatment of entrepreneurial communities compared to an empirical one is important to see both theoretical and real-life application. First, the very term "entrepreneurship" is obscure and understood differently by different scholars (Acs & Audretsch, 2003; Aldrich & Zimmer, 1986; Alvarez & Barney, 2000; Brewer & Gibson, 2014; Burt, 2002; Carsrud, Olm, & Eddy, 1986; Clifton & Badal, 2014; Cochran, 1949; Cooper, Markman, & Niss, 2000; Fayolle, 2014; Florida, 2002, 2012; 2012; Forson, Ozbilgin, Ozturk, & Tatli, 2014; Gasse, 1986; Hitt & Reed, 2000; Landstrom, 2005; Lichtenstein & Lyons, 2010; Reynolds, 2007; Sexton & Smilor, 1986). Second, the term "community" is just as obscure (Aldrich & Zimmer, 1986; Banyai, 2009; Bowman, 1932; Durkheim, 1964; Feld, 2012; Gusfield, 1975; McMillan & Chavis, 1986; Warren, 1987), and putting two obscure terms together only complicates matters more.

This definitional challenge does not mean that entrepreneurial communities cannot be studied, or that the term "entrepreneurial community" has no meaning. One can imagine the difference between an entrepreneurial community and a non-entrepreneurial community with little effort—what each looks like and feels like, what the culture is like, how people generally behave, what they value most and least, the priorities of leaders, and the life goals of long-time residents. One can imagine these different communities, but do they exist in real life? What does it really mean to be an *entrepreneurial community?*

Fortunato (2011) chose to conduct a mixed-method, multiple case study on the topic in the states of Maine, Pennsylvania, and Wisconsin. Qualitative results are presented here, following dozens of interviews of both entrepreneurs and institutional actors alike in six different communities. The qualitative interviews are particularly applicable to advancing the current literature, as they illustrate in detail how entrepreneurs and their communities interact (or fail to interact) in context in richer detail than one can find in a survey. This rich illumination is especially important for making sense of the wide variety of meanings surrounding entrepreneurship and community. Put differently, these case studies help to make sense of how the fuzzy terms "entrepreneurship" and "community" interact in an everyday context. The stories and experiences also provide accounts of both the institutional and cultural support structures encountered by entrepreneurs, with an emphasis on contrasting the different experiences in high- and low-entrepreneurship communities. The chapter briefly covers the methodology used, and then presents the findings from each community studied. Finally, a synthesis of the findings is presented that identifies key themes discriminating between high- and low-entrepreneurship communities.

The Motivations and Rationale for Entrepreneurial Community Research

This question led to studying the cultural and institutional differences between high- and low-entrepreneurship communities beginning in 2010. Growing up just outside Pittsburgh, Pennsylvania, in the hills of the southwestern part of the Commonwealth, it was (and still is) a region filled with little former steel mill towns only minutes away from posh suburbs and small historical hamlets with bustling, attractive main streets that would trail off into abandonment and decay because of the loss of local population in the wake of post-industrial economic restructuring. The Pittsburgh suburbs always seemed to have a lot to do (for suburbs), and small businesses dominated the local landscape there in an era when chain stores had not quite reached the popularity seen today. Some smaller towns farther from the city were equally capable of building viable communities among their historical assets, brick facades, and cobblestone side streets. In other towns, small businesses would appear, only to disappear within months. Main streets were abandoned and vandalized, and peppered with cheap bars and an occasional discount store standing semi-vacant like forlorn brick and stone monuments dedicated to a proud past that has long since vanished. There was poverty everywhere, and an entrenched belief that the town would bounce back—just as soon as the steel mill did. Adding to the bleakness, there was a devastating racial dimension to this dichotomy that was not discussed as openly back then. While upper-middle class minorities, who espoused the dominant cultural values of the suburbs, were embraced by suburban communities in small numbers, working-class, and impoverished minorities frequently lived in declining communities in much larger concentrations, and were tragically viewed by some as living symbols of a "less desirable" area. While the posh suburbs felt more inclusive and optimistic (at least toward the middle and upper-middle class), declining steel towns felt fractured and isolated, and seemed to embrace failure and traditional power structures, and entrenched social and economic roles more readily. Locals would make remarks about their entrepreneurial peers like, "I can't believe that guy tried to start a business here . . . what was he thinking?" It was a far cry from the posh suburbs, where one could hear locals making remarks like, "I can't believe it took us so long to get [Business X]!"

Years later, while experimenting with owning a small business in the New York City area, the work took me through a number of rural towns. Some were thriving, with local businesses lining not only the main streets but also the industrial and commercial parks as well. Others clearly thrived at one point, decades ago, and sat in a state of partial dilapidation and abandonment. The towns were often run-down, vandalized, and on more than one occasion, locals would stop to shout epithets and unwelcoming statements. Apparently looking very much like an outsider to them communicated that the researcher was not the kind of person they wanted in their town. In one such town, a local leader mentioned that one of the keystone buildings on the main street was for sale for $60,000. It needed a little bit of work, but coming from New York City, I found it was astonishing. It came to mind, "Why isn't every single entrepreneur from New York City paying that much a year in storefront rent *flocking* to towns like these? One could own a gorgeous, historic building outright and do anything with it!" Aside from the occasional heckling, it seemed almost too good to be true for an entrepreneurially minded young person.

As it turns out, this simple question touched off a project intended to elucidate why some communities seem to cultivate entrepreneurs easily, while other communities struggle to do the same. Why weren't entrepreneurs moving to some small towns in droves, even if the town had plenty of historical charm, cheap overhead, and skilled labor ready to work? What were the barriers and could they be reversed? Why were some communities so *entrepreneurial*, while others struggled to hold on to even a few businesses? It is a complex issue, made more challenging by a complicated, discordant, and multifaceted literature on entrepreneurship (see Davidson, 2008 and Fortunato, 2014 for details on the complex world of entrepreneurial scholarship).

Case Selection

This research is based on the comparison of high- and low-entrepreneurship communities in multiple regions. Yin (2015) explains that in multiple case study analysis cases must be chosen carefully to represent the case along a dimension that is either hypothesized to produce a convergent result (replication) or a divergent result for predictable reasons (as in a control group). In this case, communities are selected for the level of entrepreneurial activity that they exhibit—a phenomenon to be discussed in the section highlighting operational terms. Differences in entrepreneurship levels are expected to be associated with differences in individual-institutional-opportunity interaction, so Yin's (2015) latter suggestion about "predictable differences" between case sites is most applicable in this study.

Selecting Study Regions for Comparison

Three U.S. states, each in a different region of the United States, were chosen for research. Because of the author's participation in unrelated research in Maine, Pennsylvania, and Wisconsin, these three states were chosen for study. The choice of states could be somewhat arbitrary *as long as* the states represented three distinct areas of cultural and economic history. The term "arbitrary" is used because most states do not have a stated "small business policy," only different entrepreneurial assistance organizations and support agencies (Dabson, Malkin, Mathews, Pate, & Stickle, 2003). Additionally, Acs and Armington (2006) and Goetz (2006) found rural areas with varying degrees of breadth and depth in all regions of the United States, although there was considerable entrepreneurial growth in the intermountain West over the past decade (Acs & Armington, 2006). None of the selected states are in the intermountain West, whose growth is partially attributable to rapid growth in the general population and the attraction of lifestyle-oriented entrepreneurs like lone eagles and high flyers (Beyers & Lindahl, 1996; Sopuck, 2003). Differences in entrepreneurial assistance programs at the state level will be discussed in the community profile. Whether or not these programs play a significant role in local entrepreneurship development or the development of the individual-institutional-opportunity nexus is expected to come out in face-to-face interviews and surveys (Fortunato, 2011), although Dabson et al. (2003) suggests that such programs tend to have little effect in rural areas.

Communities in these three states were thus selected for study. These states represent the upper Midwest (Wisconsin), the Mid-Atlantic (Pennsylvania), and New England (Maine)—all areas with different cultural and economic histories, different landscapes and natural resource endowments, and different industry mixes and patterns of development. Hustedde (2007) describes the importance of local and regional culture to entrepreneurship, and no obvious factors beyond cultural, geographical, and historical attributes exist in these states that might be expected to affect entrepreneurship development substantially at the state or regional level.

Data Used for Study Site Selection

With three states selected, one high- and low-entrepreneurship community must be selected in each for comparison. To create his breadth and depth measures, Goetz (2006) utilized county economic data files from the Regional Economic Information System (REIS) of the Bureau of Economic Analysis. Interactive Table CA-30 (U.S. Department of Commerce, 2011) enables researchers to download county-specific data, including those necessary to calculate breadth and depth: the number of nonfarm proprietors, the total number of full- and part-time employment positions, and the average nonfarm proprietor's income for the county. Since this research studies rural areas, the investigation is restricted to U.S. Census-designated nonmetropolitan counties as an approximation of rural areas. Rural areas are not defined by the Census or REIS, but nonmetropolitan represents a residual category consisting of those places that are not metropolitan, generally having lower population density and, by definition, a lack of urban agglomeration effects.

Therefore, any county declared to be "metropolitan" or part of a larger metropolitan statistical area is omitted from the research.

One question that arose in designing the research was whether or not to include *farms* in the analysis of entrepreneurs, especially given the importance of agriculture to many rural economies. Richards and Bulkley (2007) call farmers the "first and forgotten" agricultural entrepreneurs (p. 1), making reference to the fact that many people do not immediately think of farmers when they think about "entrepreneurship." These authors contend that the risk-tolerant entrepreneurial culture of the United States can partially be attributed to the entrepreneurial nature of farming, especially among frontiersmen who founded farms despite the many risks of westward expansion. However, studies show that the majority of farms now earn supplemental income from off-the farm to support farming activities (Hoppe & Banker, 2006; McElwee, 2006). For many farmers and their family members, entrepreneurial, off-farm business activities have become increasingly important because they offer the flexibility and freedom to continue farming, and because losing the farm is, culturally speaking, not a viable option (Hildenbrand & Hennon, 2008). Similar analyses that are frequently cited in this work, including Acs and Armington (2006), Goetz (2006), and Henderson, Low, and Weiler (2007) chose not to include farms in their analyses. For consistency, this research will also omit farms, focusing entirely on nonfarm self-employed individuals. However, this is not to say that farms are not critical to local entrepreneurship in rural areas. Indeed, comparative research to understand how the phenomena under study in this research differentially affect farmers, farm-based entrepreneurs, and nonfarm entrepreneurs, is a rich area for ongoing inquiry and research.

Entrepreneurship Index Tabulation

Nonfarm self-employment data is used to construct *a compound index* for comparison. This compound index is the combination of two simple indices. The first is the *breadth* index, taken to be the ratio of self-employed individuals in the county to total population in that county. This ratio is then divided by the ratio of nonfarm self-employed individuals in all nonmetropolitan counties *in that state* as a proportion of total nonfarm population in nonmetropolitan counties *in that state* (this is the average ratio of self-employed workers to total population in nonmetropolitan counties in that state). This value is then multiplied by 100 so that a county with an index of 100 represents an average proportion of self-employed individuals to total population for nonmetropolitan counties of that state, higher values represent a higher proportion, and lower values a lower proportion. The breadth index can be found in this breadth index equation:

[(County nonfarm self-employed individuals) / (County population)] / [(State nonmetropolitan nonfarm self-employed individuals)/ (State nonmetropolitan population)] x 100 = *Breadth Index*

The breadth index can then be ranked from counties of highest breadth to those of lowest breadth within each state. Those counties with the highest breadth have the most self-employed individuals as a proportion of total population.

Breadth is one measure of entrepreneurial "success" based on the density of entrepreneurs in an area, but it does not measure how successful these self-employed people have been compared to other self-employed individuals. Breadth, therefore, does not necessarily correlate with *depth*, measured by the *depth* index. The depth index is taken to be the average nonfarm income for self-employed individuals in a county divided by the average nonfarm income for self-employed individuals in nonmetropolitan counties in the state. This value is then multiplied by 100 so that a county with an index of 100 represents the average income for self-employed individuals in nonmetropolitan areas of the state, while higher values represent a higher than average self-employment income and lower values a lower than average self-employment income. The depth index can be found in this depth index equation:

(County nonfarm average self-employed income) / (State nonmetropolitan nonfarm average self-employed income) x 100 = *Depth Index*

The depth index can then be ranked from counties of highest depth to those of lowest depth. Those with the highest depth have self-employed individuals earning the most income, on average, in the nonmetropolitan portion of that state. Breadth and depth may not always trend together, and some counties may rank high on one measure, and low on the other. To account for the combined effects of breadth and depth together, these two indices are averaged to calculate the average, which forms the *compound index* found in this compound index equation:

(Breadth Index + Depth Index) / 2 = *Compound Index*

The compound index is an average index of the combined effects of both breadth and depth. It should *not* be interpreted to mean that counties with indices over 100 are necessarily high in both breadth and depth; in fact, an index over 100 could mean that the county is very strong in either breadth or depth, and average in the other. However, when ranked, the highest indices are likely to be the combination of high breadth *and* depth measures, with the lowest the result of low breadth and depth measures.

The compound indices for each county are then ranked. The highest compound index represents the area of highest entrepreneurial activity, while the lowest compound index represents the area of lowest entrepreneurial activity. These two counties are selected as the *high* and *low-entrepreneurship* counties for study in that state. The selected sites, along with their compound indices, can be seen in Figure 7.1.

High Entrepreneurship	Maine	Pennsylvania	Wisconsin
County (Index)	Knox County (132.1)	Fulton County (132.9)	Buffalo County (142.2)
Community	Rockland	McConnellsburg	Alma

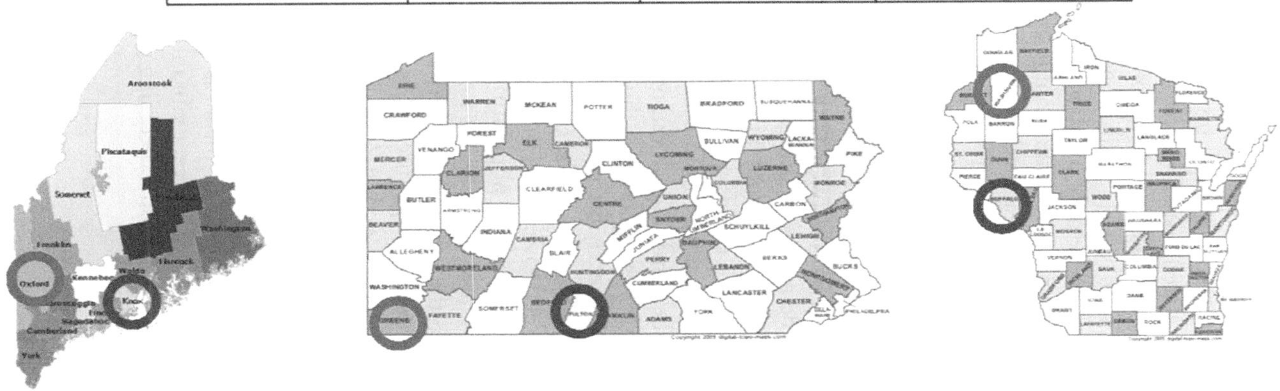

Low Entrepreneurship	Maine	Pennsylvania	Wisconsin
County (Index)	Oxford County (80.1)	Greene County (72.5)	Washburn County (61.4)
Community	Rumford	Waynesburg	Spooner

Figure 7.1 High- and Low-Entrepreneurship Study Sites with Compound Breadth/Depth Indices (Adapted from Fortunato, 2011, p. 127)

Community Selection

Within the counties that were selected based on their high- or low-entrepreneurship indices, the largest municipality within each of these counties is selected for study. Counties are often times quite large geographically, and contain multiple communities with multiple governments, chambers of commerce, and small business-related institutions. Choosing entrepreneurs randomly from across the county would lead to confusion about which entrepreneurs were interacting with which institutions. Because entrepreneurship breadth and depth data were only available at the county level, not the local level, only one community with one set of institutions could be studied within the county. Census data revealed that a substantial portion of the county's population in all six counties resided in one dense municipality (U.S. Census Bureau, 2011). In all six cases, this one "small town" was too small for the county to be defined as micro-politan by the Census, but large and dense enough to suggest that the majority of entrepreneurship in the county could be found there, since this is also where the majority of the population also lived. Since it was unclear that entrepreneurship in the largest municipality would be a good representation of the rest of the county, early interviews were used to determine if the municipality exhibited characteristics that matched with trends at the county level. If not, the second largest municipality in the county would then be selected for study (under the same criteria), then the third, and so on, until a community was identified that clearly exhibited trends reflective of the county-level analysis.

In five of the six selected counties, early interviews revealed that the largest municipality did indeed represent the expected levels of high or low entrepreneurship found at the county level. However, in Buffalo County, Wisconsin, a high-entrepreneurship county, the largest population municipality (Mondovi, Wisconsin) contained very few small businesses. The local business directory was small compared to the other communities in the study—even those with low levels of entrepreneurship. Interviews with entrepreneurs were difficult to schedule because there were so few, and the first interviews indicated that the community's employment was almost entirely dominated by Marten's Trucking, a major national logistics chain based in the small town. Informants indicated that most small business activity in the county occurred in the county's seat and second largest town,[2] Alma, which was considered by locals to be a bastion of small business and tourism. Alma became the focus of the research, and did have a vibrant Main Street with dozens of active small businesses one would expect in a county with strong county-level breadth and depth indices.

Recruiting Entrepreneurs and Institutional Actors

To truly understand what entrepreneurs are thinking, one must speak directly to entrepreneurs. However, an exclusive focus on entrepreneurs captures only one side of the story and fails to fully grasp the cultural and institutional elements that are either supporting or inhibiting entrepreneurial activity on a local level. While entrepreneurs may be open about certain local barriers, local leaders may be oblivious to these problems, or see them through a very different lens. It is expected that a failure of entrepreneurs and local leaders to see eye-to-eye on critical issues—far more than the failure of leaders to act—that may be responsible for suppressed self-employment and entrepreneurial activity in some areas.

Entrepreneurs

What constitutes an *entrepreneur* is one of the most contested, multifaceted, and long-standing discussions in entrepreneurship research, despite the fact that an entire field of research is dedicated to its study. Selecting an appropriate definition is challenging because many researchers look at entrepreneurship from the perspective of their own discipline, producing many interrelated and overlapping explanations (Low & MacMillan, 1988). Gartner (1990) empirically studied what entrepreneurs considered to be the central features of entrepreneurship. He found the most common of these to be (1) the creation of a new business, (2) new venture development, and (3) the creation of a new business that adds value (p. 20). The third feature is appropriate for a study involving communities because it is not value-laden, and leaves the determination of what "adds value" open to interpretation by local citizens.[3] Among the many definitions of entrepreneurship, *novelty, business formation* (versus casual self-employment), and *value addition* in the marketplace are all common features. Davidsson (2008) added precision to the concept of *novelty,* classifying a *new offering* as a new product or service, bundle of products and services, or price/value relation (competition based on better price, speed, or quality) (p. 17). An *entrepreneur* is defined as an individual or part of a group of individuals who has created a new business venture within a place to offer a new product or service, bundle of products or services, or price/value relationship that adds value to markets within that community. This definition is sufficiently broad to include innovative *replication,* or the introduction of a prior innovation to a new geographic market, or to an old market in a new way (Davidsson, 2008; Schumpeter, 1934).

Institutional Actor

An *institutional actor* is defined here as *an individual who is a verified member of a local institution, whose primary role in that institution involves regular interaction with small businesses or the small business community.* This definition can be true for both formal and informal groups, provided that someone outside the institution has identified the individual in the case of informal groups. For example, institutional actors can range from the mayor or city manager of a small rural city, to a "thought leader," or outspoken citizen with plenty of ideas, who is part of a local redevelopment interest group consisting of citizens who meet to discuss local development ideas over coffee every so often. Institutional actors may also be entrepreneurs themselves, but this is often not the case.

Research participants were recruited using an iterative process that involved prior identification followed by chain referral (also called "snowball sampling") that is particularly useful for populations that are hard to identify and reach, like busy entrepreneurs and institutional actors on the go (Biernacki & Waldorf, 1981; Penrod, Preston, Cain, & Starks, 2003). In this procedure, a small set of initial potential participants were identified prior to arrival at the research site. Institutions were generally contacted first, as local institutions tend to be supportive of research that may benefit their community (Fortunato, 2009). In each community, contact would be initiated with the local government and chamber of commerce by e-mail or telephone using a recruitment script. Upon contacting these institutions, the researcher would ask to interview "the individual who deals most closely with small business development." In all six sites, contact with these key institutional actors in these two institutions quickly produced the names of important entrepreneurs and other institutions related to small business.

For the entrepreneur sample, the researcher identified one or two small businesses from the local chamber of commerce business directory or the yellow pages and initiated contact by phone or e-mail to set up a meeting using a pre-written recruitment script. Then the researcher randomly selected a business or two with a presence in town that was not found in business listings, in order to try to solicit a few opinions from non-chamber members and very new businesses that were not yet listed.

From these initial interviews, all participants were asked to name any other institutions or entrepreneurs that they believed were "important to the small business community." This process was repeated until the same set of entrepreneurs, institutions, and actors were mentioned. In small communities, and in low-entrepreneurship communities, this process would typically happen after about a dozen interviews. In large- and high-entrepreneurship communities, this saturation would happen sometimes after 15 to 25 interviews. In all six sites, a genuine saturation of names was reached. Some of the individuals who were identified through interviews declined to participate, or simply failed to respond to repeated recruitment solicitations. However, this happened in less than 10 percent of all identified individuals.

Prior to the interview process, the confidentiality of participant responses was assured, and the ages of participants and their consent to participate in the research project were obtained using a signed informed consent form. All participants must have been at least 18 years old at the time of the interview. For purposes of confidentiality, it was assured that individuals' names, company names, or institutions that they represent would not be linked to their responses. For this reason, the exact type of business or organization that the participant owns or represents is suppressed, since revealing that the participant is a "baker" or "chamber of commerce representative" may indirectly identify these participants—especially in very small towns, where there may only be one baker or chamber of commerce representative. Therefore, during the course of reporting on the research, participants will only be referred to as an entrepreneur or institutional actor (although their community will be named) in order to protect their identity.

Qualitative Data Analysis

Qualitative data analysis occurs in two phases: coding and theoretical categorization. The idea of coding is to "fracture" the data (Strauss, 1987, p. 29): breaking the data into pieces and rearranging it into categories that can be directly compared within and between cases. Data cleaning is an essential part of the coding process, where extraneous answers that do not clearly relate to the theory or the research question are removed, and one- or two-word answers to complex questions are eliminated. The remaining data are then grouped into conceptual categories within cases. Second, linkages are made between the categorized data and the entrepreneurial community theories discussed, which is a process Maxwell (2005) refers to as "theoretical categorization" (p. 97). Theoretical categorization differs from "organizational" (pure description) and "substantive" categorization (theoretical concepts emerge *de novo* from the data) because data are placed "into a more general or abstract framework" that exists prior to data gathering (Maxwell, 2005, pp. 97–98). In this fashion, written transcripts are organized and continuously compared back to the theory to look for support, rejection, or contradiction surrounding the hypotheses, and to raise new insights and perspectives that offer a richer explanation of the existing theory.

In practical terms, qualitative data analysis will begin with a thorough reading of the interview transcripts. Within entrepreneurs, and again within institutional actors, responses will be organized by theoretical concept within each case. For example, the issue of insufficient access to start-up funds may be a major theme brought up by entrepreneurs, whereas this concept is conspicuously absent from institutional actor responses. Entrepreneurs may regularly cite that bankers and local government leaders make up an elite clique that is out of touch with the needs of small business, and who regularly groan that the small business sector does not produce ideas that warrant funding. Meanwhile, local leaders may never mention funding, instead saying that the small business sector seems to be doing just fine, and the presence of so many banks in town is evidence of that. In terms of theory, these responses not only illustrate discordant views about funding, and reveal the possible presence of an elite group within the community, but also more importantly to this study, they illustrate the lack of coordination, communication, and goal setting between entrepreneurs and institutional actors. If this occurs in a low-entrepreneurship community, and the high-entrepreneurship community in the same region yields similar responses about the need to address local funding from both entrepreneurs and institutions alike, then the qualitative interviews support the hypothesis that coordination on key issues like funding are associated with higher entrepreneurship rates. Moreover, it provides additional, rich insight that the local elite's restricted disbursement of funds—paired with insufficient communication with the small business sector—is more of a social barrier to entrepreneurship than simply a lack of funding options.

The focus of the qualitative results will be on reporting *concepts* rather than repeating similar statements. Without using a recording device, it is necessary for the researcher to take quick, copious notes of key informant statements. For accuracy, the researcher may ask the interview participant to repeat exact wordings to ensure the highest level of clarity of key points from the interview. Frequently, direct quotations are incorporated in the analysis to capture the essence of the underlying concept. These quotes would relate directly to the theory and offer insight as to *why* and *how* this happens, and are only used in cases where the researcher was certain to capture exact wordings, or asked the participant to verify their statements for clarity. This technique was not always possible, and in cases where the researcher was only able to capture key ideas and their contexts, direct quotes are not used. Stripping the data down to its essential components in this way is intended to provide a nice tight analysis of underlying theoretical concepts as they are manifest in the study sites. It is critical to note, however, that discrepant responses, or responses that offer alternative explanations, will *always* be included and compared to views held by the majority. At the end of the analysis, the theoretical categories are compared across study sites to determine if different themes emerged in high and low-entrepreneurship sites, or across different regions.

Results of the Face-to-Face Interviews

Research participants engaged in a face-to-face interview to discuss interaction and opportunity in their community. The written surveys provided some evidence of the extent of interaction in each community, and some information about how participants think about opportunity. They do not produce a clear picture of how interaction was initiated in each community, how that interaction has been used, what opportunities it has helped to develop, and what local barriers exist that make entrepreneurship challenging. These issues can only be understood by listening to the narratives of entrepreneurs and institutional actors, and analyzing key themes that tend to appear across these narratives, to tell the story of why the community has a high or low level of entrepreneurship. Utilizing a semi-structured interview gives respondents the freedom to describe local entrepreneurship in their own terms, to explain how the small business community evolved, to talk about its culture, and to raise any key issues that were not tested directly in the written surveys. Relevant elements of these narratives as they relate to entrepreneurship are shared in order to create a deeper understanding of how entrepreneurship in each community "works."

The face-to-face interview proceeds through four sections: *Level of Community Orientation, Defining Local Entrepreneurship and Opportunity, Nature of Local Opportunity,* and *Encouraging Local Entrepreneurship.* By thinking through these categories during the interview, participants are encouraged to provide information about what makes their community a good or bad place to do business, how their relationships with other entrepreneurs and institutions have affected that judgment, and how the small business community might yet be improved. A more nuanced understanding of how each entrepreneur or institutional actor thinks about opportunity is expected to emerge, as well as the roles each group expects the other group to play in developing these opportunity sources.

Presentation of the Data

Interviews were conducted with 84 respondents, of whom 47 were entrepreneurs, 28 were institutional actors, and 9 described themselves as both. Interviews lasted from 30- to 90-minutes across all six sites. Fewer than 10 percent of individuals recruited refused an interview, and there did not appear to be a discernible pattern of refusals in each community. Many of the responses to the questions were redundant within communities; participants in each community generally had a very complete understanding of the history and culture of their community that was rarely contradicted by other participants. Different participants did, however, go into more detail about different aspects of entrepreneurship, opportunity, and the local culture based on their own perspective. The focus of this section is how the respondents described the interactions between entrepreneurs, institutions, and sources of opportunity. Direct quotes are used to illustrate some of these points, but because of the small sample size and confidentiality constraints, these quotes are only attributed to the participant's community, and their role as either an entrepreneur, institutional actor, or both. The idea is to capture key ideas and common themes that emerged in the face-to-face interviews, with the intention of examining these findings in light of the hypotheses being tested. In cases where divergence did exist, the dissenting viewpoint will be presented as well for comparison.

Furthermore, results will be presented in a case study format. This means that data is presented site-by-site, rather than by subject, or by one's role in the community. The purpose of this is to preserve the integrity of the narrative of the community. Cases are presented state-by-state, with the findings from the high-entrepreneurship community followed by those from the low-entrepreneurship community. After the story of each community has been told, a cross-case analysis identifies key concepts and ideas that relate to the hypotheses. This analysis also examines the subtleties of how communities, and participants within those communities, either converge or differ in their views.

The community profiles are organized by state, starting with Maine, then Pennsylvania, and finally Wisconsin. Within each state, the profile of the high-entrepreneurship community is presented first, followed by the profile of the low-entrepreneurship community. To begin, the next section discusses Rockland, Maine, the high-entrepreneurship community in Maine.

Rockland, Maine

High-entrepreneurship Rockland, Maine, did not become that way by accident. A unique combination of scenic amenities, cultural ambition, institutional action, a supportive small business culture, and a limited history of extra-local corporate involvement in the city, all coalesced to create a unique environment that has turned out to be quite beneficial for local entrepreneurs. The main question to address is 'What turned a dirty, smelly fish cannery town in the late 1990s into a premier small business destination by the mid-2000s?'

" 'Renaissance' is a word you hear a lot," says one Rockland entrepreneur. "That word implies you found something sophisticated that you didn't have before. *Adaptation* is the correct term." Entrepreneurs and institutional actors who are long-time residents of Rockland can recall the city's history readily. Rockland experienced a continuous industrial "evolution," from a farming village, to shipbuilding, quarrying, commercial fishing, food processing, and finally, art, tourism, and finance. Every few generations, there was an overall change in the dominant economic driver of the town and surrounding county. "These changes from industry to industry were a 'soft sequence.' They had lots of overlap, but each one was a defined era in Rockland's history, forming a continuum," says an entrepreneur who is a lifelong resident.

> Now people point at the "new economy" of art and high-end food, but this didn't come from a renaissance. It arrived because a history of adaptation led to the success of embracing something new. This [situation] is just the next wave for Rockland.

Another local entrepreneur concurred, adding,

> This town used to make its living from harvesting a sea-based product. Once that was over-harvested, our local model was no longer relevant. Since our manufacturing base was not very diverse, many canneries left. The ones that stayed, adapted, but at first, we did not adapt as a community . . . we were the coastal version of a mill town.

INVESTMENT CATALYZES INTERACTION

The road to becoming a small business destination was not without bumps. Rockland's Chamber of Commerce and City Council tended to be aligned closely with larger, food manufacturing concerns in the 1990s, but generally did not meet the needs of small business. In terms of local strategy, "the chamber was always playing catch-up, responding instead of leading," states one entrepreneur. However, with many fish canneries departing because of diminishing catches, Rockland was left with an abundance of coastal real estate. Local officials entered talks with credit giant MBNA, whose CEO was sympathetic to relocating their data processing center offices to Rockland to take advantage of the inexpensive coastal real estate, as a scenic incentive to draw qualified employees to the area. The CEO was familiar with Rockland because he is himself an art collector and connoisseur. The elegant coastal scenery, and presence of the Farnsworth Museum and many local artists, was enough for the CEO to invest more than $5 million of the company's money into coastal improvements (including a scenic public walk) to build the new data processing center, and more than $1 million of his own money to build a downtown art gallery near the Farnsworth, with the hope of stimulating a local arts scene.

This fortuitous investment could have been representative of development *in*, rather than *of*, the community, meaning that MBNA's substantial local investments could have benefited a small group of specialized interests, rather than the entire community. Instead, the investment served as a catalyst that helped to launch Rockland out of its manufacturing-oriented paradigm, and into its current incarnation as a tourism, hospitality, and fine arts destination. As MBNA built their new facilities, existing local businesses immediately recognized the opportunities associated with hundreds of well-paid employees moving into their town. Main Street businesses recognized the need to improve Main Street as a retail location and quickly coalesced to form the Downtown Business Alliance—a strategic community alliance for entrepreneurs aimed at improving the small business climate, especially on Main Street. "People in this town have a history of working together, and giving back to the community," said an entrepreneur, "but they quickly found themselves in loggerheads with the chamber and city council." These established organizations were still in league with established canning business. "When the chamber would not cooperate, the Downtown Business Alliance took the stance of, 'fine, we'll do it without you!' "

Luckily for the Downtown Business Alliance, increased pressure from the small business community, and loss of canneries, led to a change in leadership at the chamber, with new leaders bringing with them a more pro-small business stance. Around this time, small business attendance at city council meetings, and the election of small businesspeople to city council, occurred more frequently. The chamber and Downtown Business Alliance met regularly to discuss a vision for Main Street, and eventually submitted a proposal for a community development block grant (CDBG) to refurbish Main Street, turning it into an attractive, pedestrian-friendly streetscape using existing buildings to retain a classic downtown feel. Rockland was awarded the CDBG, and this marked the beginning of a close and productive relationship between the chamber of commerce and the Downtown Business Alliance, stimulating the chamber to host monthly "Business After Hours" meetings once a month for networking, speakers, and presentations, and an opportunity for business owners to get together for the purpose of community improvement. These meetings draw dozens of local small businesspeople monthly, but the overall process of entrepreneur-institution interaction "started with a few doing the work of many," remarked a local entrepreneur. "These 'disgruntled' businesspeople started working out issues collectively, and then brought others on board when they could prove it could be done."

The success of the Downtown Business Alliance led to the development of other, "spin-off" organizations, many of whom also are affiliated with the alliance. Historic Inns of Rockland was started by an entrepreneur who wanted to turn "a lot of pretty houses" into something more strategic that could be promoted community-wide. The Historic Inns now has four bed and breakfast members who promote themselves jointly as a bed and breakfast destination. Similarly, the city's more than two dozen art galleries—many of whom were drawn by the early success of galleries closely tied to the Farnsworth and supported by MBNA—started Arts in Rockland, which features regular "art walks" across town. Through the Downtown Business Alliance, these art walks can be coordinated seamlessly with other retailers and services in town. These other businesses open their doors, often attracting additional sales and receiving consumer exposure from strolling, generally affluent, art walkers. The Farnsworth Museum has transitioned from an "island" into a community organization that promotes the arts across the community. And, stand-alone businesses often serve as "third places" for local entrepreneurs to gather and chat, including a local restaurant, a bakery, and a refurbished movie theater that shows atypical entertainment, like the Oscars, or the Metropolitan Opera Live in HD.

INTERACTING WIDELY

When asked what makes Rockland such a highly entrepreneurial community, entrepreneurs and institutional actors alike most often pointed to the city's culture of collective action as the one thing that truly separates Rockland from other small, Maine communities. "Businesses here realize that we have more local bargaining power as a collective," says a local entrepreneur, "and we do a good job working collectively, always have." Rockland has had a "work together" attitude since it was a very young settlement, and collaboration and good manners "have become part of the upbringing," said one entrepreneur. As a result, the Downtown Business Alliance and its spin-off organizations, like the Historic Inns of Rockland, have been deeply comfortable in cross-promoting and cross-supporting each other's businesses, often times in the form of special events. A number of new festivals, including the *Summer Solstice Street Festival*, the *Lobster Festival*, and the *Rockland Blues Festival*, are all the result of collaborative efforts up and down Main Street.

Local institutions have even begun to collaborate regionally. One institutional actor mentioned, "We *share* our information here; we don't believe in silos or protecting information." Another said, "We adhere to a regional mentality, working with regional development agencies who put money behind developing the entire coastline." Regional collaboration has become a highly contagious topic locally, especially as former rival towns along the coast begin to see that they have broader drawing power as the "Mid-Coast Region" rather than Rockland, Camden, or Rockport individually. The newest chamber leadership has even experimented with new intra-regional networking concepts. One particularly innovative variation is "speed dating" for entrepreneurs, where entrepreneurs from different regions take turns spending 10 minutes with one another, learning about the other person's business, and potentially sparking new interest and forming new partnerships.

Strategic interaction has essentially become a daily feature of small business life in Rockland, especially on Main Street. "We have to interact regularly!" says another. "Our customers are other small businesspeople. Bankers are in here all the time to get lunch . . . we stay engaged with our local community because these are our customers." Strong support for local small businesses has translated into entrepreneurs frequenting each other's establishments. One institutional actor said, "There is an attitude around here that if you want to support the community, you support local businesses." Local institutional actors are frequent patrons too. "You can see it everywhere," remarked one local leader, "businesses support other businesses, and that's just the mentality." When asked if these interactions led to the creation of mutual goals, the leader responded, " 'goal' is a bad word . . . we just collaborate to make Rockland better."

COMPETITION AND CONFLICT

When it comes to competition, Rockland entrepreneurs still claim to be highly competitive—just not necessarily with each other. "[I'm for] anything that brings more people downtown, even another business just like mine!" says one entrepreneur on Main Street. "We just start carving niches . . . that is how capitalism is supposed to work." Participants regularly mentioned that there was a much greater sense that entrepreneurs help one another locally, rather than compete with or undermine one another. Rather than competing for slices of the pie that is the Rockland consumer market, there is a belief that many entrepreneurs working together, even in the same industry, can create a bigger pie by attracting more people.

These passages and anecdotal stories make Rockland appear almost idyllic and utopian—a place where businesses help one another and everyone gets along. But of course, Rockland has its share of conflict as well. "When we say there is a community of small businesses, that doesn't mean everyone is a part," remarked an entrepreneur, following a sudden change in her demeanor. Another entrepreneur said, "There are two types of support on Main Street: genuine concern for your neighbor, and moral support when things are slow, because *everyone* is slow!" Not everyone is part of the support circle. "There are *definitely* entrepreneurs here who are into their own individual agendas," said another entrepreneur, "they really could care less about the community." Another Main Street entrepreneur said, "I don't want to use the word *curmudgeon,* but they are out there." What is an example of such non-participatory, or perhaps even "curmudgeonly" behavior? One example includes Main Street entrepreneurs who simply keep to themselves and fail to participate in the downtown organizations, but who still benefit from the swells in business that festivals, fairs, and art walks bring. Some entrepreneurs claim to have reached out to other such entrepreneurs, asking them to keep their doors open for special events—but they refused to stay open past 5:00 p.m. "Why are you in business then? Some small businesses do not have a customer service mentality toward their customers, or their neighbors."

OPPORTUNITY

Participants in Rockland, entrepreneurs and institutional actors alike, defined opportunity in a variety of ways. One consideration that most had in common was an insistence that opportunity is both internally situated and externally apparent. Entrepreneurs and institutional actors in Rockland, in particular, used unconventional, enlightened terminology to describe the intersection between opportunity and entrepreneurship. Some of these definitions of opportunity included individuals being inspired to do something; using small business as a way of expressing one's self; a form of creative self-expression; the chance to create your own lifestyle and do what you love to do, and to make a life around it; or seeing opportunity is about openness to your surroundings.

No matter the definition, entrepreneurs and institutional actors overwhelmingly defined opportunity as both an internal and external phenomenon. One institutional actor explained, "Conditions present themselves that are opportunistic, like a food service establishment appearing for rent. For a food service professional *specifically,* this is an opportunity. It presents itself in different ways to different people." Another institutional actor stated similarly, "What doesn't hit you between the eyes, you have to go out and create. People tend to see what goes together, what is compatible." The institutional actor stated that her organization routinely collects public data from entrepreneurs to understand their needs, and to help provide opportunities where they are lacking. However, these opportunities are very much realized by the individual. "Opportunities develop," she says, "they are both within and external to the entrepreneur, and emerge over time."

"You have to be in the right place at the right time, but you need the right background to take advantage of the opportunity," says another institutional leader. "An opportunity for you may not be an opportunity for someone else. Timing is everything."

Not all participants felt the balance was 50–50 internal-external. "I think it's 75 percent internal, 25 percent external," said one entrepreneur. "Most say, 'here's an old pair of shoes . . . what can I do with them?' " One institutional leader similarly believes it is primarily an individualistic phenomenon and ultimately up to the individual to create opportunity through action. "I'm not sure what it is about Rockland that brings this out in people, but it works." While business planning is a central feature of the discovery perspective, mostly because it assumes that entrepreneurs understand the risks they face, more than one entrepreneur disagreed with the usefulness of this practice. One said, "I did not write a business plan. It's not valid anymore 10 minutes after you open the door. And, you can make a spreadsheet do anything with the numbers." Instead, this entrepreneur believes it is an entrepreneur's adaptability and understanding of the changing needs of the customer base that keeps her business successful—an opportunistic view more aligned with the creation perspective. One institutional leader digressed, however, taking more of a discovery perspective stance. "There is a huge dose of problem-solving involved. It's mostly value-added businesses around here carving local niches—value-added lobster products, for example." Entrepreneurs find opportunity by first looking around them for problems to solve and niches to fill.

ROCKLAND'S ENTREPRENEURIAL FUTURE

Entrepreneurs and institutional representatives talked about some of the challenges that continue to face their community, and potentially how these conflicts can be resolved to create stronger support for entrepreneurship locally. A common complaint was that the State of Maine posed multiple barriers to entrepreneurship through high taxes, imposing huge worker's compensation insurance requirements that keep entrepreneurs from hiring people, and creating more jobs. The second common complaint was that "Augusta" only gives verbal support to entrepreneurship, rather than financial or assistance support. "The real focus has been on big job generators, rather than on mom and pops that make the community work," says one entrepreneur. One entrepreneur complained that Pine Tree Zones, or targeted tax abatement areas for business development, were ineffective because they are targeted at larger businesses who normally leave when the incentives dry up. An institutional actor also complained that state economic development agencies are highly fragmented, and national organizations tend to be focused on large and growth-oriented businesses, rather than the "mom and pop" businesses commonly found in Rockland. One suggestion by an institutional actor was to separate "entrepreneurship development" from "economic development" in government agencies, and to lead by showing others what entrepreneurs are already doing well, and what can be replicated easily elsewhere.

Another barrier to development has been a social division between what locals call the "home mentality" and the "away mentality." The "away mentality" refers to individuals who come to Rockland from outside the area, sometimes for only part of the year, who are drawn by lifestyle amenities and scenery. The "home mentality" is a "do-it-yourself" mentality, associated with rarely seeking outside help. This division is a barrier because it leads to divergent perspectives about Rockland's identity, and thus its small business culture. Speaking of the home mentality, one institutional actor quipped, "Maine has plenty of jobs . . . everyone has three!" Institutional actors and entrepreneurs alike resist the idea of "assistance" but appear to prefer "investment," as this builds on the rugged identity of making things happen. "When there isn't enough work, you go shovel snow," said a Rockland entrepreneur, stressing the practical nature of many Rockland residents. Combined with a tolerance for any kind of work, even low-end labor, a strong contributor to Rockland's high level of entrepreneurship may be the cultural norm of "creating work" when money is needed, paired with low stigma on the kinds of work one pursues. These beliefs appear to be culturally embedded over generations of Rockland residents.

For those individuals who have not been exposed to running a small business, but who are impressed by the local small business culture, some participants recommended some sort of entrepreneurial training or coaching program. "Otherwise," joked an entrepreneur, "you either 'have it' or you 'don't.'" While participants were not specific about the kind of entrepreneurial training they preferred, several agreed that it was a potential route to stimulating entrepreneurship among those who want to join the small business community, but do not know how.

Rumford, Maine

Rumford, Maine, is an idyllic town in the mountains, surrounded by pine forests, lakes, streams, and an enormous waterfall that cascades right through town. And, settled against the area's remarkable natural setting is a large, smelly paper mill. The mill is not only an imposing presence but also a defining feature of the local culture and mentality that has shaped entrepreneurial attitudes in the area. While historically providing an abundance of local revenue and single-handedly supporting a small town's economy, it has more recently come under fire for its negative impact on the surrounding environment in a documentary film called *Cancer Valley*; surprising, given the pristine nature of the surrounding region. Rumford is a place of contrasting views, beliefs, and activities. One finds a diversity of opinions on the town's history, on community, opportunity, and the nature of small business in rural Maine. Among the contrasts, there are also many consistencies that help to define the local identity.

THE "MOTHER MILL" EFFECT

Rumford is a town that arose around a large paper mill, and whose development was shaped by the philanthropy of industrialist Hugh Chisolm. The paper mill, opened in 1892, provided a good lifestyle for local workers for more than 80 years. Unlike many mill stories from Appalachia where workers were exploited by capitalists, and left indebted and powerless (see Gaventa, 1982), Chisolm continues to be highly regarded as a philanthropist and community builder who put workers and their families first, offering excellent wages, high-quality housing, and exceptional retirement benefits to employees. The housing he built for his workers, Strathglass Park, was among the first planned communities in the United States, and even today, the stately brick duplexes that line its streets are sought-after real estate.

The mill's prosperity, and Chisolm's legacy of competitive wages and benefits, continued until the mid-1970s, when the mill was sold to a national paper company. Amidst shrinking demand and pressures to keep costs low, the system changed from one of corporate welfare and philanthropy to cutting costs and scaling back. "With every subsequent change of ownership, there was less corporate welfare," said an entrepreneur, "but local *people* couldn't change . . . they were locked in a paradigm of corporate welfare." By "welfare," the entrepreneur is referring to a system of corporate provision through which a laborer could dedicate his working life to the mill, and in return, the company provided for his needs and the needs of his family. The high standards of such provision set by Chisolm created a mentality where people who graduated from high school typically expected to get a good job working at the mill—and historically, one would receive good pay, good housing, and excellent benefits for doing so. However, the mill "is in its last stages before closing," says another entrepreneur. "People feel pretty negative, and you can't blame them. There are already lots of retirees, low-income people, and welfare cases in the town." When asked why they don't consider starting businesses, the entrepreneur replied, "Most tax payers are mill workers . . . they're not wild thinkers, and they don't support entrepreneurship."

One entrepreneur calls the predicament the "mother mill mentality." Individuals have become so accustomed to mill labor and corporate provision, that when mill labor is not available, they switch to government welfare instead, rather than find other types of employment. One entrepreneur said, "It's a mill town . . . people associated with the mill have a very different mind-set and work ethic. You came to work in the mill, and had things handed to you when you walked in." "It is a provision mentality," says another entrepreneur, and it suppresses entrepreneurship while giving tremendous power to the mill. While mill workers are certainly concerned about potentially losing their jobs after a mill closing, entrepreneurs are just as concerned that they will lose their customer base. One entrepreneur said, "We are totally unprepared" if the mill closes. The mill, because of its employment power, is also disproportionately powerful in government decision making. "There's a lot of mill money coming into the community," said one entrepreneur. Another entrepreneur complained, "The mill continues to get tax breaks from the local government because they can't break even. Who bears the cost of the tax break? Small business. But we are struggling just as badly!" With more political support behind the mill than behind small businesses, there has been a multi-generational tendency to keep the mill alive, to survive, and to do what is necessary to preserve the status quo. Furthermore, "Assertive, smarter, younger people are going elsewhere to make a living," said an entrepreneur. There has been less talk in public discussions about innovating, trying new things, or preparing for a mill closure.

The high percentage of individuals receiving social assistance downtown has created an unusual dynamic on Congress Street, since many of the street's residents cannot afford to shop in local stores. One entrepreneur personally feels that it creates an unfair situation downtown. "Classic buildings on Congress Street are mainly occupied by government welfare services for low-income and mentally ill individuals. This [assignment of building space] hurts our Main Street . . . is this really the best place for these things? I watch potential real estate investors get in their car and leave when they see this." Another entrepreneur said, "We need social programs . . . the intent is good, it's the abuse that has been a detriment to business." The entrepreneur says that the conspicuous presence of many multi-generational welfare recipients is no trifling matter in Rumford. "It truly is a hot-button issue around here, and it could lead to more dire problems if we don't address it. It's frustrating that I work 70–80 hours a week to keep this place going, while the town has thrown away opportunity in exchange for a welfare state." The increase in downtown Section 8 housing occurred shortly after businesses began to close their doors downtown following the opening of a local Walmart. "Walmart wiped out our Main Street," says an entrepreneur, permanently changing the downtown's dynamic.

Additionally, the "mother mill" mentality is closely related to a general resistance to change in the community. When a casino company was investigating Rumford as a site for a new casino because of its proximity to major ski resorts such as Sunday Mountain, "local folks did *nothing* to bring the casino here, no pro-activity. There are jobs everywhere in the casino structure for the uneducated, semi-educated, educated . . ." said an entrepreneur. The town's selectmen (much like city council people elsewhere) turned it down. It was not a mill. "The town selectmen are not entrepreneurial, they don't get it," complained an entrepreneur. "I mean, they have to be conscious of the budget, but not too conscious!" Another entrepreneur stated, "Most selectmen have worked in the mill, and have that mentality. They are not small business friendly." The local support structure for business, especially banks and local government, normally plays a supporting role helping entrepreneurs to grow. "But we actually see business *burdened* by the support structure," says an entrepreneur. "Taxes, regulations . . . I used to think taxes were no big deal, but they really are when times are tough." A focus on regulation and keeping the status quo has stifled many local entrepreneurs, as activities from slightly modifying a Congress Street façade, to a logger pulling logs across a stream, requires a litany of permits—at least from the perspective of local entrepreneurs. Regardless, a path-dependent mentality of preserving the mill, while failing to support local business, has made Rumford a challenging place for economic survival. "I love it here," says one entrepreneur, "but it's a miserable place to make a living!"

WHAT INSTITUTIONS ARE DOING

In the face of a widely recognized "mill mentality," and an equally well-recognized understanding that such a mentality may make the community more vulnerable, local institutions have not been quiet. Whether their actions are making a difference, however, is a matter of some debate. "The town is really doing a good job at bringing people together, they've been very proactive," says one entrepreneur. "The services are excellent, and taxes are very low. The chamber is a very active group, and the Growth Council is very active." The Rumford Growth Council is an organization that was created within the town government to attract and stimulate high-growth entrepreneurship, primarily based in existing strengths, like specialty manufacturing. One institutional actor says, "[The Growth Council] has taken a big step forward. The wheels are always spinning about how to get the small business community to participate." The Growth Council also founded a technology and manufacturing incubator, utilizing an original paper mill building that had been abandoned. "Interaction among businesses is the point of the incubator," said the institutional actor. Additionally, financial institutions were reported to be very active at business and community events, said one institutional actor. "[Local institutions] are all local people, and we all grew up here, so we really care about this," she says.

Other participants, however, critiqued the local government and other institutions. "This town does not get high grades for supporting small business," says an entrepreneur. Another said, "The local government will not help you. We had to get information through the state because the town didn't know what to do." Several entrepreneurs criticized the local government for being disengaged from the small business community, and for not venturing out into town to meet small business owners. The Growth Council, too, was criticized by more than one entrepreneur, with one saying that the council has a big budget, but is not using the money wisely.

On the institutional side, institutional actors, too, generally took a *laissez-faire* stance toward small businesses, expressing that they would like to see more and better small business to improve the community's future, but that overall, things appear to be well in the small business community. One institutional actor stated, "If a business person is surviving, then they already fulfill their obligation to the community, from a commercial perspective."

While participants expressed varying degrees of support and criticism for the efforts of local institutions, both entrepreneurs and institutions widely criticized the State of Maine for misdirected efforts at supporting small business, and the community at large. One institutional actor explains, "The state and federal government are too big, and too big an economic presence here. The government used to be an economic driver, but they have made it very hard to start a business—or much of anything—here." Another institutional actor explains why, "The state Department of Environmental Protection can hold up processes for over a year, and by that time development opportunities have passed. There are a multitude of government issues, and believe it or not, high taxes were only number five on a recent survey. Working in government, people want regulation when it benefits them, but reject it when it doesn't. I'm stuck in the middle." "Yes, taxes are high, insurance requirements are high, too much red tape, too many regs," said another institutional actor, and another said, "We lost the opportunity to construct a chip mill here due to one department at the Department of Environmental Protection." Entrepreneurs, too, criticize the state government for being generally unfriendly toward business, imposing high taxes on key consumer groups like the elderly and retirees, and failing to monitor welfare abuse and the community impacts of Section 8 housing decisions. One entrepreneur stated, "We drive our retired people out of the state. These are affluent people who buy things, volunteer on boards of directors, for charities, contribute both monetarily, and intellectually. But they have a low demand for services and they contribute more than they take. We don't encourage them to stay here . . . my mother's tax liability is $30,000 less per year by living in Tucson half the year."

LOCAL CULTURE'S EFFECTS ON ENTREPRENEURSHIP

With so many Rumford residents employed by, or affected by, the paper mill, there is less of a public focus on small businesses and their importance to the community. Entrepreneurs report that there is a lack of support for small business in both the government and the local population. One entrepreneur states, "We do very little business in Rumford because there is no local appreciation for small businesses. We *do* draw our customers from a 100-mile radius, however." Some entrepreneurs have been forced to meet broader, regional needs to survive because of limited local demand. "You have to be very careful picking your niche," says an entrepreneur, "Due to the shrinking population, it's hard to sustain a customer base here, and there's limited demand. Also, our remoteness, and transportation issues, don't help. The climate is harsh here, so depending on what your business is, that can affect you." With such limited demand, tangible local customer and institutional support for small business would be critical. "This is a community that has been shrinking over the years, so businesses need to support each other," says an entrepreneur. "Small business people are running this community," says another entrepreneur. "Other than the mill, it's all we have."

With businesses attempting to attract a limited number of new customers, competition between entrepreneurs has, in many cases, trumped collaboration. One entrepreneur noted that neighbors are competitors in Rumford. "Culturally, competition is inbred here," he says, "but we have to work together to survive. We try to get together with other small businesses within our industry and work together, not against each other." Many entrepreneurs still put their business and personal status ahead of collective interests. "There is a lot of jealousy in a small town, and this breeds contempt," says an entrepreneur.

The competitive mentality of Rumford may affect the way people interact differentially, but so does a lack of time. An entrepreneur explains, "There is a small group of us interacting. Some folks are willing to put in the time after work, so they'll go meet at the chamber, the Growth Council, the Rotary. Most folks just stay home and manage their business." The chamber of commerce holds some routine after-hours events for business networking, with presentations and speakers. However, as one entrepreneur notes, "I don't participate because I have too many other obligations. I 'compare notes' informally, when I'm out and about in the community." An entrepreneur's lack of free time to interact appears to be a widely held characterization by both institutional actors and entrepreneurs in Rumford. An institutional actor stated, "Small business owners are, in my experience, too busy to interact. They mostly interact with suppliers and buyers. They are wearing too many hats." Another said, "[Businesses] gather at the Rotary Club too, but there are not too many small business owners there . . . they are too busy."

Do entrepreneurs and institutional actors ever meet to exchange ideas in Rumford? One institutional actor stated, "There has been a once-a-year business expo that has been very beneficial [for interacting with entrepreneurs], but there is no place for *institutions* to get together to interact. Businesses regularly speak with us informally out in the community." Some entrepreneur-institution collaborations have been apparent in the past, such as the *Moon Tide Festival* around the July 4 holiday: a street festival with high participation from small businesses and street vendors. "It started strong," says an institutional actor, "but interest waned over time and we lost volunteerism." Entrepreneurs and institutions alike stressed that everyone knows everyone in this small town, and that people run into one another frequently out and about in the community. But, several expressed frustration that there was no forum for meeting to talk about community strategy, and that discussing new directions for the community was futile at selectmen meetings.

COMMUNITY BENEFITS

Despite many of the challenges of running a small business, many entrepreneurs said they are still attracted to Rumford because of its community spirit and small-town feel. One entrepreneur explained what he considers to be several of the best benefits: "The recreation opportunities are just awesome here. We have world-class networking and data access, and access to fast broadband. Even though it is a small town, we can meet all our business needs in house. The people that work in this office want to be here . . . we could just as easily be in Bangor or Portland." Rumford is still large enough to contain many such amenities that make it an attractive and competitive business location, with lower real estate costs and low local taxes, and reasonable cost business services. "But," an entrepreneur warns, "I wouldn't necessarily want to do my banking, legal work, or accounting here. Everyone will know your business!"

CREATING IDENTITY IN THE WAKE OF THE MILL

With threats of a mill closure looming, developing a post-manufacturing local strategy has been difficult for those who have tried, and it has largely not been attempted by many others. The town is still considered to be a mill town according to entrepreneurs and institutional actors alike. "Modernizing the mill does not make a very modern community," says an entrepreneur. "The town has not been coordinated or cooperative enough to look at anything more than survival." An institutional leader elaborated, "The economy of the past 20–25 years does not fit here anymore. It is all manufacturing and industry here, both our weakness and our strength. It is the root of our economic prosperity, but there is too much emphasis on raw goods, and not enough emphasis on adding value." A lack of support for innovative entrepreneurship, combined with a cultural resistance to change, has kept most entrepreneurs engaged in traditional activities, like manufacturing, and personal and professional services.[4]

The fragmentation of local entrepreneurial behavior and of local institutions, and the lack of a forum or agency to handle local small business development, has prohibited a unified local development strategy from emerging. "I look out the window with my son who is a neighboring business owner," says an entrepreneur, "and I can see what this town could be. I could write a five-year plan right now. What we need is an entrepreneurship council, made up of entrepreneurs." This would, at least in theory, remedy the inability of entrepreneurs to be taken seriously at public meetings. Another entrepreneur added, "There is no clear and concise plan or way to get something new. We need clean, straightforward support for new things from local boards. There is no way to walk in and say, 'here is what I would like to do.' "

The culmination of individuals saying "here is what *I* would like to do" has so far not coalesced into a cohesive "here is what *we* would like to do." "We need goals, coordination, a one-kiosk place with community information," says one individual who is both an entrepreneur and institutional actor. "Somebody needs to tie it all in and bring it together. We have lots of ideas, but they are fragmented. We need to make sure they are not duplicating each other." The fragmentation of different ideas is potentially one reason that small business development ideas have fared so poorly with the selectmen—they are typically the ideas of one individual versus the public. "How do you get the selectmen to support new ideas? We need people and political support behind it." And, to accomplish this, coordination is necessary, although no one entrepreneur or leader appears to have taken definitive steps toward bringing the small business community together.

OPPORTUNITY

As with other research sites, Rumford participants cited a mix of discovery and creation elements when describing local opportunity, but tended to use elements of the creation perspective more often. "I am much more of a calculated risk-taker, but I fall on the creation side of things," says one entrepreneur. "You cannot be bashful or shy [in creating opportunity], or you could never sleep at night." More than one entrepreneur claimed that they see no real difference in internally or externally situated opportunity. "I can't see a difference between internal and external, same thing to me," said an entrepreneur. Another entrepreneur said, "Opportunity is out there, but you have to use your own skills to get to it." Other individuals expressed a more pessimistic view of opportunity, such as one institutional leader: "Opportunity is limited in this area." This individual took a more externally situated view, saying, "Opportunity is based on what the market offers."

McConnelsburg, Pennsylvania

An institutional actor in McConnellsburg had a unique way of describing the community where he lives and works. "It's like being on an island! Except you're surrounded by mountains, not the ocean." McConnellsburg is a very old borough, containing buildings that date back to the very early days of the United States, including the cabin of Daniel McConnell, who laid out the borough in the late 1700s. Deep in a narrow valley known as the Great Cove, McConnellsburg is bordered on one side by Tuscarora Mountain, on the other side by Thistle Ridge, and "it is 30 miles from anywhere," says the institutional actor. The distance separating McConnellsburg from other small urban centers is not trivial when it comes to entrepreneurship. "When you have to travel 30 miles in any direction to get to a chain retail store, local people adjust their business plans and find ways to provide products and services right here. That's historically how businesses have appeared," said the institutional actor, also a long-time resident.

McConnellsburg is a county seat, but is otherwise populated by dozens of small businesses, one large manufacturing firm, and virtually no national retail chains. Even the large manufacturer, unlike other large manufacturing firms examined in this research, is a locally owned and operated business serving a global market. "Businesses here do struggle with low demand," says an institutional leader, "that's why we have no Red Lobster or Walmart. We only got a McDonalds seven years ago, and a Giant five years ago. We have a Sheetz, and that's about it!" Even the large manufacturing firm was reported by several participants to flirt with closing or scaling back operations. The firm recently turned to manufacturing army vehicles under the brand name of another firm to account for slow sales in its primary market, although that contract had nearly ended at the time this research was conducted. While local demand is limited, forcing businesses to struggle with sluggish sales at times, "not having Walmart or Lowes helps our businesses," says an entrepreneur. "We have a great local hardware store, a butcher, local shops that have been here for years. Walmart just wipes out generations of businesses. Local people can't compete!"

However, other participants point out that local people *do,* in fact, compete—they just compete differently than entrepreneurs in larger cities. And instead of being competitive with one another, local stores and service providers focus on the competitiveness of their offering vis-à-vis a larger commercial marketplace. "Businesses are successful here because they operate on a smaller scale," says an institutional actor. "Ninety-day collect accounts are everybody's worst nightmare. Here customers and business owners know each other, each other's kids. That builds trust." He continued, "People offer products and services on a scale that's appropriate, and change their offering often to keep up with changing tastes and styles." Instead of driving 40 minutes to get to nearby towns such as Chambersburg or Altoona, local customers take advantage of limited—but highly tailored—local offerings. And retailers and service providers keep their eye on trends to ensure they are offering similar products and services that one can find in larger commercial hubs with national chains. This may not be innovation in the traditional sense, but could be classified as a form of replicative innovation (Schumpeter, 1934), or bringing existing goods and services to new markets where they are needed, while incurring the financial risk of doing so.

In McConnellsburg, many entrepreneurs do not sense this risk. "There's not much business turnover here," says one entrepreneur. "McConnellsburg doesn't have a lot of choices, so the regular clientele you get here helps a lot of people to stay open." Entrepreneurs and institutional actors alike commented on the strong support local consumers provide for small businesses, and that small business owners provide for each other. "People want Walmart, so they drive 30 miles to get to one," says an entrepreneur.

> When I go Christmas shopping, I go storefront shopping in places like here, Shepherdsville, Gettysburg. The community here is pretty close-knit, and willing to support local business . . . mostly for convenience, rather than going all the way to Altoona and not getting quite what you want.

One of the advantages to working with small town businesses is the ability to interact directly with the proprietor, to make deals, and make custom orders. Local banks, too, were reported to be very "helpful and friendly" to small business. Even though both community banks have recently been acquired by large, national banks, "there's still a community bank mentality," says one institutional actor, and bankers still interact regularly with local small businesses.

AGRARIAN ROOTS AND ENTREPRENEURIAL SPIRIT

Historically, McConnellsburg was primarily a trade center for the area's farms, and agrarian roots have helped to shape the entrepreneurial traditions found in the borough today. "The town is entrepreneurial out of necessity," says one institutional actor. "If you don't have something, the culture here is to pull up your bootstraps and get it for yourself. There is a culture of hard work, farming, and agribusiness in this area, so you get lots of people with an entrepreneurial way of thinking, but big agribusiness skill sets, some manufacturing too." Another institutional actor stated, "The spirit of these people is *strong,* they bounce back from hard times. The nature of rural people is to make it on their own, with little outside help. People tend to be more and more independent from generation to generation, and if a market is there, locals will try to take advantage." As a result, local entrepreneurs have leveraged their skills and resources practically, to fill local niches and improve the borough's convenience. And while practical, McConnellsburg entrepreneurs are thrifty, working on a tight budget to keep costs to the consumer low. "Might be because of how people are raised," said an entrepreneur. "There's a survival mentality here. There's not much without leaving the county, so that forced people to develop entrepreneurship skills if they want to stay."

Local businesses and institutions are perceived by participants to exude a sense of inclusiveness in the community, which is important for newcomers. One entrepreneur said, "We feel like we are more a part of this community after four years here than we did after 20 years in our old community. The personality of this community is what makes it attractive." Several participants talked about the inclusive atmosphere among downtown professionals and how easy it is to get to know people. A welcoming attitude toward in-migrant businesses has eliminated a real native/newcomer divide in the town, and many types of entrepreneurs are embraced.

One common type of entrepreneur found in McConnellsburg includes spouses of employed people. An institutional actor stated, "If there is no employment readily available for the spouse of an already-employed person, that really takes the pressure off . . . you can make a few more mistakes and still get by." Employed spouses may work at the manufacturing plant, for the county, or on a nearby farm. Regardless, it is common for many local products and services in McConnellsburg to be provided through the business ventures of spouses of local employees.

INTERACTION UP AND DOWN LINCOLN WAY

Entrepreneurs and institutional actors alike report a highly interactive, very easy-going climate on Lincoln Way, McConnellsburg's main street, and they report very little emergent conflict. One institutional actor reports, "There is a real sense of, 'If I am in trouble, I just walk into [a local colleague's] office and ask for help.'" Another institutional actor stated, "Everybody knows everybody up and down Lincoln Way, there's a good neighbor feeling downtown. People interact right on Lincoln Way! There are also street sales, golf tournaments, and so on." Festivals have emerged as the result of entrepreneur interactions along Lincoln Way, and help to draw customers into the community to boost local sales. "They keep outsiders coming into the community" so that more people discover the community's downtown culture. McConnellsburg's *Fall Foliage Festival* is a street fair that is especially popular.

Besides a healthy downtown culture, there is little divisiveness between downtown businesses and local institutions, because in many cases, downtown business owners also populate institutions. Small businesspeople are also borough board members, and the director of the chamber of commerce is an entrepreneur. As a result of this overlap, there has been a strong focus on downtown businesses by the chamber. In particular, the chamber initiated a once-a-month business networking lunch with speakers and presentations, and opportunities for strategic networking. "Word of mouth is critical for developing a business reputation, and chamber functions help businesses to do this. There is always a mix of business networking, discussion of local issues, and there is always a speaker," says a local institutional leader. "This is where I go to learn how to better serve local entrepreneurs!"

"But you see the same people participating all the time," says an entrepreneur of the chamber meetings. Like many other communities, even high-entrepreneurship communities, the community activeness of small businesses is not universal, nor always positive. The chamber, too, has not always promoted small businesses. "There's no Main Street program here, and the chamber was silent for a while," says an institutional actor. Following a change in leadership, the chamber more recently began promoting local business, capitalizing on the fact that local small businesses interacted informally, but had no forum for formal interaction. These interactions have enabled McConnellsburg entrepreneurs to create festivals, jointly promote the borough, and to anticipate trends and changes in the broader economy.

LOCAL CHALLENGES

Participants were very positive about their experience living and working in McConnellsburg, but every town presents some challenges to local economic development. One salient barrier to entrepreneurship that was frequently identified was a lack of time for local interaction and community involvement. One institutional actor said, "I think entrepreneurs *have* the opportunity to interact, but businesses do not fully utilize those opportunities to network. Being in business is hard work, and sometimes you have to ask yourself, 'Do I mow my lawn, or get dressed up for a chamber function?'" The constraints of running a business, and having a life too, are difficult for any entrepreneur, and individuals with particularly important roles at home (like mothers of small children) simply may not be able to spend the additional time working with other entrepreneurs to discuss local strategies. One entrepreneur remedied this situation by holding sales and marketing seminars in her home, but not all entrepreneurs have been able to engage in community discussions. "It's easier if you have *employees,*" says an institutional actor, "but that's not everybody."

Related to time constraints, an institutional leader noted that many local resources for entrepreneurs are under-utilized. "You would be surprised what is out there to help small business, but you would also be surprised at the resistance to help!" he says. While entrepreneurs may feel comfortable approaching their neighbors and fellow entrepreneurs for assistance, based on relationships of trust that have developed over time, entrepreneurs are less likely to approach institutions or the government for similar assistance with their business. "There are time constraints, but many folks see the government as the enemy," says the institutional leader. "They are also reluctant to do research, see what kinds of programs are out there." While McConnellsburg's downtown thrives, this institutional leader suggests that institutional solutions are out there that could help the community.

The nature of banking has also changed. Before, it was mentioned that banks maintain close ties with community entrepreneurs. While this remains true, both long-standing community banks have been acquired by larger, national banks. "This really alienated the local businesses," says an institutional actor. With national ownership came the imposition of new rules on local bankers, and new criteria for lending. A complaint from both entrepreneurs and institutional actors is that banking has become more focused on the analysis of raw numbers, and less on personal relationships. "The Obama stimulus is not encouraging banks to take risks by giving more SBA-backed loans, the way it was intended," says an institutional actor. Bringing relationships back into banking will take a concerted effort by the banking community, and financial regulators. "It takes a cultural shift," says the institutional actor, "basing loans on respect for character, experience, and sweat equity. We need to make entrepreneurship a real priority in the budget, instead of legislators just saying that entrepreneurship is the backbone of the economy."

OPPORTUNITY

As with other communities examined in this research, opportunity was commonly defined by participants using elements of both the discovery and creation perspectives, and both internally and externally controlled elements. "Both internal and external explanations make sense," remarked an entrepreneur who asked me to explain each briefly. An institutional actor commented,

> I see the logic in both standpoints. Part of creative entrepreneurship is *creating* a need and convincing people that they need a product or service. There are definitely gaps in the market too, so it really requires both! You have to find a solution that delivers both.

One institutional actor leaned toward the discovery perspective, saying, "Opportunities are out there, but it's up to the individual to get out there and find opportunity." The identification of opportunity, rather than its *de novo* creation, is a central feature of the discovery perspective.

Other individuals had unique answers that do not cleanly fit into one category or the other. One entrepreneur said, "Opportunity is *servitude*, not bringing problems, but solutions!" Solutions could conceivably be either created or discovered, but the notion of service to others as a central feature of opportunity was novel. With regard to acting upon opportunity, he also stated, "Failure is an event, not a person." He was referring to a cultural freedom to fail, making it less daunting to take risks in the first place. The entrepreneur noted that, locally, many people apply the fault of business failure to the person who owned the failed business, as if the business failed because the person is inherently a failure. "I succeeded in my first business," he says, "but that just means I barely stayed in business! I did not succeed very much!" A freedom to fail, he believes, is critical to identifying or creating opportunity—perhaps leaning toward the creation perspective, as it implies that most risk is truly unforeseen, even by the most adroit businessperson.

Waynesburg, Pennsylvania

Waynesburg, and surrounding Greene County, have reputations as places where one finds lots of "good ol' boys," according to one entrepreneur. It is a low-entrepreneurship community and, by many accounts, a very difficult place to launch a successful business. But despite the limited number of individuals who have launched a small business there, there is an unmistakable sense of pride that exudes from local leaders and entrepreneurs alike, and a faith that things can improve for the small business community. Perhaps the most striking characteristic of low-entrepreneurship in Waynesburg is the similarity in the attitudes of so many entrepreneurs and institutional actors to those found in high- entrepreneurship communities. However, many protagonists of the small business community in Waynesburg have encountered resistance to their efforts, apathy, or the inability to generate momentum. Even Waynesburg's most optimistic and community-minded entrepreneurs appear to have run aground amidst a persistent company town mentality that is openly oriented against entrepreneurship.

EXTRACTIVE ENTERPRISE AND LOCAL ENTREPRENEURSHIP

Waynesburg's economic history is dominated by the coal industry and, more recently, natural gas development in the Marcellus Shale formation. Waynesburg has historically served as an economic center for the resource-abundant southwest corner of Pennsylvania, serving as a place to gather, shop, and socialize. "There has always been big [extraction] business like coal and Marcellus gas in the area," says an institutional actor. "The rest are people who find their niche, get by. There's not a lot of middle ground." For multiple generations, employment in the coal mines gave coal companies, typically headquartered outside the region, much influence in local politics and social affairs—powers inherited by the natural gas drilling industry. "Everybody caves into coal," said one entrepreneur, "my own town is about to be destroyed by a coal plant mentality." Both institutional actors and entrepreneurs commented that local politics is divisive, and entrepreneurship challenging, because local political power is heavily influenced by the interests of the coal and gas industries—both historically and currently.

"If not for [an energy development company], this place would be a ghost town," remarked an institutional actor on the ubiquity of the extractive industries in Waynesburg. Institutional actors and entrepreneurs alike widely concurred on the effect that coal mining has had on entrepreneurship: since employment in coal and gas extraction has always been good, there is little reason to start a business. As most high school students graduate from high school, getting a high-paying job with the local extractive industries not only makes good sense but also is virtually a cultural imperative. "It is so obvious that you get a job in the mines out of college, for a lot of people, that there is actually resistance to starting your own business as a career choice," said an entrepreneur. "When you say you want to start a business, the first thing you hear is, 'why would you do *that?*'" One Main Street entrepreneur coined the term "dream stealers" to describe many of her local peers who are not entrepreneurs. "These are people who say your idea will never work," she says. When this message is repeated by enough peers, it is often enough to discourage some individuals from launching a business. "It is why I stay positive. Positive attracts positive."

Participants remarked that local opposition to entrepreneurship does not stop with discouraging locals from starting small businesses, but fewer and fewer locals turn to small, local businesses for their needs. "Main Street used to thrive, but it has gone into survival mode," says a Main Street entrepreneur. "It started about 25 years ago when the uptown business district decided that businesses should start closing their doors at 5:00 p.m. They would not change the hours to what the demographics were telling them." This entrepreneur is referring to social changes in the way Waynesburgers worked. In the wake of a global recession, many local mining and manufacturing jobs were lost to cheaper labor in other areas. As a result, there was an increase in the number of women who entered the workforce and, with more two-income families, there was less time to shop downtown—especially during the business day. "In my business," he says, "staying open late is what works for us; part of the reason we are still here."

Mining and manufacturing closures also hurt local consumerism. "About that time, we saw the rise of shopping malls," says an institutional leader. Unemployment in the area hurt family budgets, creating an opportunity for national chains to compete with local small businesses by offering lower prices. However, with unemployment rising, and personal budgets tightening—paired with the indifference of local small businesses to changing local consumption patterns—local citizens embraced low-cost national retail over goods and services offered by their neighbors. "People fought to get Walmart in here, when we need people to keep buying local!" exclaimed an entrepreneur. "There was no service mentality in this town, no support for small business." Even small businesses failed to support each other, buying from low-cost suppliers. "It's not that we have a competitive mindset downtown," states another Main Street entrepreneur, "more like a 'non-observant' mind-set. Businesses just do not support each other. One does not get the sense they care."

To complicate matters for the small business community, Waynesburg, which is home to a regionally recognized private university, fails to retain young people interested in starting a business. One entrepreneur noted that the exit of many small businesses has eliminated competition in the downtown area by eliminating competitors. "It's really limited what you can find downtown." With such little competition, Waynesburg has failed to generate a pipeline of entrepreneurs, or capitalize on the presence of the university. In fact, nearly all participants mentioned that town-gown relations are not what they could be. In Waynesburg, one rarely sees college students in the downtown area, or establishments catering to college students, even though town and campus share a long border. All parts of campus are an easy walk from downtown Waynesburg, but people—and potentially beneficial network connections—rarely cross the boundary. Institutional actors on both sides of the border state that they recognize the potential benefits, and are beginning to meet collectively to discuss strategies jointly. However, not one entrepreneur interviewed truly catered to college students, despite their conspicuous nearby presence. Nor do many college students stay in Waynesburg. "It is tough to keep them here when all you have to offer is coal mining, and most young people today don't want a job where they work seven days a week," said an entrepreneur of the mining alternative: running a small business.

RESISTING CHANGE

Related to the presence of extra-local manufacturing, path-dependent practices of multiple generations working in a large extraction company have created what one entrepreneur calls a "big union mentality." "Locals tend to be stuck in a mindset of working for a big mining company," he said. Even though a culture of "finding a job" has become locally embedded, many locals are not stepping up to take jobs that become available. "They don't pay enough. We are bringing in labor from Oklahoma, Texas, and other places!" Entrepreneurs and institutional actors alike have stated that many young people expect to graduate from high school and land a job that pays $20/hour or more to do extraction work, much like in the 1970s. But, the pay scale for labor, and the hours demanded by many extraction companies, has changed, and many young locals have either chosen not to participate in the workforce (relying on family or government subsidies for survival), or have moved elsewhere looking for other opportunities. "Entrepreneurs are stepping up though," said the entrepreneur, "we're providing services to these [out-of-state laborers]: hotels, catering, personal services. There is a lot of opportunity."

Attitudes about labor are not the only attitudes that have not changed, despite large economic changes in the region. In general, generations of individuals having worked in the same industry, and the same jobs, for similar wages (accounting for inflation), has stifled locals' tolerance for change across many aspects of local society, according to many of the participants. One institutional actor commented, "People are really disenchanted with other people who try to come in and change the town." Even institutional actors complained that other institutions have actively resisted change, instead embracing ties to older industries. This mentality has not only stifled public projects, such as the highly contested streetscape renovation on Main Street (which was finally in progress as this research took place after years of political infighting), but also is oriented at cross-purposes to an entrepreneurial mind-set, as expressed by some local entrepreneurs. "The seven dirty words of entrepreneurship: 'I have always done it that way!'" quipped an entrepreneur of the cultural resistance to change in Waynesburg. "I don't get it, many businesses think anything different is bad. Some businesses won't stay open late for festivals. They even get annoyed when they 'have to' serve customers, especially new customers." Others, she says, embrace novelty, and the entrepreneurial spirit. Across Main Street, there appears to be a mentality divide between the few new entrepreneurs one finds, and established, older businesses:[5] those who embrace change, and those who do not.

INSTITUTIONAL CONFLICT

Waynesburg is home to many local institutions designed to assist the community in local economic development. These services are offered by different levels of government and other organizations. Greene County has an economic development organization, Waynesburg has a Main Street program, both the borough and county governments have been involved in local development planning, the university has an economic development research center, and the borough has a Small Business Development Center (SBDC), offering in-person small business assistance one day a week. The chamber of commerce is very active, and the hilly farmland surrounding Waynesburg is home to many farmer's cooperatives, some of whom have even begun to offer farmer's markets. There is no shortage of development assistance in Waynesburg, which could be considered advantageous for small business. Institutional actors themselves deeply understand the breadth of assistance available to entrepreneurs—and yet entrepreneurship fails to thrive across the community.

An ongoing problem is a high degree of fragmentation in what these institutions are doing and the kinds of services they offer. This was a problem identified in Lichtenstein and Lyons (2010), explaining why a wide range of entrepreneurial assistance programs have failed to generate large numbers of entrepreneurs. However, a fragmentation of goals, mentalities, and ways of doing business also exists among local entrepreneurs. "It's hard to know which organizations are doing what," says one entrepreneur of the many institutions active in Waynesburg. Shortly after this comment, the same entrepreneur said, "Some business owners here are very successful, very involved in the community. They do everything, volunteer for everything. Others just don't." This view echoes sentiments expressed earlier, that not all entrepreneurs are equally enthusiastic about embracing change, serving the community, or supporting other small businesses. Institutions were also reported to express a very diverse range of support and opposition for local initiatives.

There is also a lack of consensus about who is to blame for low-entrepreneurship levels in the community. Institutional leaders spoke positively of the assistance programs they offer, and were curious why more entrepreneurs do not approach them for assistance. One institutional actor said, "A lot of people don't know how to access the right funds [for launching a business], but then they are sent on to more bureaucratic agencies that confuse them!" As such, entrepreneurs are often sent from institution to institution until they find a program that meets their needs, if that occurs.

Entrepreneurs, conversely, implicate local (and other) institutions for being bureaucratic, disconnected, and hopelessly fragmented. "The political structure doesn't know what to do with us!" complains one entrepreneur. "This town has such an adversarial political environment." She went on to mention that the voices of entrepreneurs are rarely heard in institutional deliberations. Another entrepreneur states, "Entrepreneurs say they get nothing out of the chamber, but they put nothing into it either. They don't even submit a business profile!" Institutional actors and entrepreneurs appear to implicate each other for not going farther in promoting entrepreneurship when, it appears, they themselves fully understand that fragmentation, and a lack of individual agency and clear roles in entrepreneurship development are the true culprits.

A lack of a well-communicated strategic purpose among local organizations and entrepreneurs has had other negative impacts on the community that have indirectly affected entrepreneurship. One important shortcoming has been an outright lack of effective city planning. One entrepreneur said, " 'Mount Walmart' [the hill near town where Walmart was built] destroyed a beloved orchard and hayfield that was important to the community. A county commissioner sold the land because he wanted the money for the county. There is no consideration of planning, environmental, or public impact to public decision makers. No green space mentality. The borough is allowing industrial storage units to go in across the street from historic real estate in the middle of town, which destroys real estate value for the whole block." Indirectly, the lack of coordinated planning and green space has impacted this particular entrepreneur's ability to attract talent and, she believes, affects the community more broadly.

AN IDENTITY CRISIS

One entrepreneur made a comment that ties together many of Waynesburg's persistent social problems, from the town/gown divide, to political infighting, fragmented institutions, apathetic entrepreneurs, and a lack of clear roles or a clear local strategy. "I think our biggest problem is finding our identity," he says. "We don't know how to capture what's unique about Waynesburg. We don't have our story straight, the community keeps changing directions." The lack of consensus has a tangible effect on the local business population. "It's hard to keep people engaged and passionate—probably the biggest challenge we face. Usually it's a core group that buys into a new initiative, but then it's harder to get broad agreement on a direction." Instead of thinking strategically or productively around potential initiatives, Waynesburg perpetuates a culture of complaining to the government about proposed changes and focusing on the negative. Several participants echoed this view, especially entrepreneurs. Even institutions do not appear to be firmly established in their roles, according to another entrepreneur who stated, "Developers are interested in us, but sometimes never even get a call back. We are really bad at having a customer service mentality."

Without clear roles, there has been even less strategic focus on supporting entrepreneurship specifically, aside from a few fragmented assistance programs. "Local politicians have an animosity toward the needs of small business," and a tendency to favor energy and extraction interests, complains one entrepreneur. Another states, "Georgia supports *college students*. Pennsylvania supports the *elderly*. Pennsylvania [vocational] schools are teaching young people to make stools. Georgia [vocational] schools are teaching them advanced aerodynamics. What does this say about our future?" Furthermore, some local entrepreneurs want the focus on entrepreneurship to go beyond downtown retail. "Food, music, culture—*this* is what makes a *community*, not retail," he says. High-tech businesses located just outside the borough have launched their capital-intensive businesses with little help from the borough, receiving direct financial assistance from national-scale technology funds. And yet, efforts are underway by the university and chamber of commerce to improve local small business conditions. Unfortunately, these efforts have not yet manifested in the creation of a broad local identity that can be used to guide efforts, and to arrive at strategies for supporting entrepreneurship.

WHAT WORKS IN WAYNESBURG

Waynesburg's story has so far focused on challenges, but the borough clearly retains multiple small businesses and robust institutions, most of whom have an interest in seeing the area improve. Despite its challenges, Waynesburg also has several strategic and lifestyle advantages that may be attractive to entrepreneurs. First, Waynesburg is set in a picturesque hill country, with a landscape similar to parts of Tuscany or Austria. It is only 60 miles from a major city (Pittsburgh), and that city's airport has low-fare connections to many domestic and a few international destinations. Most of all, Waynesburg has a small town feel, mentioned as a precious local asset by many participants. "People want to be around positive energy, but a small town is a different kind of energy," says an entrepreneur. "Here, it is the connection you make with other people. In the city, it's the connection you make with the city." Others commented that Waynesburg's culture facilitates such interactions, especially in a small business setting. "We have a loyal, multi-generational customer base, drawn to our establishments by good, honest, fair service," said another entrepreneur. "Today, customers are not getting that same level of service at most places."

And of course, Waynesburg locals are nothing if they are not optimistic. "We are one of the poorest counties in the Commonwealth," says an institutional actor, "there is so much potential here, it's *beautiful.*" "This is my community and I want to make it a little nicer, a little prettier," said an entrepreneur. "An entrepreneur's responsibility is to maintain a positive attitude, but you have to give back to the community!" Participants were keen to share their optimism for the future of the town, and its continued growth and prosperity, with the exception of one interviewed entrepreneur who wished to leave. Several participants said that Waynesburgers really love their community. "Lots of community love here," said an entrepreneur, "everyone just kinda gets along." An institutional actor took a more neutral stance, saying, "There is evidence of both cooperation and competition in this town." Evidently, conflict and competition in some aspects of community life have not destroyed enthusiasm for the community itself.

Some institutions have also made promising steps toward bridging the institutional divides mentioned earlier, "de-fragmenting" service provision, and putting a strategic emphasis on entrepreneurship. "We have a great chamber, a great Main Street program," says an entrepreneur. The chamber of commerce has taken bold new steps to form relationships between entrepreneurs and develop a Main Street identity—and even offers low-cost insurance for its small business members. The Main Street program, *Waynesburg Prosperous and Beautiful*, is focused around local events, but its ongoing role is still emerging. "Emotions are involved, and some people have left the program," says an institutional actor, but the program continues to thrive. The Main Street streetscape renovation, using a community development block grant (CDBG) from the U.S. Department of Housing and Urban Development, is a successful example of a budding relationship between the county, university, Main Street program, and others. "There was not much entrepreneur involvement," says one Main Street entrepreneur, "but there aren't many other success stories like this in the town either." The university continues to take leadership in coordinating meetings between an array of local institutions for the purpose of discussing new strategies for promoting Waynesburg and its businesses.

OPPORTUNITY

When asked to define opportunity, most entrepreneurs and institutional actors gave definitions that exhibited elements of both the discovery and creation perspectives, although definitions more closely aligned with the discovery perspective were slightly more common. "An opportunity is a void that needs to be filled or seized," says one institutional actor. Another institutional actor said, "It's a niche in the market, something untapped. You can create an opportunity, but it has to be something the market will buy into," suggesting that pre-existing market conditions likely prevail that determine the outcome of the opportunity.

Others saw opportunity as a blend of internally and externally controlled elements. "Opportunity is an open door," said an entrepreneur, "and almost anything can be an opportunity. It's both internal and external, and it goes back and forth. It's an iterative process." The temporal nature of opportunity—that it consists of internal and external components that develop cumulatively over time through an iterative process—represents a novel perspective. Other entrepreneurs suggest using a creation approach when a discovery approach does not work. "It's probably out there, but waiting to be defined," says one entrepreneur. "But markets can be created through marketing. You can convince people that they need what they don't even need!" One entrepreneur defined opportunity as "acting in order to gain," stating, "If you can't find an opportunity, then you create one by creating a reason to buy something."

Alma, Wisconsin

High-entrepreneurship Alma, Wisconsin, has been considered a "backwater town" since the 1970s, as most of the surrounding region's growth was focused on larger, manufacturing-oriented towns such as Eau Claire, Wisconsin; Winona, Minnesota; and larger cities such as Minneapolis and Saint Paul, Minnesota. Eventually, a major shopping mall's appearance in Eau Claire and the construction of a Walmart in Winona attracted many customers away from Alma's idyllic small-town Main Street. Even though storefronts were abandoned, the city of Alma did not tear down the buildings, leaving the historic street intact. Soon, tourists who passed through Alma on trips down the river, many of whom came from the Twin Cities, were inspired by the town's extraordinary scenic setting between high bluffs and the Mississippi River, and the seemingly undiscovered downtown. Purchasing real estate for very little money, those passers-by with the most entrepreneurial ambitions and a desire to leave the Twin Cities for a smaller town came to Alma, and revived what was to become one of the most active Main Streets in Wisconsin.

INFORMAL INTERACTION, LOCAL ACTION

Alma's latest wave of entrepreneurs arrived slowly, and most of them appeared within the last 15 years or less. When they arrived, the town had few institutions to support small businesses—just the municipal government, the county government, the chamber of commerce, and the local historical society. As a result, and because of the close proximity of properties on Main Street, entrepreneurs began to interact informally, stopping by one another's businesses, or just passing on the street. "Interaction? Oh, it happens a lot here," said an entrepreneur. Another said, "Most interaction in Alma is up and down Main Street. We interact without really knowing it, but there's not too much formal interaction. We are more familiar on a day-to-day basis. Mostly it's retirees that go to chamber meetings, not small business." Main Street's proximity and convenience, and the fact that few businesses in Alma are off Main Street, makes it like a giant "third place" where entrepreneurs (and the few institutional actors in town) regularly interact. New and substantive ideas have come out of these informal interactions, including Alma's yearly *Music & Art Festival*, and the *Alma Ice Breaker*, a large, social gathering.

Almost everyone in Alma's business community can be found walking up or down Main Street at some point in the day, often engaged in conversation. Among business owners, supporting local business—and the broader community—are routine features of the local culture. "All of the business owners frequent our business," says an entrepreneur. "There are a few closed-minded businesses who never come, but most of them stop by. We make a point of trying to get to know people in the small business community." Another says, "We are friends with all the 'players' in this town, they all frequent our business. And we give to every local cause. Entrepreneurship is all about giving back to the community." One entrepreneur remarked that true renaissance people (referring to creative entrepreneurs in Alma) contribute to something greater than their own coffer, and that is the community. "We are not big joiners," explains an entrepreneur, "so we take it upon ourselves to hold fundraisers that, in the eyes of the community, substitute for this participation." Support for each other, and for the community, are cultural beliefs that co-evolved as entrepreneurs came to Alma from the outside, seeking to create the ideal community atmosphere they were seeking.

Local institutions also share in the interactions. "We interact with all local institutions," says an entrepreneur. "We keep our private lives private, so our establishment is considered *neutral territory* for many people in town. Lots of organizations use this place for meetings. We want to appear non-confrontational in our community." However, most local interaction goes on throughout the course of the day, and not necessarily after-hours. Government personnel, chamber of commerce members, and other institutions frequently meet downtown to conduct business, and much of that business is informal. One entrepreneur commented that one group of actors absent from this downtown milieu is bankers, who participate little in the local small business culture, and do little for small business—although this view was not raised by all respondents.

Some institutions are more active than others. The chamber of commerce "never really had a clear mission or goal, and you don't need to be a business to be a member, you just pay $50 a year," said an entrepreneur. Not everyone partakes in chamber activities. One institutional actor stated, "The majority of interaction for the business community occurs through the chamber," although another institutional actor disagreed, saying "Most entrepreneurs do not attend because they are too busy focusing on their business." Alternatively, one entrepreneur said, "I don't participate just because I abhor meetings." Mixed attendance at chamber meetings has created barriers for the organization's effectiveness. "We were adamant about the chamber, but aside from the president, most people are not business owners," said an entrepreneur. "They want to do what's right for the *community,* but not necessarily for the *business* community. They are focusing on mainly aesthetic issues. There are lots of retirees on the board, and the same six people make all the decisions. Nobody goes to meetings except the same handful of businesses. How can you know what business owners need?" Despite this criticism, the chamber president is indeed an entrepreneur, and is well known by other Main Street entrepreneurs whose businesses he frequents.

The city of Alma is also highly involved in the affairs of entrepreneurs. Local businesses are all very familiar with the city's young mayor, the city office staff, and the city's one police officer. "The city cooperated with us over permission to have live and taped music outside our establishment. The city wanted us here, even though they wanted to control the process. They worked hard to meet our needs and make this an attractive place to come to," said an entrepreneur. Another said, "Local government, and even local inspectors, really want to help people stay in business. They work with local businesses to keep inspections realistic. In Minneapolis, they shut you down for anything. The city is great to work with, too; they work *with* you! The cooperative attitude, and a lack of excessive government intervention, is very helpful to business." Compared to localities where taxes and regulations have impeded entrepreneurs, Alma small businesses have thrived without many regulations, coordinating most of their downtown activities through informal interaction. The city council, by contrast, was cited more than once as having an anti-business attitude. "They're incompetent," exclaimed one entrepreneur, "They turn down development grants. Free money for the community."

Alma has these organizations, but because of its small size, there is only one local bank, and almost no business support services. "There is no computer support, marketing, one tax guy," says an institutional actor. "And, most locals are not part of the Internet culture here, or if they are, it's the first service they get rid of in down times." The actor praised the one local bank for its culture of local service. "Small town banking is wonderful here! They know your name, open early, and give you personalized treatment."

CULTURE, DIVERSITY, AND IDEAS

A common theme that appeared frequently in interviews relates to the way that Alma's diversity—not so much of race, religion, nationality, and age; but of *ideas*—has shaped the types of interactions that have occurred in Alma, and the outcomes of those interactions. While many small, rural towns have a large, native-born population, very few of Alma's entrepreneurs are native to the area. "Most come from the big city," says an entrepreneur. "The cost of living is considerably lower here, and the scenery drives a lot of diversity into this town." Cosmopolitan in-migrants have played a formative role in shaping the local culture. As one entrepreneur, also a long-time resident, notes, "Historically, good leadership has led to a diversity of ideas, and the best people here have ironically been from outside the community! They brought great ideas with them." As diverse ideas entered Alma via these amenity-driven, urban newcomers, these same individuals were also more receptive to ideas that were different from their own. "People here are more worldly," says an entrepreneur. "We get more people with more ideas from [places that are more diverse]. Even old-timers who are conservative are more worldly and accepting of new ideas. This view leads to a tolerant and open-minded culture that is more open to change." This tolerance in Alma stands in contrast to most other nearby towns, say several entrepreneurs, such as Winona and Mondovi. "They're more tied to themselves." As another entrepreneur put it, "There is a distinct difference between Alma and surrounding communities: people here always tried to *promote the community.*"

Being a tourist town has impacted the small business community's openness to new ideas. "You have to like people, and be open to serving people who are different than you are," says an entrepreneur. The entrepreneur noted that tourists come from all over the world to travel down the Great River Road, and a chat with these individuals exposes people to new perspectives and ways of seeing the world. It also gives Alma global exposure, especially by those that enjoy the experience of passing through.

A cultural openness to diversity and tolerance of newcomers and tourists has given Alma a very welcoming culture, but other cultural features complicate Alma's tiny local society. Despite the many ex-urban entrepreneurs on the Main Street, Alma businesses have embraced an agrarian "pull up the bootstraps" mentality. An entrepreneur and institutional actor stated, "We haven't gotten help from the USDA because people around here have that 'do-it-yourself' attitude." While the "do-it-yourself" attitude has encouraged many entrepreneurs to start their own business, this entrenched belief has also been a barrier to development. The city council has, in the past, turned down grants that were potentially beneficial to the community, and values like tolerating change and doing things yourself are not universally embraced in the town. "The 'don't change anything' mentality still prevails in some spots," says an entrepreneur, "but those folks are going away, and just shrugging their shoulders when change happens." Another entrepreneur states, "The 'old boys' network is alive and well. For a lot of these people, you only get one chance. It's hard to judge character in those circles, lots of 'keeping up appearances.'" These established networks have been in Alma since long before the latest wave of entrepreneurs arrived, and frequently petition and protest change in the community at city and Chamber meetings. Many refuse to shop at new downtown businesses. The clique is very closed to small business, and to many institutional actors. As private citizens, people do tend to support one another. "They have your back," says one entrepreneur of the local citizens, "but in this town, they know everything, and gossip can be a killer."

These persistent mentalities have created a sharp, local divide between older, incumbent natives and younger, amenity-driven entrepreneurs, and their largely touristic customer bases. This situation puts entrepreneurs in a compromised position between two distinctly different customer bases, with the potential for alienating both. Catering too strongly to tourists can drive away locals, but lead to enormous revenues when the weather is warm. The local market is more consistent, but it is much smaller, and by the accounts of entrepreneurs, more fickle. "Tourism is your gravy," says an entrepreneur, "but it's the locals who pay your bills." Another says, "If we had to rely on the local population, we would never survive. But, we also need them in the wintertime." An institutional actor commented that many businesses cater to tourists, and that locals would be very happy if more businesses catered to their needs as well. But, the demographics of the town are changing. Described by an institutional actor, "There won't be a lot of folks left that grew up here due to all the young people leaving. There seems to be a perceived lack of commitment to place, and they are being replaced by outsiders." Those outsiders, however, appear to be equally committed through their local involvement and investment in the community.

COLLABORATE LOCALLY, COMPETE REGIONALLY

One entrepreneur confidently stated, "There's nothing here that's really competing directly. We don't step on each other's toes. Competition is really against national chains elsewhere, we just have to keep our prices reasonable to attract customers." To the outsider, collaboration among local entrepreneurs appears to be ubiquitous on the surface. While this is not universally the case, a strong culture of collaborative action up and down Main Street has differentiated Alma's business culture from the culture of many other small towns. "We always make an effort to get to know new folks, even 'competitors,'" says an entrepreneur. "Every boarded-up business is a reflection on all of us. We would rather have allies than enemies, and competition can bring out the best *or* the worst in people." The collaborative spirit of the business community transcends individual effort alone, and some entrepreneurs believe strongly that their efforts both affect, and are affected by, the broader community. "We're all in this together, but it's still an individual effort too," says an entrepreneur. Another states, "People have always had the ability to work together collaboratively, and to get over personal differences." This *ésprit de corps* has lent itself to a strong sense that one's efforts are rewarding because they are rewarding to the broader community.

Naturally, a strong sense of collaboration and community has encouraged local small businesses to frequent other local small businesses. "We used local contracting in this place, and we buy produce locally, because it's fresher, *and* because it helps people in the area," says an entrepreneur, explaining benefits of buying local to both his business and the community. Another entrepreneur relied heavily on the community for support when launching, and now actively participates in community affairs. "It takes a community to get a business going," he says, "and you can't do it without community support. I had great referrals, and volunteers who helped get the business started." The culture of support across businesses approaches the strength of kin-based ties for some entrepreneurs. "Entrepreneurs here are like a brotherhood," he says. "I like to think that we can talk about anything. There is trust and confidentiality. I hate to say this, but it's not like that with the 'common folk.' There is definitely a division between the town folk and business owners in that regard." The entrepreneur, however, complained that local banks do not share in this cultural bond. "Banks think that they are above the rest, and are generally very snobby here, noses higher than all others in this town."

OPPORTUNITY

Similar to other communities, participants in Alma took a diversity of perspectives on opportunity, and generally used elements of both the discovery and creation perspective to describe what opportunity means to them. "Opportunity is a void, a need not being met, or something that is there where you put your own twist on it," said one entrepreneur, "and I think both [internal and external] explanations are true! Sometimes you can create opportunity, or you can recognize that need. *Creating* opportunity seems a little more like real life, but I see it both ways." "Opportunity is sensing a need, seeing a potential for something to happen," said a person who was both an entrepreneur and institutional actor. "It involves 'gaining' something . . . it even applies to falling in love or getting into shape!"

However, Alma residents did tend to lean toward language that reflects a discovery perspective slightly more often than participants in Maine or Pennsylvania. "I believe it is out there," says an entrepreneur, "I mean, how do you get the germ of an idea without some external coaxing?" The entrepreneur continued by reinforcing the importance of individual agency in acting upon external opportunities, saying, "A lot of people 'see' opportunity. That doesn't make them an entrepreneur! Taking the leap is what makes someone truly entrepreneurial." This perspective was novel, because few other entrepreneurs discussed the importance of taking risks in the context of opportunity. An institutional leader saw opportunity as an urgent process of assessment: "Opportunity is out there, it's a discovery process," he said. "If you don't see it, somebody else will. It's the entrepreneur's job to assess the best opportunities at any time."

Spooner, Wisconsin

Spooner, Wisconsin, faces a unique economic situation among the selected communities for study, and among low-entrepreneurship communities. Spooner is the only community to have developed under a paradigm of heavy industry, where the primary industry has shut down and moved out of the community. Spooner was once a railroading town: a hub for freight and passenger trains, and supporting industries related to the railroad, like freight handling and shipping. The last commercial railroad service to pass through Spooner made its last journey in the early 1990s. By that time, Spooner was already a vibrant community, with some industrial diversification. "We are all small businesses here, there are no businesses over 500 employees anymore" says an institutional actor. "We have food processing, like for meat jerky, some wood products, manufacturing, machine and tool operations, off-road vehicles . . . lots of recreation firms, we are a big second home-owner market. Locals cannot even live on the water anymore."

Spooner's economy has therefore diversified, but only slightly, with many businesses remaining close to traditional manufacturing, or taking advantage of tourism related to hunting, camping, and off-road vehicular recreation. While the town has fast broadband connectivity, it has not been very successful at attracting high-tech firms, or using this capability to create a telecommunications hub. And while Spooner's economic diversification was enough to keep the town from emptying following the closure of the railroad, entrepreneurship breadth and depth lag far behind other non-metro counties in the state. As the following passages will describe, Spooner has many lifestyle amenities, and it is an excellent place for recreation-minded people to live and work. The challenge to entrepreneurship in Spooner is overcoming a very embedded local culture steeped in railroading traditions, and succeeding despite mixed support for the small business community.

NO WALMART, NO CHANGE EITHER

Socially speaking, Spooner has a very strong, mutually supportive culture. "In Spooner, we generally try to look out for one another," says an institutional actor. "There's a big 'buy local' culture, and anti-Walmart sentiment." This institutional actor's comments accurately reflect observations by most other participants in Spooner. Citizens help one another, are neighborly and friendly, they dislike large national chains that could threaten their Main Street, Walnut Street, and they do frequent local businesses. The problem for entrepreneurs is that many also reject anything new or different, which has impacted the launch of many new local businesses, as locals continue to shop, dine, and drink at incumbent establishments. This concern is especially true if the entrepreneur came from outside the community.

Overcoming Spooner's local culture of stubborn attachment to existing businesses is critical to success, but barriers exist at both the consumer and institutional levels. One entrepreneur illustrated this with a story about finding start-up funding locally: "I had an easier time getting funding from out of town. Local banks said, 'There's no fried food, no liquor, no smoking . . . people won't like it.' I found there was huge institutional resistance, and cultural resistance to a lot of ideas. There is a reluctance around here to become too commercial or touristy, so anything appealing to outsiders is discouraged a bit. Bars get a lot of support here; people drink in this town. The people who stop by my business are people who live here, but are not from here. They say, 'Ah, a normal place! No onion rings? I understand why!' "

The lack of diversity within sectors, like restaurants, can be easily observed, as most restaurants and bars offer similar food and drink, all at very low prices. And, drinking alcohol at these establishments is an important social feature of the community. Perhaps carried over from the region's ancestral Swedish and German culture, sitting down for a few beers with friends and colleagues is like social glue that binds locals into a more cohesive community. "We all frequent each other's business," says an entrepreneur, "but beers after work are where you weed out the bullshit and really get down to business." The flight of locals to Spooner bars is easily observed at 5:00 p.m., and while happy hour is an important location for informal social and business interaction, it also excludes individuals who do not feel comfortable in such situations. One entrepreneur explains, "Informal interaction here is centered around alcohol. If you're not into getting a beer, the trust level declines. We have been here eight years, and it's still hard for us to break into these [after-hours] cliques because we don't follow the trends or established norms."

A few entrepreneurs used the term "stubborn" to describe the local culture, suggesting that this has historically been the case in the community. Stubbornness was related by a few entrepreneurs as the result of older Spooner residents, many of whom were employed by the railroad industry. These individuals currently occupy positions of public power and have done so for very long periods of time, and they institutionally resist change. "We need young ideas!" says one entrepreneur. "Old guys need to get off these boards and open their minds. This young generation is powerful, and the old guys don't want to change." Part of this resistance to change has been driven by a lack of understanding among locals of the perils of entrepreneurship. An institutional leader explains, "Here, if you try something and it doesn't work, you are a failure socially. Every entrepreneur understands that you fail more than you succeed." However, with relatively few entrepreneurs per capita in the local population and with many institutions populated by individuals who worked for the railroad and related industries, there is little understanding of—or tolerance for—entrepreneurial risk.

In some cases, this has resulted in an ambivalent stance toward helping entrepreneurs, even from local economic development institutions. One entrepreneur explains, "People said, 'Oh, you're a female-owned business, you'll get tons of support!' But I'm not really in a minority group, and I'm more of a hobbyist. I can't find any institutional support here." Another entrepreneur states that "Spooner has a 'live-and-let-live' attitude. But this means the town also has a reluctance to have an agenda, and institutional leaders really buy into this." An entrepreneur expressed some hope, saying, "The younger generation is starting to see and avoid these problems [of resisting change]. We are starting to collaborate with other chambers of commerce." However, she cautions, "One has to be careful, because certain folks I oppose potentially may also be customers."

Publicly supporting certain ideas, like introducing new ideas to the town, was reported to be dangerous for many entrepreneurs because of the damage it can do to their reputation among the local customer base. "Local opinions of others tend to guide business practices here," says an entrepreneur. "If someone doesn't like you, they won't do business in your store." This situation can cause the loss of customers on an individual basis, but a bad reputation can quickly spread to other parts of the population because of the presence of strong, exclusive social cliques within Spooner. "Successful interaction depends on if you are in a clique or not," says an entrepreneur. "If you go to chamber meetings and you are not part of 'the chamber clique' [established families in the area], those meetings are cold." She continues, "Cliques are why I want to stay out of local politics. It's mostly hearsay and gossip." Therefore, cliques not only serve as a social mechanism to create bonds between people within the community but also serve as a means of excluding outsiders who hold different views, for protecting and communicating local beliefs, and for keeping non-traditional voices out of the public sphere. It may also contribute to a culture where people withhold information out of fear of being judged. One entrepreneur says, "You can learn from each other, but very few people will admit their vulnerabilities. 'Everything is fine,' they say. If you can't do this, how do you offer support?"

One cultural feature that has helped entrepreneurs to thrive, however, has been the community's resistance to locating a Walmart close to Spooner. An entrepreneur said, "Walmart pulled out of plans to locate here due to the state blocking those plans. The perception around here is that local small businesses lobbied to keep them out." The closest Walmart is in Hayward, about 28 miles northeast of Spooner, and a few entrepreneurs expressed that Spooner has no ambitions to become a chain retail center like Hayward. Not everyone agrees with the prohibition of Walmart. One local institution lobbied to get a Walmart located in Spooner. A new school was constructed in anticipation of the extra tax dollars that the Walmart would eventually bring in, but under public pressure, Walmart was never given permission to build. "Walmart brings in more people with more money," says an institutional leader. "I'd be trying to pull some money off these folks if I were an entrepreneur, since local folks have such limited resources."

LOCAL COMPETITION

Socially, Spooner residents are more reserved and protected with their information, and this has created an environment where information flows about central aspects of one's business are highly restricted. "There is a somewhat competitive spirit between entrepreneurs. They are worried about others 'stealing' their market share," says an institutional actor. "They do meet over issues like parking, local festivals, and improving the physical community." They do not meet, however, to discuss business strategy. "Entrepreneurs are protective of ideas here because of limited customers, limited niches," says another institutional leader. "The local manufacturer's group disbanded for this reason, even though it was intended to bring people together for competitive advantage. Bulk and joint advertising were kicked around, but never materialized." Shrinking local markets and limited demand were mentioned as real areas of concern by more than one participant. An institutional actor stated, "When people really want to shop, they go to the Twin Cities, Duluth, Eau Claire, and so on. Entrepreneurs are concerned about declines in shopping, so they are competing more. The prices have to be correct, because locals are poor, they have low per capita income. So they really tend to shop around here for things they can't find anywhere else."

The competitive mind-set has stifled collaboration, but not completely. Some entrepreneurs still cling to a collaboration mentality, and express their frustrations with trying to bring others on board. "I am community-minded, and that makes me different from most entrepreneurs around me," says one entrepreneur. "You *should* be involved with the chamber and the Business Improvement District. By the time I got here, Walnut Street businesses were just starting to talk. Before that, it was everyone for themselves. They had trouble coordinating views." While entrepreneurs have expressed some willingness to improve the downtown, they often times did not state these intentions publicly, perhaps for fear of the cultural repercussions mentioned earlier. "If you have a problem with your town," says an entrepreneur, "don't just complain about it, get out and change it! This [mind-set] is an issue here, and everywhere." Regardless, the town's fragmented views, and the inability of entrepreneurs to discuss change meaningfully, has suppressed interaction among entrepreneurs, which has in turn suppressed the emergence of a clear, local strategy for development.

INSTITUTIONS AND ENTREPRENEURSHIP

Several institutions are active in the local business community, and offer support in various ways—although the real benefits afforded by these institutions are sometimes questioned by individuals in the business community. No matter, Spooner has a full range of institutional support organizations to support economic development more generally, and one organization specifically for small businesses in the central business district. Naturally, there is a local chamber of commerce that promotes tourism in Spooner, offers customer service training for local businesses, and hosts business networking and invited speaker events like "business after five." "Not everyone is involved in the chamber, but it's a functioning group," says one entrepreneur. Another says of the chamber, "They mostly market themselves and their own events. The focus is now changing from town promotion to thinking like economic developers." He adds, "The chamber should be promoting small business whole-heartedly," implying that small business promotion has not been central to the chamber's efforts. But entrepreneur support of the chamber has not been universal, either. "A number of businesses are not chamber members and do not interact there," says an institutional actor. "They perceive that the chamber is too focused on Walnut Street."

Unlike the chamber of commerce, the Business Improvement District (BID) was founded by entrepreneurs on Walnut Street and designed to foster interaction among downtown businesses for the expressed purpose of improving the central business district. "We love the area's railroad heritage, green spaces, and the downtown, so we started a BID on Walnut Street, and we're now expanding it north and south on River Street," says an entrepreneur. "The BID 'taxes itself' [taxes its own members] in accordance with Wisconsin Law. We choose how much we want to tax ourselves, so we agreed to pay a 0.1 percent property tax." So far, the BID has focused on downtown beautification and improving parking signage. Another entrepreneur says, "A lot of it is superficial, but superficial does a lot in making the small town a good place to shop and work." The BID may engage in other local activities, but one entrepreneur admitted, "We are still searching for a clear role for the BID, looking for a way to fill up empty storefronts in town."

The BID has had mixed success in terms of catalyzing interaction among local entrepreneurs. "The BID is where businesses really interact," says an entrepreneur. "The coffee-dinner crowd is the 'old boys' network, some bars too for happy hour." The BID has helped to give entrepreneurs on Walnut Street their own identity. One institutional actor commented, "Many businesses interact, but especially on Walnut Street." However, other downtown businesses have suggested that the BID is just another clique. One entrepreneur stated, "We turned down becoming members because I don't like how it's run. It went from being a Walnut Street initiative to being a selected, adjacency-oriented group. Why not open it to the entire community? Instead, the BID picks and chooses input. It's not representative of all the voices in the downtown." The BID therefore suffers from many of the same accusations applied to other institutions in Spooner, despite the progress it has made in stimulating interaction.

Other institutions have been focused on economic development issues, often excluding the perspectives of entrepreneurs—although these institutions may not be aware that these beliefs exist. The Washburn County Economic Development Council has the stated mission of promoting and helping small firms through large businesses, and has been actively involved in promoting the city's small business park. The efforts of this institution were panned by multiple entrepreneurs, saying that their primary goal is actually industrial recruitment, not local small business support. "They call themselves opportunity people, but promise more than they give," complains one entrepreneur. "Literally nothing is happening! I don't know if they are really doing what they say." Other entrepreneurs complained about small business financing options available through the council that carry confusing and misleading loan terms. Furthermore, many entrepreneurs associate the council with the local power structure. "My perception is that the same guys in charge of [the council] are in charge of everything. Sixty percent of the same people are on all the boards here." Whether these claims are verifiable, entrepreneurs appear to be united in their disapproval of this institution, despite some of the council's successes in attracting firms to the area.

The city council, too, has been cited as being a barrier to small business progress. "City Council needs to be supportive of the downtown," says an entrepreneur. "For example, bar patrons are causing vandalism. Better police protection would protect local businesses." The deeper problem may be that small business needs are not taken seriously by the city council, and the council is perceived by some to represent a power clique in the community. This power clique is also present in many civic groups. "These are mostly charitable organizations, and it's mostly the same people who attend," says an institutional actor. "Organizationally, we are spread pretty thin," he says, referring to the fact that Spooner has many organizations, populated by a limited number of the same members. This result may be partially because of a common problem found in this research: a crisis of time. "Balancing small business and family reduces collaboration here," says an entrepreneur. "Here, the least successful entrepreneurs are the most collaborative, because they don't spend enough time in their business." She states that unlike other institutions, the BID has been good for overcoming these obstacles in a controlled way, although not everyone agrees. Another entrepreneur states, "Businesses and the chamber and the BID do business after five, but I don't want to damage my family life to go drink with businesspeople," she says. "Same thing with morning coffees once a month."

STILL ROOM FOR A NEW IDENTITY

"What we don't have, and need more of, is interaction about opportunities!" said one institutional actor, while talking about how people in Spooner interact. "Look at what you have, like wood waste from furniture and paper production, and look for new ways to use it, like pellets for ethanol and other applications." To date, there have not been efforts to bring small businesses together to develop a cohesive strategy, or to talk about promoting a local identity. "There is no focus on creating a vision for what we want Spooner to represent, not even close!" complains one entrepreneur. Another entrepreneur says, "There is one local manufacturer who is doing his own marketing of Spooner. We need our leadership to be doing this! But none of us have time to put the pieces together. A lot of pieces are there, but the puzzle is not together yet." Independent efforts at stimulating such talks have emerged at various points, but there has been limited commitment to the process, and a lack of willingness to take the risk of starting such an initiative. "We are reluctant to truly buy into a strategy, and just doing piecemeal building for now—but there's reluctance to go all the way," explains one entrepreneur.

Part of the difficulty has been deciding what it means to do business in Spooner. "We like to pretend that we are not a tourist and recreation town," says an entrepreneur, also citing the popular local resistance to outsiders despite a recent influx of summer home dwellers. Another simply says, "We don't want to be Hayward!" meaning that Spooner will likely continue to resist the temptation to become a chain retail hub. With the exception of the BID on Walnut Street, as of this research, very little has been discussed in Spooner regarding the town's strategy, identity, or competitive advantage for the future.

OPPORTUNITY

As with other communities, Spooner participants tended to utilize elements of both the creation and discovery perspectives when defining opportunity. However, institutional actors and entrepreneurs alike tended to use discovery explanations slightly more often than creation explanations. "It's a combination of internal and external forces," said an institutional actor. "There are always opportunities. Guys that fail are people that don't do research. There is always something a person can do, and lots of people are looking for symbiosis. I have skill A, this person has skill B, let's get together and make a new product!" Though planning is a feature of this explanation, so is the symbiosis of compatible skills to create something new. An entrepreneur said, "Opportunity is seizing an opening or a need that you can fill, or a product you can make, filling a gap in your community," expressing a more discovery-oriented stance of finding existing needs in the community. Definitions related to "unfulfilled needs" were common in Spooner, and a few entrepreneurs stated that they lean toward the creation approach because it takes individual action to act upon those unfulfilled needs. However, this is really the discovery approach in disguise, as the opportunity—or unfulfilled need—existed prior to the entrepreneur's action, and the discovery perspective still relies on individual initiative to identify and act upon this extant opportunity.

Summary of Face-to-Face Interview Findings

The study communities represent a broad range of views about entrepreneurship, local interaction, opportunity, and community, and each is unique. However, key similarities do exist, especially within areas of high or low entrepreneurship that differentiate the beliefs and culture of individuals in these places. The following passages comprise a brief summary of the key findings.

Interaction in High-Entrepreneurship Communities Is Highly Strategic

Entrepreneurs and institutions in high-entrepreneurship communities regularly interact with a purpose, and that purpose is generally the support and promotion of the small business community *specifically*. Institutions play a strong role in convening small business people, and facilitating the outcomes of discussions, while entrepreneurs tend to take the lead on creating joint initiatives. Institutions have been most successful when they have given ownership of the local development process over to entrepreneurs, as in Rockland, or by keeping regulations and taxes realistic, as in Alma.

Strategic Interaction Can Have Varying Degrees of Formality

The stories of Alma and McConnellsburg illustrate that purposive interaction does not necessarily need to occur in a formal meeting. Regular, routine interactions among business owners are often just as effective in developing a supportive local culture, and in generating local strategies and ideas. While Rockland created institutions for the specific purpose of promoting small business, informal interaction continues on a day-to-day basis.

High-Entrepreneurship Communities Contain Institutions Founded by Entrepreneurs, or Existing Institutions Refocused by Existing Entrepreneurs

Institutions tend to become more focused on small business support following the involvement of entrepreneurs in that institution. These institutions are therefore manifestations "of the entrepreneurial population" rather than imposing regulations "over the entrepreneurial population." In Rockland, institutions emerged that were the novel creations of local entrepreneurs, and later given legitimacy by the interaction of these groups with other established institutions, like the chamber of commerce. In Rockland and Alma, the chambers of commerce already existed, but they became more attuned to the small business community when a small businessperson was elected as president of one of the chambers. The fundamental involvement of entrepreneurs gives the small business community ownership and control over their economic destiny, as well as a distinct identity that separates the needs of this group from those of other, larger businesses.

High-Entrepreneurship Communities Have a Cohesive, Collaboratively Created Identity

The creation of local institutions, even informal ones, has led to the development of identities that enable entrepreneurs to collaborate locally, but compete regionally. Instead of competing against one another, entrepreneurs collaborate to make their community more attractive to potential customers vis-à-vis other communities in the surrounding region, based in their local strengths. Thus Rockland competes for tourism business among affluent consumers on the Maine Coast, Alma competes for tourism consumers in the upper Midwest to differentiate its economy from surrounding manufacturing and transportation towns, and McConnellsburg has worked to create an economy of convenience, offering world-class trends in products and services locally on a small scale.

High-Entrepreneurship Communities Demonstrate High Overlap between Entrepreneurial and Institutional Roles

Related to earlier points, entrepreneurs in high- entrepreneurship communities commonly hold positions in local institutions, like the chamber of commerce, city council, or downtown groups specific to the small business community. This involvement provides a platform for the voice of the small business community to be heard among other community peers. By contrast, there is less overlap in these positions in low-entrepreneurship communities, and entrepreneurs and institutions appear to think of one another as distinct and separate groups.

High-Entrepreneurship Communities Overcome "Lack of Time" as a Boundary to Participation by Making Interaction More Ubiquitous and Less Formal

While a lack of time to interact is a constraint everywhere, complaints about time constraints emerged far more often in low-entrepreneurship communities than in high. This is due to the nature of interaction in these places. High-entrepreneurship communities have found ways to incorporate interactions with other entrepreneurs into their daily routines, and frequently take time out of the business day to "check in" with other entrepreneurs in their community. In low-entrepreneurship communities, interaction is more restricted to "functions" and "meetings," which appears to give entrepreneurs the impression that interaction is a chore, or a use of time that competes directly with time spent with family and friends. Overcoming these time constraints is critical and most easily accomplished by making regular informal interaction seem like a normal part of a daily routine. As one entrepreneur in Alma commented, "We don't even realize we are interacting!"

Low-Entrepreneurship Communities Experience Path Dependency That Is the Result of an Embedded Absence of Entrepreneurs and a Cultural Resistance to Change

An embedded culture of multi-generational employment for a large industrial firm was largely responsible for a lack of support for the small business community in low-entrepreneurship places. For generations, employment in a mill or mine gave young workers excellent benefits and incentives, and there were few competing incentives to start a small business. The resulting effect is that more individuals tended to work for an extra-local company, rather than create a new business venture, which in turn suppressed the entry of new products, services, and markets into the community. Cultural cliques, in some cases, are used to reinforce support for traditional ways of life, and to exclude or isolate individuals who may seek to change the community.

Low-Entrepreneurship Communities Show Less Support for New Small Businesses, or Entrepreneurship as a Career Option

As a result, employment for someone else became an embedded cultural feature of the lifestyle, and many local individuals who ascribe to this mind-set have had limited exposure to the entrepreneurial process. As a result, many local institutions favor large-scale industrial development to small business development, and resist changes that small businesses may bring to their community. This mentality has suppressed entrepreneurship by making it culturally undesirable, or it has restricted local demand through a cultural lack of support for new establishments.

Low-Entrepreneurship Communities Have a Fragmented Identity, with Institutions and Entrepreneurs Implicating One Another for Local Responsibility

The result of high levels of strategic interaction has been the development of strategics based around a clear local identity rooted in local strengths and assets that has encouraged entrepreneurship in high- entrepreneurship communities. In low-entrepreneurship communities, these collective discussions have often failed to take place, or have only taken place among a limited number of participants. Social fragmentation and the persistence of social cliques, plus the lack of a supportive institutional forum for holding strategic discussions, have been barriers to the development of a clear identity or a local small business strategy in low-entrepreneurship communities.

Opportunity Is Widely Defined by Participants as Being Both Internally and Externally Situated

Entrepreneurs and institutional actors alike defined opportunity using elements of both the discovery and creation perspective. This finding suggests that debates about which perspective more accurately represents the behaviors of entrepreneurs may be misplaced, when in fact entrepreneurs may regularly use features of each in an iterative process to "piece together" entrepreneurial opportunities using a combination of personal strengths and environmental conditions and circumstances. This implication is also important for entrepreneurship development, and suggests that both entrepreneurs (who control the business creation process) and institutions (who influence the local environment for small business) have distinct, important, and mutually reinforcing roles to play in cultivating a supportive and opportunistic local small business culture.

Few Differences in Responses between Individuals and Institutions

Finally, relatively few differences were found in the narratives of entrepreneurs and institutional actors. In low-entrepreneurship communities, entrepreneurs, and institutional actors were more likely to express confusion or concern over each other's actions. This consistency is to be expected in places where entrepreneurs and institutions interact less often, and where there is a sharp division in the roles played by each. However, nearly all participants expressed that their community is a healthy environment for socializing, and that "everyone knows everyone" in their town. It appears that the content and purpose of these interactions, more than the interactions themselves, may have a greater effect on the ability of entrepreneurs to thrive in the community.

Summary

This chapter has provided an in-depth exploration of the ways that local interactions, mediated by elements of the local culture, history, and environment, have affected the support for the local small business community and the ability of its entrepreneurs to thrive. The findings illustrate that entrepreneurship does not happen in a vacuum. Culture, history, and the perspectives of leaders and institutional actors have a pronounced impact on local entrepreneurial behavior and attitudes. In this network of relationships, it is not only the structure of networks that matters but also the cultural content and institutional norms inherent in those networks. By focusing on networks of human interpersonal relations beyond the firm level, the research moves toward an *ecosystem* level of understanding through which entrepreneurial action can be viewed as deeply embedded in a diverse web of different attitudes, behaviors, rules, and cultural values—not to mention diverse business strategies. Chapter 8 will analyze the case study data through the lens of theoretical frameworks presented in Chapters 2 and 3, to identify findings that can illustrate strategies for leaping cultural and leadership boundaries.

Notes

1 This chapter is adapted from the original dissertation by Fortunato (2011) on the intersection between individuals, institutions, and opportunities in high- and low-entrepreneurial communities. Select findings from this research are also published in Fortunato and Alter (2016) and Fortunato and McLaughlin (2012), although they are abridged because of the space constraints of an academic journal format. This chapter contains the full findings of the face-to-face interviews to present the entirety of the data. A full analysis of the findings is also presented here.

2 Alma became the second largest city in Buffalo County, Wisconsin, when the two delimited municipalities of the City of Alma and the Town of Alma were combined. The City of Alma is entirely encircled by the Town of Alma, which also includes the unincorporated place of Tell, Wisconsin. In U.S. Census data (2011), they are treated as one entity.

3 See Shane (2009) for an inverse approach. Shane believes that supporting entrepreneurship is bad public policy because it entrusts people without extensive entrepreneurial experience to start businesses. This concern is "bad" because such individuals often launch low-growth, low-value businesses that often fail and create few jobs. It should be clear that Shane's perspective on this matter is

antithetical to the community-oriented development approach shared from the research here, by elevating high-tech and high-growth startups by individuals who are already successful to a level of inherent superiority.

4 One observation of the researcher is that there appeared to be very few retail and restaurant establishments in this site compared to the other five—even compared to other low-entrepreneurship sites. The presence of Walmart and fast food chains like McDonalds, paired with low support for small business, may be one reason for this, echoed in the sentiments of participants.

5 Several of these individuals were not interviewed because they did not meet the criteria of having launched the business, or had not contributed substantially to the reinvention of an existing business into a new offering. They are, in fact, *owner-managers* rather than *entrepreneurs,* to use Schumpeter's (1934) terminology.

References

Acs, Z. J., & Armington, C. (2006). *Entrepreneurship, geography, and American economic growth*. New York, NY: Cambridge University Press.

Acs, Z. J., & Audretsch, D. B. (Eds.). (2003). *Handbook of entrepreneurship research: An interdisciplinary survey and introduction*. Boston, MA: Kluwer Academic Publishers.

Aldrich, H., & Zimmer, C. (1986). Entrepreneurship through social networks. In D. L. Sexton & R. W. Smilor (Eds.), *The art and science of entrepreneurship* (pp. 3–23). Cambridge, MA: Ballinger Publishing Company.

Alvarez, S., & Barney, J. (2000). Entrepreneurial capabilities. In G. D. Meyer & K. A. Hepperd (Eds.), *Entrepreneurship as strategy: Competing on the entrepreneurial edge* (pp. 63–81). Thousand Oaks, CA: Sage.

Banyai, C. (2009). Community leadership: Development and evolution of leadership in Himeshima. *Rural Society, 19*(3), 241–261.

Beyers, W. B., & Lindahl, D. P. (1996). Lone eagles and high flyers in rural producer services. *Rural Development Perspectives, 11*(3), 2–10.

Biernacki, P., & Waldorf, D. (1981). Snowball sampling: Problems and techniques of chain referral sampling. *Sociological Methods Research, 10*(2), 141–163.

Bowman, L. E. (1932). Community organization. *The American Journal of Sociology, 37*(6), 924–929.

Brewer, J., & Gibson, S. W. (Eds.). (2014). *Necessity entrepreneurs: Microenterprise education and economic development*. Northampton, MA: Edward Elgar.

Burt, R. S. (2002). The network entrepreneur. In R. Swedberg (Ed.), *Entrepreneurship: The social science view* (pp. 281–307). New York, NY: Oxford University Press.

Carsrud, A. L., Olm, K. W., & Eddy, G. G. (1986). Entrepreneurship research in quest of a paradigm. In D. L. Sexton & R. W. Smilor (Eds.), *The art and science of entrepreneurship* (pp. 367–387). Cambridge, MA: Ballinger Publishing Company.

Clifton, J., & Badal, S. B. (2014). *Entrepreneurial strengths finder*. New York, NY: Gallup Press.

Cochran, T. C. (1949). Role and sanction in American entrepreneurial history. In A. H. Cole (Ed.), *Change and the entrepreneur: Postulates and patterns for entrepreneurial history* (pp. 153–175). Boston, MA: Harvard Business School Press.

Cooper, A. C., Markman, G. D., & Niss, G. (2000). The evolution of the field of entrepreneurship. In G. D. Meyer & K. A. Hepperd (Eds.), *Entrepreneurship as strategy: Competing on the entrepreneurial edge* (pp. 115–133). Thousand Oaks, CA: Sage.

Dabson, B., Malkin, J., Mathews, A., Pate, K., & Stickle, S. (2003). *Mapping rural entrepreneurship*. Battle Creek, MI: Kellogg Foundation; Washington, DC: CFED.

Davidsson, P. (2008). *The entrepreneurship research challenge*. Cheltenham, UK: Edward Elgar.

Durkheim, E. (1964). *The division of labor in society*. New York, NY: Free Press of Glencoe.

Fayolle, A. (2014). What we know and what we need to know in the field of entrepreneurship. In A. Fayolle (Ed.), *Handbook of research on entrepreneurship: What we know and what we need to know* (pp. 1–12). Northampton, MA: Edward Elgar.

Feld, B. (2012). *Startup communities: Building an entrepreneurial ecosystem in your city*. Hoboken, NJ: Wiley.

Florida, R. (2002). *The rise of the creative class and how it's transforming work, leisure, community and everyday life*. New York, NY: Basic Books.

Florida, R. (2012). *The rise of the creative class, revisited*. New York, NY: Basic Books.

Forson, C., Ozbilgin, M., Ozturk, M. B., & Tatli, A. (2014). Multi-level approaches to entrepreneurship and small business research—transcending dichotomies with Bourdieu. In E. Chell & M. Karatas-Ozkan (Eds.), *Handbook of research on small business and entrepreneurship* (pp. 54–69). Northampton, MA: Edward Elgar.

Fortunato, M. W-P (2009). *Against the grain: What motivates entrepreneurs to locate in Pennsylvania's non-metropolitan cities and boroughs*. Saarbrucken, Germany: VDM Publishing.

Fortunato, M. W-P (2011). *The individual-institutional-opportunity nexus: Examining interaction, purpose, and opportunity in rural entrepreneurship development*. (Unpublished dissertation). University Park, PA: Pennsylvania State University.

Fortunato, M. W-P (2014). Rural entrepreneurship matters, but why? *Texas Town & City*, December 2014, 1–12. Retrieved from http://www.tml.org/p/Dec%2014%20Small%20Cities%20Corner.pdf

Fortunato, M.W-P, & Alter, T.R. (2015). Community entrepreneurship development: An introduction. *Community Development: Journal of the Community Development Society*, *46*(5), 1–12.

Fortunato, M. W-P., & McLaughlin, D. K. (2012). Interaction and purpose in highly entrepreneurial communities. *Entrepreneurship Research Journal*, *2*(1), 1–36.

Gartner, W. B. (1990). What are we talking about when we talk about entrepreneurship? *Journal of Business Venturing*, *5*(1), 15–28.

Gasse, Y. (1986). The development of new entrepreneurs: A belief-based approach. In D. L. Sexton & R. W. Smilor (Eds.), *The art and science of entrepreneurship* (pp. 49–60). Cambridge, MA: Ballinger Publishing Company.

Gaventa, J. (1982). *Power and powerlessness: Quiescence and rebellion in an Appalachian valley*. Urbana, IL: University of Illinois Press.

Goetz, S. J. (2006). *The place-based structural determinants and effects of self-employment*. Report to the Ewing Marion Kauffman Foundation.

Gusfield, J. R. (1975). *The community: A critical response*. New York, NY: Harper Colophon.

Henderson, J., Low, S., & Weiler, S. (2007). The drivers of regional entrepreneurship in rural and metro areas. In N. Walzer (Ed.), *Entrepreneurship and local economic development* (pp. 81–102). Lanham, MD: Lexington Books.

Hildenbrand, B., & Hennon, C. B. (2008). Beyond the concept of 'getting big or getting out': Entrepreneurship strategies to survive as a family farm. *International Journal of Entrepreneurship and Small Business*, *6*(3), 479–490.

Hitt, M. A., & Reed, T. S. (2000). Entrepreneurship in the new competitive landscape. In G. D. Meyer & K. A. Hepperd (Eds.), *Entrepreneurship as strategy: Competing on the entrepreneurial edge* (pp. 23–47). Thousand Oaks, CA: Sage.

Hoppe, R. M., & Banker, D. (2006). *Structure and finances of U.S. farms: 2005 family farm report*. USDA-ERS Economic Information Bulletin #12. Washington, DC: United States Department of Agriculture.

Hustedde, R. (2007). What's culture got to do with it? Strategies for strengthening an entrepreneurial culture. In N. Walzer (Ed.), *Entrepreneurship and local economic development* (pp. 39–58). Lanham, MD: Lexington Books.

Landström, H. (2005). *Pioneers in entrepreneurship and small business research*. New York, NY: Springer.

Lichtenstein, G. A., & Lyons, T. S. (2010). *Investing in entrepreneurs: A strategic approach for strengthening your regional and community economy*. Santa Barbara, CA: Praeger.

Low, M. B., & MacMillan, I. C. (1988). Entrepreneurship: Past research and future challenges. *Journal of Management, 14*(2), 139–161.

Maxwell, J. A. (2005). *Qualitative research design: An interactive approach*. Thousand Oaks, CA: Sage.

McElwee, G. (2006). Farmers as entrepreneurs: Developing competitive skills. *Journal of Developmental Entrepreneurship, 11*(3), 187–206.

McMillan, D. W., & Chavis, D. M. (1986). Sense of community: A definition and theory. *Journal of Community Psychology, 14*, 6–23.

Penrod, J., Preston, D. B., Cain, R. E., & Starks, M. T. (2003). A discussion of chain referral as a method of sampling hard-to-reach populations. *Journal of Transcultural Nursing, 14*(2), 100–107.

Reynolds, P. D. (2007). *Entrepreneurship in the United States: The future is now*. New York, NY: Springer.

Richards, S. T., & Bulkley, S. (2007). *Agricultural entrepreneurs: The first and the forgotten?* Research Paper #07–01. Washington, DC: The Hudson Institute.

Schumpeter, J. A. (1934). *The theory of economic development: An inquiry into profits, capital, credit, interest and the business cycle*. Cambridge, MA: Harvard University Press.

Sexton, D. L., & Smilor, R. W. (Eds.). (1986). *The art and science of entrepreneurship*. Cambridge, MA: Ballinger Publishing Company.

Shane, S. (2009). Why Encouraging More People to Become Entrepreneurs is Bad Public Policy. *Small Business Economics, 33*(2), 141–149.

Sopuck, R. D. (2003). *The lone eagles: Information professionals and rural economic development*. Policy Series Paper #19. Winnipeg, Manitoba: Frontier Centre for Public Policy.

Strauss, A. L. (1987). *Qualitative analysis for social scientists*. New York, NY: Cambridge University Press.

U.S. Census Bureau. (2011). *American community survey 2005–09*. Retrieved from http://www.factfinder.census.gov

U.S. Department of Commerce. (2011). *Regional Economic Information System (REIS)*. Bureau of Economic Analysis. Retrieved from http://www.bea.gov/regional

Warren, R. L. (1987). *The community in America* (3rd ed.). Lanham, MD: University Press of America.

Yin, R. K. (2015). *Case study research: Design and methods* (5th ed.). Los Angeles, CA: Sage.

8 Analysis of the Case Study Data

Considerations for Studying or Launching an Entrepreneurial Community or Ecosystem

Michael W-P Fortunato

Chapter 7 highlights high- and low-entrepreneurship in the multiple case study from Fortunato's (2011) dissertation chronicling the way that entrepreneurs and institutional actors interact—or fail to interact—to create a community that supports habits and norms of entrepreneurial venturing. The case studies focus on rural communities, as these communities lack some (though rarely all) amenities commonly found in urban areas that are useful to entrepreneurship. These six communities in Maine, Pennsylvania, and Wisconsin did not have access to local venture capitalists, research institutions, or major airports. They were sometimes off-the-beaten-path, far from major highways, and broadband coverage may or may not have been adequate depending on the side of town where one is standing. There were no noticeable industry clusters or dense networks of thousands of professionals in an interconnected, skilled local labor pool. Employees did not generally hop from company to company on the way up the career ladder, as relatively few enterprises exist, and most everyone knows of everyone else in the town. There were certainly high-tech firms and dozens of innovative business ideas, but few high-growth firms—many entrepreneurs took pride in staying small and serving their local market. With many amenity-driven factors removed from the local community, self-employment rates, and the income earned by self-employed individuals, rose and fell because of other factors that were often more social, institutional, and historical in nature.

While urban-style amenities may be helpful to stimulating entrepreneurship, these communities demonstrate that there is no shortage of entrepreneurial individuals and forward-thinking minds in rural areas as well. Without mainstream amenities, entrepreneurs in smaller communities rely more on one another, and on traditional institutional support systems such as the local government, Chamber of Commerce, and most of all, other entrepreneurs. Larger companies in the area could create opportunities, as they did in Rockland, Maine, or barriers, as they did in Rumford, Maine. A university only played an entrepreneurial support role in one community. Still, communities of this size exhibited a range of entrepreneurial behaviors, and local attitudes about entrepreneurship. The cases illustrate that an entrepreneurial community or ecosystem can be (1) created catalytically over a reasonably long period of time, and (2) can be launched in communities of nearly any size (Alma, Wisconsin, had only 781 residents at the time of the 2010 Census). However, certain considerations and expectations are important for both the study of entrepreneurial communities, and for attempting to launch an entrepreneurial community.

This chapter is an analysis of the case study in the context of this book's focus on culture and leadership. The chapter discusses central themes that have been explored in the book, and applies them to the case study data. This chapter will discuss (1) the role of culture, (2) the role of local and state leaders, (3) the role of history, (4) the roles of entrepreneurs and non-entrepreneurs, and (5) the role of local and extra-local actors. Each section will focus on how these topics have been used to remove barriers in each community. Finally, the analysis will examine the case study data in the context of the four major approaches to entrepreneurship development: (1) facilitating conditions, (2) national and regional policy, (3) entrepreneurial communities, and (4) entrepreneurial ecosystems. The strengths and weaknesses of each model will be considered for both research and practice.

The Role of Culture

"Mentality" is a word that appeared over and over again in the Fortunato (2014) case studies. Whether it was used to describe cooperation, or to describe resistance to change, a variety of "mentalities" were explored in both high- and low-entrepreneurship communities. The word "mentality" refers to a mind-set held by a portion of the population. However, what many refer to as a "mentality" is essentially what sociologists refer to as "culture," "cultural norms," and "mores." The cultural mind-set is fundamental in shaping how a person views reality, and this constructed reality often reinforces and reproduces the culture over time (see Berger & Luckmann, 1991). The idea that culture shapes reality, from the way people react to entrepreneurs to the propensity of an entrepreneur to launch, is a long-standing focus in sociology. Granovetter (1985) states that all economic action is deeply embedded in social relations, which are themselves affected by culture. This approach does not "rob" the entrepreneur of his or her agency and individuality in launching a business, as Shane (2012) warns. Instead, it recognizes that even individualistic action is deeply—even fundamentally—influenced by what people in a community consider to be good, honorable, honest norms of human behavior. If the community believes that entrepreneurship is a noble, celebrated pursuit, one can almost expect there to be a high degree of needed support for entrepreneurs. When entrepreneurship is seen as a frivolous, foolish activity for "weirdos" and "crazy people," it can have the pervasive effect of suppressing the aspirations of people who might otherwise become entrepreneurs, and leave those who do launch feeling lonely, isolated, and undervalued.

Borrowing from the field of sociology, communities follow a pattern of social role occupation (see Goffman, 1959; Merton, 1957), through which life can be viewed as an *ecology* of different roles, each with different, socially constructed expectations. A person may be a mother, a banker, a chess player, a movie buff, a foodie, a daughter, a community volunteer, and an evening MBA student at the same time. Each role carries different expectations and connotes different behaviors considered to be appropriate at any one time. However, this "role set" (see Merton, 1957) can also pass from one generation to another, especially if this woman's mother had many of the same interests, much like her mother before her. Many of these roles are deeply and socially influenced, and based on expectations of a person's performance. Both high- and low-entrepreneurship communities often struggle with issues of local participation. Even getting committed entrepreneurs to the table for collective meetings and events is a challenge for places with high entrepreneurship rates. The major difference between high- and low-entrepreneurship communities, however, is that high entrepreneurship communities tended to target *an entrepreneur's entire role set,* while low-entrepreneurship communities focused more on entrepreneurs as entrepreneurs. The difference: communities like Rockland, Maine, are aware of the time constraints of entrepreneurs, and work to create organic events (networking-based meet-ups, artsy festivals) blending recreation, the need to mingle, and human interest with matters of importance to the entrepreneurial community. Smaller communities like McConnellsburg, Pennsylvania, and Alma, Wisconsin, did so more informally, by blending conversations about local collaboration seamlessly with everyday interactions up and down the Main Street, as a deliberate feature of the local culture. Time-strapped entrepreneurs were drawn to these interactions because they fulfilled other needs besides business needs, and addressed the "whole person," all while supporting the broader community. In low-entrepreneurship communities, social fragmentation, and excessive competitiveness suppresses this kind of action.

One of the major cultural attributes in these cases supporting entrepreneurship is collaboration among entrepreneurs. This cultural value respects the individuality of entrepreneurs, but recognizes that there are occasionally situations that transcend the immediate needs of an individual business, such as the survival of the town. In Alma, Wisconsin, it was mentioned that a boarded-up Main Street is a reflection on the entire community, and that the local culture suggests that even competing entrepreneurs can get ahead together if they work together strategically. Each of the high-entrepreneurship communities had a culture of routine interaction that take a variety of forms—from formal meet-and-greet events to informal interactions up and down the Main Street. Much of the strategic work of entrepreneurs is done quite informally, often while patronizing each other's businesses. The community quickly includes others in the loop, and discussions are frequently focused on helping the entire community to succeed through the creation of festivals, events, downtown groups, and joint marketing. It should be noted that entrepreneurs in these communities primarily interact with other entrepreneurs and not necessarily institutional actors, who are at times seen as resource providers rather than peers. For this level of interaction to occur, entrepreneurs also rely on norms of trust and reciprocity. This behavior is the case in McConnellsburg, Pennsylvania, where there are few 90-day accounts, and definitely *not* the case in Rumford, Maine, or Waynesburg, Pennsylvania, where entrepreneurs believe that other entrepreneurs may steal their ideas, market share, or standing in the community. Alternatively, many entrepreneurs in Waynesburg, particularly, are simply "non-observant" of the rest of the entrepreneurial community, and make little effort to reach out to fellow entrepreneurs or new customers.

Furthermore, interaction requires inclusivity and a cultural *openness to diversity*. The cultural openness to serve diverse outsiders who see the world differently is most pronounced in Alma, Wisconsin, whose entrepreneurs bring these values from larger cities. As one McConnellsburg entrepreneur stated, they felt "more a part of the community after 4 years than 20 in our old community." Such deliberate inclusion serves to welcome newcomers and different thinkers critical to maintaining a high level of local innovation, rather than isolating them or creating an insider/outsider divide like the one found in Spooner, Wisconsin. In Alma, entrepreneurs regularly reach out, and give back to the community when they can—effective practices espoused by Feld's (2012) *Boulder Thesis*. Openness to diversity not only facilitates openness across the community of entrepreneurs but also with customers as well. Entrepreneurs in Alma, for example, enjoyed strong summer sales figures from a wide diversity of tourists along the Great River Road, although this sometimes isolated them from local customers whose support was needed in the wintertime. Openness to customers diverges from the feeling of "having to help people" found in Waynesburg, which was also cited as a major barrier.

A cultural sense of *adaptability* was also an important advantage in high-entrepreneurship communities. Each of these communities had either experienced a history of economic change over time, was sufficiently remote to rely on a "pull up your bootstraps" mentality, or both. McConnellsburg was highly adaptable in its offerings, and customers appreciated the ability to work directly with proprietors to place custom orders and make special deals in this isolated town. This contrasts with Waynesburg, where entrepreneurs mentioned that many of their peers espoused the "seven dirty words" of entrepreneurship: "I have always done it that way!" In that city, entrepreneurs catering to their traditional customer bases had difficulty reaching across the road to a college campus to attract new customers because of a local aversion to change and adaptation. In Spooner, resistance to change kept many entrepreneurs from providing innovative offerings, and sometimes presented them with challenges in finding funding for such offerings. Participants in both Spooner and Waynesburg commented about the local "good ol' boys" network—individuals who enjoy a relative share of power, and tend to oppose challenges that might upset that power structure.

Several entrepreneurs and institutional actors alike felt that the lack of a cohesive, local identity was a major barrier to pulling both groups together more effectively. Fragmentation across institutions, and across entrepreneurs, leads to a cultural embrace of "what *I* would like to do" instead of "what *we* would like to do." Oftentimes, institutional actors and entrepreneurs see eye-to-eye about how to better support small business in the community, but run afoul of other groups with different cultural incentives, such as city councils who have an interest in preserving the community in its current state. Even in mill towns, a lack of collective identity was cited for holding the community back from taking new directions, even if entrepreneurs and some institutional actors are ready to go. High fragmentation can lead to informational silos or, even worse, cliques (as was the case in Spooner). While low participation at public events was found to harm both types of communities in the case studies, low-entrepreneurship communities suffered especially from low public participation and entrepreneur engagement because of social fragmentation.

Finally, a major cultural difference stems from the difference between the "mother mill" or "company town" mentality and the "opportunistic" mentality of high-entrepreneurship communities. This difference reflects two different cultural dimensions of economic life: Provision versus creation. In cultures that rely on provision, the most honorable path to economic self-sufficiency is to pledge loyalty to a mill, railroad, or mining company. These companies are owned by entities outside the community, and they tend to pay reasonably high salaries to workers right out of high school and provide honest, consistent work, although salaries and benefits are diminishing. Historically, loyalty to such a company for a period of 25 to 35 years could provide an entire family with a good life, and retirement benefits for the worker. When these jobs are at stake because of economic restructuring—the most salient popular and governmental response is to preserve the employer at all costs. Community growth is pursued through a variety of industrial recruitment techniques to provide more wage employment jobs, should the original company eventually fold or pull out of the community.

A provision culture diverges sharply from a creation culture, where individuals feel that they are empowered—and indeed *should* be empowered—with creating their own economic destiny through entrepreneurship. Cultures that value creation are often more forward looking and generative, willing to try new things and tolerate failures if they occur. A high value is placed on novelty and experimentation above stability and consistency. When situations go wrong, such as a plant closure, it can be paralyzing to a provision-minded community. As in Rumford, there may be a high number of individuals utilizing social services until new jobs appear, or they may leave the community altogether like Waynesburg's college students. Some individuals may even try entrepreneurship, but out of necessity rather than opportunity. In high-entrepreneurship communities, a culture that values creation over provision also supports opportunistic action, where it is acceptable to "dream big," identify opportunities strategically, and attract sufficient funding prior to launch.[1]

Leaping Cultural Boundaries

As evidenced in the case studies, norms of inclusivity, openness to diversity, collaboration, creation rather than provision, working across boundaries, regular and routine formal and informal interaction, adaptability in business offerings and business hours, and an opportunistic mind-set are all present in high-entrepreneurship communities more often than in low-entrepreneurship communities. While there are exceptions to these norms in all communities under study, there is a local perception that cultural pathways, or "mentalities," are responsible for shaping a variety of attitudes and behaviors.

A community's culture is a difficult mind-set to change, and anyone who tries to implement change is likely to meet substantial resistance. New cultural pathways can easily be perceived as threats to established pathways, especially if they redistribute power from formal authority figures to new actors like entrepreneurs. However, this path is not the approach taken by entrepreneurs in the case study. While terms like "culture change" may be popular, entrepreneurs in high-entrepreneurship communities do not change the dominant culture—*they create a space for an alternative culture to emerge*. This very important insight shifts the focus of entrepreneurship from a conflict frame (i.e., changing the "bad" culture of others) to an attraction frame (i.e., our downtown group is the place for innovative thinkers!). Even in high-entrepreneurship Alma, participants noted that the community of entrepreneurs is still isolated from older retirees in the area who resist change. Rather than attempting to combat the culture, Main Street entrepreneurs create their own downtown culture of innovation and collaboration. By deliberately reaching out to others, like-minded individuals are quickly welcomed into the group. Resisters are generally left alone, and despite their efforts to suppress change, often times reluctantly accept the productive actions of the entrepreneurial community. The door is left open for resisters to join, even if they were initially skeptical. Similarly, in Rockland, downtown business groups like the Historic Inns and the greater Downtown Business Alliance created cultural enclaves where entrepreneurs could go to be with other entrepreneurs. In low-entrepreneurship Rumford, there was still a recognition that an entrepreneurial interest group was needed: "What we need is an entrepreneurship council, made up of entrepreneurs," said one Rumford entrepreneur.

This approach relies on a "pull" model rather than a "push" model, attracting like minds until a critical mass is reached, beyond which point the group is far less likely to encounter mainstream cultural resistance. The culture change is never complete—there are always resisters. But, as the communities attract more entrepreneurs, they in turn attract new types of customers, new residents, and people who appreciate the efforts of the small business community.

A major turning point in the cultural transformation of communities is the formal recognition of individuals bearing alternative cultural views as mainstream leaders. In both Rockland and McConnellsburg, when the leadership of the local Chamber began to include entrepreneurs, this then brought an entrepreneurial perspective to those organizations. At this point, small business issues begin to be taken seriously in decision-making forums addressing commercial issues, or community issues more broadly.

Leaping cultural boundaries requires the creation of a space where entrepreneurs can interact purposively and collaboratively to better the community. Oftentimes it is entrepreneurs who create organizations dedicated to supporting small business interests, and these can take on an innovative flair. Entrepreneurs in communities outside this study create their own incubators and co-working spaces as a place where entrepreneurs can interact, and where innovation is highly supported. These "connector" organizations (see Feld, 2012) can also serve as educational hubs for learning about entrepreneurship, small business development, and a variety of innovative applications (i.e., technology, manufacturing, marketing). Spaces such as these should adopt an open door policy to maximize attraction, and create early working relationships with local government, mainstream business organizations, and the media, who can help to promote the efforts of the group. With effective promotion, the group may serve as a "strange attractor" to potential entrepreneurs from outside the community, drawing them in to the ecosystem. Members of these organizations should be encouraged to pursue leadership positions in local government, and on the boards of other local organizations.

Entrepreneurs commonly create these types of culturally supportive spaces, but forward-thinking leaders in local government and economic development can do the same! In these cases, it may be necessary to reach out to entrepreneurs at the very beginning of the creation process. Doing so will ensure that local entrepreneurs' perspectives are incorporated right from the start. This approach may also help to alleviate concerns that the new cultural space belongs to a non-entrepreneurial organization in a community, such as a government or chamber. Even if these groups are viewed positively in the community, ensuring that cultural spaces belong to entrepreneurs also protects the initiative from any negative feelings that the broader community may have toward the larger, established organizations coordinating the launch. Established organizations can still play an important and active supporting role, and it is likely that empowering entrepreneurs from the beginning will solidify the trust with participants necessary to view the established organization as a full partner, equal participant, and a vanguard of innovative thinking.

The Role of Local and State Leaders

Politicians were frequently identified by entrepreneurs to be barriers to their success, and to the construction of a healthy entrepreneurial community. These leaders are often at both the state and local levels, although disappointment with leadership was not universal in the study. At the state level, the state government of Maine was repeatedly mentioned as creating excessive barriers to small business development, for example. From excessive bureaucracy and regulations to the prioritization of larger industries, many participants viewed Maine's government as oriented against small business. Similarly, participants in Pennsylvania stated that entrepreneurship should be a real priority for government, not just legislators saying that it is the backbone of the economy. One entrepreneur also viewed Pennsylvania's government as providing vocational education geared toward the past, rather than incentivizing the future. Overall, Feld's (2012) and Isenberg's (2010) views that policymakers more often dis-incentivize and mis-incentivize entrepreneurs because governments have very different incentives than entrepreneurs is consistent with the findings here.

On a local level, as well, many entrepreneurs were critical of their municipal governments and local organizations, although this was not a universal finding. A major identified barrier was that local government often times does not understand entrepreneurs, or understood the incentives of large industry better. In Rumford and Waynesburg, entrepreneurs complained that their governments had "caved in" to big industry, providing incentives that are often siphoned away from smaller businesses in the form of taxes. Low-entrepreneurship communities note that their local institutions often do not know what to do with entrepreneurs, have low levels of training regarding launching a business (or outsourced this knowledge to an established organization, like the SBDC), or fail to communicate with or be responsive to entrepreneur concerns.

Entrepreneurs in both high- and low-entrepreneurship communities reported feeling isolated from their local government councils—unless one eventually won a seat on the board. Much like Feld's (2012) entrepreneurial ecosystem, entrepreneurs tended to champion small business issues more effectively than other leaders. Organizations that can provide leadership, like banks, are sometimes lumped into the same category local governments, as was the case in Alma. And entrepreneurs were themselves not free from criticism. In Waynesburg, many small business owners were perceived to put very little effort into organizations like the chamber of commerce.

However, not all interactions with local government were negative. Several participants reported having good relations with local government agencies, and in some places, praised governmental leaders for trying to make a positive change for entrepreneurs, even when these efforts were not immediately successful. In Alma, entrepreneurs reported that local government worked closely with entrepreneurs to ensure that regulations were reasonable, taxes were low, and that government was responsive to the needs and queries of entrepreneurs. This attention contributes to a working relationship that was seen as highly advantageous for entrepreneurs.

Leaping Leadership Boundaries

According to Feld (2012) and Isenberg (2010), government is not the best entity to try to stimulate an entrepreneurial community, and the case studies do little to contradict this idea. This view may unfortunately downplay the potentially positive steps that local and state leaders can play in supporting entrepreneurship. For readers in the fields of economic development, local government, or public administration, these steps can be quite meaningful and catalytic.

The first boundary to overcome is the absence of a small business voice in local organizations. Even if local institutional actors know a lot about entrepreneurship, the inclusion of entrepreneurs in major, local institutions is both symbolic and substantive. These individuals can raise issues that are completely unknown outside the local circle of entrepreneurs. They can also provide solutions that incorporate a different set of incentives than those of government and local institutions. By *empowering* entrepreneurs in these spaces, rather than trying to lead (see Feld, 2012), entrepreneurs can feel free to speak on behalf of the entire community of entrepreneurs about what really matters to them.

Second, rather than taking decisive action as a government or institution, consider removing existing barriers instead. This *via negativa* approach (Taleb, 2012) involves the systematic identification of barriers to entrepreneurship, and removing them as much as possible. Entrepreneurs should be fundamentally involved in both the identification process and in creating the solution. Simple incentives, like regulatory fees, may seem reasonable to a large institution, but could look very different to an entrepreneur. Progressive taxes, incentives, and regulations can help entrepreneurs, but so can regular communication and trained staff members who understand small business dynamics. Removing excessive local regulations while encouraging entrepreneurs to create their own self-governing agreements can produce many of the same results with greater ownership and without imposing laws.

Third, encourage entrepreneurs to interact widely. Local leaders can make a difference quickly by serving as a convener of entrepreneurs, especially if the convening centers on something relevant to entrepreneurial life: social networking, learning, creativity, innovation, and fun. Effective leaders can encourage entrepreneurs to launch their own organizations that local leaders then attend and support. Be ready to promote this organization and its efforts, as they are likely to be transformative if enough people are involved. Funding these efforts may be a good investment too, as entrepreneurs can often create jobs and tax revenues while raising much of their own funding—as long as local leaders are savvy about where to find resources and incentives for entrepreneurs (a partnership with an SBDC branch is one way of bridging this gap). The amount of self-organized action that can arise from this simple step was remarkable in Rockland, for example, and it requires very few resources.

Finally, encourage entrepreneurs to run for city council, or to take leadership positions locally. The presence of entrepreneurs in major institutions will ensure that the small business voice is heard in a forum for legitimate decision making (see Clevenger & Miao, 2017). While local leaders may not themselves lead an entrepreneurial revolution, the case study suggests that good government can be an important supporter of these efforts, and can, at the very least, remove critical barriers to entrepreneurial success.

The Role of History

There were several unanticipated findings in this research, but none resonated quite as strongly as the effect of cultural history on self-employment rates. High-entrepreneurship communities were each very different, and took different paths to high entrepreneurship. Rockland had experienced a history of industrial change, with a new primary industry taking root every two generations or so. The rise of new industries, and eventual collapse and obsolescence of the old, seems highly Schumpeterian (1934), and this history of market turnover has prevented institutional lock-in and path dependence (David, 1994) from taking root. New entrepreneurial ventures were therefore easy for the population to embrace, as few were wedded to one singular economic model.

For Alma, the history of entrepreneurship began in cities like Chicago and Minneapolis, from which most of the town's entrepreneurs migrated. These entrepreneurs slowly occupied a nearly abandoned Main Street with little resistance. Bringing their urban norms of openness to diversity and co-opetition with them, an institutionalized culture of collaboration developed naturally. Most entrepreneurs who arrived in Alma already knew "the rules" of how to engage with other entrepreneurs, or quickly learned them. For McConnellsburg, the entrepreneurial climate evolved directly out of an agrarian "bootstrap" culture. If a product or service did not exist in isolated McConnellsburg, it was up to locals to find a way to provide it locally. Richards and Bulkley (2007) called farmers the "first and forgotten" entrepreneurs, and McConnellsburg's entrepreneurs exemplify the connection between innovative venturing and agrarian self-reliance.

Low-entrepreneurship communities, by stark contrast, could have in many ways been the very same community. Entrepreneurs reported that the local culture showed a strong preference for traditional forms of economic development, such as recruiting industrial development. Additionally, many entrepreneurs remark that they felt isolated from the rest of the community, and that locals frequently made disparaging remarks about their business:

often predicting the business' failure, or using demeaning language to describe the business. Community leaders were often times keenly aware of the importance of entrepreneurship, but expressed some doubt about how to best support them given the local cultural constraints. In some cases, entrepreneurs complained that their governments appeared to be fragmented, and did not communicate effectively about entrepreneurship. Larger businesses and industries could outmuscle the local government in some cases by threatening to close their operations if more incentives were not provided, and new businesses from outside the community could sometimes negotiate local economic incentives not available to entrepreneurs.

Put simply, it was not just cultural, leadership, and institutional norms that mattered in each place—it is the *history* of cultural, leadership, and institutional norms that shaped outcomes. Those places with higher entrepreneurship levels sprung forth from areas that historically valued transformation, diversity, openness, resourcefulness, and innovation via both opportunity and necessity. They lacked a central, dominating industry, or if one emerged, it was eventually replaced. Those places with lower entrepreneurship levels were universally dominated by an externally owned mill, plant, or drilling operation. Wage employment was historically valued above self-employment and the pursuit of higher education. These cultures tended to be more collectivist and conforming to established norms, and value stability and tradition over change and novelty. Entrepreneurs in these communities frequently complained about not quite fitting in with the local culture or institutions, or not being part of the "in" crowd. No matter the situation, these cultures did not emerge overnight. Rockland's situation was unusual in that the city transformed from a fairly dangerous, pungent cannery town to a tourist destination hosting cruise ships in about a decade—although this quick turn was based on a history of quick turns from one industry to another. Generally, community cultures affecting entrepreneurship developed over very long trajectories, multiple major shifts in the local economy, and many generations of local action.

Leaping Historical Boundaries

The time dimension is especially important because it is one that is often forgotten when thinking about entrepreneurial communities. The history of any community carries with it a cultural legacy of the leaders and entrepreneurial agents of another era, sometimes tracing all the way back to the early days of the community. It is a powerful form of institutional memory through which the local culture and its social and institutional norms are produced and reproduced over time with different players playing similar roles. As can be seen in the case study communities, social expectations about what is acceptable and what is unacceptable, what can and cannot occur, which roles are respected and which are not, are as much a matter of history as they are a matter of facilitating conditions, policy, or the presence of certain entrepreneurial amenities.

For the researcher, understanding the temporal dynamics of community is critical. An examination of entrepreneurs in their community context should contain some understanding of how the community originated, the dominant economic paradigms over time, and which dominant cultural values have endured. A community that originated as a company town with little to no change in the dominant industry over time is likely to exhibit very different entrepreneurial potential than a pioneer community that began with risk-bearing landholders staking claims for themselves.

The long institutional memory of communities may be discouraging for local leaders and economic development practitioners who wish to make a change in the community's entrepreneurial culture. To be sure, the data supports the idea that there will be more cultural barriers in places without a history of economic transition. However, even high-entrepreneurship communities experience pockets of resistance. To create a more entrepreneurial culture, practitioners should heed the advice of Feld (2012), who stressed that entrepreneurs must make a long-term commitment to building the community. That sounds easy enough, but Feld is correct in mentioning the tenacity, patience, and commitment required to build an entrepreneurial community, as it can take a very, very long time. Cultures do not change overnight, but they can change over time. As we see in the cases, this change almost always began very small, with few people doing most of the work, and eventually overtaking and stifling other community norms favoring industrial development and status-quo approaches.

The Roles of Entrepreneurs and Non-entrepreneurs

Entrepreneurs and non-entrepreneurs can each play a critical role in supporting entrepreneurship. Besides entrepreneurs, local customers, buyers, suppliers, financial institutions, governments, and support services can all work together to better understand how entrepreneurship works locally. Just because a Chamber of Commerce, a local economic development company, or a bank exists is not sufficient to believe that these entities are well versed in the needs and business patterns of entrepreneurs. "We need support from local boards," said one Rumford entrepreneur, who noted an "us" versus "them" mentality between entrepreneurs and local selectmen (city council members). In McConnellsburg, support from local banks was identified as an advantage, while in Spooner, resistance from local banks was a critical barrier. Along with local governments and organizations, banks and other financial institutions can be a central partner in developing a space for entrepreneurs, as enhanced understanding among the financial services community can make the lending and investing climate more friendly toward entrepreneurs.

Customers may be the most important non-entrepreneurial entity in any community, as this is the lifeblood of small business revenues. Waynesburg had difficulty winning local consumers over to downtown businesses from low-cost competitors like Walmart. Conversely, entrepreneurs in

McConnellsburg retained customers from leaving the area by competing in areas where large chains are weak: local convenience, special deal making, service, and customization. Alma struggled somewhat with its customer base, as summer customers wanted different products and services as year-round customers, and year-round customers tended to avoid tourism-oriented establishments. Keeping stores open only on weekdays and closing at 5:00 p.m. was cited as a barrier to attracting customers in a modern, 24-hour world where more adults are in the workforce than in the past. In all, communities that embraced adaptability and a willingness to create offerings not found in local chains appeared to fare better than communities whose entrepreneurs are opposed to change. Additionally, locations can provide dual offerings for locals and extra-locals alike so there is something for everyone, and welcome entrepreneurs from out of town into the community. Likewise, governments and local organizations can play an important role in convening entrepreneurs, and providing newcomers and visitors to the community opportunities to interact with the local entrepreneurial scene through festivals, special events, and creative place making. Local branding can be very effective in introducing the community's unique offerings to outsiders, and this advocacy can help to differentiate local products on the shelves of more mainstream retailers. Also, local leaders and entrepreneurship organizations may consider taking a "welcome wagon" approach to newcomers to the community by providing gifts, local business directories, events calendars, and coupons for local establishments. By promoting locally, insiders and outsiders alike become more aware that a local scene exists in the first place, which can entice more customers and entrepreneurs to discover what the community has to offer.

The Four Approaches to Entrepreneurship Development

This section briefly analyzes the case studies with regard to the four approaches to entrepreneurship development detailed in Chapter 3: *Models of Entrepreneurial Community and Ecosystem Development*. In this research, one of the objectives was to understand which elements of the four approaches appears to make the greatest contributions to developing a community that supports entrepreneurship and entrepreneurial action. Each approach is listed, along with key insights about the approach from the case studies in Chapter 7.

Facilitating Conditions Approach

Facilitating conditions are typically discussed as being either present or absent in a community. These conditions can be physical objects like infrastructure, or more complex phenomena like a supportive culture. In the case studies, facilitating conditions appeared from time to time, particularly when talking about local amenities. Scenic amenities such as coastlines and forests provided a geographically important backdrop for the local entrepreneurship scene; however, entrepreneurs did not speak at great length about how this improved their business. More complex social processes were occasionally discussed using facilitating conditions language, such as the presence or absence of an entrepreneurial alliance or council, or a local city council that values entrepreneurial action. Looking across areas of presence and absence, it appears that high-entrepreneurship communities are more likely to have formal or informal spaces for interaction, a supportive culture, and in some cases, institutions that are responsive to the needs of entrepreneurs. Several participants valued scenic amenities and infrastructure. In Waynesburg, the presence of a university was not particularly helpful to local entrepreneurs in contrast to the spillover effects found around higher education institutions (Audretsch & Lehmann, 2005), largely because of a town-gown divide that isolates these two groups.

Overall, the facilitating conditions approach is a sub-dominant theme in the case studies. Participants in the study were more eager to talk about human and institutional processes that were either enhancing or inhibiting their experience as entrepreneurs. While understanding the latter as the primary focus of this research, it is surprising that amenities were not discussed more often. One reason for this may be that business amenities, once acquired by a community, fade into the background as standard tools and processes of the working world. Also, in these rural communities, amenities may be less of a focus for entrepreneurs, since most either grew up in a rural area with few urban amenities, or moved to a rural area with full knowledge that such amenities would not be available. Regardless, in these rural places, there was a much stronger emphasis placed on processes of human interaction than on facilitating conditions. Entrepreneurial success had more to do with dynamic processes, and less to do with static circumstances.

National and Regional Policy

Somewhat surprisingly, the national and regional policy approach was widely panned by entrepreneurs, and occasionally by institutional actors, who see government interference as bad for entrepreneurship. Multiple participants viewed state-level legislators and decision makers as contributing to serious regulatory, tax, and bureaucratic barriers or burdens that suppress entrepreneurship. This view was especially the case in Maine and Pennsylvania, where the state government is perceived to be unfriendly toward small business and entrepreneurs. Local governments were also scrutinized as entrepreneurs complained that departments within the local government had poor training on entrepreneurship and on the needs of entrepreneurs. This perception made local governments appear to be blind to the basic needs of local enterprise, if they responded to entrepreneurs at all. Entrepreneurs also commonly felt that their local city councils, in particular, were oriented against change, and that this restricted the range of products, services, marketing, and place making that entrepreneurs could undertake. A poor opinion of government was not universal, and in a few cases, local governments are praised for their willingness to be responsive, to work with entrepreneurs, and to try their best to support entrepreneurs irrespective of the actual outcome.

The national and regional policy approach fundamentally supports the idea that governments can actively stimulate a more entrepreneurial culture through a mix of policy solutions. At no point in these case studies does that appear to be true. Naturally, the external generalizability of six case study sites is limited, but it is surprising that national and regional policy makers were never mentioned in a positive light. This reflection could be due to a general dissatisfaction with government, but it should be noted that the negative and neutral comments made by participants seem to represent the inverse of the national and regional policy approach: creating barriers to entrepreneurship rather than removing them.

Entrepreneurial Communities

The entrepreneurial communities approach is partially supported by the case study data. Entrepreneurs and institutional actors alike put a great deal of emphasis on human interaction, regularly noting interpersonal and institutional advantages and barriers in their community. This interconnectedness, built upon dense local networks that cross institutional boundaries, can especially be seen in high-entrepreneurship communities and are exemplified by social networking events and downtown business groups. Even the tendency of entrepreneurs to interact widely partially supports the entrepreneurial communities approach. Since inclusiveness is central to entrepreneurial communities, high-entrepreneurship communities particularly exemplify this dimension of interaction, and have stated that it helps build camaraderie among local entrepreneurs.

However, the entrepreneurial communities approach falls somewhat short when describing the nature of interaction in the study communities. Entrepreneurial communities models are often targeted at local leaders, and they exemplify a diversified support system of which entrepreneurs only make up one portion. Put differently, entrepreneurs are not as central to the entrepreneurial communities approach as they are to the entrepreneurial ecosystems approach. While supportive, participatory governments and local institutions are cited as essential to building entrepreneurial communities, this situation was not always the case in high-entrepreneurship communities. Entrepreneurs, and some institutional actors who support entrepreneurship, often found themselves at odds with local governments and organizations, and succeeded despite institutional resistance. It was not until entrepreneurs had themselves infiltrated these organizations that they began to adjust their organizational culture to address the needs of entrepreneurs. Furthermore, many elements of entrepreneurial communities, such as education and mentorship, were absent in these locations. Most entrepreneurship development was done through peer-to-peer mentorship, and was focused around informal interactions rather than deliberate development efforts aimed at entrepreneurs themselves. The entrepreneurial communities approach is therefore highly instructive about interaction and inclusivity, but less instructive about the role of entrepreneurs and institutions, and the generative stages of entrepreneurship development.

Entrepreneurial Ecosystem

An entrepreneurial ecosystem appears to be the closest framework available to describe the case study data. While entrepreneurial communities helped to explain elements of building an inclusive, purposive, multi-institutional support system, the ecosystem approach more accurately demonstrates the emergent and iterative process of entrepreneurial community development. In every community, high- and low-entrepreneurship participants mentioned the importance of finding "niches" in the local economy. This strategy is particularly important in the face of national chain development. Entrepreneurs must readily differentiate their offerings from larger competitors who benefit from economies of scale. However, the ways that these entrepreneurs approach the issue differs somewhat: entrepreneurs in low-entrepreneurship communities find niches to survive in a complex environment, while entrepreneurs in high-entrepreneurship communities look at the situation more opportunistically, as a way to diversify local offerings and compete on customization and service.

Conclusion

While a wide range of research has shown that urban-style amenities are helpful to businesses, many of the cultural and leadership relationships exposed in these smaller communities have been found to be important in urban communities as well. Norms of trust, reciprocity, the willingness of entrepreneurs to collaborate and self-organize, institutional involvement (while not necessarily taking the lead), and a "support local" mentality concur with the literature that these cultural and leadership are essential to supporting entrepreneurial action on a geographic scale [sources].

This chapter analyzed the case studies presented in Chapter 7 with an eye on identifying specific strategies that can be used to overcome local cultural and leadership boundaries to developing a community that is more supportive of entrepreneurship. These strategies reflect those that appear to be already working in high-entrepreneurship communities, and on the stated needs of entrepreneurs and institutional actors in low-entrepreneurship communities. Oftentimes there is consensus on what is working and what could work better. These strategies are intended to assist practitioners, government and local organization officials, and interested entrepreneurial leaders to overcome common problems in cultivating local support for entrepreneurship. For researchers, the chapter attempts to highlight connections between these findings and other findings in the literature, and also presents a starting point for new research on local entrepreneurship development strategies.

This analysis was followed by an analysis of the case study based upon the general approaches to entrepreneurship development in Chapter 3. It was found that participants in the studies most commonly cited elements of both the entrepreneurial communities and ecosystem approaches as important to supporting local entrepreneurship. Some facilitating conditions are mentioned, such as access to Internet, banks, and scenic or geographic amenities. However, entrepreneurs especially appear to reject the national and regional policy approach, raising complaints about how state and local governments have handled entrepreneurship development and created regulatory, bureaucratic, and tax barriers. Overall, this research supports the idea that both the entrepreneurial communities and ecosystem approaches make unique contributions to understanding this research topic, although it should also be noted that the choice of research topic lends itself to these approaches. Further research may explore the situations and circumstances in which each approach may be helpful and useful to entrepreneurship at the community level.

Note

1 See Dana (1995) and Williams (2009) for excellent examples of how culture can structure opportunity- versus necessity-oriented entrepreneurship in two very different scenarios: A sub-arctic community, and the United Kingdom's informal economy.

References

Audretsch, D. B., & Lehmann, E. E. (2005). Does the knowledge spillover theory of entrepreneurship hold for regions? *Research Policy*, *34*(8), 1191–1202.

Berger, P. L., & Luckmann, T. (1991). *The social construction of reality: A treatise in the sociology of knowledge* (10th ed.). London, UK: Penguin.

Clevenger, M. R., & Miao, C. (2017). Transformational leadership to build an entrepreneurial community. In M. W-P Fortunato & M. R. Clevenger (Eds.), *Toward entrepreneurial community development: Leaping cultural and leadership boundaries* (pp. 126–151). New York, NY: Routledge.

Dana, L. P. (1995). Entrepreneurship in a remote sub-Arctic community. *Entrepreneurship Theory and Practice*, *20*, 57–72.

David, P. A. (1994). Why are institutions the 'carriers of history?' Path dependence and the evolution of conventions, organizations and institutions. *Structural Change and Economic Dynamics*, *5*(2), 205–220.

Feld, B. (2012). *Startup communities: Building an entrepreneurial ecosystem in your city*. Hoboken, NJ: Wiley.

Fortunato, M. W-P (2011). *The individual-institutional-opportunity nexus: Examining interaction, purpose, and opportunity in rural entrepreneurship development.* (Unpublished dissertation). University Park, PA: Pennsylvania State University.

Goffman, E. (1959). *The presentation of self in everyday life*. Garden City, NY: Doubleday.

Granovetter, M. (1985). Economic action and social structure: The problem of embeddedness. *American Journal of Sociology*, *91*(3), 481–510.

Isenberg, D. J. (2010). How to start an entrepreneurial revolution. *Harvard Business Review*, *88*(6), 40–50.

Merton, R. K. (1957). The role-set: Problems in sociological theory. *The British Journal of Sociology*, *8*(2), 106–120.

Richards, S. T., & Bulkley, S. (2007). *Agricultural entrepreneurs: The first and the forgotten?* Research Paper #07–01. Washington, DC: The Hudson Institute.

Schumpeter, J. A. (1934). *The theory of economic development: An inquiry into profits, capital, credit, interest, and the business cycle*. New York, NY: Transaction Publishers.

Shane, S. (2012). Reflections on the 2010 AMR decade award: Delivering on the promise of entrepreneurship as a field of research. *Academy of Management Review*, *37*(1), 10–20.

Taleb, N. N. (2012). *Antifragile: Things that gain from disorder*. New York, NY: Random House.

Williams, C. C. (2009). The motives of off-the-books entrepreneurs: Necessity-or opportunity-driven? *International Entrepreneurship and Management Journal*, *5*(2), 203–217.

9 Entrepreneurial Community Success

Psychological Characteristics, Experiences, and Identity

Ellen E. Newell

An entrepreneurial community consists of many interrelated elements, including entrepreneurs, locally owned businesses of varying sizes, governments, economic development boards, educational systems, local and regional formal leadership, and residents devoted to living and working in the community (Breazeale & Hustedde, 2017; Clevenger, 2017; Fortunato, 2017). These actors all come together to help support entrepreneurial endeavors within a successful entrepreneurial community. Education programs can provide courses in entrepreneurship and business planning, entrepreneurial leadership can remove legal and regulatory barriers to allow small businesses to launch and potentially thrive, and local residents can be encouraged to embrace a culture of supporting entrepreneurship endeavors. *Entrepreneurial community* refers to an all-encompassing community made up of many groups of people and their intertwined roles in creating a community that supports the launch of new ventures (Clevenger, 2017; Fortunato, 2017).

An entrepreneurial community cannot exist without entrepreneurs, and an understanding of entrepreneur's psychological experiences can shed light on entrepreneurial community development. Psychology as a field scientifically examines how behavior and mental processes intertwine. In the past, psychological research of entrepreneurs tended to focus on how single psychological elements (e.g., only personality factors; Nielsen, Klyver, Evald, & Bager, 2012) could be used to identify successful entrepreneurs. The field of psychology now takes an integrative view of the human experience, with many psychological theories accounting for multiple features, such as cognitive processes, emotions, or how physiological functioning can impact outcomes (Nielsen et al., 2012). Psychology does not usually provide clean cut answers. There is no fail-safe guide to success, and any text that attempts to give the guaranteed psychological techniques for successful entrepreneurial community development are, to be blunt, bogus. Rather, this chapter will demonstrate that all conditions—the entrepreneurs' characteristics, their motivations, previous experiences, their identities, all need to coalesce to create a successful endeavor. An understanding of relevant psychological theories and findings provides entrepreneurs with essential techniques for creating a productive and collaborative entrepreneurial community.

Additionally, this chapter makes a distinction between *entrepreneurial communities* and *entrepreneurial social groups*. An *entrepreneurial social group* is a group of entrepreneurs who share similar entrepreneurial identities and have shared group norms, values, and goals (Haslam, van Knippenberg, Platow, & Ellemers, 2003). *Entrepreneurial communities* more broadly include other community actors and organizations who support entrepreneurship (Clevenger, 2017; Fortunato, 2017). The entrepreneurial social group can be considered a part of the entrepreneurial community, but it is important that the entrepreneurial social group be considered a distinct entity when discussing the psychological traits of entrepreneurs, specifically.

This chapter will examine the thoughts, actions, and behaviors of the entrepreneurs themselves. First, it will examine common characteristics that many people believe, often incorrectly, creates successful entrepreneurs. A few examples of entrepreneurs' attitudes, thoughts, behaviors, and the external situation are offered, demonstrating how these collectively can support entrepreneurial success. A holistic understanding of psychological elements affecting entrepreneurship can lead to a better understanding of how the community can assist entrepreneurs (e.g., via educational opportunities), and how entrepreneurs can work together to make an entrepreneurial community thrive. Relevant psychological characteristics and experiences that influence desire and propensity to become a successful entrepreneur will be identified. Then the chapter examines entrepreneurial identity and how it can impact entrepreneurial community involvement. Entrepreneurs often focus on individualistic goals, as their key priority is to create a novel and unique venture or initiative. This process leads to potential challenges when asking entrepreneurs to build a collective identity that allows them to cooperatively work together to create a strong entrepreneurial community. Psychological theories and findings will be used to offer suggestions for building a strong community where successful entrepreneurial collaborations are a part of the community's foundation. Insights will be offered for how entrepreneurs can be cultivated and recruited for entrepreneurial community development. Finally, this chapter concludes with a discussion of some of the challenges of being an entrepreneur within an entrepreneurial community.

The Elephant in the Room: The Entrepreneurial Personality, Does It Exist?

> You know, there's not a lot different in what my typical day like is now than then except for I think that back then, I would start drinking around, like, 6:00 or 7:00 p.m. while I was working 'cause I was just so stressed out. Now I have a 2-year-old, so I'm up at, you know, 5:00 a.m. And I don't really go to bed until 2:00. But my typical day was waking up really early in the morning, going to work, dealing with every problem that you can have 'cause in the restaurant industry, there's always something wrong. And then you work and you try to motivate and inspire the rest of your cooks and stay motivated and inspire yourself. And you just work until you're closed. And then you kind of wrap it all up and do it again the next day. I mean, I still

> work seven days a week. I still work over 90 hours a week. But when you own something and you're doing it for yourself, it's, like, you don't look at it as, like, work. I don't look at it as, like, a job. You know, I look at it as, like, my life, and it's what drives me.
>
> ~ Chef Danny Bowien, *Fresh Air* interview, January 21, 2016

The quote from entrepreneurial restaurateur Danny Bowien, co-founder of three independent restaurants around the United States, describes the challenges of opening, operating, and maintaining a successful entrepreneurial business venture. In it, he explains a set of psychological experiences common to many entrepreneurs. He is tired, overworked, and stressed to the max because he is trying to launch a completely novel business venture while balancing the pressures of work and home. Adding to the pressure is the knowledge that it is his job to inspire and motivate his employees to embrace the mission of the organization. Yet, despite these extreme challenges, he describes the entire experience as a key part of his identity. Being an entrepreneur is who he is, and this identity encapsulates all parts of his life. Entrepreneurs are often perceived as being driven to independently develop novel business ventures (Alvesson, 2000). It is also common for entrepreneurs to feel they will be completely at fault if the venture fails. These feelings can lead to a solitary (Shepherd & Haynie, 2009) and stressful existence (Cardon & Patel, 2015) as an entrepreneur. Devoted entrepreneurs such as Danny Bowien, are the people who will build the roots of an innovative small business–type culture that comprises an entrepreneurial community. Through their fruitful endeavors, entrepreneurs and business owners will be able to provide leadership, mentorship, and support for members of the entrepreneurial community.

Identifying individuals, such as Danny Bowien, who have either launched a business, or a nascent entrepreneur who is interested in launching a serious venture, is an important first step to creating an entrepreneurial community. Researchers have long attempted to identify consistent characteristics of entrepreneurs. Identifying stable entrepreneurial characteristics is attractive because they would help identify potential entrepreneurs by simply administering a basic personality or job aptitude test. Characteristics that make up a successful entrepreneur, however, are never this simple or straight forward.

It is very common for people to believe that individuals are born to perform certain jobs, meaning that they have certain natural characteristics that make them well suited for particular careers (e.g., "that kid is a *born* leader!"). This belief is so engrained that a recent study on perceptions of entrepreneurs found that an entrepreneur described as having a 'natural talent' for entrepreneurship, as compared to an otherwise identical entrepreneur who was described as having had to work hard to learn his or her entrepreneurial skills, was perceived to be higher achieving and better performing during a business proposal presentation (Tsay, 2016). Further,

Tsay (2016) found that people were more willing to support the business plan of 'natural' entrepreneurs, even if their qualifications were lower than those entrepreneurs who had to work to gain their skills. Focusing on natural, ingrained personality traits can therefore be a slippery slope for those looking to build an entrepreneurial community. So much attention has been devoted to determining the personality characteristics of the entrepreneur that limited discussion will be covered here. For reviews of relevant personality and psychological factors see Baum, Frese, and Baron (2007); Begley and Boyd (1987); Brandstätter (2011); Brockhaus and Horwitz (1986); Carsrud and Brännback (2009); Korunka, Frank, Lueger, and Mugler (2003); Rauch and Frese (2007a); Shaver (2014); and Zhao, Seibert, and Lumpkin (2010).

Personality refers to an individual's characteristics that remain relatively stable across various situations. Early personality research tried to match specific personality traits with specific outcomes. For example, are people who are open to new experiences inherently more likely to succeed (Barrick & Mount, 1991)? For decades, researchers did not find a consistent pattern between personality and entrepreneurship—measured by either entrepreneurial success or propensity. This futility led to a call to discontinue personality and entrepreneurship research (Aldrich, 1999; Brockhaus & Horwitz, 1986; Gartner, 1989). More recently, researchers have suggested that meta-analysis techniques utilizing previously existing studies, and therefore larger sample sizes and various methodologies, may be able to establish a personality profile for entrepreneurs (Rauch & Frese, 2007a).

Since that time, some interesting relationships between entrepreneurial success and personality traits have been found (Brandstätter, 2011; Schmitt-Rodermund, 2004; Stewart & Roth, 2007; Zhao et al., 2010). For example, Rauch and Frese (2007b) conducted a meta-analysis that included 116 independent samples and found that some traits could be used to predict business success and creation among owners. Some have found that need for achievement, a personal drive to master significant skills, and an ability to accomplish challenging tasks, is correlated with success among entrepreneurs (Collins, Hanges, & Locke, 2004; Rauch & Frese, 2007b). In addition, Zhao and Seibert (2006) conducted a meta-analysis that compared entrepreneurs with managers on several personality traits. Entrepreneurs tended to score higher on conscientiousness, openness to experience, and need for achievement when compared to managers. In contrast, entrepreneurs scored significantly lower on neuroticism and agreeableness when compared to managers. Further, those who founded their own business, as compared to those who took over an already functioning business, were found to be more assertive (Brandstätter, 1997).

Several researchers have considered whether entrepreneurs are naturally drawn to risk taking. They have debated over whether this propensity for risk taking is helpful in allowing them to secure advantages on opportunities that others might deem too risky (see Stewart & Roth, 2001 for a review). Via meta-analysis, Stewart and Roth (2001, 2004) showed that entrepreneurs tended to score higher on risk taking when compared to business managers. In addition, entrepreneurs who were motivated to grow their endeavor scored significantly higher on risk taking, as compared to entrepreneurs whose motivations were to provide income for their families. Notably, Miner and Raju (2004) conducted follow-up meta-analyses to examine risk-taking tendency comparisons between entrepreneurs and managers using an alternative measure of risk-taking and found some conflicting results. Zhao et al. (2010) recently conducted an additional meta-analysis and examining personality traits and entrepreneurship. They specifically expanded their hypotheses to examine both intent to become an entrepreneur and performance as an entrepreneur as separate variables. They found that entrepreneurial intention was related to propensity for risk taking; however, propensity for risk taking was unrelated to performance suggesting understanding the context is important for understanding when risk-taking personality traits can predict entrepreneurial behaviors.

The disparities in these findings highlight the common claim that significantly more research needs to be done on entrepreneurship (Hisrich, Langan-Fox & Grant, 2007; Rauch & Frese, 2007a; Shaver, 2014). A significant amount of entrepreneurial personality research, in particular, has been criticized for low effect sizes, small sample sizes, poor theoretical framework, and chiefly correlational designs. Operationalizations of constructs and debates over methodologies (Miner & Raju, 2004; Stewart & Roth, 2004) highlight that clarifications are needed within the field. Additional research needs to be conducted to help build and understanding of possible entrepreneurial characteristics. Overall, questions like "does the entrepreneurial personality exist?" pose significant problems for researchers. Humans do not exist in a stagnant environment. Actions, personality traits, personal motivations, and so on, that help entrepreneurs in one situation may not be helpful when that situation changes (Krueger, 2003; Magnusson & Endler, 1977; Rauch & Frese, 2007a).

In addition, how does one define a successful entrepreneur? A personality trait that helps with one type of "success" (e.g., making a significant sale) may be completely unrelated to other types of success (e.g., developing an innovative idea; Rauch & Frese, 2007b). Thus a focus on identifying entrepreneurs exclusively from a personality profile may not be particularly fruitful (Brockhaus & Horwitz, 1986; Gartner, 1989). Recent researchers in the field of entrepreneurship have stressed that to understand the entrepreneur we must understand the interaction between personality characteristics, other psychological characteristics (e.g., motivations), and situations (Davis, Hall, & Mayer, 2015; Mischel & Shoda, 1998; Rauch & Frese, 2007a). This comprehensive approach, that has been embraced by psychologists for decades, is embodied within a model proposed by Rauch and Frese (2007a). They propose that various types of personality traits, previous skills and abilities, individual goals and motivations, and the specific business environment must all be considered when trying to predict entrepreneurial success. Rauch and Frese (2007a) suggest that a focus on personality traits, or indeed any one factor, may be a detriment to understanding entrepreneurial success:

> We should not reify individual differences: They may not be causal agents, even if they predict behavior; we need to be able to describe the dynamics of how individual differences have an influence on behavior. A good understanding of individual differences "requires an integrated conceptual scheme that classifies not only behaviors, but specifies their determinants and key mechanisms through which they operate" (Bandura, 1999, p. 200).
>
> (Rauch and Frese, 2007a, p. 42)

Baum and Locke (2004) offer one example of how situation, motivation, and individual traits can all come together to lead to success. Through a six-year longitudinal study, they showed that individual skills (e.g., ability to find funding for a new venture), individual traits such as passion and tenacity for the endeavor, and self-confidence that they could perform the needed tasks (i.e., self-efficacy), along with the situational variables of how much entrepreneurs felt they had a company vision that was shared with their employees and whether the organization had set goals, can all come together to predict significant growth. Importantly, tenacity, passion, and skills did *not* directly predict venture growth. Instead, vision, goals, and self-efficacy mediated the relationships with growth. Thus a theoretically based model that takes into account several aspects of the entrepreneurship experience will help researchers better understand the relationship between personality traits, entrepreneurial outcomes, as well as possible mediators and moderators of these relationships.

The important reflection of this research is that looking for "born leaders" or "natural talents" may not be the best way to seek out potential entrepreneurs to contribute to entrepreneurial communities. Similar goals (e.g., intention to develop a successful venture), similar motivations (e.g., an interest or propensity in risky activities), and similar identities (e.g., describing being an entrepreneur as an important part of yourself), however, can bring people with like characteristics together (Ellemers, Haslam, Platow, & van Knippenberg, 2003). Which leads to a better understanding that all aspects of a situation (e.g., a person's thoughts, feelings, behaviors, and business climate) can influence entrepreneurial successes and failures. Further, a knowledge that these successes and failures can have a direct influence on the entrepreneurial community can help all community members come together to refine the actions and decisions of the community to better support its members. For example, an entrepreneurial community may come together to develop strategies for helping to protect entrepreneurs as they take some level of necessary risk.

The best advice for practitioners and entrepreneurs who are looking to build an entrepreneurial community is to be aware of the fundamental attribution error (Ross, 1977). This common cognitive error states that many people are quick to assume that someone's actions (etc.) are a result of their underlying personality traits. It is common for people to discount that actions can actually result from many reasons variety of reasons (e.g., education, previous experiences). As a result, anyone looking to build an entrepreneurial community must realize that it is possible for a person to become a valuable member of an entrepreneurial community—even if they do not initially seem to possess traits thought to be required among entrepreneurs. This is an emerging and iterative process that takes time, interaction, and ongoing support at multiple levels.

Additional Psychological Phenomena That May Predict Successful Entrepreneurship

Beyond personality, there are a number of psychological factors that may be helpful in predicting who is likely to become a successful entrepreneur. Considerable reviews of psychological entrepreneurship have suggested that elements like feeling personally in control over the outcome of a situation (Begley & Boyd, 1987; Korunka et al., 2003), *self-efficacy* (see Krueger, 2003, and Locke & Baum, 2007 for reviews), and psychological motivations to succeed, like *grit* (Duckworth, Peterson, Matthews, & Kelly, 2007), may be related to entrepreneurial intentions and ultimately success.

Self-Efficacy

Self-efficacy refers to an individual's belief that they have the skills and ability to control the outcome of a situation (Bandura, 1997). Self-efficacy is often situationally based; one may feel high in self-efficacy when it comes to accomplishing a challenging project at work, but the same person may feel limited self-efficacy for tasks outside of work (e.g., low belief in their ability to change a flat tire). Thus self-efficacy may be helpful in predicting entrepreneurial success within particular contexts. Others have suggested that a sense of general self-efficacy is also important for entrepreneurial success (Poon, Ainuddin, & Junit, 2007).

After several decades of research in entrepreneurship, it has become clear that psychological constructs, like self-efficacy, have not always consistently led to a direct relationship for entrepreneurial intentions or success, and sometimes no relationship has been observed at all (Schoon & Duckworth, 2012). More recently, it has been suggested that there are additional variables needed to understand these relationships (i.e., possible mediators or moderators; Hisrich et al., 2007; Rauch & Frese, 2007a). For example, Poon et al. (2007), found no direct relationship between general self-efficacy and how well people felt their businesses were performing. Instead *entrepreneurial orientation*, how much the management tried to have the organization embody key entrepreneurial characteristics such as innovation and risk taking, mediated the relationship between a sense of general self-efficacy and how well entrepreneurs felt their businesses were performing. Finally, very often these variables, such as perceptions of control or self-efficacy, *are* the mediators or moderators between factors like risk-taking propensity and entrepreneurial intensions as was observed by Zhao, Siebert, and Hills (2005).

Grit and Personal Beliefs about Abilities

More recent research has begun to examine multiple factors that can be used to predict success, as compared to focusing on single concepts like a personality profile or perceptions of self-efficacy. *Grit* is a relatively new construct that encompasses people's motivation to work hard over a long period of time to accomplish a goal (Duckworth et al., 2007). A gritty person is high in passion, conscientiousness, self-control, perseverance, and has very stable goals and interests. Through a series of studies, Duckworth et al. have shown grit can predict success in a variety of situations. For example, they provide evidence that gritty novice teachers will become the most effective educators over time (Robertson-Kraft & Duckworth, 2014) and that gritty spelling bee participants will persevere the longest (Duckworth et al., 2007). Further, they show that grit can predict which first year cadets at the U.S. Military Academy, West Point will successfully complete extremely challenging and tedious training activities (Duckworth et al., 2007). While it is common to hear about grit's potential for the success of entrepreneurial endeavors (Williams, 2014), relatively few researchers have explicitly examined grit among entrepreneurs (Baum & Locke, 2004; Curtis, 2008; Syed & Mueller, 2014). Early results suggest that grit may influence entrepreneur's ability to focus on long-term goals, stay on track of their goals, and development of new skills needed to accomplish their entrepreneurial goals (Syed & Mueller, 2014).

A precursor to grit, Dweck (1986, 2008) conducted significant studies showing that a person's motivational perspective can impact task performance. She has argued that some people feel their abilities (including innate IQ) are fixed whereas others believe their intelligence (and corresponding skill set) is changeable and can adapt from learning, effort, and new experiences. Those who feel their abilities are not fixed are willing to work harder, persist longer, and challenge themselves on novel tasks (Smiley & Dweck, 1994). Those who feel their abilities are fixed are less likely to work as hard, presumably because they do not feel the additional effort will benefit themselves as their abilities are stable. In addition, praising children for having a high IQ (e.g., "Great job! You're so smart!") led to them working less hard on subsequent challenging tasks, whereas children who were praised for their hard work on a task (e.g., "Great job! You worked so hard!") continued to persevere on challenging tasks. Focus on intelligence and innate skill when recruiting entrepreneurs to join a community may be tempting (Tsay,

2016), although this practice may actually be a hindrance when looking for people who will use innovation and creativity to solve novel problems in the community (Dweck, 2008). Further, constant comparison and focus on previous entrepreneurial accomplishments may actually hinder new innovations, as it is similar to reminding them that they are "naturally smart."

Much of this research examines psychological phenomena outside of the field of entrepreneurial communities. There are many opportunities for increased entrepreneurship research in these areas. It is worth hypothesizing, however, that if these motivations can be used to predict success in a variety of areas, then they may be useful to harness when developing a community that values hard work and embraces a communal entrepreneurial vision. As with all psychological constructs, these motivations should always be considered along with an understanding of relevant ecological factors, supporting entrepreneurs, social networks, and community dynamics.

Early Experiences Influence Entrepreneurial Motivations

Several scholars have hypothesized that having parents or role models who are entrepreneurs early in life influences one's likelihood to become an entrepreneur (Brockhaus & Horwitz, 1986; Schmitt-Rodermund, 2004). A relatively new line of research is examining how experiences throughout childhood and adolescence, beyond merely receiving exposure to entrepreneurial role models, may predict future entrepreneurial likelihood. Personality characteristics, interests, and activities in adolescence (e.g., taking on early leadership roles) may help forecast whether an individual is likely to become an entrepreneur (Obschonka, Silbereisen, & Schmitt-Rodermund, 2010, 2012; Schmitt-Rodermund, 2004). Further, early innovative behaviors (e.g., participation in activities like music or woodworking), early leadership experience, and early entrepreneurial activities such as creating and selling items to friends during adolescence may actually predict later entrepreneurial successes (Obschonka, Silbereisen, Schmitt-Rodermund, & Stuetzer, 2011).

While not a focus here, it is well worth noting that women entrepreneurs often experience significant challenges that differ from men's experiences. Many of these differences may stem from adolescence. Women may receive less mentoring, financial support, or encouragement earlier in life that may discourage them from pursuing entrepreneurship (Schoon & Duckworth, 2012). Having supportive parents, education, and developing relevant social skills earlier in life may help alleviate some of the gender differences in entrepreneurship (Brockhaus & Horwitz, 1986; Schoon & Duckworth, 2012).

A key part of any community is its educational system (Clevenger, 2017), although many researchers doubt that an educational system can create an entrepreneur out of absolutely anyone (Clifton & Badal, 2014). Much of this skepticism likely stems from the previously discussed assumption that entrepreneurs have predictable personality characteristics that are necessary for successful entrepreneurship. Some scholars have suggested, however, that a potential student must approach academic entrepreneurship training via their own motivations to be an entrepreneur. Once they make this initial step, they are then able to learn significant skills within formal educational settings (Mullins, 2006).

Most entrepreneurial endeavors are risky with a high chance of failure. Education can help potential entrepreneurs create goals, business plans, and offer mentorship. Educational opportunities—at all educational levels—provide benefits to an entire entrepreneurial community beyond simply helping an individual entrepreneur to succeed (Clevenger, 2017). A major advantage of an entrepreneurial community is that entrepreneurs are often motivated to create jobs that will employ members of the local community more broadly (Neck & Greene, 2011). Subsequently, most entrepreneurial educational programs include training on job creation (Katz, 2007). A cyclical relationship between educational institutions and the overall economic health of the community via the productive efforts of entrepreneurs is created. Research on grit is in the early stages and it is too early to know whether the motivation can be taught among students. Bandura (1993), however, believed that teaching about beliefs and abilities like self-efficacy were a valuable aspect of education. An educational system embedded within an entrepreneurial community should be encouraged to evaluate these phenomena and associated research findings for appropriate incorporation into relevant curricula. This opportunity will allow educational branches of the community to help train prospective entrepreneurs, and then these entrepreneurs can eventually play an essential role in providing viable job opportunities within the community.

Innovation and Creativity

Innovation and creativity are key components in the entrepreneur process (Clevenger, 2017). For entrepreneurs, being distinctive and innovative is a key part of their lifestyle. They seek to find unique business undertakings that will provide value-adding outcomes. Consider some of Danny Bowien's restaurant reviews that speak highly of his creative and innovative entrepreneurial abilities. "Many of the old dishes [are] marked as much by Mr. Bowien's *freethinking approach* as by the burn and tingle of chiles and Sichuan peppercorns" (Wells, 2015, emphasis added). "The West Coast chef has his talents as a cook, but *his real genius is for creating a grand sense of occasion*" (Platt, n.d., emphasis added). It is Bowien's ability to develop completely new combinations of flavors as well as creating a unique dining atmosphere that highlights his entrepreneurial talents. When entrepreneurs succeed, they are also not the only ones to benefit: the community can significantly benefit from the unique business opportunities in their community as well as when entrepreneurs offer their innovation and creativity to community development. Entrepreneurs can find imaginative ways to create jobs, produce multiple business ventures, and provide various forms of support within their community (e.g., by bridging relationships between diverse groups).

Innovation involves two major components: ideas and execution (Clevenger, 2017; Runco & Jaeger, 2012; Unsworth, 2001). The first is the ability to inventively come up with novel ideas, whether they are a new service, product, or process, or a new way to structure an organization to promote efficiency (Clevenger, 2017). Second, it is not enough for an entrepreneur to merely develop new ideas; they must also be able to launch the new ideas, promote them, and convince others—often with a focus on those with money or status within the community—that the new concept is useful and needed. In other words, the entrepreneur needs to see novel ideas come to fruition. Creativity, therefore, is an important skill for many entrepreneurs.

Rauch and Frese (2007a) recently commented on the surprising lack of creativity-oriented research within the field of entrepreneurship. The following is a brief review of some recent studies that are helpful in enhancing the creative environment of entrepreneurial communities. Some of this work is theoretical, and not all of these findings have been directly tested within the field of entrepreneurship, suggesting a continued need for research.

Psychological Factors Concerning Innovation and Creativity

Positive mood is consistently linked to creativity (Ashby, Isen, & Turken, 1999), although the type of task under study and the contextual situation may impact this relationship. Positive moods lead to more flexibility in thinking, however negative moods can facilitate creative solutions in situations that are serious and require concentration (De Dreu & Nijstad, 2008; see Cropley & Cropley, 2015 for a review). Some mood states, such as depression, may fully deter creativity. Interestingly, people in a positive mood may actively avoid choosing negative tasks that presumably dampen their mood (Hirt, Devers, & McCrea, 2008). When people in positive mood have to complete a task that may dampen their mood, they are still likely to come up with more creative responses as compared to those in other mood states. Further, conjuring these additional creative thoughts may actually buffer a person's positive mood throughout a task that may instill negative mood. While the direct connection between mood and entrepreneurship is still fairly abstract at this point, there are hypotheses that can be drawn about the effects of mood state and entrepreneurial productivity. For example, entrepreneurship can be a high stress career (Cardon & Patel, 2015) and stress can have negative effects on mood (Het & Wolf, 2007). Therefore, entrepreneurs may be at higher risk for negative mood thus impacting the type of creative processing they are able to employ.

Exhibiting creative behaviors can be linked to certain personality traits, but situational details may determine when this link exists. For example,

George and Zhou (2001) conducted a study examining personality and creativity among employees at a large drilling company in the United States. They found that people who rank high on the personality trait openness to experience were the most creative on a task that required flexibility in its requirements (e.g., the task may be somewhat ambiguous with objectives of the task changing overtime) when they received positive feedback. In addition, openness to experience predicted increased creativity when participants felt they could choose the way in which to tackle the problem and received positive feedback. This view suggests that, like positive mood, positive feedback may help facilitate creativity along with feeling some control over the method used to address the problem.

Diversity, Multicultural Experiences, and Creativity

Multicultural experiences may provide special training for those looking to create a varied and diverse entrepreneurial community. Specifically, living abroad has been associated with increased creativity and professional success (Maddux & Galinsky, 2009; Tadmor, Galinsky, & Maddux, 2012). This association is driven by perceived identification with both cultures and use of integrative complexity, which means that the more individuals can see the world from the perspective of both cultures and use these potentially diverging viewpoints to inform their decisions, actions, and outputs, the more creative uses they find for a relatively benign object (i.e., a brick; Tadmor et al., 2012). Notably Tadmor et al. (2012) found integrative complexity moderates the relationship between identity and creativity within a classic experimental psychology laboratory setting as well as within business environments. Specifically, they found that among Israeli professionals working in Silicon Valley, the more participants identified with both cultures (the United States and Israel) and the more they considered and integrated varying perspectives within their decisions, the more work related innovations they had made (e.g., how many businesses they had started), the more likely they were to receive a promotion, and the higher their performance was rated. It is also worth noting that the relationship between creativity and living abroad was only found when participants had fully lived abroad—mere travel does not produce this effect (Maddux & Galinsky, 2009).

Using similar logic, Henderson and Robertson (1999) proposed that multicultural relationships are essential for the success of many entrepreneurial businesses, arguing that business educators should pay particular attention to these topics within their entrepreneurial curricula. In addition, Steffens, Terjesen, and Davidsson (2012) found that diverse new venture teams have better long-term venture performance when compared to less diverse teams. Even with all of its benefits, incorporating diversity policies can have complex implications. Richard, Barnett, Dwyer, and Chadwick (2004) found that, among firms that reported high levels of innovations (e.g., number of new services/technologies (etc.) created over a five-year period), productivity and racial diversity were positively related. This relationship, however, was multifaceted. The highest productivity happened among firms with the most racially diverse management as well as within organizations that reported high levels of innovation. This positive relationship was not seen among organization who reported low racial diversity or low innovation.

Policies and practices enhancing diversity can also be challenging to implement and can be even more difficult to design and enforce. Kaiser et al. (2013) report that diversity policies, such as statements of commitment to diverse hiring practices or diversity training programs that are carelessly implemented can cause more harm than good among the workforce. When incorrectly executed, diversity policies can give the false sense that discrimination is not happening and a false sense that the needs of diverse members are being met. Further, unmonitored strategies can even lead to negative treatment for those who claim discrimination when a protocol is in place; the mere presence of a policy can make people ignore the actual experiences of workers simply because it feels like the issue has been resolved. This negative effect can theoretically be ameliorated if people are trained in understanding that biases toward intentionally or unintentionally ignoring discrimination exist. Policies and practices can potentially help change the norms of a situation and allow community members to become more accepting of diversity (Paluck, 2011). All efforts to become more open, diverse, and welcoming, however, must be structured using empirically based procedures. Simply enacting a community-wide diversity mind-set without appropriate instruction could backfire and cause more harm than good for the entrepreneurial community (Kaiser et al., 2013). Regardless of these challenges, entrepreneurial communities should strive to create an environment where diverse individuals feel welcomed and where policies are structured to embrace diversity and differing perspectives. Diverse communities have the potential to increase the collaborative opportunities within the community by involving many people with many perspectives in the community's strategic decision making. In this way, the community itself can play an active role in recruiting more entrepreneurs and developing critical mass behind a culture that values innovation.

Entrepreneurial Identity and Collaborative Work Within Communities

Entrepreneurs produce many advantageous outcomes in communities. Among these benefits, entrepreneurs help provide jobs and transformational community leadership (Clevenger & Miao, 2017). Creating a community full of independent entrepreneurs also comes with significant challenges. How can entrepreneurs and local leaders encourage individual entrepreneurs to come together to create a unified community that, in an ideal world, offers a supportive and constructive environment focused on creative ventures? The following sections will address how entrepreneurs can converge as an entrepreneurial social group that collectively influences the entrepreneurial community. This section will also address the possibility that the entrepreneurial social group may be a challenge to create and maintain.

People generally see themselves as both individuals and as members of social groups (Brewer, 1991; Ellemers, Spears, & Doosje, 2002; Hogg & Terry, 2000). A person may describe herself as a woman, an entrepreneur, an innovator, and a mother, with all aspects contributing to the person's sense of who she is. The importance the person places on each membership may depend on what situation she is in, who she is with, or what she just happens to be thinking about (Spears, Oakes, Ellemers, & Haslam, 1997). For example, while at work, a self-identified entrepreneur may feel key aspects of their entrepreneurial identity (e.g., being an independent, creative individual) are the most central part of who they are. When the same entrepreneur is at home with their children they may feel that being a good parent who promotes loving collaborative interactions is the most important part of who they are. Furthermore, individuals may place more importance on particular identities and far less on others, with a tendency to favor identities that bolster self-esteem (Haslam, Powell, & Turner, 2000). These various categorizations (and the corresponding degree of importance placed on them) can impact a person's actions, their comparisons of themselves with other group (or non-group) members, as well as how people feel about themselves (i.e., their self-esteem; Tajfel & Turner, 1979, 1986; Turner, Hogg, Oakes, Reicher, & Whetherell, 1987).

Identifying with a group is associated with both positive (e.g., feeling less stress because of social support from group members, Haslam et al., 2005) and negative outcomes (e.g., lower self-esteem when your group is discriminated against, McCoy & Major, 2003). The entrepreneurial identity, however, is somewhat understudied. It is not as straightforward as many other social identity groups because entrepreneurs often do not band together as a group; instead they assume positions of high status and power as the, frequently, single person who developed a venture (Baron, Frese, & Baum, 2007).

Entrepreneur Identity

Even though many entrepreneurs share core beliefs about entrepreneurship (McGrath & MacMillan, 1992), entrepreneurs often focus on their individual identity rather than their memberships within collective social groups (Shepherd & Haynie, 2009). They are stereotyped as being unique; they often strive to be seen as different; they are their work, and their work is them. Consider the quote that opened the personality section of the chapter. Danny Bowien leads a restaurant; he motivates and works with colleagues around him, but it is more than a job. The venture makes up a key component of who he is: "You don't look at it as, like, work. I don't look at it as, like, a job. *You know, I look at it as, like, my life, and it's what drives me*" (Briger & Bowien, 2016, emphasis added). He sees himself as an entrepreneur who is a key (maybe even *the* key) to the endeavor's success.

Several scholars have suggested that the entrepreneur is strongly an independent personal identity (Wiklund, 1999). Alvesson (2000) contends that, while some identify as an entrepreneur in the collective group sense, many others assume that the entrepreneur is a person who keeps their identity focused on individual needs. Alvesson (2000) states, in context of predicting an entrepreneur's faithfulness to an organization,

> Defining one's self without invoking a specific group (the client, the profession, the work group) does not include elements of a social identity, as there is not a "we" entrepreneurs offering social belonging. Being an "entrepreneur," defining oneself in opposition to bureaucracy involves an inclination towards exit rather than loyalty to the employer.
> (p. 1111)

Alvesson's argument suggests that people who identify as entrepreneurs are more likely to highlight their individuality as an entrepreneur. It is natural for all people to want to be seen as unique individuals (Brewer, 1991). People like recognition for their individual contributions and like to be seen as distinct from others. For an entrepreneur it may be especially important to be seen as an individual as it may help with them to initiate entrepreneurial behaviors (Farmer, Yao, Kung-Mcintyre, 2011). Entrepreneurship is often equated with people who are persistent, who create unique and novel solutions to problems, sometimes even identifying problems that others in the community do not see (Baker & Nelson, 2005). In many cases the entrepreneur's ideas may also challenge the status quo by pushing limits with their ideas beyond what many others feel are necessary (Baker & Nelson, 2005; Choi, 2007; see also Weick, 1979).

Entrepreneur Identity: Predicting Entrepreneurial Potential

Similar to meta-level personality traits, some recent research suggests that an entrepreneur identity can be used to predict whether individuals will take steps to actually become an entrepreneur. Farmer, Yao, and Kung-McIntyre (2011) show that possessing an entrepreneur identity can help predict whether an individual will forever hope to become an entrepreneur, or whether a person will actually take initiative to become one. In their study, entrepreneur identity was measured as perception of one's image of oneself, including perceived abilities and whether these correspond with abilities commonly used by entrepreneurs. Entrepreneur identity was positively correlated with desire to become an entrepreneur. Farmer et al. then showed that the more that people desire to become an entrepreneur, the more likely they are to have taken actual steps to become an entrepreneur by launching an innovative idea. This process includes having taken steps to come up with a creative business idea, as well as steps to actually launch the venture. The authors hypothesize, therefore, that seeing oneself as having the *constitution of an entrepreneur*—more innovative than the constitution of a small business owner or some other role in a commercial occupation—is a driving force between desire to become an entrepreneur and actually taking steps to become one. Importantly, the authors found that prior start-up experience strengthened the relationship between desire to become an entrepreneur and taking steps to become an entrepreneur. Farmer et al. did not distinguish, however, between prior start-up success or failure when determining start-up experience; thus, experience, regardless of ultimate outcome of the previous venture, is likely valuable in actually becoming an entrepreneur.

Identity Creation Within Entrepreneurial Endeavors

Entrepreneurs are in the unique position of being at the very center of the development of a venture's identity. Thus an entrepreneur's values, stemming from characteristics of their own personal identities, can help determine what values are central to the venture's ideology. This initially takes place when the founding entrepreneur hires the venture's first employees. Stewart and Hoell (2016) recently proposed a model for how this process might take place. They utilize an example of a founding entrepreneur who identifies with classic entrepreneurial characteristics (e.g., being an innovator) as well as an environmentalist. Being an environmentalist is a characteristic central to this individual person's identity, but is not necessarily to that person's entrepreneurial identity. When the entrepreneur is able to hire their first employee, they are likely to hire someone who shows potential for developing an identity within the organization that embraces the venture's mission for their product or service as well as for their environmental objectives. Further, Stewart and Hoell (2016) suggest that the entrepreneur would be protective of their entrepreneurial identity by hiring initial employees who can perform tasks less relevant to the entrepreneur's personal identity (e.g., payroll) so that the entrepreneur can focus on the aspects that make them distinct (i.e., namely innovating). This action allows the entrepreneur to protect their distinctiveness (and subsequently their self-esteem) while also promoting the shared social identity of the venture by ensuring that all employees are equally committed to the venture's mission and ideals. While this model still remains largely untested, one could hypothesize that entrepreneurs, as founders, may actually *reduce* innovation in subsequent generations of employees *if* an entrepreneur maintains these initial hiring practices designed to maintain their distinctive entrepreneurship identity rather than by cultivating new innovators.

It may be possible for a founding entrepreneur to hire employees with entrepreneurial proclivities and still maintain the venture's key goals. Several have suggested that it is possible to develop an entrepreneurial orientation within an organization that promotes collaborative efforts among colleagues. Poon et al. (2007) proposed that managers can help set up an entrepreneurial orientation at work and this orientation may mediate the relationship between self-efficacy and performance. The entrepreneurial orientation is one where management encourages innovative behavior and is protective of those who take risks to help further the venture's mission and goals that were originally defined by the founding entrepreneur (Lumpkin & Dess, 1996). Therefore, an entrepreneurial orientation is one where employees are encouraged to act as an entrepreneur, but always with the venture's intentions in mind. When done properly, this orientation could assist entrepreneurs in feeling comfortable hiring fresh, potential-future entrepreneurs, and still see collaborative entrepreneurial style behaviors among colleagues. Perhaps most importantly, these techniques will allow for the cultivation of multiple entrepreneurial generations within a community. Recall that Farmer et al. (2011) found that previous start-up experiences, as well as the ability to perceive one's self as having the necessary qualities to become an entrepreneur, can be used to predict who will actually launch an entrepreneurial venture. Mentoring young potential entrepreneurs within functioning entrepreneurial ventures can provide future generations with entrepreneurial role models who are often key to future entrepreneurial success (Obschonka et al., 2010, 2012; Schmitt-Rodermund, 2004).

Entrepreneurial Social Groups

Despite the individualistic entrepreneurial identity, entrepreneurs can often gain valuable resources from inclusion within social groups (e.g., feelings of belonging, self-esteem, social status; e.g., Haslam et al., 2000; Tajfel & Turner, 1986). Individual identities include our sense of what makes us unique and different from others (Brewer, 1991), but collective identities within social groups provide a sense of group association that is critical to human well-being. Communities can provide individuals with peer networks. These networks can consist of larger institutional support networks. They can also be made up of peers with similar goals, lives, and entrepreneurial identities. Identifying with other similarly minded individuals can provide lots of positive benefits. For example, an entrepreneur can feel a boost to their self-esteem when they feel that entrepreneurs, in general, are respected members within the entrepreneurial community (Tajfel & Turner, 1979, 1986). In addition, both receiving support from (Cohen & McKay, 1984; Haslam, O'Brien, Jetten, Vormedal, & Penna, 2005) and giving support to (Cosley, McCoy, Saslow, & Epel, 2010) community members could help an entrepreneur master stress. Finally, entrepreneurs can also receive advice for mastering entrepreneurial tasks from other entrepreneurs; who are, theoretically, the only other people who face the same entrepreneurial challenges within the community.

Identifying with similar others can also benefit all members of the entrepreneurial community because entrepreneurs can collaboratively work together to fulfill special community needs (e.g., job creation) that other branches of the community may not be able to provide. Entrepreneurs, however, are unlike many other social groups because they are often in direct competition with each other. Subsequently entrepreneurs may be reluctant to join a group of entrepreneurs to collaborate on tasks to help the entrepreneurial community. Entrepreneurs, therefore, may be able to significantly help the entrepreneurial community as a group, but whether this collaboration will take place at all is somewhat unknown. Additional research is needed to understand these relationships fully. Is it possible, for a person to describe *being an entrepreneur* as key to their unique individual identity but also to use *being an entrepreneur* to provide them with an entrepreneurial social group where they feel included among entrepreneurial peers?

Challenges with the Entrepreneurial Social Group Aspect of Identity

If a key characteristic of the entrepreneur identity is to be individualistic and unique, then this leads to a variety of unsolved questions about how entrepreneurs may act together. Is it possible for entrepreneurs to share a social identity with other entrepreneurs, who also share similar norms, preferences, and values? Perhaps more importantly, what is the likely relationship between entrepreneurs? Do they work collaboratively, or are they in competition? The next few sections will attempt to shed light on what research has been conducted on entrepreneurial communities and entrepreneurial identification.

Shepherd and Haynie (2009) suggest that the solitary existence of the entrepreneur poses a significant problem. Humans need each other as communal beings who derive power in numbers for basic safety and security, as well as to undertake large goals that cannot be accomplished individually (Baumeister & Leary, 1995). Because of an innate need to be social, people can gain important benefits from membership in various social groups (e.g., self-esteem, Tajfel & Turner, 1986). Being accepted in groups is so important to survival, in fact, that feeling ostracized from others is one of the worst feelings anyone can have (Williams, 2007, 2014), and this status can have severe negative effects for well-being (Gonsalkorale & Williams, 2007). In contrast, recent findings by Wu, Liu, Kwan, and Lee (2016) suggest identification with a work organization can significantly mediate the negative relationship between feeling ostracized at work and taking unsolicited actions to help the workplace community. Self-identifying as an entrepreneur could alleviate some of the negative effects among entrepreneurs who feel ostracized from others. For the nascent entrepreneur this presents a conundrum. Do they focus on themselves and their entrepreneurial intentions, and sacrifice the benefits of group membership, or do they utilize the benefits of group membership, but at cost of their entrepreneurial individualized identity motivations? Further, if the credit of being an entrepreneur goes to the individual, then how can one encourage entrepreneurs to behave as community members, and likewise retain a spirit of individualistic innovation balanced with cooperative group work?

The benefits and goals of a particular identity (whether it be individual, as a solitary entrepreneur, or collective, as a member of a valued workgroup) may determine which identity is salient at any particular time (Haslam et al., 2000). One solution offered by Shepherd and Haynie (2009) is that entrepreneurs may be able to focus on their need to be a unique and distinctive individual while at work, or during interactions with other entrepreneurs. They can also satisfy their communal needs when outside of work with family members and other social groups. In other words, entrepreneur may be less negatively impacted by not having a social network at work if they can feel they have social support from people outside of work. There are pros and cons to this approach. First, if successful, it may provide needed social support that can reduce feelings of ostracism and protect well-being. It is not, however, always that easy to promote simply switching roles in various situations. Work life balance is a challenge that many struggle to achieve. In addition, feeling isolated at work is correlated with lower job satisfaction and lower well-being (McCoy, Newell, & Gardner, 2013). Thus fulfilling different needs by focusing on different identities may work for some, but is unlikely to be the only solution needed for this problem.

As a possible solution, Ellemers, de Gilder, and Haslam (2004) proposed that there are situations at work when individuals may be enticed to identify with a collective workgroup. Specifically, people may be motivated to identify with a workgroup if it is perceived to be successful, distinct, or has a unique likelihood of success in the future. In all of these cases, identification and involvement with the efficacious workgroup may help increase a person's status within the organization. This finding may extend to entrepreneurs who are motivated to create an entrepreneurial community. By teaming up with other entrepreneurs, they may be able to develop a distinct, high status, group within the community that highlights their leadership, their job creation, and other significant contributions. Furthermore, working within a group of entrepreneurs collaboratively may help the entrepreneur (and subsequently the community) by offering a chance for meaningful social interactions in a group with shared group identity. This cohesion creates a sense of community among entrepreneurs where group work, initiative, and collaboration offer the opportunity for workers to be seen as distinctive, both within the organization, and collectively within the broader community. This focus also suggests that those who identify as entrepreneurs can embed themselves within a collaborative community of entrepreneurs and subsequently feel the benefits of group membership—even when one of the central, cultural values is a relative state of independence.

These potential positive consequences for entrepreneurial shared community identity must be approached cautiously. Sometimes working with others does not lead to effective outcomes (e.g., groupthink; Janis, 1972, 1982). In addition, in many contexts it may not be raw identification, but rather an individual's *commitment* to a group, that predicts emotional and behavioral outcomes (Ellemers et al., 2003). For example, Ellemers, de Gilder, and van den Heuvel (1998) found that a person's level of commitment to their work group was a better predictor of whether a person would help their colleagues than how much that person identified the with their organization as a whole. Further, those who were more committed to their own career—and ultimately their own future success—were less likely to help their colleagues.

A focus on individual versus collective motivations and goals can have significant implications for professional group relations. In a study of financial service employees, Ellemers et al. (1998) found that workgroup commitment positively predicted better performance evaluation scores; however, overall individual career commitment was unrelated to performance evaluation scores. In addition, identification with the organization as a whole predicted whether an employee wanted to stay or leave the organization, but it was commitment to career that predicted whether employees would actually make a career change. While the differences between commitment to an organization versus commitment to an entrepreneurial community require further study, this does provide some insight for how an entrepreneur may respond to a community consisting of entrepreneurial peers, who also may be their competition. Members will need to actually be invested in the group and embrace their goals and ideals for a community-driven group of entrepreneurs to be successful. Members of the group who are participating merely for their own entrepreneurial personal gain may be less likely to help the development of an entrepreneurial community, leading to a less-successful group. In sum, various types of group identification and group commitment must be considered when attempting to predict the success of an entrepreneurial social group.

The specific elements of entrepreneurial groups are still understudied. To be a true social group, members must have shared norms, interactions with each other, and often will work together for the accomplishment of a community goal (Tajfel & Turner, 1986). The question remains as to the extent to which entrepreneurs will embrace the entrepreneurial social group identity. The strong individualistic entrepreneurial identity and corresponding individual goals may prevent a strong shared identity with other entrepreneurs. Entrepreneurs who can adopt the entrepreneurial social identity, however, will be able to reap the many known benefits of social identity. Further, this shared identity could have significant benefits for the general entrepreneurial community. Entrepreneurial social group members may be able to collaborate on projects that require creativity (and other entrepreneurial skills) that benefit the community. Tasks such as developing community fundraisers, slogans, or novel ways to bring consumers into the community will all benefit from assistance from entrepreneurial social groups whose members are committed to the entrepreneurial social group and are invested in the entrepreneurial community.

Conclusion

Entrepreneurs are vital components of entrepreneurial communities. They can provide a multitude of benefits including job creation and creative decision making to the community. Further, their very existence within the community can be an indication of an entrepreneurial community's success in valuing and promoting entrepreneurial endeavors. In the early stages of entrepreneurial community development, successful (or potentially successful), entrepreneurs must be identified for involvement and inclusion within the community. As reviewed, however, this process is not easy. A thorough understanding of an individual, the situation, and their previous experiences is necessary when identifying those who may bring entrepreneurial benefits to the community. The advantage to this complexity, however, is that many types of people have the potential to contribute to an entrepreneurial community that is structured to foster entrepreneurial development. Excellent educational systems that promote entrepreneurial role models and early entrepreneurial experiences, a community-wide appreciation and acceptance for multicultural perspectives, and a community designed to protect some level of risk taking can all help encourage entrepreneurs to join the community.

Once entrepreneurs have joined the geographic community, they can potentially band together as an entrepreneurial social group. This group of entrepreneurs can combine their unique creativity and innovation skills to provide the community with outcomes that non-entrepreneurs cannot provide. The entrepreneurial social group, however, relies on entrepreneurs developing a shared sense of identity with each other. This may, or may not happen because it is hypothesized that many entrepreneurs emphasize their own individualistic entrepreneurial abilities as a principle part of their self-identity. An entrepreneur is charged with developing a new idea and then they must implement these changes to bring the venture to fruition. An entrepreneurial community places the entrepreneur in a different position. Rather than assuming complete control over their own personal venture, they need to engage in collaborative activities with other entrepreneurs and community members. These collaborations can lead to positive outcomes. They can also be a challenge because the people entrepreneurs often have to interact with the most in entrepreneurial communities are other entrepreneurs, who also retain individualistic identities.

It must be stressed that research in the area of entrepreneurial identity and in-group collaboration is understudied within the context of entrepreneurial communities. Much of the collaborative research between the psychology and entrepreneurship fields has been correlational. This deficit makes it a challenge to concretely draw conclusions about exactly which psychological factors, under which circumstances, will lead to successful, collaborative, entrepreneurial communities. If a shared entrepreneurial social identity that promotes commitment to collaboration with other entrepreneurs can be created, then the overarching entrepreneurial community can significantly benefit from their unique contributions. Overall, an understanding of empirical psychological research can provide valuable resources for those interested in developing entrepreneurial communities that are rich in innovation, collaboration, and entrepreneurial involvement.

References

Aldrich, H. E. (1999). *Organizations evolving*. London, UK: Sage.

Alvesson, M. (2000). Social identity and the problem of loyalty in knowledge-intensive companies. *Journal of Management Studies*, *37*, 1101–1123.

Ashby, F. G., Isen, A. M., & Turken, A. U. (1999). A neuropsychological theory of positive affect and its influence on cognition. *Psychological Review*, *106*, 529–550.

Baker, T., & Nelson, R. E. (2005). Creating something from nothing: Resource construction through entrepreneurial Bricolage. *Administrative Science Quarterly*, *50*, 329–366.

Bandura, A. (1993). Perceived self-efficacy in cognitive development and functioning. *Educational Psychologist*, *28*, 117–148.

Bandura, A. (1997). *Self-efficacy: The exercise of control*. New York, NY: Freeman.

Bandura, A. (1999). Social-cognitive theory of personality. In D. Cervonce & Y. Shoda (Eds.), *The coherence of personality: Social-cognitive bases of consistency, variability, and organization* (pp. 185–241). New York, NY: Guilford Press.

Baron, R. A., Frese, M., & Baum, J. R. (2007). Research gains: Benefits of closer links between I/O psychology and entrepreneurship. In J. R. Baum, M. Frese, & R. A. Baron (Eds.), *The psychology of entrepreneurship* (pp. 347–373). Mahwah, NJ: Lawrence Erlbaum Associates.

Barrick, M. R., & Mount, M. K. (1991). The big five personality dimensions and job performance: A meta-analysis. *Personnel Psychology*, *41*, 1–26.

Baum, J. R., Frese, M., & Baron, R. (Eds.). (2007). *The psychology of entrepreneurship*. Mahwah, NJ: Lawrence Erlbaum Associates.

Baum, J. R., & Locke, E. A. (2004). The relationship of entrepreneurial traits, skill, and motivation to subsequent venture growth. *Journal of Applied Psychology*, *89*, 587–598.

Baumeister, R., & Leary, M. R. (1995). The need to belong: Desire for interpersonal attachments as a fundamental human motivation. *Psychological Bulletin*, *117*, 497–529.

Begley, T. M., & Boyd, D. P. (1987). Psychological characteristics associated with performance in entrepreneurial firms and smaller businesses. *Journal of Business Venturing*, *2*, 79–93.

Brandstätter, H. (1997). Becoming an entrepreneur—a question of personality structure? *Journal of Economic Psychology*, *18*, 157–177.

Brandstätter, H. (2011). Personality aspects of entrepreneurship: A look at five meta-analyses. *Personality and Individual Differences*, *51*, 222–230.

Breazeale, N. D., & Hustedde, R. J. (2017). Understanding the impact of culture in entrepreneurship. In M. W-P Fortunato & M. R. Clevenger (Eds.), *Toward entrepreneurial community development: Leaping cultural and leadership boundaries* (pp. 104–125). New York, NY: Routledge.

Brewer, M. (1991). The social self: On being the same and different at the same time. *Personality and Social Psychology Bulletin*, *17*, 475–482.

Briger, S., & Bowien, S. (2016, January 21). The audacious Korean-American chef who mastered 'Mission Chinese Food.' In T. Gross & D. Miller (Executive Producers), *Fresh Air*. Philadelphia, PA: National Public Radio. Retrieved from http://www.npr.org

Brockhaus, R. H., & Horwitz, P. S. (1986). The psychology of the entrepreneur. In D. L. Sexton & R. W. Smilor (Eds.), *The art and science of entrepreneurship* (pp. 25–48). Cambridge, MA: Ballinger Publishing Company.

Cardon, M. S., & Patel, P. C. (2015). Is stress worth it? Stress-related health and wealth trade-offs for entrepreneurs. *Applied Psychology: An International Review*, *64*, 379–420.

Carsrud, A. L., & Brännback, M. (Eds.). (2009). *Understanding the entrepreneurial mind: Opening the black box*. New York, NY: Springer.

Choi, J. N. (2007). Change-oriented organizational citizenship behavior: Effects of work environment characteristics and intervening psychological processes. *Journal of Organizational Behavior*, *28*, 467–484.

Clevenger, M. R. (2017). Perceptions of entrepreneurs and community: From historical roots to a contemporary kaleidoscope. In M. W-P Fortunato & M. R. Clevenger (Eds.), *Toward entrepreneurial community development: Leaping cultural and leadership boundaries* (pp. 10–50). New York, NY: Routledge.

Clevenger, M. R., & Miao, C. (2017). Transformational leadership to build an entrepreneurial community. In M. W-P Fortunato & M. R. Clevenger (Eds.), *Toward entrepreneurial community development: Leaping cultural and leadership boundaries* (pp. 126–151). New York, NY: Routledge.

Clifton, J., & Badal, S. B. (2014). *Entrepreneurial strengthsfinder*. New York, NY: Gallup Press.

Cohen, S., & McKay, G. (1984). Social support, stress and the buffering hypothesis: A theoretical analysis. In A. Baum, S. E. Taylor, & J. E. Singer (Eds.), *Handbook of psychology and health* (pp. 253–267). Hillsdale, NJ: Lawrence Erlbaum Associates.

Collins, C. J., Hanges, P. J., & Locke, E. A. (2004). The relationship of achievement motivation to entrepreneurial behavior: A meta-analysis. *Human Performance*, *17*, 95–117.

Cosley, B. J., McCoy, S. K., Saslow, L. R., & Epel, E. S. (2010). Is compassion for others stress buffering? Consequences of compassion and social support for physiological reactivity to stress. *Journal of Experimental Social Psychology*, *46*, 816–823.

Cropley, D. H., & Cropley, A. J. (2015). *Psychology of innovations in organizations*. New York, NY: Cambridge University Press.

Curtis, T. (2008). Finding that grit makes a pearl: A critical re-reading of research into social enterprise. *International Journal of Entrepreneurial Behaviour & Research*, *14*, 1355–2554.

Davis, M. H., Hall, J. A., & Mayer, P. S. (2015). Developing a new measure of entrepreneurial mindset: Reliability, validity, and implications for practitioners. *Consulting Psychology Journal: Practice and Research*, *68*, 21–48.

De Dreu, C. K. W., & Nijstad, B. A. (2008). Mental set and creative thought in social conflict: Threat rigidity versus motivated focus. *Journal of Personality and Social Psychology*, *95*, 648–661.

Duckworth, A. L., Peterson, C., Matthews, M. D., & Kelly, D. R. (2007). Grit: Perseverance and passion for long-term goals. *Journal of Personality and Social Psychology*, *92*, 1087–1101.

Dweck, C. S. (1986). Motivational processes affecting learning. *American Psychologist*, *41*, 1040–1048.

Dweck, C. S. (2008). *Mindset: The new psychology of success*. New York, NY: Ballantine Books.

Ellemers, N., de Gilder, D., & Haslam, S. A. (2004). Motivating individuals and groups at work: A social identity perspective on leadership and group performance. *The Academy of Management Review*, *29*, 459–478.

Ellemers, N., de Gilder, D., & van den Heuvel, H. (1998). Career-oriented verses team-oriented commitment and behavior at work. *Journal of Applied Psychology, 83*, 717–730.

Ellemers, N., Haslam, S. A., Platow, M., & van Knippenberg, D. (2003). Social identity at work: Developments, debates, directions. In S. A. Haslam, D. van Knippenberg, M. J. Platow, & N. Ellemers (Eds.), *Social identity at work: Developing theory for organizational practice* (pp. 3–28). New York, NY: Psychology Press.

Ellemers, N., Spears, R., & Doosje, B. (2002). Self and social identity. *Annual Review of Psychology, 53*, 161–186.

Farmer, S. M., Yao, X., & Kung-Mcintyre, K. (2011). The behavioral impact of entrepreneur identity aspiration and prior entrepreneurial experience. *Entrepreneurship: Theory and Practice, 35*, 245–273.

Fortunato, M. W-P (2017). Models of entrepreneurial community and ecosystem development. In M. W-P Fortunato & M. R. Clevenger (Eds.), *Toward entrepreneurial community development: Leaping cultural and leadership boundaries* (pp. 51–103). New York, NY: Routledge.

Gartner, W. B. (1989). "Who is an entrepreneur?" is the wrong question. *Entrepreneurship Theory and Practice, 12*, 47–68.

George, J. M., & Zhou, J. (2001). When openness to experience and conscientiousness are related to creative behavior: An interactional approach. *Journal of Applied Psychology, 86*, 513–524.

Gonsalkorale, K., & Williams, K. D. (2007). The KKK won't let me play: Ostracism even by a despised outgroup hurts. *European Journal of Social Psychology, 37*, 1176–1186.

Haslam, S. A., O'Brien, A., Jetten, J., Vormedal, K., & Penna, S. (2005). Taking the strain: Social identity, social support, and the experience of stress. *British Journal of Social Psychology, 44*, 355–370.

Haslam, S. A., Powell, C., & Turner, J. C. (2000). Social identity, self-categorization, and work motivation: Rethinking the contribution of the group to positive and sustainable organisational outcomes. *Applied Psychology: An International Review, 49*, 319–339.

Haslam, S. A., van Knippenberg, D., Platow, M. J., & Ellemers, N. (Eds.). (2003). *Social identity at work: Developing theory for organizational practice.* New York, NY: Psychology Press.

Henderson, R., & Robertson, M. (1999). Who wants to be an entrepreneur? Young adult attitudes to entrepreneurship as a career. *Education and Training, 41*, 236–245.

Het, S., & Wolf, O. T. (2007). Mood changes in response to psychosocial stress in healthy young women: Effects of pretreatment with cortisol. *Behavioral Neuroscience, 121*, 11–20.

Hirt, E. R., Devers, E. E., & McCrea, S. M. (2008). I want to be creative: Exploring the role of hedonic contingency theory in the positive mood cognitive flexibility link. *Journal of Personality and Social Psychology, 94*, 214–230.

Hisrich, R., Langan-Fox, J., & Grant, S. (2007). Entrepreneurship research practice: A call to action for psychology. *American Psychologist, 62*, 575–589.

Hogg, M. A., & Terry, D. J. (2000). Social identity and self-categorization processes in organizational contexts. *Academy of Management Review, 25*, 121–140.

Janis, I. L. (1972). *Victims of groupthink*. Boston, MA: Houghton Mifflin.

Janis, I. L. (1982). *Groupthink* (2nd ed.). Boston, MA: Houghton Mifflin.

Kaiser, C. R., Major, B., Jurcevic, I., Dover, T. L., Brady, L. M., & Shapiro, J. R. (2013). Presumed fair: Ironic effects of organizational diversity structures. *Journal of Personality and Social Psychology*, *104*, 504–519.

Katz, J. A. (2007). Education and training in entrepreneurship. In J. R. Baum, M. Frese, & R. A. Baron (Eds.), *The psychology of entrepreneurship* (pp. 209–235). Mahwah, NJ: Lawrence Erlbaum Associates.

Korunka, C., Frank, H., Lueger, M., & Mugler, J. (2003). The entrepreneurial personality in the context of resources, environment, and the startup process: A configurational approach. *Entrepreneurship Theory & Practice*, *28*, 23–42.

Krueger, N. F. (2003). The cognitive psychology of entrepreneurship. In Z. J. Acs & D. B. Audretsch (Eds.), *Handbook of entrepreneurship research: An interdisciplinary survey and introduction* (pp. 105–140). Dordrecht: Kluwer Academic Publishers.

Locke, E. A., & Baum, J. R. (2007). Entrepreneurial motivation. In J. R. Baum, M. Frese, & R. A. Baron (Eds.), *The psychology of entrepreneurship* (pp. 41–65). Mahwah, NJ: Lawrence Erlbaum Associates.

Lumpkin, G. T., & Dess, G. G. (1996). Clarifying the entrepreneurial orientation construct and linking it to performance. *Academy of Management Review*, *21*, 135–172.

Maddux, W. W., & Galinsky, A. D. (2009). Cultural borders and mental barriers: The relationship between living abroad and creativity. *Journal of Personality and Social Psychology*, *96*, 1047–1061.

Magnusson, D., & Endler, N. S. (1977). Interactional psychology: Present status and future prospects. In D. Magnusson & N. S. Endler (Eds.), *Personality at the crossroads; Current issues in interactional psychology* (pp. 3–36). Hillsdale, NJ: Lawrence Earlbaum Associates.

McCoy, S. K., & Major, B. (2003). Group identification moderates emotional responses to perceived prejudice. *Personality and Social Psychology Bulletin*, *29*, 1005–1017.

McCoy, S. K., Newell, E. E., & Gardner, S. K. (2013). Seeking balance: The importance of environmental conditions in men and women faculty's well-being. *Innovative Higher Education*, *38*, 309–322.

McGrath, R. G., & MacMillan, I. C. (1992). More like each other than anyone else? A cross-cultural study of entrepreneurial perceptions. *Journal of Business Venturing*, *7*, 419–429.

Miner, J. B., & Raju, N. S. (2004). Risk propensity differences between managers and entrepreneurs and between low- and high-growth entrepreneurs: A reply in a more conservative vein. *Journal of Applied Psychology*, *89*, 3–13.

Mischel, W., & Shoda, Y. (1998). Reconciling processing dynamics and personality dispositions. *Annual Review of Psychology*, *49*, 229–258.

Mullins, J. (2006). Can we teach entrepreneurship? *Business Strategy Review*, *17*, 13–17.

Neck, H. M., & Greene, P. G. (2011). Entrepreneurship education: Known worlds and new frontiers. *Journal of Small Business Management*, *49*, 55–70.

Nielsen, S. L., Klyver, K., Evald, M. R., & Bager, T. (2012). *Entrepreneurship in theory and practice: Paradoxes in play*. Northampton, MA: Edward Elgar.

Obschonka, M., Silbereisen, R. K., & Schmitt-Rodermund, E. (2010). Entrepreneurial intention as developmental outcome. *Journal of Vocational Behavior*, *77*, 63–72.

Obschonka, M., Silbereisen, R. K., & Schmitt-Rodermund, E. (2012). Explaining entrepreneurial behavior: Dispositional personality traits, growth of personal entrepreneurial resources, and business idea generation. *The Career Development Quarterly*, *60*, 178–190.

Obschonka, M., Silbereisen, R. K., Schmitt-Rodermund, E., & Stuetzer, M. (2011). Nascent entrepreneurship and the developing individual: Early entrepreneurial competence in adolescence and venture creation success during the career. *Journal of Vocational Behavior*, *79*, 121–133.

Paluck, E. L. (2011). Peer pressure against prejudice: A high school field experiment examining social network change. *Journal of Experimental Social Psychology*, *47*, 350–358.

Platt, A. (n.d.). Mission Chinese Food—Lower East Side—New York Magazine restaurant guide. *New York Magazine*. Retrieved from http://www.nymag.com

Poon, J. M. V., Ainuddin, R. A., & Junit, S. H. (2007). Effects of self-concept traits and entrepreneurial orientation on firm performance. *International Small Business Journal*, *24*, 61–82.

Rauch, A., & Frese, M. (2007a). Born to be an entrepreneur? Revisiting the personality approach to entrepreneurship. In J. R. Baum, M. Frese, & R. A. Baron (Eds.), *The psychology of entrepreneurship* (pp. 41–65). Mahwah, NJ: Lawrence Erlbaum Associates.

Rauch, A., & Frese, M. (2007b). Let's put the person back into entrepreneurship research: A meta-analysis on the relationship between business owners' personality traits, business creation, and success. *European Journal of Work and Organizational Psychology*, *16*, 353–385.

Richard, O. C., Barnett, T., Dwyer, S., & Chadwick, K. (2004). Cultural diversity in management, firm performance, and the moderating role of entrepreneurial orientation dimensions. *Academy of Management Journal*, *47*, 255–266.

Robertson-Kraft, C., & Duckworth, A. L. (2014). True grit: Trait-level perseverance and passion for long-term goals predicts effectiveness and retention among novice teachers. *Teachers College Record*, *116*, 1–27.

Ross, L. (1977). The intuitive psychologist and his shortcomings: Distortions in the attribution process. In L. Berkowitz (Ed.), *Advances in experimental social psychology* (Vol. 10, pp. 173–220). New York, NY: Academic Press.

Runco, M. A., & Jaeger, G. J. (2012). The standard definition of creativity. *Creativity Research Journal*, *24*, 92–96.

Schmitt-Rodermund, E. (2004). Pathways to successful entrepreneurship: Parenting, personality, early entrepreneurial competence, and interests. *Journal of Vocational Behavior*, *65*, 498–518.

Schoon, I., & Duckworth, K. (2012). Who becomes an entrepreneur? Early life experiences as predictors of entrepreneurship. *Developmental Psychology*, *48*, 1719–1726.

Shaver, K. G. (2014). Psychology of entrepreneurial behavior. In A. Fayole (Ed.), *Handbook of research on entrepreneurship* (pp. 262–280). Northampton, MA: Edward Elgar.

Shepherd, D., & Haynie, J. M. (2009). Birds of a feather don't always flock together: Identity management in entrepreneurship. *Journal of Business Venturing*, *24, 316–337.*

Smiley, P. A., & Dweck, C. S. (1994). Individual differences in achievement goals among young children. *Child Development*, *65*, 1723–1743.

Spears, R., Oakes, P. J., Ellemers, N., & Haslam, S. A. (Eds.). (1997). *The social psychology of stereotyping and group life*. Oxford: Blackwell Publishers.

Steffens, P., Terjesen, S., & Davidsson, P. (2012). Birds of a feather get lost together: New venture team composition and performance. *Small Business Economics*, *39*, 727–743.

Stewart, S. A., & Hoell, R. C. (2016). Hire someone like me, or hire someone I need: Entrepreneur identity and early-stage hiring in small firms. *Journal of Small Business & Entrepreneurship*, *28*, 187–201.

Stewart, W. H., & Roth, P. L. (2001). Risk propensity differences between entrepreneurs and managers: A meta-analytic review. *Journal of Applied Psychology*, *86*, 145–153.

Stewart, W. H., & Roth, P. L. (2004). Data-quality affects meta-analytic conclusions: A response to Miner and Raju (2004) concerning entrepreneurial risk propensity. *Journal of Applied Psychology*, *89*, 14–21.

Stewart, W. H., & Roth, P. L. (2007). A meta-analysis of achievement motivation differences between entrepreneurs and managers. *Journal of Small Business Management*, *45*, 401–421.

Syed, I., & Mueller, B. (2014). Finding the passion to persevere: An exploration of the mechanisms by which passion fuels entrepreneurial grit. *Frontiers of Entrepreneurship Research*, *34*, 1–14.

Tadmor, C. T., Galinsky, A. D., & Maddux, A. D. (2012). Getting the most out of living abroad: Biculturalism and integrative complexity as key drivers of creative and professional success. *Journal of Personality and Social Psychology*, *103*, 520–542.

Tajfel, H., & Turner, J. C. (1979). An integrative theory of intergroup conflict. In G. Austin & S. Worchel (Eds.), *The social psychology of intergroup relations* (pp. 33–47). Monterey, CA: Brooks/Cole.

Tajfel, H., & Turner, J. C. (1986). The social identity theory of intergroup behaviour. In S. Worchel & W. G. Austin (Eds.), *The psychology of intergroup relations* (pp. 7–24). Chicago, IL: Nelson-Hall.

Tsay, C-J. (2016). Privileging naturals over strivers: The costs of the naturalness bias. *Personal and Social Psychology Bulletin*, *42*, 40–53.

Turner, J. C, Hogg, M. A., Oakes, P. J., Reicher, S. D., & Whetherell, M. S. (1987). *Rediscovering the social group: A self-categorization theory*. Oxford, UK: Blackwell Publishing.

Unsworth, K. (2001). Unpacking creativity. *The Academy of Management Review*, *26*, 289–298.

Weick, K. E. (1979). *The social psychology of organizing* (2nd ed.). Reading, MA: Addison-Wesley.

Wells, P. (2015, June 9). Restaurant review: Mission Chinese Food on the Lower East Side. *The New York Times*. Retrieved from http://www.nytimes.com

Wiklund, J. (1999). The sustainability of the entrepreneurial orientation—Performance relationship. *Entrepreneurship Theory and Practice*, *24*, 37–48.

Williams, D. K. (2014, December 1). Do you have enough grit to make it as an entrepreneur? *Forbes*. Retrieved from http://www.forbes.com

Williams, K. D. (2007). Ostracism. *Annual Review of Psychology*, *58*, 425–452.

Wu, C.-H., Liu, J., Kwan, H. K., & Lee, C. (2016). Why and when workplace ostracism inhibits organizational citizenship behaviors: An organizational identification perspective. *Journal of Applied Psychology*, *101*, 362–378.

Zhao, H., & Seibert, S. E. (2006). The Big Five personality dimensions and entrepreneurial status: A meta-analytical review. *Journal of Applied Psychology*, *91*, 259–271.

Zhao, H., Siebert, S. E., & Hills, G. E. (2005). The mediating role of self-efficacy in the development of entrepreneurial intentions. *Journal of Applied Psychology*, *90*, 1265–1272.

Zhao, H., Seibert, S. E., & Lumpkin, G. T. (2010). The relationship of personality to entrepreneurial intentions and performance: A meta-analytic review. *Journal of Management*, *36*, 381–404.

10 Leaping Cultural and Leadership Boundaries

Catalyzing Entrepreneurial Communities

Michael W-P Fortunato and Morgan R. Clevenger

Entrepreneurship is a phenomenon that research suggests can be culturally and institutionally supported. Perhaps the most burning question for researchers and practitioners is, "how?" The ideas presented in this book demonstrate a variety of ways to begin to cultivate a better community environment for leaders and feeders focused on entrepreneurs—those who launch businesses, and those who support new businesses. The same culture and leadership initiative that can support entrepreneurship can also inhibit entrepreneurship, however. In many places with a long history of corporate enterprise that supports wage employment, the cultural and institutional support systems for launching a new enterprise may not be present or are purposely suppressed. This approach can inadvertently lead to the creation of social and institutional boundaries through a lack of understanding of entrepreneurship, prioritization of other local initiatives over small business development, unwillingness to support local businesses as customers, excessive taxation and regulation, cliquishness, and institutional fragmentation. These barriers can be more pervasive and subtle than other, more commonly cited barriers, such as a lack of access to capital or poor access to infrastructure. This book does not make the presumption that cultural and institutional barriers matter *more* than a more traditional focus on financial and regulatory support for the firm. Taking a cue from Granovetter (1973), the concepts presented in this book simply attempt to elevate the importance of human interactional factors that are less common in the literature. The literature on the link between communities and entrepreneurs is growing, and some scholars have positioned this nexus as the next frontier in entrepreneurship research (Lyons, Alter, Audretsch, & Augustine, 2012). This book takes the stance that those actions that serve to strengthen the community as a whole may also strengthen the local platform for entrepreneurial action—particularly if entrepreneurs themselves have opportunities to engage in formal and informal leadership. This chapter discusses the issue of boundaries and mitigating them. Final thoughts are shared regarding the process of entrepreneurial community development. Limitations of this book are shared along with future research relating to the topic. Finally, while information and ideas are important, the co-editors create a *call to action* to apply and share ideas in fostering a healthy entrepreneurial community.

Leaping Local Entrepreneurial Boundaries

Entrepreneurial community development is more complicated than it sounds for several reasons. First, there is a strong temporal dimension. On one hand, the course of history strongly shapes the cultural landscape of any community. Changing that culture may prove to be futile or very slow, meaning that the best option for culture change is to create spaces where alternative ethics—like a positive view of entrepreneurship—can be practiced openly and where others can easily join the movement. If entrepreneurship is perceived to be threatening to the dominant culture, then social and institutional barriers can appear quickly that disparage entrepreneurial efforts and reinforce the dominant social paradigm of wage employment, pride in the current local identity, and the reinforcement of long-standing traditions.

Second, the results are unpredictable. The creation of vibrant entrepreneurial ecosystems is an uneven, stochastic process that evolves over time, with many actors playing many different roles over the course of the community's development. Those roles often cannot be predicted in advance, nor can the leaders and feeders who participate. Additionally, an ecosystem approach accounts for the inevitability of failure among firms, and effectively redistributes talent and energy in the face of a firm exit. With so much noise and uncertainty endemic to the system, ecosystems can only be "designed" at the macro-level, advancing a series of system ethics supportive of entrepreneurial action rather than a set of concrete growth and development plans. This view makes planning very challenging, and the idea of key performance indicators, while important to institutional stakeholders, may be misguided.

Third, there remains a major tension in the literature, and in this research, about *who* should lead. Newer literature from the entrepreneurial ecosystem school suggests that it is entrepreneurs who are best suited to lead a local entrepreneurial revolution, as these individuals have different incentives than institutional actors (Feld, 2012). While there is some support for this idea from the data in Chapter 7, such an approach may also prematurely discount the prominent "feeder" roles that other local leaders with an entrepreneurial vision can play. The secret, it seems, parallels the secret to building any strong community: interact widely, inclusively, and with purpose. When such interactions become public and are promoted in a positive light, a message is sent that the community cares about entrepreneurship, innovation, diversity, and novel approaches to solving problems. Expanding boundaries occur as a natural dynamic of complexity from other agents, actors, or networks (Avolio & Bass, 1988; Scott, 2003).

Sometimes boundaries are established for clarity or convenience. As the neighbor in Frost's original 1941 poem *Mending Wall* constantly said, "Good fences make good neighbors" (Frost, 2012, p. 3). But often challenging the maintenance of walls opens opportunities. The following sections create a list of general ideas and strategies that may be useful in leaping local cultural boundaries. Challenging boundaries can open domains, broaden or change structure, rebalance resources, spark creativity, enact opportunities, and increase entrepreneurship.

Use Ecosystem Logic

Ecosystems are stochastic and difficult to predict, but much like firms, they carry the cultural "DNA" of their founders. The values and norms that were used to launch the ecosystem will often persist even as the ecosystem grows well beyond its original founding group. This concern is what is considered design at the macro-level. Rather than creating a specific plan for an ecosystem, with flat, uninspiring performance indicators and institutional incentives, focus on creating a *system ethic*. The feel of the ecosystem, what is valued there, how people interact, and important rituals and cultural symbols matter more at this stage than creating a concrete plan.

More "Boulder Thesis," Less Policy

Feld's (2012) *Boulder Thesis* exhibits four components: (a) entrepreneurs must lead the start-up community, (b) the leaders must have a long-term commitment, (c) the start-up community must be inclusive of anyone who wants to participate in it, and (d) the start-up community must have continual activities that engage the entire entrepreneurial stack (Feld, 2012, p. 25). What Feld (2012) also mentioned, supported by the case studies in this book, is that policy-driven approaches to stimulating entrepreneurship do not tend to work well because they operate on short political cycles, lack the long-term commitment needed to launch an ecosystem, and are grounded in different incentives than those favored by entrepreneurs. However, a bottom-up approach that empowers entrepreneurs from the beginning—building ownership and a spirit of mentorship right from the start—empowers the capability of starting small and adapting deliberately to meet changing market conditions. This tactic is very different from an approach that starts large, where a major initiative is launched (and many dollars spent) based on models built upon current (or past or perceived) economic conditions, where change is centrally administered rather than devolved to the individuals who must themselves bear the brunt of market risk. If there is one major contribution that governments and large organizations can make to supporting the community, it is the removal of legal, regulatory, and financial barriers to entry and allowed expansion for entrepreneurs.

Facilitating Conditions Matter

Social processes are the primary focus of this book, but facilitating conditions can oftentimes override what would otherwise be a vibrant entrepreneurial community. A lack of access to critical resources (i.e., financing, information, and infrastructure) presents formidable barriers to any entrepreneur. The book subtly suggests that these conditions sometimes receive too much attention, where the focus should be on human interaction through culture and institutions. This discussion does not mean that facilitating conditions do not matter. One major contribution of ecosystem feeders is the continued removal of barriers to accessing finances, information, and excessive policies.

A Stronger Role for Feeders

While Feld (2012) downplays the role of "feeders" as subordinate to entrepreneurial leadership, the research presented here shows that feeders are often times key collaborators who can be catalysts themselves—as long as they involve entrepreneurs from the beginning. Local governments are well positioned to improve a community's infrastructure, promote the community, and remove legal barriers to starting a business. Deliberately reaching out to entrepreneurs to participate in public processes not only gives these feeders a front-row seat to the entrepreneurial climate but also enhances their ability to attract funding to local efforts by promoting the ways it will support a self-sustaining entrepreneurial community. Large companies and nonprofits can welcome more entrepreneurs into chamber events and development functions, as entrepreneurs can oftentimes collaborate with larger industry and nonprofits to solve not only business problems but also social and environmental problems—all from a new perspective. Academics can equally interact more with entrepreneurs, creating knowledge exchanges that lead to innovation transfer and providing formative opportunities for students. These actions are simple gestures, but they require a place for interaction to occur productively.

Generative and Transformational Leadership Matter

As discussed in Chapters 2 and 5, leadership is an important function of multiple actors in a community. The efforts of leaders in any community function—individual, nonprofit, government, or organizational—is no easy task (Lakey, Lakey, Napler, & Robinson, 1998; Svara, 1995; Tierney, 2006). Dynamic communities encounter constant change, thus leadership also changes. Transitions, new ideas, and new personalities also take time to adjust to function in a high capacity (Avolio & Bass, 1988; Bunker & Wakefield, 2005; Goodyear & Golden, 2008; Lakey et al., 1998; Sendjaya & Sarros, 2002; Svara, 1995).

Generative leadership focuses on innovation and innovative activities (Lane & Maxfield, 1996; Surie & Hazy, 2006). "On its own, innovation leads nowhere" (Gerber, 1995, p. 122). Innovation must be harnessed for productivity and economic output. So innovation and entrepreneurship are both needed to advance an entrepreneurial community.

The entrepreneurial leader is focused on the firm or enterprise internal functionality while simultaneously enacting the organization in the open system of the community and a given industry (Aldrich, 2002; Baumol, 1990; Feld, 2012; Gupta, MacMillan, & Surie, 2003; Isenberg, 2010; Kuratko, 2009, 2016; Kuratko & Morris, 2013; Zacharakis, Spinelli, & Timmons, 2011). Kuratko (2016), Kuratko and Morris (2013), McGrath and MacMillan (2000), and Zacharakis et al. (2011) isolate *entrepreneurial leadership*, but the context relates to the focus in either an entrepreneurial firm-level concept or as "an approach" to any organization or arrangement with innovative leadership (e.g., corporate entrepreneurship, social entrepreneurship, single entrepreneur, etc.). However, Zacharakis et al. (2011) note that key attributes of such leaders emphasize the quick ability to learn and think, resiliency, integrity, and entrepreneurial culture building in a firm or organization. Gupta, MacMillan, and Surie (2003) believe "entrepreneurial leadership has much in common with transformational leadership" as the goal is appealing to the higher needs of followers and constituents (p. 245). Entrepreneurs need a supportive climate and culture—an entrepreneurial community—to try to succeed, but with the allowance to fail. This dynamic, open environment allows for doing and learning, which, hopefully, eventually yields success. The ongoing process embeds entrepreneurs, and opportunities create leaders. The overall process allows for higher performance and satisfaction, thus the transformation of an entrepreneurial community.

A Space for Culture to Emerge

A simple first step in catalyzing an entrepreneurial community or ecosystem is to create a space to anchor human interactions (Adler & Kwon, 2002; Hoang & Antoncic, 2003; Shane & Cable, 2002; Stam, Arzlanian, & Elfring, 2014). This space should come packaged with an ethic for productive engagement: anyone who wants to be part is welcome, diversity across many dimensions of life is encouraged, and most of all, the space will *focus on supporting entrepreneurs*. This space could be an event space, an incubator, a well-known public venue, or just an informal meeting spot (e.g., a café or restaurant) where people already like to get together. Feeders, like universities, governments, and businesses, can be pivotal in providing a physical environment for interaction, and encouraging their own people to stop by from time to time. Meetings should be deliberate: it is about supporting the local entrepreneurship community. Leaders and feeders alike can stimulate this kind of action by reaching out broadly.

Create Alliances Broadly and Deliberately

Social networking is a common feature of effective communities, but there is a difference between networking and creating a purposive alliance. Granovetter (1973) stressed the importance of having lots of "weak ties" in a system, as new knowledge about opportunities tends to flow over these informal ties of acquaintanceship. However, Burt (1995) also notes that the location of these ties matter. For leaders and feeders alike, it makes sense to reach out to organizations that are a strategic fit for entrepreneurs, but also those that seem to be isolated from the entrepreneurial discussion, or those who have historically been exclusive within the community. These "siloed" organizations may contain deep knowledge, connections, and mentors that can help the community. It takes deliberate effort to reach out to siloed organizations. Be sure to keep inviting members of these groups to the table, and leave the door open even if they say "no" at first. These individuals or organizations may simply be more risk averse than yours, or late adopters of new forms of organizing.

Marketing and Social Networking for Success

Marketing requires thoughtful planning and attention. Both traditional mediums and social media are helpful tools to communicate, inform, and create opportunities for others to engage in entrepreneurship. These opportunities happen through people—social networks.

As elaborated in Chapter 6, social networking is also a process and requires thoughtful planning and attention. Leveraging strong ties and utilizing weak ties allows connectivity to increase ideas, sharing of information, solving issues, maximizing resources, and fulfilling opportunity needs through other people. Building on the basic concepts of trust and trustworthiness, fulfilling expectations, and delivering on promises is what social network—and ultimately marketing—are all about.

Manage Collaboration Among Individualists

Just like snowflakes or fingerprints, individuals are all different. Build on diversity. The biggest challenge in managing collaborations among individuals is investing in the time to foster and solicit ideas and interactions to determine the best information and ideas possible. Managing collaborations—just like marketing and social networking—takes time and requires thoughtful planning and execution. Throughout the process, focus on strengthening social networks while leveraging resources. Most individuals ultimately want to contribute to the process in supporting a community and its myriad of businesses and organizations. However, care is often presented in challenging ways. Likely the best way to leap boundaries here is to listen.

Measure and Maintain Accountability

What gets measured is what gets done. Everyone wants to feel progress and believe advancements are being made. The only way to capture these achievements—or when to know to adapt or change—is to create goals and milestones and write them down. From the desired goals and milestones, list needed (and available) resources as well as specific dates and objective checkpoints. Hold one another mutually accountable, but be flexible. Interdependence takes time (Scott, 2003). Additionally, attention to process, people's needs, and stewardship of resources are valued in the enactment and measurement of goals.

Celebrate the Collective

Even in the world of entrepreneurship, meetings are not always fun, and merely checking progress items off a list can feel like tedium. Celebrating the successes of the group not only builds morale and reaffirms the group's mission but also shows everyone else how much fun a group is having. This milestone celebration is an important way of communicating to others that (a) the group really cares about entrepreneurial success, (b) outsiders are missing the best party in town, and (c) it is easy (and encouraged) to become an insider. Pause to celebrate successes. Give praise and recognition where it is due. Encourage those who need encouraged. It's that simple. These efforts, though, need to be made in appropriate timing and not delayed. Even a "thank you" has little demands on resources yet goes a long way in building social capital and strengthens the social network and community.

Pass the Baton

Entrepreneurial community development is not a one-time exercise. To keep any initiative going requires stability and sustainability in the organization. This balance can be a challenge in an entrepreneurial community or ecosystem that is constantly evolving as well as being based on random innovations and a changing set of players and roles. Nonetheless, complex systems that change are often times quite stable at the system level, and stress and change is needed for the organization to develop (see Taleb, 2012 for an illustration). If an individual has been fortunate enough to lead and catalyze an entrepreneurial community, it is vital to pass the baton to someone who else is willing to serve, able to make a nontrivial commitment, and perhaps most of all, who is *different*. Keeping leadership fresh, engaging, and full of different ideas can eventually help a system to thrive, as long as it is not chaotic. New leadership should also remain committed to the norms and ideals that the community worked so hard to create, but open to new directions and ideas emerging from the bottom up. The best candidate for the job may be the person who is capable of listening the best and cheerleading the most. It may be difficult to let go, so be sure to properly plan overlap time in responsibilities—where warranted—for mentoring, historic documentation, and smooth transition.

Entrepreneurial Community Development: A Process

Baumol (1990) notes entrepreneurship varies among societies. Regardless of culture, entrepreneurship focuses on productive new ideas and generating innovative directions for communities, regions, states, and countries. The key to remember is that development of an entrepreneurial community—much less an entrepreneurial ecosystem—takes time and is a process. Among various aspects of entrepreneurial action in process development are purpose, resource utilization, and exchange.

The process of setting goals, identifying and utilizing resources, and creating positive exchanges takes time. Barbosa (2015) provides important questions regarding establishment and maintenance of boundaries in the process:

> *Who* decides upon the establishments of boundaries (for the emerging organization, project, social movement, etc.)?
> *When* and *where* does the establishment of boundaries take place?
> *What* boundaries are established?
> *Why* are these specific boundaries established?
> *How* is the decision upon the establishment of boundaries structured and implemented?
> *What* are these specific boundaries established *for* (what are the intended and unintended consequences of it)? (p. 405)

Answering these questions and exploring possibilities is what undergirds the entrepreneurial community development process.

Limitations

This book represents the authors' and editors' best efforts to integrate the academic and practitioner literature across a rapidly evolving space in a way that is useful and practical to both academics and practitioners. The research portion of this book focuses on case studies from six communities in three states in the United States. Naturally, the external generalizability of such a study is relative—the research is not intended to examine the incidence of entrepreneurial culture across a wide swath of geographic terrain, but to understand the fuzzy relationship between entrepreneurs and their communities in rich detail. A comparative lens is used to understand how this relationship may differ across areas of low- and high-entrepreneurship, and different cultural zones within the United States. However, this is just the starting point. Additional research is needed to uncover different cultural features in different regions and nations that may not have been present in the focus communities. Additionally, much progress has been made quickly in the theoretical development of ecosystems since the research was conducted. While Feld's (2012) and Isenberg's (2010) works are highly informative and illustrative, they largely rely on the combined experience of these scholars to describe the work anecdotally or using single cases. This research did not deliberately investigate some key elements of ecosystems, such as business failure and how it was tolerated, or direct inquiry about what the term "ecosystem" means to entrepreneurs. These would be very interesting opportunities for future research, to address the understanding of the term itself among entrepreneurs in a critical frame, and to learn more about the less-pleasant, stochastic issues of business cycles and entrepreneurial failures.

Future Research

The authors along with other colleagues are currently planning some future research on various topics discussed in this book. Investigating factors supporting and inhibiting entrepreneurial community development continues to emerge. Future research will take place in different cultural regions both inside and outside the United States, and will use mixed methods to maximize the benefits of both qualitative and quantitative modes of study. As the focus on entrepreneurs and communities deepens and a collective understanding grows results and additional suggestions for developing and maintaining entrepreneurial communities and entrepreneurial ecosystems will be shared.

Call to Action

This book would mean very little if it were intended to sit on a shelf, collecting dust, or anchoring a stack of desk papers with the occasional passer-by saying, "Oh, that one looks interesting," or just ignoring it altogether. True, this book covers a good deal of concepts, some heavy research, and unpacks some ideas that still puzzle and delight entrepreneurial thinkers. Your authors, however, are not sit-on-the-shelf, office-bound academics in real life! While committed to maintaining an academic tone throughout this book, both of the primary authors are dedicated to researching *and* practicing the idea of transforming communities through entrepreneurship. Between the two of us, we not only conduct applied research on the ground in real communities but also get our students involved as well. We teach people how to start businesses, and we work with communities to solve both business and non-business problems through entrepreneurial thinking. We share what we learn with others, and that exchange only deepens our own knowledge about what entrepreneurship is and why it matters. Even in our line of academic work, we take pride in bringing a spirit of entrepreneurship and innovation into the classrooms and communities that we serve, and it is our goal to spread that passion for entrepreneurship far and wide. It was a conscientious choice to invite authors to the table who share our zest for the topic.

The end of a book is a great time to put it down, get out of your chair, stretch a bit, call some friends and colleagues, and to start implementing any ideas you may have had while reading. We offer several strategies for getting started, and we encourage you to take these strategies, try them out, alter and adjust them, and make them your own. And if something different is working for you, we would love to know about it! The study of entrepreneurs and entrepreneurship is much like entrepreneurship itself: a kaleidoscope that is likely much more experimental rather than authoritative, it is evolutionary and adaptable rather than staid and consistent, and there is always room for a new approach or perspective that really works. We hope that, through your creative efforts, you may continue to innovate as scholars and practitioners and embrace novelty and risk—especially when those risks seem large to others, but small to you.

So what are you waiting for? The hardest thing about catalyzing an entrepreneurial community or ecosystem may be the biggest barrier of all: taking the first step. However, this undertaking is one of the easiest acts one can do as an entrepreneurial leader or feeder. Are you an entrepreneur? Walk over (don't e-mail, text, or call) and talk to another entrepreneur whom one might think is interested in promoting the whole community. Over coffee and a Danish, perhaps think of an organization or group who could launch to bring more entrepreneurs into the community. As entrepreneurs, see what can be done to make it better than all the other entrepreneurial assistance groups that are out there. What would be different? What innovative touches could be added? What makes more sense to people in this community that current offerings are lacking?

Is there a leader in a community who would like to see more entrepreneurship? Please put this book down immediately and walk over (again, don't e-mail, text, or call) and talk to an entrepreneur in the community about launching an interest group or organization to support small businesses locally. Over coffee or a smoothie, listen to everything they say. What steps would an entrepreneur take that have not been considered? What linkages are there between local entrepreneurs and your organization that have not been explored? Can you think of a way to start bridging this gap *tomorrow*? Who else might get involved that would be beneficial to entrepreneurs? How might these efforts look different from less-successful efforts that may have occurred in the past? Ask entrepreneurs what they would do differently—they will tell you.

Are you an academic who enjoys studying entrepreneurship? By all means, put down this book immediately and walk over (don't e-mail, text, or call) and talk to some entrepreneurs in the community—just informally at first. What kinds of questions are on *their* minds? What sorts of answers do they seek that would make the whole community of entrepreneurs successful? Over lunch or a happy hour, perhaps discuss some ways that students, colleagues, and fellow researchers could get more involved in the community of entrepreneurs. In fact, these entrepreneurs may be able to serve as out-of-classroom mentors to the students who are interested in entrepreneurship. There is no rule saying that networking cannot begin prior to completing one's degree, and this simple step helps to inject new talent into the local ecosystem, while elevating academic quality through applied experience. Such a relationship also enhances research by ensuring that your program of work remains on-the-ground-relevant at all times.

Wilkinson (1991) defines community as being framed through three key elements: (1) a locality, (2) a local society, and (3) a set of locally oriented collective actions. The third concept sits at the nexus of entrepreneurship and community (Davidsson, 2015). In closing, try to create a symbiotic positive relationship between multiple actors and sectors—instead of parasitic ones—at this nexus (Mazzucato, 2013). The creation of positive relationships built on trust is arrived at through action. These actions require good faith and follow through. We resound McMullen and Shepherd's (2006) idea that "entrepreneurship requires action" (p. 132). Going one step further, building an entrepreneurial community also requires action.

References

Adler, P. S., & Kwon, S. W. (2002). Social capital: Prospects for a new concept. *Academy of Management Review*, *27*, 17–40.

Aldrich, H. (2002). Entrepreneurial strategies in new organizational populations. In R. Swedberg (Ed.), *Entrepreneurship: The social science view* (pp. 212–228). New York, NY: Oxford University Press.

Avolio, B. J., & Bass, B. M. (1988). Transformational leadership, charisma, and beyond. In J. G. Hunt, B. R. Baliga, H. P. Dachler, & C. A. Schriesheim (Eds.), *Emerging leadership vistas* (pp. 29–50). Boston, MA: Lexington Books.

Barbosa, S. D. (20154). Revisiting entrepreneurship research from a decision-making perspective. In A. Fayolle (Ed.), *Handbook of research on entrepreneurship: What we know and what we need to know* (pp. 389–426). Northampton, MA: Edward Elgar.

Baumol, W. J. (1990). Entrepreneurship: Productive, unproductive, and destructive. *Journal of Political Economy*, *98*(5), 893–921.

Bunker, K. A., & Wakefield, M. (2005). *Leading with authenticity in times of transition*. Greensboro, NC: Center for Creative Leadership.

Burt, R. S. (1995). *Structural holes: The social structure of competition*. Boston, MA: Harvard University Press.

Davidsson, P. (2015). Entrepreneurial opportunities and the entrepreneurship nexus: A re-conceptualization. *Journal of Business Venturing*, *30*, 674–695.

Feld, B. (2012). *Startup communities: Building an entrepreneurial ecosystem in your city*. Hoboken, NJ: Wiley.

Frost, R. (2012). *The early works of Robert Frost: Featuring the road not taken, birches, after apple-picking, mending wall and more!* Seattle, WA: CreateSpace Independent Publishing Platform.

Gerber, M. E. (1995). *The myth revisited: Why most small businesses don't work and what to do about it*. New York, NY: Harper Collins.

Goodyear, M., & Golden, C. (2008, November). Leadership transitions: Keys for success. *Educause Quarterly*, 52–54.

Granovetter, M. (1973). The strength of weak ties. *American Journal of Sociology*, *78*(6), 1360–1380.

Gupta, V., MacMillan, I. C., & Surie, G. (2003). Entrepreneurial leadership: Developing and measuring a cross-cultural construct. *Journal of Business Venturing*, *19*, 241–260.

Hoang, H., & Antoncic, B. (2003). Network-based research in entrepreneurship: A critical review. *Journal of Business Venturing*, *18*, 165–187.

Isenberg, D. (2010, June). The big idea: How to start an entrepreneurial revolution. *Harvard Business Review*, 1–10.

Kuratko, D. F. (2009). The entrepreneurial imperative of the 21st Century. *Business Horizons*, *52*(5), 421–428.

Kuratko, D. F. (2016). *Entrepreneurship: Theory, process, and practice* (10th ed.). Independence, KY: South-Western College Pub.

Kuratko, D. F., & Morris, M. H. (2013). *Entrepreneurship & leadership*. Northampton, MA: Edward Elgar.

Lakey, B. M., Lakey, G., Napler, R., & Robinson, J. M. (1998). *Grassroots and nonprofit leadership: A guide for organizations in changing times*. Gabriola Island, Canada: New Society Publishers.

Lane, D., & Maxfield, R. (1996). Strategy under complexity: Fostering generative relationships. *Long Range Planning*, *29*(2), 215–231.

Lyons, T. S., Alter, T. R., Audretsch, D., & Augustine, D. (2012). Entrepreneurship and community: The next frontier of entrepreneurship inquiry. *Entrepreneurship Research Journal*, *2*(1), 1–26.

Mazzucato, M. (2013). *The entrepreneurial state: Debunking public vs. private sector myths*. New York, NY: Anthem Press.

McGrath, R. G., & MacMillan, I. C. (2000). *The entrepreneurial mindset*. Boston, MA: Harvard Business School Press.

McMullen, J. S., & Shepherd, D. A. (2006). Entrepreneurial action and the role of uncertainty in the theory of the entrepreneur. *Academy of Management Review*, *31*(1), 132–152.

Scott, W. R. (2003). *Organizations: Rational, natural, and open systems* (5th ed.). Upper Saddle, NJ: Prentice Hall.

Sendjaya, S., & Sarros, J. C. (2002). Servant leadership: Its origin, development, and application in organizations. *Journal of Leadership and Organization Studies*, *9*(2), 57–64.

Shane, S., & Cable, D. (2002). Network ties, reputation, and the financing of new ventures. *Management Science*, *48*, 364–381.

Stam, W., Arzlanian, S., & Elfring, T. (2014). Social capital of entrepreneurs and small firm performance: A meta-analysis of contextual and methodological moderators. *Journal of Business Venturing*, *29*, 152–173.

Surie, G., & Hazy, J. K. (2006). Generative leadership: Nurturing innovation in complex systems. *E:CO*, *8*(4), 13–26.

Svara, J. H. (1995, Winter). Institutional powers and mayoral leadership. *State and Local Government Review*, *27*(1), 71–83.

Taleb, N. N. (2012). *Antifragile: Things that gain from disorder*. New York, NY: Random House.

Tierney, T. J. (2006, Summer). The leadership deficit. *Stanford Social Innovation Review*, 26–35.

Wilkinson, K. P. (1991). *The community in rural America*. New York, NY: Greenwood Press.

Zacharakis, A., Spinelli, S., & Timmons, J. A. (2011). *Business plans that work: A guide for small business*. New York, NY: McGraw-Hill.

Index

Note: Entries in italics indicate figures and tables.

For Product Safety Concerns and Information please contact our
EU representative GPSR@taylorandfrancis.com Taylor & Francis
Verlag GmbH, Kaufingerstraße 24, 80331 München, Germany